The Far East
in World Trade

PRAEGER SPECIAL STUDIES IN
INTERNATIONAL ECONOMICS AND DEVELOPMENT

The Far East in World Trade

DEVELOPMENTS AND GROWTH SINCE 1945

Alfred K. Ho

FREDERICK A. PRAEGER, Publishers
New York · Washington · London

The purpose of the Praeger Special Studies is to make specialized research monographs in U.S. and international economics and politics
available to the academic, business, and government communities. For
further information, write to the Special Projects Division, Frederick
A. Praeger, Publishers, 111 Fourth Avenue, New York, N.Y. 10003.

FREDERICK A. PRAEGER, PUBLISHERS
111 Fourth Avenue, New York, N.Y. 10003, U.S.A.
77-79 Charlotte Street, London W.1, England

Published in the United States of America in 1967
by Frederick A. Praeger, Inc., Publishers

Library of Congress Catalog Card Number: 68-14159

Printed in the United States of America

PREFACE

In this study I have attempted to trace the development of international trade in the Far East since the close of World War II. Chapter 1 describes the amount of trade of the Far East to provide the reader with an over-all picture of the relative position of the Far East in world trade. Chapter 2 deals with the theoretical basis of the trade of the Far East. The doctrine of comparative advantage applies to the trade of the Far East in a general way, but some of the basic assumptions underlying the doctrine may have to be modified. In this chapter the terms of trade of the Far Eastern countries are clarified, the problems of their balance of payments examined, and their foreign-exchange and tariff policies discussed. Chapters 3 through 5 approach the trade of the Far East from the point of view of the Western powers, describing their commercial operations and attempting to ascertain their competitive positions. Emphasis is placed on the roles played by the Sino-Soviet Bloc, the United Kingdom, West Germany, and the United States. Chapters 6 through 10 approach the trade of the Far East from the point of view of the Far Eastern countries: describing their activities, discussing their policies, and demonstrating how trade is being used as a means to further their economic development. Chapter 11 summarizes some of the findings of the book and speculates on how trade can be promoted for the mutual benefit of the West and the East.

The author owes a debt of gratitude to the National Science Foundation for the grant of the science fellowship which enabled him to carry on a year's uninterrupted research and study at the University of California, Los Angeles, in 1965. It was during this period that the manuscript was written and revised. The author is grateful to President John Lombardi, Dean Robert Holcomb, Professors Sooren Frankian, Richard Carney, and C. Dawn Sander of Los Angeles City College for their support and advice. The supervision and inspiration of Professors Harold M. Somers, William R. Allen, Sven Arndt, and M. D. Intriligator of the University of California, Los Angeles, Professor Joseph E. Haring of Occidental College, and Dr. Charles Wolf Jr. of the Rand Corporation have made the year of work at the University a very interesting and fruitful one. To all of them the author is deeply grateful. None of them, of course, bears any responsibility for the content of the book.

Finally, I owe a debt to my wife, Marjorie, for her help in editing and typing the manuscript. To her the book is dedicated.

A. K. H.

Los Angeles

CONTENTS

LIST OF TABLES

xi

LIST OF FIGURES

GEOGRAPHIC TERMS

Only the major countries are listed. The terms are defined as used in this book.

Asia	includes Burma, Ceylon, Mainland China, Hong Kong, India, Pakistan, Indonesia, Japan, Malaya, Singapore, the Philippines, Thailand, Taiwan (Formosa), Laos, Cambodia, North Vietnam, South Vietnam, North Korea, South Korea, Ryukyu, West New Guinea, Sarawak, Brunei, North Borneo, Dutch Asia, and Portugese Asia.
Common Market Countries	include Belgium-Luxemburg, Italy, France, West Germany, and the Netherlands.
Economic Commission for Asia and the Far East (ECAFE)	includes Afghanistan, Australia, Burma, Cambodia, Ceylon, Formosa, Malaya, Singapore, India, Indonesia, Iran, Japan, Laos, Mongolia, Nepal, New Zealand, Pakistan, the Philippines, South Korea, South Vietnam, Thailand, and Hong Kong.
European Free Trade Association	includes Austria, Denmark, Norway, Portugal, Sweden, Switzerland, and the United Kingdom.
Far East	includes Asia and Oceania.
Middle East	includes Aden, Cyprus, Ethiopia, Egypt, Iraq, Iran, Israel, Jordan, Lebanon, Libya, Sudan, Syria, and the United Arab Republic.

Non-sterling Continental Organization for European Economic Cooperation (OEEC)	includes Austria, Belgium-Luxemburg, Denmark, France, West Germany, Greece, Italy, the Netherlands, Norway, Portugal, Sweden, Switzerland, and Turkey.
Oceania	includes Australia, New Zealand, Fiji, Papua, Australian New Guinea, New Caledonia, French Polynesia, and Guam.
Other Western European Countries	include Iceland, Ireland, Finland, Greece, Spain, Turkey, and Yugoslavia.
Sterling Area	includes OEEC Sterling countries, which include Iceland, Ireland, and the United Kingdom. Sterling Middle East includes Aden, Cyprus, Jordan, and Libya.
Sterling America	includes Jamaica, Trinidad, Barbados, Bahamas, Bermuda, British Honduras, Leeward Islands, Windward Islands, British Guiana, and Falkland Islands.
Sterling Africa	includes Kenya, Uganda, Tanganyika, Rhodesia, Nyassaland, Gambia, Ghana, Mauritius, Union of South Africa, Nigeria, Sierra Leone, Zanzibar, and Pemba.
Sterling Asia	includes Burma, Ceylon, India, Pakistan, Malaya, Singapore, Sarawak, Brunei, North Borneo, and Hong Kong.
Sterling Oceania	includes Australia and New Zealand.
Western Europe	includes the Common Market Countries (EEC), the European Free Trade Association (EFTA) and other Western European countries.

The Far East
in World Trade

CHAPTER **1** THE MAGNITUDE OF
THE TRADE
OF THE FAR EAST

An understanding of the trade of the Far East is possible
only if the economic, political, and social conditions of the Far
East as a whole are considered. The Far East in the postwar
period is a changing world, with drastic and, in some instances, revolutionary changes of all types happening simultaneously. It is the objective of this book to observe the
development of trade in the changing world of the Far East to
find out how trade has been affected by these changes.

Economic recovery in the postwar years came early for
some countries and relatively late for others. A large number
of nations in this region were originally colonies of Western
powers and had gained political independence in the postwar
period. Some gained independence earlier and through peace-
ful means--for instance, the Philippines, in 1946; and some
gained independence quite late--for instance Malaya, in 1957.
For a few, the transfer of political power came only after long
years of strife, as in the cases of Vietnam and Indonesia. For
some countries, this was a period of economic nationalism
aimed at self-reliance in goods and services and a bigger share
for their own nationals in the nation's business activities. This
was also, for most countries, a period of industrialization,
with varying degrees of government planning and leadership. The
trade of the Far East, of course, became quite different from
what it was in the prewar days, reflecting the economic,
political, and social transition of the region.

To give a general background survey of the trade of the Far
East, this chapter attempts to show the magnitude of the trade,
so that there can be some estimate of the position of the Far
East in world trade.

Although the Far East constitutes a large area of the world,
the scope of the present study is limited to the trade of the major
countries in the area. Even for some of the major countries,
such as North Korea and North Vietnam, there is lack of information. The Far East, in the present study, consists of two
large areas: Asia and Oceania. Asia can be divided into the

following parts: Japan; Continental Asia including Communist China, South Korea, North Korea, Hong Kong, and Formosa; Southeast Asia including Burma, Thailand, Laos, Cambodia, North Vietnam, South Vietnam, and Malaysia; South Asia including the Philippines and Indonesia. Oceania includes largely Australia and New Zealand.

Table 1

Comparison of Far Eastern Trade with World Trade
(billions of U.S. dollars)

	Exports		Imports	
	World	Far East	World	Far East
1928	30.8	4.8	33.6	4.6
1938	20.5	3.8	22.9	3.6
1949	54.3	7.7	59.2	9.2
1950	56.1	8.8	58.9	8.0
1951	75.9	12.5	80.8	13.0
1952	71.9	9.9	79.9	12.5
1953	74.9	10.3	76.7	11.7
1954	77.7	10.3	79.8	11.9
1955	84.6	11.6	89.3	13.1
1956	93.9	12.3	98.6	14.6
1957	100.9	13.2	108.2	16.9
1958	96.1	11.9	101.1	14.4
1959	101.8	13.7	106.5	15.1
1960	113.2	14.8	118.6	17.9

Sources: International Monetary Fund, International Financial Statistics, Washington, D.C., June, 1962, pp. 38-41; United Nations, A Study of Trade Between Asia and Europe, Geneva, 1953, p. 1.

In 1960 the exports of the world amounted to $113.2 billion, while that of the Far East amounted to $14.8 billion, about 13.1 per cent of the world total. For the same year the imports of the world amounted to $118.6 billion, while that of the Far East amounted to $17.9 billion, about 15.1 per cent of the world total.

Table 2

Trade of the Far East
(values in billions of U.S. dollars)
(shares in percentages of world)

	Exports				Imports			
	Value		Share		Value		Share	
	Asia	Oceania	Asia	Oceania	Asia	Oceania	Asia	Oceania
1928	4. 8	...	15. 4	...	4. 6	...	13. 7	...
1938	3. 0	0. 8	15. 0	3. 6	2. 8	0. 8	12. 2	3. 3
1949	5. 4	2. 3	9. 9	4. 2	7. 3	1. 9	12. 3	3. 1
1950	6. 8	2. 0	12. 1	3. 5	6. 2	1. 8	10. 6	3. 1
1951	9. 7	2. 8	12. 8	3. 7	9. 9	3. 1	12. 2	3. 8
1952	7. 4	2. 5	10. 3	3. 5	9. 6	2. 9	12. 0	3. 6
1953	7. 5	2. 8	10. 0	3. 7	9. 6	2. 1	12. 5	2. 7
1954	7. 8	2. 5	10. 0	3. 2	9. 2	2. 7	11. 5	3. 4
1955	9. 0	2. 6	10. 6	3. 1	10. 0	3. 1	11. 2	3. 5
1956	9. 5	2. 8	10. 1	3. 0	11. 7	2. 9	11. 9	2. 9
1957	10. 1	3. 1	10. 1	3. 1	13. 9	3. 0	12. 9	2. 8
1958	9. 4	2. 5	9. 8	2. 6	11. 4	3. 0	11. 3	2. 9
1959	10. 7	3. 0	10. 5	2. 9	12. 1	3. 0	11. 4	2. 8
1960	11. 8	3. 0	10. 0	2. 7	14. 2	3. 7	11. 9	3. 1

Sources: International Monetary Fund, International Financial Statistics, Washington, D.C., June 1962,
pp. 38-41; United Nations, A Study of Trade Between Asia and Europe, Geneva, 1953, p. 1.

The Far East referred to here includes Asia and Oceania. If
we single out Asia, its share of the exports of the world in the
1950's was about 10 per cent, which was lower than its share in
1938 at 15 per cent and its share in 1928 at 15.4 per cent. Meanwhile, the Asian share of the imports of the world in the 1950's
was about 12 per cent, approximately the same as its share in
1938, but lower than its 1928 share of 13.7 per cent. In other
words, Asia's position in world trade has declined in the last
thirty years.

Even at the 1928 figures, Asia's position in world trade
could be greatly improved, particularly considering the fact

that Asia has more than half of the world's population.   The
dream that Asia, the land of teeming millions, would become
a gigantic market for goods and services is still very far
from realization.   There are a number of reasons for this low
rate of trade.

Asia has seldom been completely free from military conflicts.   Immediately after World War II, there were the civil
war in China, the Korean War, and civil wars in Indonesia and
Vietnam.   There were also guerrilla operations of Communist
terrorists in the Philippines, Malaysia, Burma, and Laos.
The only nations which have enjoyed peace in the postwar period are Japan, Thailand, and India.   Even in India there has
been bloodshed--between Moslems and Hindus at the time of the
partition and in sporadic conflicts subsequently.   The inability
of the peoples of Asia to achieve peace and order, of course,
is among the main factors impeding economic progress and
the growth of trade.   Communist China, North Korea, and
North Vietnam still pose military threats to the rest of Asia,
but, as the new nations are gaining experience and internal
stability, domestic peace and order should gradually become
realities.

In Asia there has been a tendency toward economic fragmentation which tends to create more obstacles for the trade
of the region.   Before 1937 Burma was a part of India, and
before 1947 Pakistan and India were one political entity.
Indochina was originally one colony, at least in the economic
sense, but after the war it was divided into three parts:
Laos, Cambodia, and Vietnam.   Subsequently, Vietnam was
further divided into North and South Vietnam.   Korea, Formosa, and Japan were one economic unit before World War
II.   Formosa, or Taiwan, is now under the Nationalist
Government of China, and Korea has been subdivided into
North and South Korea.   All these political divisions have
created economic barriers and have reduced the free flow of
goods and services.   In most cases the fragmentation results
in economic dislocations with one part having raw materials
but no processing or manufacturing facilities and the other
part having the facilities but no raw materials; or with one
part having the population centers and the other part the food sup-

plies. With fragmentation, instead of keeping the free movements of goods and services to meet the needs of different
regions, there is the tendency of establishing tariff walls and
trade controls for each part to gain self-sufficiency in an awk-
ward environment. This, of course, will further intensify
economic dislocations.

The experience of Europe in the establishment of the Common Market and the Free Trade Association has demonstrated
a trend toward custom union and economic consolidation which
seems to point to a solution to the problem of economic fragmentation. It is hoped that the Asian countries will learn from
the European experience and take steps to reverse this tendency of economic fragmentation while still keeping their individual
political independence.[1]

The population of Asia is too large for the land to support at
a decent standard of living. The growing population has become
a burden. Any increase in production is consumed by the increase in population, leaving little savings for investment.
This lack of capital has retarded economic growth. Exportable
surpluses are low and importing capacity is small. Under
these circumstances, trade development in the postwar period
has had its limitations.[2]

Asia, as a supplier of raw materials to Europe and North
America, lost ground during the war because the area was largely
under Japanese occupation. Europe and North America, de-
prived of this source of materials, were forced to develop resources in their own areas, or seek new resources in other
areas such as Africa and Latin America, or develop substitutes. Japanese occupation ended with the war, but Asia is
not likely ever to fully recover its lost markets because Africa
is closer to Europe and Latin America is closer to North
America. The synthetic industries did not die at the end of
the war but, in some instances, such as that of synthetic
textile fiber, have grown stronger.[3]

The Far East, except Japan, is an area of underdeveloped
economy, and of low technological attainment in business
management and in scientific and engineering fields. This is
largely due to its inadequate educational facilities and the high

degree of illiteracy of the people. As a result, the export trade of the majority of the nations of the Far East is dominated by primary products. World trade has grown faster among the industrial nations than among the primary producing nations.

The people of the Far East are industrious and diligent, but their efforts are hampered by the lack of modern business organization which is essential in the pooling of resources and manpower for large-scale business endeavors. Entrepreneurship implies not only hard-working individuals but also the ability and the techniques of business organization which are lacking in the Far East.

Economic nationalism in the narrow sense is prevalent in some of the Far Eastern countries due to the feeling of the newly gained power of self-determination. After long periods of Western domination, the strong desire to manage their own affairs without outside interference is natural and understandable. However, the application of economic nationalism in its narrow sense may mean unnecessary international trade barriers and restrictions.

All these military, political and economic factors have restrained the trade of Asia, leaving much to be desired in the over-all situation of the economy of the area. The Far Eastern nations are conscious of their economic backwardness and are striving in all earnestness to improve their production and income. There is a firm determination and drive to bring about progress as exemplified by such countries as Japan, India, and Formosa, and improvement of the share of the Far East in world trade is certainly possible.

In the 1950's Oceania's share in world trade was a little less than the pre-war figure for 1938. This may have been caused by greater self-sufficiency of food production in the United Kingdom and the tariff policy of Continental Europe.

In the 1950's, Oceania sent out about 3 per cent of the world's exports, and received about 3 per cent of world imports. This should be considered a well-developed trade, taking into consideration the fact that Oceania has only 0.4 per cent of the world population.

Notes to Chapter 1

1. United Nations, Regional Market Arrangements with Reference to the ECAFE Region (Bangkok, 1961), pp. 4-5.

2. United Nations, Department of Economic and Social Affairs, A Study of Trade between Asia and Europe (Geneva, 1953), p. 2.

3. United Nations, Department of Economic and Social Affairs, World Economic Report (New York, 1948), pp. 113-14.

CHAPTER **2** THE THEORY
OF THE TRADE
OF THE FAR EAST

To develop a theory of the trade of the Far East, it is
necessary to state first of all the goals of this investigation.
It is hoped that in the orderly pursuit of these goals an explanation for the trade behaviors of the nations in the Far East
can be found. The goals that we have in mind are answers to
a few basic questions: (1) What is the basis for national
specialization? In other words, what are the determining factors for nations in the Far East to export certain items and import others? (2) How are the terms of trade determined? Is
trade beneficial to all? Which nations are getting the better
part of the bargain? (3) How are the payments made for
trade? Are the international payments balanced for these
nations? If not, where do the pressures come from and what
are their consequences? (4) What are the commercial policies of these nations? Is there a conflict between trade theory
and growth theory? Would free trade or protection better
promote economic growth in the Far East?

NATIONAL SPECIALIZATION

A large part of the theory of trade deals with the topic of
national specialization, seeking an explanation for the division
of labor among nations. There are different doctrines with
different areas of emphasis: labor productivity, monetary
costs, factor endowments, etc. These doctrines are for-
mulated to explain the trade of the world as a whole and are
not especially intended to explain the trade of the Far East in
particular. It is possible to borrow the pure theory in general to explain the regional Far Eastern trade in particular, but
caution must be exercised. Otherwise, either we would not
do justice to the doctrines, or our generalizations would not
be applicable to the situation in reality. The task here is

not to repudiate theoretical doctrines by saying that they do
not apply to the situation in the Far East at all, nor to accept
them in their entirety.   The intention here is to point out
what conceptual modifications or clarifications are necessary
so that the doctrines in their new form can be more realistic
in explaining the trade of the Far East.   Between the Far
East and the West there are differences in moral judgments,
in behavioral patterns, and in economic structure.   These
differences cannot be ignored if we want to understand the
trade of the Far East.

The specialization of the Far Eastern countries in international trade is reflected in their major exports:

Japan: fish products; cotton, silk, and woolen textiles;
    clothing; chemical fertilizer; synthetic fiber;
    iron and steel products; electric appliances;
    machine tools; machinery; instruments; and ships.

Communist China: food, tea, coal, metal ores, textiles,
    iron and steel products, machine tools, and
    machinery.

India: tea, cotton textiles, jute manufactures, leather
    goods, metal ores, iron and steel products, and
    machinery.

Australia: wool, butter, hides, skins, leather goods,
    metal products, chemicals, paper, machinery,
    and electric equipment.

New Zealand: wool, meat, butter, and cheese.

Taiwan: sugar, rice, tea, cement, coal, steel products,
    and aluminum products.

Hong Kong: cotton textiles, clothing, footwear, furniture,
    machine tools, and machinery.

Philippines: sugar, coconut products, tobacco, fruits,
    wool, paper, cotton textiles, cordage, metal pro-
    ducts, and machinery.

Other underdeveloped countries: rubber, tin, rice, tea, sugar, cotton, jute, petroleum, and coconut products.

Since the Far Eastern countries enjoy comparative advantages in the above commodities, they can offer them on the international market at comparatively low prices. In turn, buyers on the international market purchase these commodities from the Far Eastern Countries because the prices are lower than those of domestic or other international sources.

The Far Eastern countries, except Japan, do not have an abundant capital supply and their rates of domestic capital formation are low due to the low per capita income and the high consumption function. However, in these countries, the large population and high rate of population growth create an abundant labor supply. This labor supply is largely unskilled, with a small portion of skilled labor at the low technological level. There are shortages of technicians, engineers, and professionals. As a result, these countries specialize in primary production which is labor intensive because agriculture and mining with primitive methods can better utilize a large unskilled labor force. This explains the large agriculture and mineral primary products content of the exports of most of the Far Eastern countries, especially the underdeveloped ones. The primary products commonly appearing among the major exports of these countries are: rubber, tin, metal ores, rice, tea, sugar, jute, coconut products, cotton, and silk.

Using the Heckscher-Ohlin concept, a country exports those commodities produced with relatively large quantities of the country's relatively abundant factor. Can this concept be applied to the trade composition of Japan? Tatemoto and Ichimura have investigated factor intensities of Japanese trade commodities. Because Japan's position in trade relative to other Far Eastern countries is not the same as its position relative to the advanced countries, Tatemoto and Ichimura do not treat Japan's exports to the world as a whole. Instead, they divide Japan's exports into two groups: exports to the advanced countries and exports to the underdeveloped countries. They find that Japan's exports to advanced countries are labor intensive, but its exports to underdeveloped countries are

capital intensive. Similarly, Japan's imports from advanced
countries are capital intensive and its imports from underdeveloped countries labor intensive. Japan is relatively capital
abundant compared to other Far Eastern countries, but relatively
labor abundant compared to advanced countries. This characteristic indicates that Japan occupies a unique and important position in the trade of the Far East. Japan imports
heavy and technical equipment from advanced countries, and
with this it produces capital-intensive manufactures for export
to other Far Eastern countries. Then it imports from other
Far Eastern countries labor-intensive primary products which
it reprocesses and exports to advanced countries. [1]

Another way to express the comparative advantage that
the Far Eastern countries enjoy in their major exports is by
their relatively high labor productivity, which can be measured
by the relatively high output to labor ratios. In the Far Eastern countries wages are relatively lower than the West, but,
for most products, output per unit of labor is lower too. It
is only in these major exports that the Far Eastern countries
enjoy relatively higher output to labor ratios. In the primary
products of agriculture and mining, the higher labor productivity is not due to the skills of labor, since mostly unskilled labor is employed, but it is due to the favorable natural
resources: the fertile soil, an abundant water supply, and
the proper climate for the growing of rubber, rice, tea,
sugar, cotton jute, coconuts, oil seeds, etc. ; the rich and
easily accessible resources in Asia for the mining of tin, coal,
and other metal ores; the abundant land supply in Oceania for
raising cattle and sheep for meat, butter, cheese, wool, hides,
and skins. These natural resource advantages are reflected in
the high output to labor ratios. In some Far Eastern countries
such as mainland China, India, Taiwan, Australia, Hong Kong,
and the Philippines, where industrialization has started, there
is relatively high labor productivity due to the improvement
of skills of labor in light manufactures and simple capital goods.
Therefore, among their major exports are cotton, textiles, clothing, paper, cement, iron and steel products, electric appliances, machine tools, and simple machinery. Japan now
enjoys higher labor productivity not only in certain fields of
light manufactures but also in some fields of heavy industries;

not only higher labor productivity relative to other Far Eastern
countries, but also in some cases relative to the West.   Therefore, among its major exports are chemical fertilizers, synthetic fibers, electric appliances, optical and precision instruments, machine tools, ships, rolling stock, and many
types of machinery. In Ricardo's concept, the composition
of trade is determined exclusively by international differences
in relative output to labor ratios. Assuming in a model of two
commodities and two countries, a_1, a_2 are the output-factor
ratios for commodities 1 and 2 in country I, and b_1, b_2 are
the output-factor ratios for commodities 1 and 2 in country II.
Here only one factor, labor, is involved. Country I will export commodity 1 and import commodity 2, if
$$a_1/a_2 > b_1/b_2 \text{ or } a_1/b_1 > a_2/b_2.$$
We can generalize this model to include many commodities
for the two countries. Here, instead of comparing the output-
factor ratios of two commodities, we rank commodities by
their output-factor ratios on a list. It will always be true that
each of a country's exports on the upper part of the list will
have a higher output-factor ratio than each of its imports on
the lower part of the list. As to where the dividing line is,
this is a matter of the demands of the two countries for each
other's goods.[2]

We now have two theories on hand to explain the trade
composition in the Far Eastern countries. While the Ricardian doctrine assumes the same production function, which is
the capital labor proportion used in production for the different countries, it explains the composition of trade exclusively by the difference in the relative output to labor ratios. The
Heckscher-Ohlin theory assumes the opposite, that there is
the same labor productivity for different countries, and explains the composition of trade exclusively by the differences
in the production function (the capital labor proportion used
in production). If we are engaged in a discussion of the pure
theory of international trade, we are obliged to choose one
of the two because they are mutually exclusive. However,
we are interested here in the explanation of a real situation--
the trade composition of the Far Eastern countries. Neither
of the two theories gives the perfect explanation because in
these countries there are differences in labor productivity
and in factor endowments. Probably, in the light and heavy

manufactures, where technology is important, the theory of labor productivity will hold better, but in the primary products, where largely unskilled labor is used, factor endowment will hold better. A practical businessman will continue to import these commodities from the Far East as long as there is comparative advantage, and he does not insist on one exclusive theory. The comparative advantage could be caused by many factors. For that matter, a practical businessman is not directly concerned with pure theory of international trade in the first place.

After establishing these theories in principle, we can proceed to their modifications, clarifications, and to the refining of their concepts so that the theories can be better applicable to the trade of the Far East.

1. Labor in the Far East is more heterogeneous than in the West, while the Ricardian doctrine assumes homogeneous labor. There is very often a dual economy in the Far Eastern countries, with a modern sector (largely along the coasts) using developed production techniques and financed to a large extent by foreign interests and a traditional sector (in the interior) using primitive methods of production and based entirely on domestic capital and resources. For instance, in Southeast Asia, in the localities where Europeans have developed rubber plantations, tin mines or petroleum plants, modern communities have developed with higher standards of living than the traditional sector. The labor supply is better trained and wages are higher. In the Western economy, the prosperity of one sector may have a linkage effect on other sectors, as the profits of one sector may be invested in other sectors, and the technological advancement of one sector may reduce costs of other sectors. But this is not the case in a dual economy. Foreign investments will be limited to the few special fields where raw materials are produced for the advanced countries. Foreign capital seldom goes into the traditional sector. There is no clear technological linkage between the two sectors. The traditional sector may remain poor while the modern sector prospers, resulting in two sets of wage rates--one for each sector. If the labor supplies of the two sectors were competitive, the difference of wage rates would tend to gradually disappear. This may have happened in some countries like

Japan, but not in others. For instance, in a Southeast Asian
country, an intelligent worker with high industrial aptitude may
remain in the traditional sector due to the lack of transportation facilities, to the requirement of a large initial fund to
support himself before he finds the job which fully utilizes
his talents, to his lack of training, to his cultural tradition
preferring farming over commercial occupation, or to his
political position choosing not to work for foreign interests.
His wage would not relate to that of a similar worker in the
cities. The dual economy is not a fixed concept and may gradually fade away as the traditional section becomes modernized.
Then its labor force may acquire the necessary training and
become more competitive with the labor force in the modern
sector and labor mobility may improve. The dual economy as
a barrier to competition may be strong in some countries and
weak in others. In the West, labor is to some extent heterogeneous, and labor mobility from area to area and from industry
to industry is also not completely free. The trade of the Far
East concerns mainly the modern sector, as the traditional
sector is essentially a closed economy with very little of its
products entering into the world market. To be realistic,
it is necessary to consider that the labor in the Far Eastern
countries is in varying degrees more heterogeneous than the
labor force in the West as long as dual economy in these countries exist.

    2. The competition of trade for the Far Eastern countries
is changing all the time. Ricardo, in describing the trade between England and Portugal, assumes the two countries at a-
bout the same stage of industrial development. But Gerald M.
Meier, in describing the trade of developing countries, contends that at any time the international economy will be composed of countries which have attained different levels of
development as measured by per capita real income, that over
a period of time the several countries will also experience
different rates of advance, and, moreover, that each country's pattern of internal development may vary in accordance with
particular leading and lagging sectors and different intercon-
nections between sectors. [3] This is to say that in developing
countries, a commodity may rank low by labor productivity at
one time and be an import, but may shortly move up the list,
due to the improvement of labor productivity, and enter into the

world market as an export. This does not repudiate the Ricardian doctrine, but makes the task of determining the composition of trade more complicated. It is simply that as the young industries in the Far East develop, the trade composition will change. The share of raw materials in their export trade may decline, while the share of manufactures may rise. The share of manufactures in their import trade may decline, while the share of capital goods in their import trade may rise.

3. In the Far East there is some degree of international mobility of factors. While the Ricardian doctrine assumes perfect internal mobility of factors and no international mobility of factors, Myint observes that in the Far East there is probably better international mobility than internal mobility as capital is still coming to Southeast Asia from the West and a labor force is still coming to Southeast Asia from China and India. [4] Of course, this has been the case ever since the very beginning when the Far East was opened to the West for trade. The development of colonial economies has been largely due to the international mobility of capital, production techniques, and resources, with the first two coming to the Far East, and the last going out from the Far East. We may consider Singapore and Hong Kong enclaves of the economy of England. There is good international mobility of factors between Singapore and Hong Kong and between both of them and England. A merchant in Singapore may have his imports financed by a local bank or by a bank in England. He probably finds it cheaper to import a certain merchandise from India by sea than trying to bring it out of the jungles in the hinterland of the country. Therefore, bank rates, foreign-exchange rates, and wage rates in Singapore may be more closely related to England than to the interior region of the traditional sector of Malaysia.

Another example of this phenomenon is Japan. Japan exports a number of commodities without abundant domestic supplies of raw material, or in some cases without any domestic supplies at all. For instance, Japan does not have any domestic production of raw cotton, raw wool, and crude oil, but has a large export trade of cotton and woolen textiles and petroleum products. [5] Japan has developed these industries entirely on international supplies.

4. In the Far East, comparative costs considerations should not be confined to just the manufacturing costs, but should include all the costs the buyers in the international market have to pay until the commodities are brought to them. According to the Ricardian doctrine, comparative costs can be measured by the output-labor ratios. But there are other cost factors in addition to labor costs. Furthermore, in the Far Eastern countries, wage rates are different. Can we explain the trade composition of the Far Eastern countries by the output-labor ratios, ignoring other cost factors and ignoring the difference in wage rates?

Kravis supports the Ricardian doctrine by investigating the wage rates of the United States and Japan. The fact that there are several particular wage rates in each of the two countries instead of one general wage rate does not disturb the picture of comparative advantages, because wage rates are higher in the export industries than in the import industries in both countries, and, futhermore, the ranking of industries by wage rates for the two countries is almost identical. In other words, there are wage differentials in both countries, but the inter-industrial wage structure happens to be identical for them. Consequently, the wage differentials would not disturb the picture of wage bill comparison. According to Kravis, the only thing that matters is the labor productivity, thus sustaining the Ricardian doctrine. Another observation of Kravis' is the tendency of competition in the labor market to cause each country's wage rates to "cluster around the national average afforded by the nation's general level of productivity." This means that labor productivity would be a stronger predictor of the composition of trade between two countries of similar levels of productivity.[6]

Bhagwati is not satisfied with Kravis' findings, contending that Kravis has gone only halfway in proving the Ricardian doctrine. To Bhagwati, the average total cost is measured by $(L/O)(w)(TC/W)$, where L is the units of labor used, O is the output, w is the wage rate, TC is the total cost and W is the wage bill. By showing that the inter-industrial wage structure is identical in Japan and the United States, Kravis succeeds in proving that labor productivity will be reflected in the wage bill. But, to Bhagwati, Kravis has left the TC/W ratio un-

touched. Bhagwati will not be satisfied unless it can be
shown that TC/W is also the same in both countries. [7]

In the Far East, the ratio TC/W is not identical for all
countries, because there are other cost factors (capital bill,
taxes, customs duties, transportation costs, insurance
charges, etc.), and these cost factors may not be proportional
to the wage bill. To an economist faithful to the Ricardian
tradition, if a commodity enjoys better labor productivity, it
will be included in the list of exports. But in reality, it will
not be exported unless a practical-minded buyer in the international market buys it, and this buyer will not buy it
just because of the advantage in labor productivity. He will
have to seriously investigate the customs duties, taxes, transportation costs, and insurance charges. He cannot assume
all these cost factors identical for all countries, nor can he
assume these cost factors constant in the same country at all
times. Far Eastern countries may readjust customs duties
and taxes from time to time. Transportation facilities and
insurance services are not uniformly developed in the Far
East, and their costs may vary from country to country. The
classical economists tended to over-simplify matters; for instance, transportation costs were not given the proper attention. To the classical economists, since European countries
are close together, transportation costs of a foreign source
of supply were assumed to be not too much different from
that of a domestic source. However, most of the merchandise from the Far East may have to travel halfway around the
world to reach an industrial center in the West. The classical
economists usually assumed free trade in their discussion of
the doctrine of comparative advantage; yet in the Far East
tariffs cannot be ignored. There is no doubt as to the general
applicability of the doctrine of comparative advantage. But to
make the doctrine depict the trade of the Far East, the comparative advantage is better considered with all the cost factors included, rather than in the narrow concept of manufacturing costs alone.

5. In the Far East the labor supply is not fixed and often
not fully employed. The Ricardian doctrine assumes that the
resources of a country are fixed and fully employed before it
enters into the international market. The function of trade is

reallocation of a country's resources more efficiently between
domestic and trade requirements in the light of the new set of
relative prices now open to the country. With given techniques
and full employment, export production can be increased only
at the cost of reducing some fields of production for domestic
consumption. This theory describes the developed West better than the Far East. Because of fast population growth, the
labor force in the Far East is constantly increasing and often
is not fully employed unless the economy can keep growing
fast enough to create job opportunities for it. Therefore, for
the overpopulated countries in the Far East, there is the
constant pressure of a surplus labor force. According to
Adam Smith, trade is the vent for surplus. To Smith, trade
helps the nation to ship out the surplus part of the products
of its land and labor (or the products made with its surplus
land and labor for which there is no domestic demand) and to
bring back in return other products which are in demand.
Trade overcomes the narrowness of the home market, provides an outlet for the surplus products above domestic requirements and creates additional employment for surplus
land and labor. By widening the extent of the market, trade
improves the general level of production and promotes employment within the country. Adam Smith's concept of trade
is not static in the sense that he does not keep production to
a fixed level for domestic requirements. Production is
forever urged on by the new outlets of world markets. This
incentive for larger and better output would bring about in-
novations and efficiency, and thereby yield, in addition to
the first transaction gains of trade, secondary indirect productivity gains. This concept of indirect gains was later fully
developed by John Stuart Mill. Smith was not only for free
trade (in removing all trade barriers), but he advocated the
positive promotion of exports to improve growth. [8]

Compared to later comparative cost theory, Smith's concept more fittingly describes the trade of the Far East. The
surplus resources concept has no place in the comparative cost
theory, as the theory assumes either a perfect market, or at
least a high degree of mobility of factors within the country and
flexibility in the adjustments of production and consumption.
Thus, the resources not required for export production will be
absorbed into domestic production. The theory describes the

economy of the industrial West with good markets for the distribution of products and for the allocation of resources.   The
surplus resources concept of Smith implies imperfect market,
inflexibility of adjustments of production and consumption, internal immobility of factors and specificity of resources.
This is a good description of the Far East, where the transportation and communication facilities are poor, cultural tradition and social customs put a low prestige value on occupations
in the fields of manufacturing and commerce, and people are
tied to the land due to lack of training and capital. [9]

A good harvest for the Far Eastern countries will mean a
possible expansion of exports, as, in Smith's words, trade is
the vent for surplus.   A decline in the rubber market would
create surplus resources which cannot be readily absorbed
for domestic production.   Governments and businessmen in the
Far East are quite aware of the importance of trade as a
source of additional income and as a solution to the problem
of gaining full employment of surplus manpower.

6. Some commodities are exported by Far Eastern countries not because of the comparative advantage in doing so, but
because of government promotion. Classical economists usually assume laissez faire economy for the trading nations, with
the governments playing a very limited role so that the competition of trade is largely a matter of free decisions of private business based on comparative-advantage principles.
However, this has, so far, not been the case for the Far Eastern countries in the postwar period.   There has been a tendency for the various Far Eastern governments to take an
active role, in varying degrees, in promoting economic development through industrialization.   Very often the governments
will help industries by promoting the export trade of their
manufactures so that these industries can enjoy expanded
markets and can improve their foreign-exchange earnings (with
which they can acquire from abroad the necessary machinery
and raw materials for expansion).   Many measures are used
to promote the export trade of industries: reducing or removing the customs duties of their imports, giving them
tax advantages, allowing them to buy as much foreign
exchange as they need at regular official rates or at lower
rates, allowing them to sell their foreign-exchange earnings

to the government or on the black market at higher rates, or
giving them subsidies. The composition of trade of the Far
Eastern countries is thus distorted by government promotion.
Of course, extreme cases are the Communist countries in the
Far East where the composition of trade is completely a matter of government policy in carrying out its economic plans.
Should the Far Eastern countries revert to the laissez faire
economy, the composition of their trade might be quite different from what it is today.

7. There are cases where the exports of some Far Eastern countries are not manufactured by them. According to
the Heckscher-Ohlin theory, if heavy machinery is exported
by Hong Kong and Singapore, Hong Kong and Singapore then
must have abundant supplies of the factors which are used in
large quantities in the production of heavy machinery. If by
production we imply manufacturing, then the statement is far
from being true. Hong Kong and Singapore do not manufacture heavy machinery for export at all. They are entrêpot
trade centers; they only re-export what they have imported.
Merchants of England and European countries send their
merchandise to Hong Kong and Singapore, where the merchandise is distributed to the neighboring Far Eastern countries.
Merchandise from the neighboring countries would also go
first to Hong Kong and Singapore and from there continue on
to England and Europe. This came about because merchants
of Hong Kong and Singapore have the language ability, the
knowledge of local conditions and the contacts with business
firms in the neighboring countries. Hong Kong and Singapore
do not contribute any factors for the manufacturing of heavy
machinery they re-export, but they handle the marketing and
distribution aspects in providing banking, shipping, insurance, repackaging, advertising, and some processing
services. The Heckscher-Ohlin theory is not especially
designed to explain the entrepôt trade of the Far East, but
can be clarified to cover the entrepôt trade if the word production is not limited to manufacturing but is broadened to
include marketing and distribution.

Again, it is not the intention here to repudiate the comparative advantage principle as a basis for the theory of
trade of the Far East. On the contrary, these pure theories

are well established generalizations of world trade as a whole, and they apply to the West as well as the Far East. However, as pure theories, they are not particularly designed to provide a perfect explanation of the trade of the Far East with full consideration given to all its peculiar characteristics. Therefore, in applying the pure theories to a practical situation, it is necessary to point out these peculiarities and to suggest certain clarifications, modifications, and refinements of the theoretical concepts so that the general pure theories can be brought closer to the real situation and thus provide a better description of the trade of the Far East.

TERMS OF TRADE

In the discussion of trade and development, the concept of the terms of trade has received considerable attention, because the terms of trade provide significant indications of a country's international position and the welfare effects of trade on its economy. The terms of trade have become a necessary tool in trade analysis. There has been some difference of opinion among economists on the recent development of the terms of trade for primary products exporting countries; therefore, a study of the terms of trade of the Far East is of great interest.

There has been the often-repeated contention that poor countries have suffered deterioration in their net barter terms of trade. We find this view in the reports of the United Nations and in the writings of Raul Prebisch, W. A. Lewis, Gunnar Myrdal, A. H. Imlah, and C. P. Kindelberger. As indicated in Table 3 by the statistics of the United Nations, the terms of trade for all developing countries have on the average deteriorated 9 per cent for the period 1953-62. On the basis of inference of the United Kingdom's net barter terms of trade, it is believed that a given quantity of primary products would pay on the eve of World War II for only 60 per cent of the quantity of manufactured goods which it could buy at the beginning of the second half of the 19th century. [10] This finding is contradictory to the classical position that the operation of diminishing returns in primary production would cause the prices of primary products to rise relative to the prices of manufactures.

Among others, one reason given for this deterioration of the terms of trade for developing countries is that there has been a relative decrease in the demand for primary products.

This change of demand can in turn be traced to two factors: (1) Engel's law which states that as our income goes up the portion of the income for the expenditures of certain products, such as foodstuffs, goes down and (2) because of technical progress in manufacturing, the amount of industrial raw materials used per unit of output has been reduced. [11]

If the alleged terms of trade deterioration are true, there can be only a pessimistic outlook for the poor countries because they can not exist without trade. However, with trade there would be an international transfer of income away from the poor countries, and this decrease in purchasing power could be significant in reducing their capacity for development.

There is now another school disagreeing with these terms of trade deterioration position. Some question the validity of the conclusion that the terms of trade of the poor countries, in the long run, actually have deteriorated.

Theodore Morgan considers the study of the United Kingdom's terms of trade not broad enough to provide a sufficiently strong foundation for any adequate generalization about the long run terms of trade of poor countries. The various poor countries have highly diverse demand and supply experience for the different primary products. [12]

Evaluating the United Nations statistics, A. K. Cairncross holds that the deterioration should not be considered a general trend, but rather an expected readjustment from the unusually high primary prices during the 1951-53 period of the Korean War boom. He points out that the value of exports of underdeveloped countries increased for the period 1950-57 by 50 per cent, or 6 per cent per annum, not far below that of the industrial countries. Cairncross considers that there may be a decline in the demand for some existing primary products because of the use of substitutes; however, he insists that we

must not overlook the fact that there will be increasing demand for additional new primary products as the world standard of living improves. He points out that aluminum, rubber,
newsprint, synthetic fibers, etc., are all new requirements created in the 20th century. [13]   There is no worry
about the international position of a country rich in resources
of uranium, for instance, when the world has come to the
stage of using atomic energy for commerce and industry.

Some accept the contention that there has been terms of
trade deterioration for poor countries, but attribute it to reasons other than the lowering of the demand. The fact that the
United Kingdom paid less for imports of primary products
can be explained by the lowering of the transportation costs
which are often included in the import prices of these products. Others contend that the United Kingdom received
relatively higher prices for exports because of the higher
wage costs of production or higher quality of these products.[14]

Observation of the Terms of Trade for Far Eastern Countries

As there have been differences of opinion as to whether
the terms of trade have a tendency of deterioration in the Far
East, it might be well to look into the statistics. As indicated
in Table 3, according to United Nations statistics, the terms
of trade for all developing regions for primary products have
deteriorated 9 per cent in the period from 1953-62. [15]   But the
terms of trade for the ECAFE region for primary products
for the same period have fluctuated within the range from 92 to
105 and rested at 101 for 1962 showing no deterioration. There
is a slight deterioration if the 1962 index is compared to the
1951 index at 127, but the 1951 index was abnormally high due
to the Korean War boom.

As indicated in Table 4 the over-all terms of trade for
the period 1953-62 have fluctuated within the range of 96 to 106
and rested at 99 in 1962, showing hardly any deterioration at
all. Except for the high index of 120 in 1951, the 1962 index for
the region compares favorably to 90 for 1948 and 83 for 1938.[16]

Although, as indicated in Table 3, the export prices for the

ECAFE region for food and minerals have deteriorated, the
prices for agricultural nonfood products have been stable.
The over-all export prices have deteriorated but the prices
for imports have also deteriorated, resulting in rather stable
terms of trade for the region. This means that the Far East
has been, on the whole, able to make adjustments in their
trade to face the advanced nations on equal grounds. The
pessimistic outlook that some theoreticians have for the trade
of primary producing countries does not apply to the Far East.

   The gross barter terms of trade, or the quantum ratio
between exports and imports as indicated in Table 4, have
deteriorated drastically from 100 in 1953 to 84 in 1962, which
is almost half of that for 1938 at 160. This does not mean
that the ECAFE countries have in recent years exported smaller
quantities of exports; in fact the quantum index for exports
has been continuously increasing: from 100 in 1953, to 134 in 1962,
which is even higher than 128 registered for 1938. The deterioration of the gross terms of trade is due to the fast
increase in the quantities of imports, with its quantum index
going up from 100 in 1953 to 159 in 1962, whereas the index
for 1938 was 80. This means although the quantities of exports of the Far Eastern countries have gradually improved to
slightly exceed the prewar level, the quantities of their imports have grown to twice the prewar level. This fantastic
rise in the quantities of imports can be explained by the reconstruction, industrialization, militarization, and urban-
ization programs being carried out in the Far Eastern
countries. These different phases of growth have gone beyond the level that can be adequately provided for by domestic
supplies. The fact that the rise of the quantities of exports has
not caught up with the rise of the quantities of imports can be
explained by the universal population growth in all countries
and the higher level of per capita consumption in some.

   The deterioration of the gross barter terms of trade
brings up the question of how the Far Eastern countries are
able to pay for the import surpluses. As indicated in Table 5,
the index of the capacity to import for the various countries
has improved. The index of capacity to import is the product of the quantum index for exports and the net barter terms
of trade. The latter are stable for some countries and have

Table 3

Developing Regions: Unit Value Indexes and Terms of Trade for Primary Exports
(in U.S. dollars, 1953=100)

	Imports		Primary exports								Terms of trade	
			All developing regions				Developing ECAFE region[c]					
	All developing regions[a]	Developing ECAFE region	Food	Agricultural nonfood[b]	Minerals	General	Food	Agricultural nonfood	Minerals	General	All developing regions (6)/(1)	Developing ECAFE region (10)/(2)
	(1)	(2)	(3)	(4)	(5)	(6)	(7)	(8)	(9)	(10)	(11)	(12)
1950	89	93	...	...	...	...	89	127	103	112	...	120
1951	105	115	...	...	...	...	94	189	111	147	...	127
1952	107	110	101	116	102	105	100	129	110	117	98	106
1953	100	100	100	100	100	100	100	100	100	100	100	100
1954	96	95	117	101	102	109	105	96	94	99	113	104
1955	97	96	98	108	103	102	95	118	99	107	105	111
1956	99	96	97	106	104	101	90	110	101	101	102	105
1957	103	101	100	102	110	103	90	109	103	92	100	92
1958	99	96	95	92	110	98	93	99	104	98	99	102
1959	97	94	84	101	102	93	90	125	96	107	96	113
1960	98	98	80	105	100	92	89	130	92	107	94	109
1961	97	96	78	95	99	88	91	109	92	99	91	103
1962	96	95	78	91	99	87	94	101	91	96	91	101

Source: Unless otherwise indicated, all tables are compiled by the ECAFE Secretariat based on government or United Nations statistics. For the present table, columns (1) to (6) and (11) are taken from United Nations, Monthly Bulletin of Statistics; columns (7) to (10) and (12) are compiled by the ECAFE Secretariat.

[a] Latin America, Africa excluding South Africa, Middle East and developing ECAFE region.

[b] Includes nonfood products of forests and fisheries.

[c] For country coverage, see infra, Asian Economic Statistics, Table 1.

Table 4

Developing ECAFE Region:[a] Quantum Indexes, Unit Value Indexes, and Commodity Trade Balance
(Value in million U.S. dollars; indexes: 1953=100)

	Quantum index			Unit value index			Value		
	Exports	Imports	Quantum ratio (1)÷(2)	Exports	Imports	Terms of trade (4)÷(5)	Export	Import	Balance
	(1)	(2)	(3)	(4)	(5)	(6)	(7)	(8)	(9)
1938[b]	128	80	160	35	42	83	2,650	2,370	+ 280
1948	81	75	108	105	117	90	5,210	6,020	- 810
1950	106	88	120	101	93	109	6,440	5,650	+ 790
1951	107	104	103	140	115	122	9,050	8,300	+ 750
1952	98	106	92	114	110	104	6,800	8,100	-1,300
1953	100	100	100	100	100	100	6,040	7,020	- 980
1954	103	100	103	96	95	101	5,980	6,670	- 690
1955	110	110	100	102	96	106	6,840	7,370	- 530
1956	117	125	94	97	96	101	6,910	8,370	-1,460
1957	119	136	88	97	101	96	7,070	9,480	-2,410
1958	112	123	91	93	96	97	6,410	8,240	-1,830
1959	120	189	84	99	94	105	7,210	8,420	-1,210
1960	121	149	84	104	98	106	7,650	9,830	-2,180
1961	127	149	85	97	96	101	7,500	10,020	-2,520
1962	134	159	84	94	95	99	7,730	10,430	-2,700

Source: United Nations, Monthly Bulletin of Statistics, Statistical Yearbook and Yearbook of International Trade Statistics.

[a]Excluding Iran.

[b]Figures adjusted to approximate trade of present customs areas except trade between India and Pakistan. For details, see United Nations, Yearbook of International Trade Statistics.

28

deteriorated for others, but the former has improved for all the listed countries except Pakistan. Taiwan and Japan were able to pay, in 1962, 75 per cent and 70 per cent more, respectively, for imports in volume than they did in 1953. This improvement in their ability to pay for imports has helped, but is still far from being sufficient to meet their requirements, thus resulting in the increasing deficits in the merchandise accounts for the entire region as indicated in Table 4. The deficits are eventually made up by tourist spending, foreign private capital investments, incoming remittances, foreign government expenditures, the United States special procurement expenditures, foreign aid, bank loans, and the outflow of gold. Some countries, in providing supplies for the Allied Nations in World War II, managed to accumulate substantial foreign-exchange and gold reserves which are now being used to pay for imports.

As long as the net barter terms of trade are stable for the Far East, any improvement in productivity will result in favorable factoral terms of trade, which is the product of productivity and the net barter terms of trade. In other words, trade has been beneficial to the Far East. Bhagwati maintains a theoretical possibility of "immizerizing growth" which implies that productivity improvement may reduce the factoral terms of trade and even hurt a country as its net barter terms of trade drop faster than the rise of productivity.[17] This will not happen in the Far East if the net barter terms of trade stay stable as they have in recent years.

Although the net barter terms of trade are stable for the region as a whole, it does not mean that they are stable for every country. Actually, the performance of the terms has been quite varied, showing stability for some but wild fluctuations and a tendency to deteriorate for others.

Table 6 gives the terms of trade for the various countries for the period from 1948-62. Invariably there is a high plateau in 1951 due to the Korean War boom. There are also relatively high indexes for 1954-55 and 1959-60 for most countries, showing the effect of the prosperity of the United States and Japan, which are the two countries of considerable importance as trade partners of the Far East.

Table 5

ECAFE Countries: Terms of Trade and Capacity to Import, 1962
(in U.S. dollars, 1953=100)

	Quantum index		Ratio of quantum indexes (1)÷(2)	Unit value index		Terms of trade (4)÷(5)	Index of capacity to import (6)x(1)	Ratio of import capacity index to import quantum index (7)÷(2)	Ratio of export to import
	Exports	Imports		Exports	Imports				
	(1)	(2)	(3)	(4)	(5)	(6)	(7)	(8)	(9)
Ceylon	122	101	121	93	89	105	128	127	109
China (Taiwan)[a]	204	152	134	84	98	86	175	115	77
India	120	182	66	107	94	114	137	75	63
Federation of Malaya	149	183	82	112	84	133	199	109	107
Pakistan[a]	82	156	53	111	135	82	67	43	54
Philippines	159	118	135	86	110	78	124	105	94
Thailand	154	175	88	91	101	90	139	80	84
Viet-Nam, Republic of	167	95	176	65	90	73	121	128	21
All developing countries[b]									
Excluding India	137	154	89	92	95	96	132	85	79
Including India	134	159	84	94	95	99	133	84	76
Japan	177	199	89	90	93	96	170	85	87
Australia[c]	156	168	93	75	110	68	107	64	104
New Zealand	132	140	95	92	104	88	116	83	106

[a]Quantum index derived from indexes of unit value and of total value in U.S. dollars.
[b]Includes countries listed above as well as Afghanistan, Burma, Indonesia, Portuguese India, Timor, Macao, West Irian, and Ryukyu Island.
[c]Year ending June.

Table 6

Net Barter Terms of Trade of Far Eastern Countries
(1958=100)

	1948	1950	1951	1952	1953	1954	1955	1956	1957	1958	1959	1960	1961	1962
Japan	...	87	93	89	95	94	91	91	88	100	106	106	105	104
Taiwan	...	...	...	117	115	103	114	103	112	100	97	91	96	90
India	99	103	128	99	99	109	102	102	94	100	108	111	112	113
Malaya	77	115	137	111	96	100	125	116	104	100	123	125	106	101
Thailand	...	...	...	...	...	109	106	98	94	100	107	109	104	109
Philippines	132	121	116	92	118	109	100	100	98	100	106	102	93	92
Ceylon	66	97	100	72	81	103	107	89	94	100	102	102	94	88
Indonesia	...	139	146	109	106	114	128	128	120	100	132	114	111	93
Pakistan	...	218	230	192	138	151	137	122	117	100	97	114	155	113
Vietnam	...	116	137	124	114	102	114	112	107	100	109	100	85	79
Burma	65	52	90	128	158	132	111	120	105	100	106	101	93	102

Source: Economic Survey of Asia and the Far East, 1956, Bangkok, 1957, p. 213; 1960, Bangkok, 1961, p. 138; 1963, Bangkok, 1964, p. 222-23. The Economic Commission for Asia and the Far East has published the terms of trade index numbers with different base years which have been converted to 1958 here.

The reason that some underdeveloped countries suffer from
a deterioration of the terms of trade is given by Kindleberger and
Cairncross as the poor factor mobility which may result in the
poor adjustments of the trade to meet adverse market conditions.
Sometimes, facing a decline in the prices of some exports, a
country may have to make adjustments shifting its production
away from these exports, and here factor mobility becomes important.   In the underdeveloped countries it is assumed that, due
to the low level of social overhead capital, the transportation
and communication facilities may be inadequate, resulting in the
difficulties of transferring factors from one region to another and
from one industry to another.   There are also the slow capital
formation process and the lack of technical personnel which make
it difficult for these countries to develop new exports.   In addition,
a very important element, the structural inflexibility of
the export trade, causes a situation in which a country's exports
are rigidly confined to a very few items.   The over-concentration
of the export trade is almost a universal feature of a colonial
economy in the sense that only a few primary products have been
developed by the colonial power to meet the needs of the mother
country, while the rest of the colonial economy is left behind.
Most of the colonies in the Far East have gained their political
independence, but their economies still maintain the colonial
pattern.   If there is a decline in the prices of the limited number
of exports, it is very difficult for these countries to make any
adjustment in the content of their export trade because, except
for these few items, they are far behind in productive efficiency.
Thus, diversification in the export trade will offer them some
degree of freedom of action in making trade adjustments.

Table 7 is an attempt to indicate the relative factor mobility and export structural flexibility of these countries.   Countries that compare favorably in these respects are placed at the
top of the table.   The export concentration index is calculated
by Benton F. Massell, using 1959 information in most cases.
The grouping of export industries is based on the three digit
standard international trade classification (SITC). [18] Japan's
high degree of diversification indicates its high level of development. [19] Facing the weakening of the markets for silk and cotton
textiles, Japan in recent years has gradually reduced its export
content of silk and cotton textiles and replaced them with

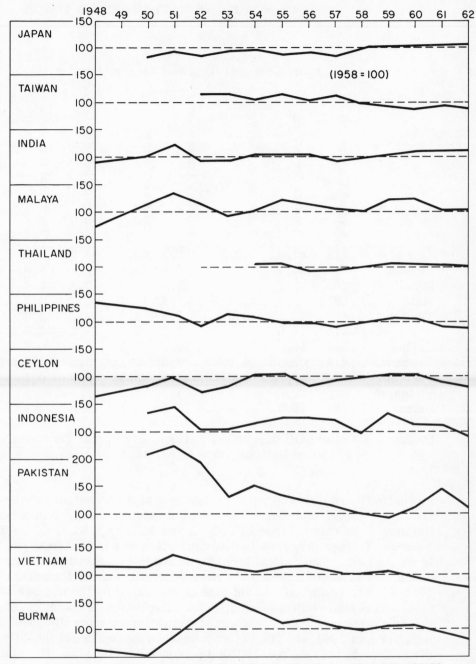

FIGURE I. THE NET BARTER TERMS OF TRADE OF FAR EASTERN COUNTRIES

Source: Based on information given in Table 6.

33

Table 7

Export Concentration and Factor Mobility

	Export Concentration	Capital Formation	Telegraphic Service	Railway Passenger	Railway Freight	Shipping Service	Technical Student
Japan	.215	47.3	100.2	187.5	61.9	94.9	13.8
Taiwan	...	26.1	...	40.2	23.0	...	6.8
India	.280	...	...	17.9	...	2.3	0.4
Malaya	.697	...	5.6	9.7	12.1	...	0.7
Thailand	.490	...	9.0	8.9	4.9	...	2.0
Philippines	.414	14.9	...	3.6	0.7	13.3	2.6
Ceylon	.649	16.0	...	22.2	3.8	...	0.2
Indonesia	.417	...	6.9	7.9	...	3.5	1.1
Pakistan	...	...	4.5	13.1	8.8	3.3	0.1
Vietnam	...	...	3.2	3.7	1.0	...	0.5
Burma	.691	18.3	3.0	8.8	4.2	...	0.3

Source: Statistical Office, United Nations, Statistical Yearbook,
1962, United Nations, New York, 1963, pp. 345,364,411-1

synthetic fibers. This is possible because of its technical efficiency
and better factor mobility. There was a moderate degree of divers
fication of the export trade of Taiwan and India in 1953, and, as Ta
7 shows, further progress in diversification was made in the period
from 1953-62. The capital formation rate is measured by the percentage of national income for gross-domestic-capital formation in
1962.[20] The technical student rate is measured by the number of
technical school students per 1,000 population for 1953-54.[21] The
railway passenger rate is the passenger-kilometer per 100,000
population in 1961.[22] The railway freight rate is the net ton-kilo-
meter freight service per 100,000 population in 1961.[23] The shipping rate is the gross registered tons per 1,000 population in 1961.
The telegraph rate is the telegraphic messages per 100,000 population in 1961.[25]

Figure 1 shows the graphs of the net barter terms of trade of some of the Far Eastern countries; they are drawn from the information given in Table 6. There is a good correlation between Figure 1 and Table 7. Japan, Taiwan, and India are countries with better export flexibility and factor mobility, and their terms of trade show a high degree of stability. Countries like Indonesia, Pakistan, and Burma have poor export flexibility and poor factor mobility, and their terms of trade show both a long-run tendency of deterioration and a short-run tendency of fluctuation. The contention is that facing the unstable primary-product world markets, the Far Eastern countries can make better trade adjustments if their economy is kept active and flexible. There is, of course, a trade-off between specialization and diversification. In specialization a country will gain in productivity, but there is the danger of market catastrophies; while in diversification, a country may be better prepared to meet the poor markets, but there is necessarily a loss of productivity. In the case of over-concentration of the export trade to the extent of decreasing returns to scale, diversification is imperative.

An observer of the trade of the Far East cannot but be curious about the wide fluctuations of the terms of trade which occur from time to time for some countries. This is often explained by the instability of the world markets and the inelastic demand and supply of these primary products. This type of explanation comes naturally and can be accepted without question, as it follows the traditional market-price analysis which forms a basic part of our economic concepts. But such violent fluctuations as those which occurred in Malaya (from 115 in 1950 to 137 in 1951, an increase of 19 per cent in one year, and from 137 in 1951 to 96 in 1953, a 30 per cent drop in two years) warrant further investigation. Undoubtedly, political and military factors disturbing the normal patterns of trade and causing violent terms of trade fluctuations have to be taken into consideration. Economists tend to close their eyes to these factors as they belong to another discipline. The Far East has not yet come to the stage of military and political equilibrium; military and political factors are often among the very dynamic forces causing disturbances and, at the same time, pushing developments of the region. The operation of these forces can be summarized in two categories: (1) war and cold war, and (2) monopoly and government controls.

War and Cold War

In time of war or when war is impending, the terms of
trade move in favor of the nonbelligerent countries and
against the belligerent countries, yielding windfall profits for
the former. Upon cessation of hostilities, the terms will
begin to approach the normal level. European economists
seldom include war as a factor in trade theory. This is natural because when war starts in Europe all nations will be
involved and trade is reduced to nil, leaving no special advantage to any. But for the United States, wars in Europe
have played a very significant role in helping this country
become the leading power of the commercial world. To
substantiate this, one has only to follow the commercial
progress made by this country during and after World Wars
I and II.

Far Eastern countries, not involved in the hostilities of
World War II, were able to realize tremendous gains in trade.
During World War II, long-term contracts were entered into
by the United Kingdom and the Commonwealth nations for the
procurement of foodstuffs and essential materials. The annual quantity bought was usually stipulated in the contract,
while the price was either fixed or subject to periodical negotiations. The bulk buying during the fifteen years from 1940-
55 proved to be satisfactory in achieving the following objectives: It ensured a steady flow of foodstuffs and materials to
the United Kingdom and withheld these supplies from going into the enemy countries; it saved the United Kingdom hard currencies, which otherwise would have to be spent on non-Com-
monwealth sources; it provided adequate market for the
exports of Commonwealth nations; and it stabilized the prices
of these exports. The terms, of course, moved in favor
of the Commonwealth nations not directly involved in the war.
However, it was also beneficial to the United Kingdom
because without long-term bulk-buying contracts, the
United Kingdom would have had to pay the fluctuating
prices which could be even higher than the long-term stable
ones. During World War II, India's exports expanded while
her imports were curtailed due to the shortage of shipping, resulting in large trade surpluses each year. There was also

considerable Allied military spending in India. Because of
all these, India was able to repay its external debts (over
$120 million, U.S.) and also to accumulate a large foreign-
exchange reserve of about $5.2 billion U.S., which was kept
in the Sterling pool at London.[26]   This is one of the sources
of funds that India can use in carrying out its economic development programs in postwar years.

Malaya is the center of the rubber market in the Far East.
Rubber supplies from Indonesia and other neighboring sources
are brought into Malaya where, together with the domestic supplies, they are processed and graded for export. Since 1946
when the United States started its stockpiling program, it has
become the largest buyer of rubber from Malaya. The large
quantity purchases of the United States caused the price of
rubber steadily to rise. In 1950, on the eve of the Korean War,
Communist China, Russia, and the United States competed for
the supplies of rubber in Malaya, thus causing rubber price to
go up from $0.45 to $2.40 per pound in a matter of a few
months--a rise of 530 per cent. A number of rubber dealers
made fabulous fortunes in a short period of time. After the
Korean War the price of rubber gradually settled back to normal. In 1955 and 1960, again, there were sharp rises in the
price of rubber due to large United States purchases.[27] This
explains the wide fluctuations of the terms of trade of Malaya
in Figure 1, as rubber is the most important export item of
Malaya.

In 1953 Ceylon and Communist China concluded an agreement for Ceylon to ship 50,000 tons of rubber in exchange for
270,000 tons of rice from Communist China. The price of
rubber quoted here relative to the price of rice was far above
the international market level, and, therefore, the terms of
trade were completely in favor of Ceylon. Ceylon was behind
Malaya in the productivity of rubber and was losing out to Malaya its markets in Communist China and the United States from
1950-51. Ceylon was quite bitter about this and was desperate
to improve its rubber market. In 1951, with the outbreak of
the Korean War, the United Nations established an economic
embargo on Communist China, and rubber was on the prohibited
list. Ceylon was not signatory to the embargo agreement. On
the contrary, it took the opportunity to send a supply of rubber

to Communist China. This, of course, irritated the United States
and brought on a strong protest from the United Nations. In
1952 Ceylon and the United States negotiated for rubber, but
they could not agree on the price. While the United States was
willing to pay the lower, Singapore's international market price,
Ceylon insisted on the higher price that prevailed in her local
market. Ceylon obtained the favorable terms of trade in the
1953 agreement with Communist China by taking advantage of
the United Nations embargo. Communist China agreed to this
high price for two compelling reasons: (1) Ceylon was the only
source of rubber open to it, and (2) Communist China was using
the high price to encourage other Asian countries to violate the
embargo. [28]

Monopoly and Government Controls

One group of economists, including W. A. Lewis and
F. Meha, contends that productivity has improved the terms of
trade for advanced nations, but caused them to deteriorate for
the underdeveloped countries because the gains from increased
productivity have been distributed in the form of high wages and
profits for the advanced countries, whereas the gains in productivity in the poor countries have been distributed in the form of
price reduction. [29] This assumes that labor unions are stronger
in the advanced countries, resulting in higher wages, while the unlimited labor supply of poor countries tends to depress the wage
rate. There is also the implication that big firms in advanced
countries have good control of not only domestic markets but
international markets as well, resulting in higher profit rates,
while the poor countries compete more in price. However,
wage-pushed inflation and oligopoly fixed price may not improve
the terms of trade of advanced countries, but on the contrary,
they may weaken their international position if there is active
competition among the advanced countries. Suppose Japan is
competitive to the United States in certain fields. Any improvement of productivity in the United States is quickly
matched by similar improvement in Japan. Would there be an
improvement of the terms of trade for the United States due to
higher wages and profits? Or would the prices of these products be going down due to the competition? Lewis' position
implies some degree of monopolistic control of the international
market by advanced countries. The question then is how strong

is the monopolistic control, if that control exists?

The trade pattern of the Far Eastern countries is not similar to that of independent economies of similar sizes dealing with one another on equal terms. They trade in groups: the Communist Bloc, the Sterling Area, and the Dollar Area. In each of the areas there are dominant economies, for instance: Soviet Russia in the Communist Bloc, the United Kingdom in the Sterling Area, and the United States in the Dollar Area.

Inasmuch as the trade is kept within the group and the dominant economies are the only sources of capital goods and technical services, a partial monopolistic position exists for the dominant economies. Actually, this should be considered the principal rewards for their leadership and their having to shoulder the burden of the foreign aid and mutual security programs. To the extent that trade does cross group lines, the monopolistic advantage of the dominant economies will diminish. Businessmen in the poor countries would not mind quoting a little lower price to the biggest buyer so as not to lose that very important market, and they would not mind paying a little higher price for the capital goods from the dominant economy, because that can be the major source of supply and that is where better technical services and financial terms can be obtained. As the biggest firms in a domestic economy enjoy some external economy due to the scale in buying and selling, so can there be better terms of trade for the dominant economies in the Far East.

The trade between Communist China and Russia is not conducted by private business firms in a free market, but rather through barter negotiations by state agencies. Communist China supplies raw materials and agricultural products to Russia and obtains industrial equipment and supplies from Russia in return. As Russia is the only source of capital goods for China, but could obtain agricultural products and raw materials elsewhere, it appears that Communist China is weaker in its bargaining position. Furthermore, Communist China has to rely on Russian credits for these purchases. However, the Communist Chinese government has proclaimed that in its trade with Russia the terms of trade have been fair. By comparing the prices of Russian and Communist Chinese trade

with the United Nations statistics of world market prices,
Robert F. Dernberger finds that the terms of trade have been
fair on the whole. Dernberger was converting ruble to yuan at
the rate of 1 to 1.67. But C. M. Li contends that in clearing
accounts, the conversion rate had ranged from 1 to 2.177 to
1 to 2.5. Therefore, the terms of trade have been fair to
Communist China in appearance by the market rate of conversion, but in reality unfair to Communist China by the unfavorable conversion rate at the time of payments. [30]

Sometimes it is possible for a small country to gain monopolistic control of the market of a certain material temporarily, and by government action the terms of trade may be ma-
nipulated in its favor. Before World War II, Burma was the
major exporter of rice, sharing the market with Indochina,
Thailand, Korea, and Taiwan. Burma exported nearly 3.5
million tons annually. Much of its rice went to India, Ceylon,
and Malaya. When war broke out, the British Government set
up a Rice Control Board which bought the entire exportable
surplus of Burmese rice. In 1942 when Burma was occupied
by Japan, Japan monopolized the Burmese rice trade. At the
end of the war, Burmese rice trade was restored to private
enterprise. In 1948 Burma gained independence from the
United Kingdom, and the socialistic government established a
monopoly of its rice trade under the management of the State
Agricultural Marketing Board which, acting as the sole agent,
buys all the exportable rice of Burma and sells it abroad.
Formerly, when the rice trade was in the hands of European,
Indian, and Chinese dealers, competition among them had kept
the price of rice low; but now, because of the Board's monopoly,
the price of rice went up. Furthermore, Burmese rice farms
did not suffer much damage during World War II. By 1950 her
rice production was restored to normal, while Taiwan, Indochina, and Korea still could not produce enough rice for their
domestic consumption. The international rice market in the
Far East was temporarily in the hands of Burma. This international and domestic monopoly resulted in favorable terms of
trade for Burma. Meanwhile, the domestic price of rice was
kept low, as the Board was the sole buyer for the export trade.
The difference of the external and internal price levels was
the margin of profits for the Board. The Board was doing
quite well. The Burmese Government position, ironically,

was the opposite of the American Government position as far
as farm products are concerned. The Burmese Government
bought rice on the domestic market at a lower price and sold
it abroad at a higher price, while the United States Government has been doing the opposite. This profitable rice monopoly for Burma lasted until 1953 when other rice producing
nations had restored their prewar level rice outputs. This
is mainly why the terms of trade for Burma steadily improved from 52 in 1950 to 158 in 1953 (with 1958 as the base
year, as shown in Table 6).[31]

Countries in the Far East compare favorably with other
primary-product exporting countries in the sense that their
terms of trade have been comparatively stable. However,
some of them stand to gain by more efforts along the lines of
improving the flexibility, diversification, and factor mobility
in their economies. The study of the terms of trade is funda-
mental to the understanding of a country's international position. However, governments still tend to use the balance of
payments as a basis for their policy decisions. This is probably because the concept of terms of trade is more difficult
for the general public to grasp and its statistics are not as
readily available, whereas the balance of payments presents
an over-all picture of a country's international position and
is closer to individual household budgetary experience.

BALANCE OF PAYMENTS AND
FOREIGN-EXCHANGE POLICY

Commercial policies of the Far Eastern countries are
developed largely to serve two purposes: to promote economic growth and to balance the international payments. It is not
always easy to attain two objectives at the same time. There
are always the urgent needs to overcome food shortage and to
meet the pent-up effective demand for consumer goods. This
plus the extraordinary requirements for machinery, transport
equipment, and materials for economic growth certainly will
create problems in international payments. Imports required for economic growth must be kept at a high level, but
the imports of nonessentials must be reduced to a minimum.
This imports-selection policy is tightened or liberalized from

time to time as necessitated by the fluctuations of export earnings and other sources of foreign exchange.

Balance of Payments

In the 1920's there was for the countries now included in the ECAFE a pattern of multilateral trade and payments which had developed on two inseparable premises: (1) The merchandise trade balance formed an interlocking network where trade surpluses in one direction were offset by deficits in other directions; and (2) the movements of capital and payments for invisible items such as financing, insurance, and freight generally offset the remaining trade surpluses and deficits.

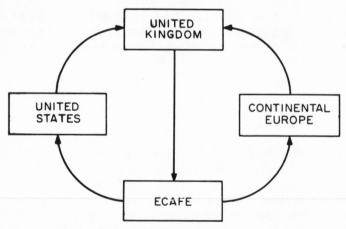

FIGURE 2.   MERCHANDISE TRADE BALANCES,
ECAFE, 1920'S

Source: United Nations, A Study of Trade between Asia and
Europe, Geneva, 1953, p. 6.

The merchandise trade balances showed two major trade circuits, and in each of them the ECAFE region formed one corner of the triangle. In the first place, the ECAFE region had a considerable trade surplus with the United States, which in turn had a trade surplus with the United Kingdom. Secondly, the ECAFE region had a considerable trade surplus with continental Europe, which in turn had a trade surplus with the United Kingdom. Both circuits were closed by the consistent export surplus of the United Kingdom with the ECAFE region.

These merchandise trade balances were again compensated by the payments for services and the capital flow. In the period 1920-29, the United States had a trade surplus with the world to the amount of $750 million annually and was able to export capital to the amount of $650 million annually. The United Kingdom had a trade deficit with the world to the amount of $1,200 million annually, and continental Europe had a trade deficit with the world to the amount of $1,100 million annually. These deficits were financed through receipts of invisible items estimated at some $2,000 million annually for the United Kingdom and about $1,000 million annually for continental Europe. The ECAFE region had deficits on invisible accounts with the United Kingdom and continental Europe. The payments on invisible accounts were made possible by the merchandise surplus of the ECAFE region as well as by the inflow of long-term capital and occasional short-term borrowing. These sources were also sufficient to finance considerable imports of gold and silver as reserves. [32]

This pattern of multilateral trade and payments weathered the depression of the 1930's, but came to an end during World War II. In the postwar period many Asian countries are suffering trade deficits with the world in general and with the United States in particular. Mainland China operates its trade as a state monopoloy, and by strict controls it managed to create a surplus for the years 1956-58. For the period from 1954-59, Ceylon, Cambodia, Malaya and Singapore, Indonesia, New Zealand, and Thailand had surpluses in their trade with the United States. This, of course, would help in relieving payments pressure, but a general equilibrium of international trade and payments for the Far East as a whole is not expected in the near future.

A major difficulty of international payments for the Far Eastern countries lies in the very large investment needs of

imports of capital goods for their economic development. It
is impossible to expect these countries to pay for the long-run
capital needs with current export earnings. Long-term foreign investments have to be encouraged to finance the long-run
capital needs. However, currently, foreign investments have
not come to the Far East in large quantities. This is because
of the political and military insecurity of the region and the restrictive and sometimes unfriendly policies of some of the
governments of the Far East regarding foreign investments
during the immediate postwar years. Some of the governments
of the Far East did not like to see high returns go to foreign investors; they applied heavy taxes on these returns, or they restricted the repatriation of capital, dividends, and interests.
This would certainly discourage foreign investments. In recent years there has been a change of policy in some Far Eastern countries to encourage foreign investments. There must
be a clear understanding on the part of the governments of the
Far East that if long-term foreign investments are necessary,
high returns will have to be paid and the rights of the investors respected. Only when there is a friendly investment
atmosphere to attract foreign investments can there be hope
for the optimum economic development and the general equilibrium in trade and payments. On the other hand, there has
been a tendency of foreign business to use its superior position to create monopolies in the market to crowd out smaller
domestic producers. There has been also the tendency of
foreign business to interfere with politics and exert undue influence on the governments of Far Eastern countries. This
will lead to ill feeling, suspicion, and hostilities. The relationship between foreign business and local government has
not been satisfactory the world over. A better relationship
can be cultivated if both respect each other's rights. Joint
ventures with foreign and local interests participating together probably will encourage mutual respect and confidence,
as they will have the very valuable experience of working together for a common goal. There is a disequilibrium of the
capital in the world, with relative surplus in the advanced
countries and relative shortage in the underdeveloped countries. Freer flow of capital is called for so that there will
be fuller utilization of capital and higher returns. There
will have to be freer flow of capital before there can be freer
flow of capital goods which are constituting an increasingly

important sector of the trade between the Far East and the
West.

Foreign-Exchange Policy

Most of the Far Eastern countries have difficulty, from
time to time, maintaining their balance of international payments. The consequences of prolonged adverse balance of
payments are either excessive fluctuations of the exchange
rate or an outflow of gold--or both. The former will disturb
trade and the latter two will weaken the monetary system.

According to the classical tradition of free trade, there
is no need of any controls over foreign-exchange and gold
movements. The so-called price-specie-flow mechanism,
worked out by David Hume, Adam Smith, John Stuart Mill,
and Alfred Marshall, is supposed to operate automatically to
bring about equilibrium of balance of payments.

The price-specie-flow mechanism works like this. A
deficit in international payments leads to gold exports in the
short run. This loss of gold, however, reduces the amount
of money in the country, since either gold is money or the
banking system keeps the supply of money adjusted to the
quantity of gold reserves. According to the quantity theory of
money, a decrease in the money supply of the country will
lead to a decline in commodity prices. Lower commodity
prices will increase exports, as foreigners find the country
a cheaper place in which to buy. This increase of exports will
bring about the country's equilibrium in trade and international
payments, and there even may be an increase in employment.

The simple price-specie-flow mechanism, however, has
been unable to stand the test of time as an effective adjustment process. The mechanism is based on the operation
of the gold standard of the old days. At the present time,
the gold standard does not exist in the Far East. While gold
flows may be effective in correcting payment deficits for a
while, they evidently cannot be continued indefinitely. A
country cannot sustain gold exports over a lengthy period
without running out of its gold stock. Modern economists
have inserted qualifications into the mechanism concerned
with the effects of gold movements on the supply of money

and the effects of change in the supply of money on commodity prices. While the classical economists stress, in the price-specie-flow mechanism, the importance of price changes induced by gold flows as a factor in bringing about adjustments, modern economists do not exclude the effects of price changes. They are inclined to think that the major burden of adjustments is carried by change in income. Since all the Far Eastern countries have extremely low gold stocks, they would like to improve their gold stock to provide a stronger backing for their currencies. Gold certainly is not expendable as a factor of adjustments in international payments. To supplement and protect their gold reserves, most countries in the Far East have established, in their central banks, reserves in foreign exchange. A favorable balance of payments will improve the foreign-exchange reserves, and an unfavorable balance will reduce them, leaving the gold stock untouched.

Even if we suppose that the Far Eastern countries have enough gold to allow free outflow, and even if we accept a direct simple link between the gold movements and the price-level changes, still this type of policy is difficult for the Far Eastern countries to accept because the adjustment process of the price-specie-flow mechanism for adverse balance of payments calls for a lowering of the domestic price level which is supposed to promote exports. Far Eastern countries are now in the process of industrialization and the promotion of national income; they certainly would not want to allow deflation to occur too frequently. Deflation would slow down their progress more than anything else, as business adjustment to deflation is usually contraction. Deflation may reduce business confidence, which in turn may bring about recession.

A free foreign-exchange market in which governmental authorities never intervene is hardly possible, especially in the Far East where for most countries there is a long-run tendency of import surpluses. Since 1957, with improvements in her balance of payments position, Japan has started a program of gradual relaxation of controls. It is the only country in the Far East approaching the establishment of a free foreign-exchange market. In the Sterling Area, there is easy convertibility between pound sterling and Commonwealth currencies.

Due to the persistent adverse trade and payments balances, most Far Eastern countries have resorted to foreign-exchange controls. Here the task is to directly restrict imports to the level of exports, or to impose controls to limit expenditures on foreign services, or to restrict the movements of capital as well. In actual practice, the government would require all foreign-exchange earnings through trade, services, and investments to be surrendered to the central bank in exchange for the domestic currency at the official rate, thereby establishing government control of the sources of foreign exchange. Users of foreign exchange would have to come to the government to apply for foreign exchange. The government could use its discretion to discriminate against users for undesirable purposes. The essence of foreign-exchange control is the rationing of the short supply of foreign exchange for the necessary payments.

In rationing, the authorities attempt to set some social standards. They may restrict the imports of "luxuries," while permitting the imports of "essentials." This is discrimination by commodity. In rationing, the authorities may be very strict in scrutinizing the applications for a currency in critical shortage, while quite lenient in the case of a currency of relative abundance. Thus, they encourage imports from the latter and discourage imports from the former. This is discrimination by country. For instance, imports of Japanese equipment are favored over American equipment if there is a more severe shortage of American dollars than yen.

A widely used system of foreign-exchange control in the Far East is the clearing system. Under this system, for instance, Formosa keeps an account in Tokyo, with all the earnings of its exports to Japan paid into it and all its imports from Japan paid out of it. By this system, Formosa can limit its imports in value from Japan to the value of its exports to Japan. A comparable account is created at Taipei by Japan. The purpose of this is to insure a bilateral balance of payments between Japan and Formosa.

Whenever there is foreign-exchange control, there is the likelihood of the existence of a black market. Due to the shortage of foreign exchange, foreign-exchange rates on the black market may be much higher than the official rates.

Importers of luxury items, for instance, who cannot obtain
foreign exchange from the government will go to the black
market willing to pay the higher rates. The black market is
supplied with illicit sources of foreign exchange such as
foreign tourists or foreign servicemen who sell foreign currencies on the black market for higher rates. The authorities, in order to maintain control of foreign exchange, will
have to try to stamp out the black market, which is not
always easy to do. When the black market rates are very
much higher than the official rates, even legitimate merchants may risk government prosecution and sell their
earnings of foreign exchange on the black market. Gradually, this will dry up the source of supply of foreign exchange
for the government and, thus, present difficulties in the
foreign-exchange control operation. To reduce this tendency, the authorities will have to improve the official
rates to bring them in line with the black market rates.
This would mean occasional devaluation of the domestic currency from time to time. In a sense, the official rates are
artificial, while the black market rates more realistically
reflect the shortage and the high demand for foreign exchange. Occasional adjustments of the official rates are
only natural and realistic. Of course, here we cannot
overlook the risk factor of the black market rate. The
higher the risk, the higher black market rate will be asked,
and the risk factor is determined by the effectiveness of
government prosecution.

Another reason for this occasional devaluation of the
domestic currency is the inflationary tendency of countries
in the Far East. Using the purchasing-power-parity theory
of Gustav Gassel, it is natural for the foreign-exchange
rates to fluctuate to reflect relative changes in price levels.

Some countries use the devaluation of domestic currency as a means to promote exports. This occurs when
the devaluation is greater than what is necessary to counterbalance the inflation factor. Whether this will improve the
country's balance of payments depends a great deal on the
elasticity of demands of its exports and imports.

In actual practice, the occasional devaluation of domestic currencies in countries of the Far East has been
made largely with the aim of bringing the official rates
closer to the black market rates. It is not often used as

a deliberate policy to improve the balance of payments, because the effects of the devaluation on the quantities of exports and imports have not been carefully studied.

It is not easy to say that foreign-exchange control has
restricted trade and that, therefore, the advanced nations
should negotiate with the Far Eastern countries for the re-
moval of the control. This approach is not likely to be very
successful as long as there is the tendency of adverse balance
of payments for the Far Eastern countries.

TARIFF POLICY

A very controversial aspect of the trade theory deals
with tariffs. The classical school advocates free trade, but
in reality trade is seldom completely free. While most of
the advanced countries impose tariffs or import restrictions
on agricultural imports, underdeveloped countries do the
same on manufacture imports. While the classical economists concentrate their attention on the general equilibrium
under ideal conditions, protectionists take a more realistic
approach and concern themselves with less idealistic
peculiarities.

The Theory of Protection

Protectionists do not base their arguments entirely on
trade concepts; their arguments sometimes are based on
economic development concepts. To them, trade itself is
not a goal but a means, while the economic development of
the countries involved is usually the ultimate purpose. There
are a few special occasions where the justification of protection may be argued.

1. Industrialization through Protection
It is generally accepted that protection is justified in the
case of infant industries which cannot withstand the competition of well-developed imports. The tariffs will be eventually
removed as the industries mature. The cost of this protection
to the country is the high prices it has to pay for the products

of the infant industries when tariffs are applied. But the country will stand to gain when and if the industries mature, because there will be technical advancement, improvements of production and better employment opportunities for the country.

The main objections to the infant industry argument are: (1) When the pressure of international competition is removed, the infant industry will not grow, or will not grow as fast; and (2) this temporary protection has a tendency to develop into a long-term subsidy, as the infant industry will always want to hang on to its protected market. These objections can be overcome if tariffs are granted carefully only to those infant industries which have the potential to develop to meet international competition in a short period of time, and if the tariffs are granted only on short-term basis and are subject to frequent reviews for their termination as the industries mature, as is the practice in India.

Underdeveloped countries are now attempting to bring about industrialization through protection. It is not a matter of one or two infant industries being promoted under protection, but of the entire economy undergoing industrialization under protection. In this case the infant industry argument is extended on a very large scale.

In 1929, when the Australian Government was contemplating industrialization under protection, Australian economists developed a lengthy argument for tariffs. Many heated debates on the Australian tariff followed. In 1937, in an essay, W. B. Reddaway used a system of seven equations which, if their structure correctly depicted the Australian economic system, proved that the tariff reduced national income, but raised real wages. This controversy in the 1930's involved Taussig, Haberler, and Viner[33] and left economists with mixed views. Viner considers that protection of manufacturing would increase real income if a country has a comparative labor advantage, but that monopoly would hold wages so high in manufacturing that imports would undersell them. However, he continues that free trade, which would force the monopolist to reduce wages and cause the comparative advantage o manufacturing to be reflected in market prices, would accomplish the same effect. Haberler stands for protection of manufacturing if wages for equivalent labor are higher in manufacturing than in agriculture. Welfare in the economy may be increased by producing manufactured goods at home, even though they are more expensive relative to agricultural products at home than abroad, and manufacturing can survive at home only if protected. In this case higher aggregate real income is purchased at the cost of some unemployment.[34]

Another way of looking at the controversy of free trade versus protection is the discrepancy found in the optimal allocation of given resources from the trade theory viewpoint on the one hand and from economic development viewpoint on the other. Both viewpoints would aim at the most efficient use of resources, but the difference seems to be that the trade theory would place the emphasis on the comparative advantages the country enjoys now, while the development theory would place emphasis on the promotion of economic growth in the future. The time element is of importance here.[35] In an article on "Comparative Advantage and Development Policy," Chenery very ably pinpoints the conflicts between the trade theory and the development theory.[36] According to the trade theory, gains of trade are of primary importance, and they can be maximized by free trade. But according to the development theory, trade gains may be sacrificed for development gains which can be maximized by a development program, and tariffs may be necessary for implementing such a program.

Manoilesco in his book, Theory of Protection and International Trade, in 1931, argues that the average income for the underdeveloped countries can be improved by industrialization as the productivity of labor and wages are higher in industries than in agriculture. Myrdal shares the same view that there is a wide gap in real wages between industry and agriculture.[37] Kuznets, from his studies of the sector distribution of income for 14 countries over a long period of time and for 45 countries in recent years, finds that industrial wages paid to workers fresh from the country are considerably above agricultural incomes. The wage disparity exists in underdeveloped and advanced countries alike and it is a persistent long-run phenomenon. Hagen says it is an empirically observed fact that when the per capita income is rising rapidly and secularly in a country, the output of manufacturing and mining grows secularly relative to that of agriculture and inputs required in manufacturing and mining likewise grow relative to those in agriculture. In this case, except in the hypothetical situation of perfect geographic and occupational mobility of labor, wages in manufacturing must be higher than in agriculture. If they are not higher, manufacturing will not be able to obtain the continuing stream of added labor that it needs. This wage disparity is consistent with full employment. As a result of the wage disparity, manufacturing industry, having a real comparative advantage, will be undersold by imports. Protective tariffs which permit such industry to exist will increase real income in the economy. However, Hagen concedes that a subsidy per unit of labor equal to the wage differential will increase real income further, and if combined with free trade will permit optimum income improvement.[38] Hagen finds economic growth through industrialization, with continuing rise in per capita income over the long-run is characteristic of the entire Western world, and it may be beginning now in China, India, and other nations in the Far East.[39] Anthony Koo raises some questions about the statistical basis in Hagen's comparison of the wages between manufacturing and agricultural working forces in that there may be discrepancies in productivity, age composition, the cost of living or the discomfort of city life which are not fully accounted for. Hagen would not mind some readjustments of the statistics to better account for these factors, but he insists that wages of laborers of equivalent capacity must be higher in industry than in agriculture in order to cause this continuing flow of labor.

2. Factor Immobility

According to the classical school: Labor is homogeneous, factor mobility within a country is free and easy, and the country's production can adjust to the changing world market with ease, so that the equilibrium under free trade will provide full employment and efficient allocation of resources. However, modern economists question the assumption that labor is homogeneous and factor mobility is free and easy. According to Cairnes, labor is differentiated by the social class structure and by the structure of vocational training; therefore, instead of homogeneous labor, there are noncompeting groups each for a special field of production, one of which is not always substitutable for another. Pigou shares this position, pointing out that in the industrial world, brain labor, trained hand labor, and muscular labor are noncompeting in the sense that against those who pass from one to another there is a great and often insurmountable gulf. If trade should induce the country to reduce the production of an industry using factors of low substitutability, it will worsen the income position of these factors.

If factor immobility is accepted, then free trade may not lead to full employment and efficient allocation of resources. Ohlin puts it this way: A nation may have a comparative advantage in manufacturing when costs are measured in terms of homogeneous labor, but if the divergence of wage levels between manufacturing and agriculture is much greater than that of the country it trades with, its money cost advantage may lie in agricultural products; hence the country is likely to specialize entirely in agriculture. In this case free trade may lead to a lower national income than will protection of manufactures. [40]

Taussig made an effort to save the classical position by maintaining that if the structure and relative wages of noncompeting groups are similar from country to country, and if the input requirements of any given product for members of these groups are about the same from country to country, then the classical position stands in its original form. [41] However, realistically speaking, noncompeting groups are not the same for the Far East and the industrial West, as the social class structure and the structure of vocational training are not the same for the two parts of the world.

If we take the position of classical economists that labor is highly mobile, adjustments in the allocation of the labor force would prevent any surplus labor to form in any sector. However, if we concede that labor is not very mobile, then

there is in a dwindling sector possible surplus labor refusing
equilibrium adjustments. In the underdeveloped countries,
faced with fast population growth and limited employment in
primary production, surplus labor often results. To solve
the problem, according to Gunnar Myrdal and Manuel Gottlieb,
protective tariffs to accelerate industrialization are called
for. The higher wages offered by protected industries may
improve labor mobility by helping the labor force to make its
equilibrium adjustments.[42] According to Raul Prebisch, surplus labor in primary production may also result from productivity improvement. Again, he advocates protective tariffs
to induce industrialization because they will limit the adjustments to those new branches of industries that should be developed within a given period of time. If these tariffs are
applied gradually, high import prices could be absorbed by
general increase in productivity without seriously affecting
the price level of the economy--provided that protection has
not been exaggerated to shelter inefficiency. He adds that it
will be a very mistaken policy to advocate technical progress
in primary production without a parallel policy of industrialization, as the surplus labor created will cause lower wages
or disguised unemployment.[43]

3. Internal and External Economics

The classical trade theory generally assumes the production functions of trading countries with constant returns to
scale or constant opportunity costs. Countries can expand or
contract the scale of production of different sectors without
worrying about changes of real or opportunity costs. Modern
economists introduce the concept of internal economy due to
scale into the trade theory and sometimes arrive at conclusions different from those of the classical position. The controversy over F.D. Graham's case for tariff protection in
the 1920's illustrates this point. Graham's basic contention
was that a country with a comparative advantage in increas-
ing-cost goods and a comparative disadvantage in decreas-
ing-cost goods may be worse off under free trade than with no
trade, or at least could better its free trade position by protection. Graham constructs the case of two countries producing two commodities: wheat, which is subject to diminishing

returns, and watches, which are subject to increasing returns.
Costs are stated in terms of output per unit of labor time.
When trade opens between these countries, the one with a comparative advantage in wheat expands its wheat production and
contracts its watch industry. After specialization has pro-
ceeded some distance, the output per unit of labor input has
fallen for watches and wheat because of diseconomies of small
and large scale, respectively. The opposite occurs in the country whose watch industry expands and whose wheat industry
contracts; its output per unit of labor input has risen. In the
unfortunate country specializing in wheat, labor productivity
shrinks at about the same rate in both industries as trade expands, while the international terms of trade stay constant.
Comparative-cost logic may continue to dictate specialization
in, and export of, wheat, but real income may consist of less of
both commodities than it would in the absence of trade.

There have been some objections to the Graham case for
protection, but all turn not on its consistency but on its em-
pirical plausibility. 44 While in an advanced country, where
there are good factor mobility and effective competition behaviors, it is unlikely for a country to enjoy comparative
advantage in a diminishing return industry for long. But in an
underdeveloped country, the Graham--Tinbergen case for protection may find its application. Due to technical backwardness, a Far Eastern country has comparative disadvantage in
manufacturing. Trade would induce the country to specialize
in primary products. As the country pushes further and further into the specialization of primary production, diminishing returns may result due to the shortages of land and natural
resources. International trade may reduce the real income of
the country as it goes further and further into such specialization
in a diminishing return industry.

The classical trade position not only overlooks the internal
economy of scale, but also pays little attention to the external
economics of linkage. External economies to a firm refers to
the situation where, without any internal improvements, the
firm enjoys better profits because the industry as a whole expands or makes improvements. External economies to an industry refer to the situation where, without any internal
improvements, the industry enjoys better profits because other

related industries expand or make improvements. Industries
are classified on several levels: for instance, marketing,
manufacturing of consumer goods, manufacturing of capital
goods, basic metal industries, transportation and communications, utilities, etc. The level closest to the consumers is
placed at the top, and that farthest from the consumers at
the bottom. Each level supports a level above and is in turn
supported by a level below. Industries are related to one
another with strong or weak external economies. External
economies can be of two types: horizontal or vertical.
According to Fleming, the horizontal type refers to the
effects of one industry on another of the same level: for instance, the prosperity of one consumer-goods industry may
lead to the prosperity of another through increased purchasing power and consumer spending of the community. However, according to Pranab Bardhan, the horizontal type
refers to the interdependence of production functions of industries of the same level: For instance, the efficiency improvement of one consumer goods industry may lead to the
efficiency improvement of another. The vertical type refers to the effects of the expansion or improvements of one
industry on the profitability of another industry of a different level. The vertical external economies can be again
divided into two types: forward and backward. The forward
type refers to the effects on the level above, and the backward on the level below.

It has been the experience of numerous poor countries to
show considerable growth in their trade, but only a very slow
rate of economic development in contrast with what would be
expected from classical analysis. According to Bardhan,
trade has not helped the poor countries as much as it has
helped the developed countries. For the poor countries, the primary production promoted by trade has very
weak externality effects on their economies, while for the developed countries the production of manufactures of consumer
goods and capital goods promoted by trade has much stronger
forward and backward externality effects. Therefore, Bardhan
concludes, protection for manufactures is justified in that
faster development in manufacturing will be more likely to
lead to faster economic growth for the poor countries. [46]

In the beginning of industrialization, Western nations also
started out with an emphasis on some primary or staple com-

modities for exports: for instance, cotton and wool textiles for
Britian, timber for Sweden, dairy products for Denmark,
cotton and wheat for the United States, and silk for Japan.
Why did the expansion of exports of these primary or staple
commodities bring about faster economic development for the
Western countries than the primary products are now doing
for the underdeveloped countries? Gerald M. Meier provides
two reasons for this discrepancy: the too-rapid population
growth and the dual economy in the underdeveloped countries.
This view is shared by Bardhan and Hirschman. Bardhan observes that for the underdeveloped countries the primary export sector, despite considerable expansion in the 19th century, did not serve as a propulsive sector, because the export
sector is an economic enclave of the metropolitan country.
Externality effects of the primary export sector of the underdeveloped country are stronger on the metropolitan country
than on the underdeveloped economy. Hirschman adds that the
small linkage effects of primary production in the underdeveloped countries are due to the fact that only a very small
fraction of the products receive elaborate processing in these
countries. [47] In the United States, the cotton plantation, cotton
textile industry, and cotton textile machinery manufacturing,
exist side by side; prosperity of one would have profound effects on the others. Malayan rubber plantations are largely
financed and managed by British interests. The expansion of
the rubber plantations in Malaya will improve the profits of
the rubber products manufacturing in England rather than in
Malaya, because very little of the manufacturing industry
exists in Malaya. To improve the linkage between trade and
economic growth, the underdeveloped countries will have to
encourage the processing and other manufacturing industries
related to primary products to develop in their own countries,
as some of the underdeveloped countries have done. Chenery
has observed that in the underdeveloped countries there is already evidence of the beginning of external economies due to
the expansion in machinery, transport equipment, metals, and
some intermediate goods industries. [48]

The justification of tariff protection on the grounds of external economies is conditioned by the irreversibility of such
effects. That is, when an enterprise is protected, its expansion will create favorable externality effects on other related
industries, and these effects will continue even after the pro-

tection is withdrawn. If the external economies are reversible, then whatever gains due to the protection will be wiped out when the protection is withdrawn, or protection once imposed will have to be made permanent. The case of irreversible external economies is similar to the case of infant industry, where temporary protection will yield permanent gains. An example of this is: The expansion of a manufacturing industry due to protection may give its input-providing industry a sufficient stimulus to go over the hump and reap internal economies of scale, and this enhances, in turn, the profitability of the protected industry using cheaper inputs.

4. Technological Progress

A major factor causing the slow economic growth of the underdeveloped countries is their technological backwardness. There are many reasons for this: inadequate education, lack of scientific aptitude, a nonmaterialistic way of life, etc. According to Harry Johnson, national specialization in primary products for trade has not helped these countries to overcome this shortcoming, but on the contrary has held their technological progress at a very slow rate. Technological backwardness has caused these countries to specialize in primary products, and this specialization in turn has made fast technological progress impossible.[49] Therefore, according to H. M. Singer, the underdeveloped countries should not allow themselves to be tied down to the specialization of primary products, but should try to promote industrialization-- by protection if necessary. A most important element of industrialization is the growing dynamic way of life and resilience that goes with urban civilization. Possibly, there may be a transfer of the population from low productivity occupations to high productivity occupations, thus achieving a rise in real income for these countries.[50] Bardhan shares this view, considering that an advantage of protection is the learning experience and the technological progress gained from the expansion of the import-competing industries. This technological progress will bring about better efficiency in the use of factors of production and will yield a higher level of income.[51] Chenery considers that the possibility of rising efficiency, as labor and management acquire increasing experience in actual manufacturing, has long been recognized.[52]

5. Capital Formation

For the developed countries, free trade stimulates capital
formation. As Ohlin points out, when the comparative advantage of these countries lies in capital intensive commodities,
extension of international trade raises the real reward to capital. If the supply function for savings is positively sloped,
this means that the rate of capital formation is accelerated.
However, for the underdeveloped countries, protection may
stimulate capital formation (a position taken by Alvin Johnson).
Protection tends to alter the distribution of income in favor of
the entrepreneurs of the protected industries. Compared
to other groups, these entrepreneurs are more thrifty because
they need capital and can better utilize the capital to equip-
their growing industries. Thereby, protection will accelerate
the rate of capital formation and investment. F. D. Graham
agrees with free-traders on the point that more capital could
be accumulated under free trade than under protection, but he
takes the position that protection tends to concentrate income in
the hands of people who are the best savers and investors. The
increasing returns of the growing industries under protection
will provide strong incentive for the entrepreneurs to save and
invest as fast as they can manage so that their industries can expand to reach an efficient size. [53]

Free-Trade Position Restated

Although there are a few special occasions where justification for protection may be argued, it is necessary not to
overlook the classical position as a general principle and to re-
state the advantage of free trade.

While protection tends to create obstacles in business
transactions, free trade will encourage free flow of goods and
services and should help the developing countries to grow, as
these countries would require all types of materials and equipment for their development programs. This is probably why
free ports such as Hong Kong and Singapore enjoy relatively
better prosperity than the neighboring countries of higher
tariffs. The experience of the fast economic growth in the Com-

mon Market countries of Western Europe certainly would give testimony to the advantage of free trade among themselves, although it may be difficult mathematically to measure the relationship between economic integration and economic growth. It stands to reason that better business freedom as promoted by free trade would tend to accelerate business activities in contrast to the obstructions created by protection.

Free trade will encourage competition both in the domestic market and in the international market, while protection tends to shield business from such competition. Excessive protection will harbor inefficiency and encourage laziness. For the young developing economy of the Far East, the competitive spirit should be encouraged rather than inhibited, although competition may be an uncomfortable environment for the business concerns involved. The people and the governments of the Far East should realize that protection is often requested by business concerns on the pretense of social needs, but its real purpose may actually be the creation of a partial monopoly of the protected markets, and the end result is for the community to pay for the inefficiency and laziness of these business concerns.

If the dual economy is the cause of the noncompeting groups of manpower and resources, then the dual economy will have to be eliminated. The demarcation line between the coastal modern sector and the interior traditional sector can be modernized. The labor forces of the two sectors may become more substitutive for one another if they have similar training and qualifications. The traditional sector does not have to limit itself to primary production but can gradually take on processing and manufacturing. The coastal modern sector does not have to be completely dominated by foreign interests. The governments will have to take on more responsibilities in vocational training to reduce the specificness of the labor force, so that the labor force can adjust to the changing domestic and international markets.

The problem of surplus labor force on primary production, a basis for protection to accelerate manufacturing, can be approached through a birth control policy. It is futile to expect that higher and higher tariffs can be used to solve the problem of repeated population explosions. Too rapid population growth would make it difficult for countries to have any improvements of real per capita income.

As long as the Far Eastern countries have the urge to promote economic growth through industrialization, their trade policy will largely be dictated by development theory concepts and will not follow, completely, the free trade position. However, at the same time, it is also wrong to assume that the Far Eastern countries would take the all-out protection position, relying on tariffs to solve all their economic problems. In synthesizing development theory considerations and trade theory considerations, it is important to put first things first. A free-trade position must be considered the general principle, and protection the deviation. Each policy should be justified by its own merits. Free trade must be the ultimate goal, although protection may be necessary to handle specific maladjustments from time to time. Free trade is the condition for general equilibrium, and protection should be used only as a matter of expediency.

Free trade would lead to the optimal allocation of resources for best utilization, while protection would often result in distortions. By favoring a few selected industries, protection provides better and larger manpower and material resources for these industries, but the unprotected industries must suffer. Protection is a discretionary policy, and it is favoritism. If carried too far, protection would create a situation where industries do not compete efficiently but fight for government favors in tariffs. The general public would end up paying high prices for the products of those inefficient industries that could apply the strongest political pressures.

Free trade would lead to lower prices through competition and better supplies of goods and services; protection would tend to create inflation due to shortages and obstructions.

Protection as a means to accelerate industrialization may be justified to an extent, but its effects should not be overstressed. Industrialization for a country calls for a variety of factors. Military insecurity and political unrest are not conducive to steady economic growth. Unless there is

peace and order, there may be a flight of capital out of the
region, rather than a substantial influx of foreign capital.
There should be a fast expansion program for transportation
and communication facilities to provide a workable market
system and to promote factor mobility. The modern factory
system of mass production cannot function without the marketing and shipping facilities to handle its products and resources.
A modern education system with the emphasis on physical and
social sciences, engineering, and business techniques will
have to be promoted to balance the traditional cultural preference for literary, philosophical and religous pursuits. Before
there can be industrialization, there must be a period of technological progress. There must be new products, new production techniques, new management methods, new market
channels, etc. Industrialization is the outcome of the best
efforts of scientists, laboratory workers, engineers, businessmen, social scientists, government personnel, etc. It is
the combined efforts of all the people in a country reflected in
its economy, and it is not achieved merely by the enactment of
a tariff law.

If factor mobility, a basis for protection, is due to obstructions caused by certain features in the social class
structure or the structure of vocational training, then these
features will have to be eliminated. It is costly for the community to have those with industrial aptitude tied down
to agriculture just because there is a higher social prestige
for farming over business. The Far Eastern way of life
traditionally holds contempt for ambition and competition.
However, if modernization and industrialization are desired,
the way of life has to accept some modifications, as the competitive spirit forms the basis of the business world. Free
public education or subsidized education will have to be instituted so that professions or desirable occupations are not
limited to the privileged classes. If nepotism is strong in
government and business personnel management, then there
should be reforms. Open competitive examinations should be
the basis of appointments, rather than family relations or
personal favors. The improvement of factor mobility is not a
simple matter; tariffs alone are hardly adequate for solving
the problem.

Reality of Commercial Policies

With all the arguments of free trade and protection influencing the thinking of the policy makers in the Far East, what has actually happened in the development of their postwar commercial policies? A brief review of the postwar development yields a few general observations common to most of them. (The detailed description of the experience of each of these countries is covered in later chapters.)

1. Most of the effective tariff laws were enacted in the 1950's with only a few occasional minor modifications in recent years. This indicates that tariffs are long run policies designed to regulate trade in such a way as to meet their long run revenue and development needs. This stability of tariffs is desirable in the sense that disturbances of tariffs on business transactions are reduced to the minimum. The short run adjustments to meet the fluctuations of international payments are left to import restrictions and foreign-exchange controls.

2. Tariffs are partially designed for revenue purposes with varying rates for the different countries as needed. Customs revenues, as percentages of government revenues, range from 5 per cent, as in the case of Japan, to 50 per cent in the case of Ceylon.

3. Tariffs are imposed also for protection purposes. High duties are imposed on imports of manufactures which tend to compete with domestic products. The number of industries covered by protection varies with countries, but generally speaking the rates are lower than in prewar days. The Far Eastern countries in the postwar period do not go all out for protection; on the contrary, tariff rates are modest. We find in the Philippines an interesting example. During the period of American control, the tariffs of the Philippines were regulated by the United States. The Philippines had always clamored for higher protection, but after the country gained independence, by choice it enacted in 1957 a tariff law with protection rates much lower than those of 1909 under American control. For most countries in the Far East, once an industry is given protection, the the protection tends to last indefinitely. India is the only ex-

ample where protection is granted on a temporary basis and in
the 1950's a large number of industries were actually removed
from the protection list.

4. Tariffs are also imposed to select imports. Essential
imports such as food, raw materials, and capital equipment
are either admitted free of duty or subject to very low rates,
while luxury consumer goods are subject to heavy duties. This
is to economize on the use of limited sources of foreign exchange.

5. Import restrictions by quotas or by licensing and foreign-exchange controls are short run devices to correct the
fluctuations of international payments. They are tightened up
in times of serious deficits and liberalized in times of equilibrium. In recent years in Japan, when there have been improve
ments in international payments, these short run controls are
almost totally removed.

6. The preferential tariffs, a system giving the mother
countries especially low rates, were started in the 1930's, but
have been preserved in the Far East in the postwar period even
after the colonies gained independence. There are exceptions. Burma has terminated its preferential tariffs for
the United Kingdom. South Vietnam does not have preferential tariffs for France, but includes France in a group of
some twenty nations enjoying favorable rates. The Philippines is gradually terminating its preferential tariffs for the
United States.

7. Most of the Far Eastern countries are members of the
GATT through which some reductions of tariffs have been
accomplished.

Among the different countries in the Far East, the experience of trade controls has been varied, with each one having
a unique system to meet its needs. Of course, a country's
trade controls would naturally reflect its economic and political ideology. Among the Communist countries in the Far East
including Communist China, North Vietnam, and North Korea,
government controls of trade have been tightening up. But in
most of the pro-West countries--for instance, Hong Kong,

Malaysia, Japan, and the Philippines--where the capitalistic philosophy prevails, there is a tendency of relaxation of trade controls, and this tendency is more pronounced when these countries are making good progress in economic development, growing more confident of its production, and are in a better position to manage their international payments.

Notes to Chapter 2

1. J. Bhagwati, "Pure Theory of International Trade," Economic Journal, March, 1964, p. 25.

2. ibid., pp. 4-5.

3. Gerald M. Meier, International Trade and Development (New York: Harper and Row, 1963), pp. 4-5.

4. Myint, "The Classical Theory of International Trade and the Underdeveloped Countries," Economic Journal, June, 1958, pp. 326-27.

5. Ministry of Foreign Affairs, Japan's Foreign Trade (Tokyo: Ministry of Foreign Affairs, 1958), p. 47.

6. Irving B. Kravis, "Wage and Foreign Trade," Review of Economic and Statistics, February, 1956, pp. 14-30; "Availability and Other Influences on the Commodity of Trade," Journal of Political Economy, April, 1956, pp. 143-46.

7. Bhagwati, op. cit., p. 8.

8. Myint, op. cit., pp. 317-19.

9. Myint, op. cit., pp. 320-21.

10. United Nations, Department of Economic Affairs, Relative Prices of Exports and Imports of Under- developed Countries, 1949, p. 72; A.H. Imlah, Economic Elements in the Pax Britannica (Cambridge: Harvard University Press, 1958), Chapter IV, Table 8; C.P. Kindleberger, The Terms of Trade, a European Case Study (New York: John Wiley & Son, 1956), pp. 53 ff.

11. H.W. Singer, "The Distribution of Gains between Investing and Borrowing Countries," American Economic Review, Papers and Proceedings, May, 1950, p. 479; Raul Prebisch, "Commercial Policy in Underdeveloped Countries," American Economic Review, Papers and Proceedings, May, 1959, pp. 261-64.

12. Theodore Morgan, "The Long-Run Terms of Trade between Agriculture and Manufacturing," Economic Development and Cultural Change, October, 1959, pp. 6-17.

13. A.K. Cairncross, "International Trade and Economic Development," Economica XXVIII (August, 1961), reprinted in his Factors in Economic Development (New York: Frederick A. Praeger, 1962), pp. 237-46.

14. ibid.

15. Kindleberger, op. cit., p. 173.

16. United Nations, Economic Commission for Asia and the Far East, Economic Survey of Asia and the Far East, 1961, Bangkok, 1962, pp. 11-12.

17. Meier, op. cit., pp. 49-51.

18. Economic Survey of Asia and the Far East, 1963, op. cit., Bangkok, 1964, p. 38.

19. The diversification of the export trade of Japan is calculated from the composition of its exports. United Nations, Statistical Office, Yearbook of International Trade Statistics, 1959, New York, 1960, Part I, pp. 321-25; Yearbook of International Statistics, 1953, New York, 1954, Part I, p. 261-68.

20. United Nations, Yearbook of National Accounts Statistics, 1960, New York, 1961; 1963, New York, 1964.

21. Economic Survey of Asia and the Far East, 1958, op. cit., Bangkok, 1959, p. 76.

22. United Nations, Statistical Office, Statistical Yearbook, 1962, New York, 1963, p. 345.

23. ibid.

24. Statistical Yearbook, 1962, New York, 1963, p. 364.

25. ibid., pp. 411-15.

26. International Monetary Fund, Balance of Payments Yearbook, VI (Washington, D.C., 1955), 7.

27. T.H. Silcock, The Economy of Malaya (Singapore: Donald Moore, 1957), pp. 8-12; Joan Wilson, The Singapore Rubber Market (Singapore: Eastern University Press, 1958), pp. 34-36.

28. Alec Nove and D. Donnelly, Trade with Communist Countries (London: Hutchinson & Co., Ltd., 1960), pp. 149-50; Hsin Ying, Foreign Trade of Communist China (Hong Kong: Union Research Institute, 1954), pp. 106-11.

29. W.A. Lewis, "Economic Development with Unlimited Supplies of Labor," Manchester School of Economic and Social Studies, XX (1954), pp. 183-84; F. Mehta, "The Effects of Adverse Income Terms of Trade on the Secular Growth of Underdeveloped Countries," Indian Economic Journal, VI (July, 1958), pp. 9-12.

30. Choh-ming Li, Economic Development of Communist China (Berkeley: University of California Press, 1959), pp. 177-78.

31. Jonathan V. Levin, The Export Economics (Cambridge: Harvard University Press, 1960), pp. 250-61.

32. United Nations, A Study of Trade between Asia and Europe, Geneva, 1953, p. 6.

33. loc. cit.

34. Richard E. Caves, Trade and Economic Structure (Cambridge: Harvard University Press, 1963), pp. 67-68.

35. Everett E. Hagen, "An Economic Justification of Protectionism," Quarterly Journal of Economics, November, 1958, pp. 476-79.

36. Meier, op. cit., pp. 151-53.

37. Hollis B. Chenery, "Comparative Advantage and Development Policy," American Economic Review, March, 1961, pp. 18-19.

38. Meier, op. cit., p. 133.

39. Hagen, op. cit., pp. 501-2.

40. Hagen, op. cit., p. 498.

41. Hagen, op. cit., p. 499; Caves, op. cit., pp. 59-65.

42. ibid.

43. Meier, op. cit., p. 125; Caves, op. cit., p. 247.

44. Raul Prebisch, "Commercial Policy in the Underdeveloped Countries," American Economic Review, May, 1959, pp. 251-60.

45. Caves, op. cit., pp. 169-72.

46. Pranab Bardhan, "External Economics, Economic Development and the Theory of Protection," Oxford Economic Papers, March, 1964, pp. 47-52.

47. Meier, op. cit., p. 159.

48. ibid.

49. Caves, op. cit., p. 159.

50. H.W. Singer, "Distribution of Gains Between Investing and Borrowing Countries," American Economic Review, May, 1950, pp. 477-80.

51. Bardhan, op. cit., p. 45.

52. Chenery, op. cit., p. 24.

53. Caves, op. cit., pp. 252-53.

CHAPTER 3 WESTERN EUROPEAN TRADE WITH THE FAR EAST

In the past thirty years, the trade of ECAFE region has followed a general pattern which can be summarized in Tables 8 and 9.

These tables indicate the competitive positions of the major countries in the trade of ECAFE regions, as each one tries to improve its position at the expense of some of the others.

Generally speaking, about one third of the region's trade has been with western Europe, less than one fifth with the United States and Canada, and about one fifth with the region itself. Of the remaining 30 per cent, half has been accounted for by eastern Europe, the Soviet Union, Japan, and Communist China.

Some important shifts in the direction of the region's export trade have occurred in the last 30 years or so. Before World War II, the present EEC area remained a declining market, and the present EFTA area an expanding market. But since the war, the EEC area has become an expanding market, while the EFTA has been a declining market.

The region's import trade has also changed: Since World War II the share of the EEC area has improved and that of the EFTA area has declined.

North America's share in the region's export trade has fluctuated around the one fifth level in the past 30 years, with a decline after the depression and a rise in the immediate postwar years. A spectacular change has occured in the fast rise of North America's share in the region's import trade, from 9.6 per cent in 1928, to 20 per cent in 1959-61, with an all time high of 25.6 per cent in 1948.

Table 8

Exports of ECAFE Region by Destination
(percentage distribution)

	1928	1938	1948	1959-61 Average
Western Europe	35.6	36.0	34.5	32.9
EEC	18.8	16.0	12.5	13.8
EFTA	15.7	19.3	20.5	17.3
U. K.	14.9	18.1	18.0	15.6
Eastern Europe & USSR	0.7	1.5	2.7	4.8
U. S. A. & Canada	18.4	17.7	21.4	17.8
Japan	6.0	5.0	1.4	8.3
ECAFE Region	22.2	22.7	20.7	20.0
Mainland China	6.9	4.3	2.7	1.9
Others	10.1	12.7	16.5	14.2
Total	100.0	100.0	100.0	100.0

Source: United Nations, Economic Survey of Asia and the Far East, 1962, New York, 1963, p. 8.

Japan's share in the region's trade suffered a setback during the immediate postwar years, but it has recovered so fast in recent years that Japan's share is much higher now than in any prewar year.

While in the past 30 years Eastern Europe and the Soviet Union have made some improvements in their shares in the region's trade, Communist China's share has declined. The combined share of the Soviet Bloc in the region's trade has seldom gone beyond the 7 or 8 per cent level. The ECAFE region has always been and still is an area dominated by the trade of the West.

Of course, the Far East is a much larger area than the ECAFE, as it includes in addition: Communist China, North Korea, North Vietnam, Japan, Australia, and New Zealand. In order to show the trade pattern of the Far East as a whole, we will have to consider the trade of these additional countries.

Table 9

Imports of ECAFE Region by Provenance
(percentage distribution)

	1928	1938	1948	1959-61 Average
Western Europe	42.3	35.4	32.4	32.8
EEC	15.7	15.8	9.3	15.7
EFTA	26.4	19.2	22.7	16.6
U. K.	24.7	17.6	20.1	13.8
Eastern Europe & USSR	1.4	2.0	0.8	2.2
U. S. A. & Canada	9.6	11.8	25.6	20.0
Japan	5.7	7.9	2.6	11.8
ECAFE Region	29.3	29.0	15.9	18.6
Mainland China	7.2	6.4	4.6	4.2
Others	4.5	7.6	18.1	10.5
Total	100.0	100.0	100.0	100.0

Source: United Nations, Economic Survey of Asia and the Far
East, 1962, New York, 1963.

GROUP TRADING OF THE FAR EAST

The trade of the Far East is not that of countries trading
with one another on an individual basis, but rather the trade of
three groups of countries: the Sterling Asia, the Dollar Asia,
and the Soviet Asia. In ideology, in political and military
alignment, or merely through closer contacts, countries of
the Far East are differentiated into these three groups with
each functioning as a trade unit. Members in each group trade
largely with one another and maintain fairly stable exchange
rates with one another. Through years of association and adjustments, not entirely without economic conflicts due to de-
velopmental changes of members, the economies of each group
have become compatible with one another. Each group has a
dominant Western power of advanced economy, one or two
industrialized Far Eastern countries, and a number of primary producing Far Eastern countries.

Before World War II, France had French Indo-China, a colony in Asia, and the Netherlands had Indonesia; but both colonies have become independent. France was able to maintain its economic domination over its former colony until 1952; however, by now French Asia and the Netherlands Asia have about become extinct.

For each member of the group there is a specific role. The dominant Western nation provides the bulk of capital goods and some light manufactures for the group. It operates most of the transoceanic transportation and communication facilities, and offers financial, insurance, and market research service. It is also responsible for the technological advancement of the group to a large extent. The industrialized Far Eastern countries provide light manufactures and some capital goods. They operate regional transportation and communication facilities and offer some minor services. The primary producing Far Eastern countries specialize in farming and mining.

The Sterling Asia, as a part of the sterling area, is a formal institution providing specific privileges and obligations for its members. The position of the United Kingdom in the trade of Sterling Asia was at its peak in the 1950's, but has suffered a decline in recent years. The Dollar Asia is by comparison a loose term referring to the informal group where the United States and Japan have developed a predominant position in trade. It follows largely the scope of the American aid and mutual security programs. The Soviet Asia, as a component of the Soviet Bloc, is more than a trade group; it is an economic entity in the large sense. The position of Soviet Russia in the trade of the Far East was at its best in the late 1950's and has suffered deterioration in recent years.

There is always intergroup rivalry among the Western nations, with each trying to improve its trading position in other camps. There is also intragroup competition between the Western nations and the industrialized Far Eastern countries in light manufactures and capital goods, as well as in services. There is again the possibility for the industrialized Far Eastern countries to develop trade outside their groups because they have some capital and transportation and communication facilities at their disposal. But the freedom of action for the primary Far Eastern countries is quite limited.

Table 10

Trading Groups in the Far East

	Western Powers	Industrialized Far Eastern Countries	Major Primary Producing Far Eastern Countries
Sterling Asia	United Kingdom	India	Australia, New Zealand, Burma, Ceylon, Malaysia, Hong Kong, Pakistan, Sarawak, Brunei, N. Borneo.
Dollar Asia	United States	Japan	Philippines, Formosa, South Korea, Thailand.
Soviet Asia	Soviet Russia	Mainland China	North Korea, North Vietnam.

THE TRADE OF STERLING ASIA

The United Kingdom began its trade with the Far East at the end of the 16th century. It was in 1588 that the first British ship, the Hercules, returned to London from the Far East with the richest load of cargo ever known to have come to England. The ship carried indigo and cotton from India, cinnamon from Ceylon, pepper from Sumatra, and nutmeg, clove and mace from Molucca. Through unceasing commercial, political, and military activities, the United Kingdom in time created in the Far East a large group of Commonwealth nations, some of which are self-governing now. The self-governing Commonwealth nations in the Far East are Ceylon, India, Pakistan, Australia, New Zealand, and Malaysia. The Commonwealth areas that are not self-governing are Hong Kong and Brunei. Burma, a former colony of the United Kingdom, is no longer within the Commonwealth. The United Kingdom

has, traditionally, been the leading trading partner of the Commonwealth nations, taking the largest shares of their exports
and supplying them the largest shares of their imports.

In 1956 the trade of the Commonwealth nations in the Far
East followed a general pattern. These nations, as agricultural nations with their exports dominated by raw materials
and foodstuffs, had a large portion of their trade with industrial nations--over 60 per cent in most cases. Half of this
trade was with the United Kingdom, while the balance was
distributed among the common market (EEC), the European
Free Trade Association (EFTA), the United States and Japan.
The other 40 per cent of their trade was divided between the
other Commonwealth nations and the rest of the world. There
were some deviations from the general pattern. New Zealand
leaned very heavily on trade with the United Kingdom, which
took well over half of its trade. The United Kingdom's share
of trade with Hong Kong, Malaya and Singapore was rather
small, because these are world entrepôt centers where a large
part of the trade of the Far East is handled.

The British have, through the years of commercial activities in the Far East, established a fine system of business
channels which certainly have helped to direct the trade of the
Commonwealth nations toward the United Kingdom. To men-
tion a few examples of this system: There are British shipping
facilities to carry the trade, British telecommunications facilities to transmit business correspondence, a large network of
British firms of exporters, importers, wholesalers, and local
distributors to handle the merchandise, and British advertising facilities to sell their products. As long as these facilities
work satisfactorily, the merchants of the Far East will use
them instead of establishing new channels. Other European
countries, the United States and Japan, which do not have such a complete system of business facilities, sometimes have to use
British facilities to handle their trade. Therefore, at the out-
set, these nations suffer a disadvantage in competing with the
United Kingdom.

Preferential trade arrangements, provided by the United
Kingdom and the Commonwealth nations for each other's trade,
contribute to the close commercial relationship among them.
Preferential trade arrangements can mean a number of things:

Table 11

Direction of Trade of Commonwealth Nations, 1956

	UK	EEC	EFTA	US	Japan	Total Industrial Nations	Common-wealth Nations	Other
Exports (in percentages of their total exports)								
Australia	31	23	4	7	13	75	19	6
Ceylon	30	10	1	8	1	50	26	24
India	30	10	1	15	5	61	16	23
Malaya	16	17	2	15	8	58	20	22
New Zealand	64	16	1	7	1	89	8	3
Pakistan	16	26	1	9	13	65	21	14
Hong Kong	9	3	1	4	10	27	23	50
Imports (in percentages of their total imports)								
Australia	43	10	4	13	2	72	16	12
Ceylon	21	12	1	2	7	43	24	33
India	25	20	5	11	5	66	13	21
Malaya	18	7	2	5	6	38	16	46
New Zealand	54	6	2	8	1	71	24	5
Pakistan	18	18	2	28	6	72	14	14
Hong Kong	11	8	4	9	18	50	13	37

Source: The Economist Intelligence Unit, The Commonwealth
and Europe (London: The Whitefriars Press, 1960), p. 5.
EEC is the European Economic Community, generally
referred to as the Common Market, or the inner six comprising Belgium, France, Italy, Luxemburg, the Netherlands, and West Germany. EFTA stands for the European
Free Trade Association, generally referred to as the Outer
Seven, including the United Kingdom, Austria, Denmark,
Norway, Portugal, Sweden, and Switzerland. The figures
here for EFTA do not include the United Kingdom and Portugal.

preferential tariff rates, quotas system, long term contracts, credit arrangements, and discriminatory measures against outsiders.

The preferential quotas system refers to the practice that the United Kingdom carries out from time to time: commitments to import some definite quantities of certain commodities from the Commonwealth nations.   The quota supplies may be duty free or subject to reduced tariff rates.   This practice obliges the United Kingdom to buy its needed imports first from the Commonwealth nations before it buys elsewhere.

Long-term contracts are often entered into by the United Kingdom and the Commonwealth nations for certain imports. The annual quantity bought is usually stipulated in the contract, while the price may be fixed or subject to periodical negotiations.   An example of this was the United Kingdom's procurement of foodstuffs and essential materials from the Commonwealth nations during and immediately after World War II.   The wish to protect the value of sterling by the sparing and judicious use of foreign exchange played the foremost part in the import policy of the United Kingdom.   To ensure supplies (and in some cases to withhold them from the enemy), it was often necessary to negotiate contracts which in scope and content went beyond the financial capacity of private businessmen.   The fifteen-years experience of bulk buying under long-term contracts from 1940-55 proved to be satisfactory.   It assisted the colonies by enabling them to maintain their export earnings; it ensured a steady flow of essential commodities to the United Kingdom to meet its requirements; it saved the United Kingdom dollars, as these supplies were paid with Commonwealth currencies; and it enabled the United Kingdom to obtain essential supplies at lower prices than the world market.   After the war, the United Kingdom gradually reduced the scope of bulk buying, and commodity after commodity in the import trade was restored to private business, for two main reasons.   After the war, prices of raw materials fell, and the United Kingdom wanted the freedom to buy at the prevailing prices of the falling market instead of commiting itself to fixed long terms. The other reason was that it was difficult to meet the peace-time raw material requirements by fixed long-term contracts, as the requirements were constantly changing in quantity and quality specifications.

The United Kingdom may give the Commonwealth nations favorable credit terms to facilitate their purchases. This is necessary especially in the case of purchases of capital goods. Of course here the United Kingdom faces competition from the United States.

Long-term capital investment is another instrument to promote trade. Until recently the United Kingdom has been a major lending power to the Commonwealth nations.

There are two aspects to be considered in long-term capital flow: private and government sources. As far as private sources are concerned, the predominance of the United Kingdom as a source of investment indicates the continued importance of the freedom of capital movements between the United Kingdom and the Commonwealth nations. But the financial circumstances of the United Kingdom and the huge needs of the Commonwealth nations have made it impossible for the United Kingdom single-handedly to adequately fulfill the role as the source of private capital during recent years. Large amounts of private capital have come from the dollar area.

As far as government source of capital is concerned, the United Kingdom recently has become less important as a lender to the Commonwealth nations, except for some minor Commonwealth territories which still rely extensively on British government loans. Apart from India's borrowing from West Germany and Soviet Russia, and South Africa's borrowing from continental Europe, government loans and grants to the Commonwealth nations are coming increasingly from the United States and from international institutions such as the United Nations and the International Bank for Reconstruction and Development. [1]

Australia and New Zealand are attractive to private foreign investors and have been obtaining private capital from the United Kingdom and other sources in large amounts. Ceylon, India, Malaya, and Pakistan are turning more and more to government sources of capital, partly because they are less attractive to private capital due to their prevailing political climate, but also because private enterprise is no longer regarded as the most suitable instrument for developing basic services and industries. [2]

Table 12

Long-Term Capital Inflow by Area, Cumulative
1954-58
(in million pounds sterling)

	UK	Other Sterling Areas	Non-sterling Europe	Dollar Area	Other	Total
Australia						
Private	197.1	...	...	98.9	41.2	337.2
Government	---	---	---	---	54.8	54.8
Ceylon						
Private	-6.2	-0.3	-0.2	-0.1	---	-6.8
Government	4.5	-0.2	---	---	4.1	8.4
India						
Private	30.9	...	3.1	20.5	36.3	90.6
Government	12.1	...	15.3	160.8	150.3	338.4
New Zealand						
Private	43.4	9.3	4.4	4.5	---	0.2
Government	30.9	2.3	---	22.9	---	56.2

Source: The Commonwealth and Europe, p. 29.

Discriminative measures against outsiders, mostly
against Japan and the United States, were taken in the early postwar years by Commonwealth nations to maintain their close economic ties with the United Kingdom and to relieve payments pressure. Australia, New Zealand, and India discriminated against
Japanese imports in their quotas and licensing policies in the
early postwar years. This discrimination was steadily modified and finally abolished by Australia in 1957 and by New Zealand and India in 1958.[3]

Australia, New Zealand, India, and Pakistan, following
the general policy of the sterling area, practiced discrimination against the dollar area. Pakistan abolished dollar discrimination in 1955, and Australia and New Zealand did the
same in 1960. India ended the dollar discrimination for consumer goods in 1959, but retained the discrimination against
capital goods.[4]

The most important factor ensuring close economic ties between the United Kingdom and the Commonwealth nations has been the preferential tariff. The beginning of the system dates back to the turn of the century when some Commonwealth nations began to give preferential tariff treatment to goods from the United Kingdom. In 1919 the United Kingdom, in turn, gave preference to goods imported from the Commonwealth. In 1932, with the passing of the Import Duty Act and the negotiation of reciprocal preference at Ottawa, the system reached its fullest development. The Ottawa Agreements are generally given the credit for swinging Commonwealth trade towards the United Kingdom during the early 30's. Of course there were many other factors which helped to create this course of development.

Only six years after Ottawa, the first modification was made in the system when the United Kingdom abolished its preference on Commonwealth wheat in accordance with the terms of the Anglo-American Trade Agreement of 1938. During the war and in the early postwar years, the influence of Commonwealth preference was probably minimal. It has been calculated that between 1937 and 1948 the share of the United Kingdom exports to the Commonwealth receiving preference fell from over 55 per cent to around 50 per cent and that the average margin of preference on these goods fell from over 20 per cent to 15 per cent. The corresponding figures for Commonwealth exports are from about 60 per cent to 55 per cent and from 20 per cent to around 12 per cent.[5]

The margin of preference is defined as the difference between the duty paid on the products of countries receiving most-favored nation treatment from the United Kingdom and the duty paid on Commonwealth products.

Three factors were responsible for the reduction of preference margins: changes in the tariff schedules of the United Kingdom and Commonwealth nations; tariff cuts made in the course of international tariff negotiations through the General Agreement on Tariffs and Trade (GATT); and the erosion of preference on specific duties as world prices have moved upwards. Most of the preferences were based on ad valorem duties-- that is, a percentage of the value of the imports. However, some preferences are specific rates, such as one based on so many shillings per physical unit of the imports. If the prices of imports have gone up but the number of shillings per unit remains the same, the rate of preference margin is reduced. The erosion of preference margins particularly affected Australia and New Zealand exports to the United Kingdom. To compensate for this loss, Australia by an agreement in 1957, and New Zealand by an agreement in 1958, were given the power to reduce preference margins. It is expected that the reduction in preference margins, both specific and ad valorem, will continue.

The smaller share of preferential goods in the trade between the United Kingdom and the Commonwealth nations is partially caused by the changes in the composition of trade. For instance, the United Kingdom gives preferences to more foodstuffs from the Commonwealth than to raw materials. As the United Kingdom is importing more raw materials than foodstuffs from the Commonwealth, the proportion of preferential goods in their trade is thus reduced.[6] About 80 per cent of the foodstuffs, petroleum, and manufactures from the Commonwealth nations are given some preference by the United Kingdom as compared to less than 30 per cent of the raw materials.

To sum up, the preferential tariffs probably do no more than raise the shares in each other's total trade by a few per cent, since the tariffs are fully effective only over a limited range of goods. Many Commonwealth exporters are fully aware of their limited effectiveness (at least in respect to what they can get for their exports), yet would be reluctant to see the preference disappear entirely.

Another factor instrumental in sustaining the close economic ties between the United Kingdom and the Commonwealth nations is the sterling area, which is a system of multilateral payments. This system was established at the turn of the century. Under this system, Commonwealth nations hold their international reserves in sterling balances; they maintain their currencies in a fixed relationship with the pound sterling; they keep their surplus dollar earnings in terms of sterling in a pool maintained in London; and they use London banking facilities to discharge their obligations

incurred on international accounts. This system developed
out of Britain's then leading position in international trade, the
stable value of the pound sterling, and the free convertibility
of pound sterling into gold and other currencies. By joining
the sterling area, Commonwealth nations enjoy the advantages of added stability to their currencies and the easy convertibility from their currency to pound sterling and to other
currencies. The disadvantages are that they have to surrender their surplus dollar earnings to the pool at London
and their withdrawals from the pool are subject to agreement
by the United Kingdom. When the United Kingdom relin-
quished the gold standard, Canada left the sterling area and
has been considered a country of the dollar area. The sterling area is not limited to the Commonwealth nations, however; other countries such as Egypt, Portugal, the Scandinav-
ian countries, the Baltic countries, Iran, Hungary, Greece,
and Yugoslavia have joined it.

    In the postwar years, when some members had an increased
need for hard currencies and the withdrawals allowed were limited, there was some dissatisfaction with the system. Now
India, Australia, and Ceylon hold some independent gold and
dollar reserves.

    As a member of the sterling area, a country must keep
a sterling balance at London. The sterling balance is kept
in two accounts: the unrestricted account from which sterling
can be withdrawn and converted into other currencies freely,
and the restricted account from which sterling cannot be withdrawn without the agreement of the United Kingdom. The bulk
of the sterling balances at London is held in the form of treasury bills bearing interest at 0.5 per cent. Interests are paid
to holders of unrestricted accounts.

    Under the sterling area arrangement, the United Kingdom
in its trade with members may enjoy favorable terms of trade
if the members do not have adequate monetary sterling reserves. Members need sterling to pay into the pool. There
is a high demand for sterling in excess of the demand for current commercial purposes, resulting in a premium on sterling.
Once the members have adequate sterling reserves, the premium disappears. If the members of the sterling area have
more than adequate monetary sterling reserves, the process
is reversed. The supply of sterling is greater than that for
commercial needs. Sterling stands at a discount and thus

the terms of trade move against the United Kingdom.

The sterling area was established when the sterling was the basic currency of the world and used as an international medium of exchange among the members. Now, in the post-war world, the United States has emerged as the most power-ful financial power, and the dollar has become increasingly important. The United States has a larger import capacity than the United Kingdom. Now raw material producers look to the United States as the major potential buyer. This was illustrated by the effects of the stockpile program of the United States during the Korean War, which brought about prosperity to a number of countries in the Far East. In the 1930's, the world adjusted its prices to the United Kingdom prices, but now the world is more susceptible to the market forces of the United States. Some members of the sterling area began to speculate on whether they should remain in the sterling area or switch to the dollar area. Remaining in the sterling area, they can count on larger trade with the United Kingdom, but their trade with the United States will be re-stricted as they do not have the free use of their dollar earn-ings. However, if they should leave the sterling area, they will have to maintain on their own a stable exchange relation-ship between their currencies and the dollar. This would re-quire large dollar reserves which are difficult to accumulate as most of the Commonwealth nations do not have a favorable balance of trade with the United States.

In the postwar years, there was a general pattern in the contributions to, and the withdrawals from, the dollar pool made by the Commonwealth nations. Burma, India, Pakistan, and Hong Kong have been withdrawing heavily from the pool, while Ceylon and Malaysia have been making contributions to the pool as they have continuously had surplus trade with the United States. Australia and New Zealand have had surplus trade with the United States from time to time. [7]

In recent years the United Kingdom has been unable to adequately supply the Commonwealth nations with the neces-sary capital goods and essential materials, resulting in the needs of the Commonwealth nations for imports from out-side. This dependence on outside imports in turn has re-sulted in increased demands for withdrawals from the pool.

Consequently, the sterling area, as a system of multilateral payments, has not functioned as smoothly and effectively as it did in the prewar days.

All these factors mentioned above--the political ties, economic compatibility, established business channels, preferential trade arrangements, the sterling area, and capital investment--have contributed to the special position of the United Kingdom in the trade of Sterling Asia. These factors were most effective in the 1930's, and the share of the United Kingdom in the trade of these nations was at its height. Subsequently, these factors have been weakened by the war, the political independence of these nations, the competition from Japan, the United States, and the continental European nations, the changing nature of the economy of the members, and economic difficulties in the United Kingdom. Consequently, the share of the United Kingdom in the trade of Sterling Asia had declined.

If attention is focused on the shares of the United Kingdom in the export trade to the Sterling Asian nations, it is apparent that they were smaller in 1962 than they were in 1938 for a number of nations, namely Burma, Ceylon, India, Malaysia, Australia, and New Zealand. It is only in Hong Kong and Pakistan that the United Kingdom had larger shares in 1962 than in 1938.

In the import trade of the Sterling Asian nations, the United Kingdom's shares in 1962 were smaller than in 1938 in the following nations: India, Malaysia, Australia, and New Zealand. However, its share in 1962 was larger than in 1938 in Hong Kong.

The United Kingdom has improved its trade position with some nonsterling Asian countries. For instance, its share in the export trade of Thailand and its share in the import trade of the Philippines were larger in 1962 than in 1938. Nevertheless, the over-all trade of the United Kingdom in the Far East has suffered a decline since 1938.

By an agreement in 1959, the European Free Trade Association (EFTA) was established, and the organization came into being in 1960. This group includes the United Kingdom, Austria,

Table 13

United Kingdom's Trade with the Far East

	1938	1948	1952	1956	1959	1962
Share in the Exports of Far Eastern Countries (in percentages of their exports)						
Burma	13.9	8.5	9.5	7.4	8.8	9.8
Ceylon	50.0	30.1	27.8	28.8	27.4	30.1
Hong Kong	3.5	4.9	...	9.3	13.1	16.1
India	34.2	21.2	20.5	30.5	27.6	29.6
Indonesia	3.4	4.3	2.7	8.9	21.9	3.2
Japan	5.9	8.2	...	2.7	3.5	2.2
Malaya, Singapore	14.2	13.9	20.8	16.5	14.6	10.1
Pakistan	...	9.2	12.8	15.9	18.4	17.7
Philippines	2.0	1.0	...	1.5	1.6	1.2
Thailand	1.3	1.5	0.7	3.1	2.9	5.0
South Korea	...	...	...	3.6	4.7	2.9
Australia	63.5	43.6	38.7	30.8	27.0	19.3
New Zealand	85.6	73.3	65.3	64.5	56.5	49.2
Share in the Imports of Far Eastern Countries (in percentages of their imports)						
Burma	18.4	47.0	22.5	21.2	19.2	15.1
Ceylon	20.6	17.5	22.6	21.2	24.7	20.8
Hong Kong	9.6	14.5	...	11.9	11.5	11.4
India	30.8	28.6	18.6	25.5	19.4	16.9
Indonesia	7.8	10.1	7.1	6.1	6.6	6.6
Japan	1.3	0.2	...	2.7	2.6	1.9
Malaya, Singapore	18.4	19.2	21.1	18.2	17.6	16.8
Pakistan	...	26.8	20.2	16.3	17.6	18.0
Philippines	2.0	0.9	...	3.0	4.2	4.6
Thailand	13.6	9.3	13.1	11.5	10.3	9.2
South Korea	...	...	...	0.6	2.8	1.5
Australia	42.8	41.7	37.0	37.1	31.9	30.5
New Zealand	46.3	50.7	45.6	47.0	42.0	42.1

Sources: United Nations, International Monetary Fund, Inter-

national Bank for Reconstruction and Development, Direc-
tion of International Trade, New York, Series T., V. 4,
No. 1/2, pp. 100-3; V. 8, No. 7, pp. 136-38; V. 11,
No. 9, pp. 171-73; Annual 1958-62, pp. 134-36.

Denmark, Norway, Portugal, Sweden, and Switzerland. In 1960
the EFTA cut tariffs on industrial products by 20 per cent, and
by 1950 these countries will have established among themselves
free trade on industrial products. For agricultural products
special arrangements are made. For instance, by an agreement
between Denmark and the United Kingdom, Danish bacon, pork,
and dairy products are given free entry to the United Kingdom.
Since the EFTA is mainly confined to tariff reduction on industrial products, it would not affect the trade of the Far East to
any large extent. In negotiating with other members on tariffs
on agricultural products, the United Kingdom certainly will
keep the interests of the Commonwealth nations in mind. There
could be some gains for the Commonwealth nations in their export trade of raw materials. For instance, the British leather
industry may import a larger quantity of raw hides and skins
from India for processing and re-exporting to its EFTA partners. Better cooperation with the EFTA members in economic
development may induce higher import requirements of raw
materials from the Far East. [8]

A study of the composition of the trade of the United Kingdom will show clearly that the imports from the Far East are
concentrated in a small number of products, (mainly foodstuffs,
tobacco, and raw materials), while the exports to this area con-
tain a large variety of products ranging from consumer goods,
industrial materials, machinery, appliances, and transport
equipment. The imports of the United Kingdom from the Far
East tend to be stable. The United Kingdom for years to come
will remain a major market for their beef, butter, wheat, tea,
rubber, and wool. However, the exports of the United Kingdom to the Far East may undergo changes. [9] As countries in
this area are striving to become industrialized, consumer goods
exports of the United Kingdom may decline, while certain
industrial materials and capital goods exports may expand.
Therefore, the future of the export trade of the United Kingdom to the Far East depends a great deal on the ability
of the United Kingdom to provide the right kinds of materials
and capital goods in the right quantities to meet the needs of

these countries at attractive prices and with liberal credit
arrangements. The effectiveness of the preferential tariff
has often been exaggerated. Actually, the 10 or 15 per cent
preferential margins to promote the export of capital goods of
the United Kingdom would be to no avail if the goods were not
available or priced much higher than Japanese products, or
if they did not carry the kind of credit arrangements which
are being provided by American firms.

Because of the decline of British exports in the Far East
in the postwar period, the Federation of British Industries
sent a mission to the Far East in 1961 to search for ways to
improve British trade and investment from first hand information. The mission's report reveals some concrete sug-
gestions. Realizing that the Far East is in the midst of a
transition, moving into industrialization, where the people
are earnestly trying to diversify their production and exports,
to expand their national income and trade, and improve their
foreign exchange position, the mission suggests that British
firms cannot afford to be even second in involvement in the
formative stages of this economic and trade development. It
believes that unless the United Kingdom makes its best effort
now, however difficult the task, a pattern of trade will emerge
without the British. It cautions that the Far East cannot be
treated as though it were the American or European market.
The countries with newly gained independence still have their
strong fear of a new form of exploitation. Many British firms
are working in the spirit of collaboration, which is the spirit
required. The development plans of the Far Eastern countries
offer great opportunities of supplies of capital goods. But the
attempt to supply them will often fail unless the supplier is
prepared to cooperate in technical and credit assistance.
Technical assistance is not confined to large inter-governmen-
tal schemes, but should also be provided in the process of
trade. British firms will need to cooperate more closely
with their local agents in the training of local technical personnel in the setting up of training schools and demonstration centers in the use of their products which they wish to
sell. The specifications of capital goods to sell must be
worked out in close collaboration with local manufactures.
The British firms should also be ready to provide assistance
in financial arrangements with the types of credits that are
competitive with those offered by other sources.

Twenty or thirty years ago, one would expect the mission's report to place great emphasis on the tariff problem, but interestingly enough, it is not the case now. A very important aspect of the trade between the Far East and the West deals with capital goods for which tariffs are low. The real problems now facing this trade are the technological and financial difficulties. To promote trade in the Far East, the British firms would have to send out representatives of the highest technical capability and investment judgment so that they can judge what types of capital goods would meet the production requirements of these countries and whether the credits are granted on a solid basis. [10]

Under the leadership of the United Kingdom, the Colombo Plan was launched to develop the economy and trade of Southeast and East Asia. The plan was financed by capital and technical aid largely from the United Kingdom, Canada, Australia, and New Zealand.

For the period 1950-62, the United Kingdom gave a total of $864 million in grants and loans under the Colombo Plan. This does not include withdrawals of $705 million from the sterling balances by India, Pakistan, and Ceylon. The distribution of the United Kingdom's aid is as follows:

	(million U. S. dollars)
Malaya and Singapore	205.6
North Borneo and Sarawak	60.1
India	441.3
Pakistan	98.0
Indus Basin Development Fund	58.2
Laos	0.4
Vietnam	0.6

In addition, the United Kingdom has given another $20.6 million of technical aid to these countries.

Canada gave $377.1 million of capital and technical aid, Australia gave $96.8 million, and New Zealand $23.9 million in the same period.

After ten years of development, the Consultative Committee of the Colombo Plan reports that for the countries covered, there is a rise in agricultural output by 40 per cent, industrial output by 75 per cent, national income by 42 per cent, and per capita income by 17 per cent. The over-all economic growth is not extraordinary but there has been good expansion of industrial output in fields such as iron and steel, electricity, paper and paper board, rubber manufactures, chemicals, cement, electric appliances, and transport equipment. 11

<h2 style="text-align:center">CONTINENTAL EUROPE'S TRADE
WITH THE FAR EAST</h2>

Among the nations of continental Europe which trade heavily with the Far East are France, the Netherlands, West Germany, Italy, Switzerland, Belgium, and Luxemburg. Of this group, the first three nations have long been interested in the Far East. It was during the second half of the 19th century that France established its colony of French Indochina. France had firm control of this colony until World War II, when it was lost to Japan in 1942. In 1945 France regained the colony from Japan, but war broke out between France and native Communist forces. It was not until 1954 that a settlement was reached. Now, Indochina is divided into four parts: North Vietnam, South Vietnam, Laos, and Cambodia. North Vietnam is under the control of a native Communist regime, and is economically a nation in the Soviet Bloc. The other three are independent states but seperately associated with France. The Netherlands gained its colony as far back as 1800. The colony fell under Japanese rule from 1942-45 during World War II. After the war a movement for independence started and Indonesia gained complete independence in 1950. Germany had colonies, such as Tsingtao on the China coast, and the Pacific islands, including the Marianas, the Carolines, and the Marshalls. All these colonies were wrested from Germany during World War I.

Under the European colonial system, there was heavy trading between the European mother countries and their colonies. In the period after World War II, with the colonies becoming independent, this colonial pattern of trade began to break down. Former colonial powers may still take a large share of the trade of their erstwhile colonies due to long established business channels, well entrenched markets, good

shipping services, convenient financial facilities, and preferential trade arrangements, but it is apparent that the trade of
former colonies has been redirected away from their mother
countries. West Germany, because of its fast recovery and
growing industrial strength, has been making impressive new
gains in the markets of the Far East.

The Trade of France with the Far East

During the colonial period, France held rigid control over
the economy of its colonies. Industrial production, distribution, trade, and shipping were all in the hands of French nationals. The local economy of the colonies was well co-
ordinated with the economy of France.

Table 14

France's Trade with the Far East

	1938	1948	1952	1956	1959	1962
Share in the Imports of Far Eastern Countries (in percentages of their imports)						
Indochina	76.0	84.0	84.0	...	...	...
South Vietnam	...	...	...	23.4	23.4	13.3
Cambodia	...	...	...	16.4	30.3	18.5
Laos	...	...	...	15.3	5.9	7.6
India	0.9	0.5	1.7	2.4	2.1	1.1
Share in the Exports of Far Eastern Countries (in percentages of their exports)						
South Vietnam	...	...	...	67.2	31.7	38.2
Cambodia	...	...	...	28.2	30.8	26.0
India	3.6	1.6	1.0	1.1	1.3	1.2
Malaya, Singapore	7.5	3.5	4.3	4.6	3.4	6.6
Australia	8.1	11.7	9.1	8.7	6.4	4.7

Source: Direction of International Trade.

Local currencies of the colonies were tied to the French franc, and their exchange rates were based on the Paris official market rates. There was preferential tariff for the trade between France and its colonies. It was not until 1954-55 that South Vietnam, Laos, and Cambodia had gradually gained their full economic sovereignty.

In the early postwar years, France's export to its colonies before their independence actually increased, reaching a peak in 1952 at over $300 million U. S. For the period 1956-62, France's position in the trade of South Vietnam has declined.

From South Vietnam and Cambodia's point of view, France is still an important market, taking about 30 per cent of their exports. To compensate for the loss of trade in former colonies, France has been successful in improving its position in other Far Eastern countries such as India and Malaysia since 1952.

The Netherlands Trade with the Far East

From 1928 to its independence in 1950, Indonesia conducted one-fourth of its trade with the Netherlands, but after independence the Netherlands' share greatly declined. In 1959, the Netherlands took 1 per cent of Indonesia's exports and provided 3. 7 per cent of its imports. This decline has been much more drastic than that suffered by France or the United Kingdom in their trade with their former colonies. This can be partly explained by the long bitter years of fighting between the Netherlands and Indonesia during the war of independence and the subsequent quarrel over the territory of West New Guinea. In 1957 the Indonesian government started the wholesale expulsion of the Dutch community from the country and has placed all Dutch commercial, banking, industrial, and utilities interests under government custody. As a consequence, there is hardly any normal trade relation between the two. Indonesia has adopted a nationalistic commercial policy. This policy aims at taking over the control of the nation's economic activities from the hands of foreign merchants, not only the Dutch but also the Chinese, and placing it in Indonesian hands. It promoted the diversification of production and trade so as to lessen the country's reliance on the exports of a small number of commodities. [12]

To compensate for the loss of exports to Indonesia, the Netherlands has been successful in developing markets in other Asian countries: for instance, Australia, Malaya, Singapore, Japan, India, the Philippines, and Thailand. In the postwar years, there has been an impressive increase in the value of Dutch exports to all of these countries.

Table 15

Netherlands' Trade with some Far Eastern Countries

	1938	1948	1952	1956	1959	1962
Share in the Imports (in percentages of their imports)						
Indonesia	21.8	21.3	12.8	10.6	3.7	0.5
Malaya & Singapore	1.0	0.9	1.8	1.8	...	...
Australia	0.6	0.9	1.2	1.4	1.9	1.3
Philippines	2.1	0.1	...	2.0	2.6	3.2
Share in the Exports (in percentages of their exports)						
Indonesia	19.9	33.2	21.2	19.5	1.0	2.1
Malaya & Singapore	1.0	2.0	2.8	3.5	...	...
Philippines	1.7	0.9	...	8.6	7.8	6.8
Thailand	0.2	2.6	3.6	5.9	5.7	...

Source: Direction of International Trade

The Netherlands' imports from Indonesia steadily declined from 1952 on; however, Indonesia is still the leading source of supplies in Asia for the Netherlands. Other nations providing the Netherlands with large supplies are mainland China, Japan, Malaya, Singapore, the Philippines, India, and Australia.

West Germany's Trade with the Far East

The most spectacular development in the postwar trade of the Far East has been the expansion of its trade with West Germany. When war ended, the trade of West Germany was almost nil, but it recovered very rapidly. By 1951 West Germany's trade with Asia had already exceeded the prewar level in 1938. In 1959 the value of West Germany's exports to Asia was 3.5 times that of 1938 and the value of its imports 1.7 times that of 1938. In the postwar years, there has been a steady increase in the value of West Germany's exports to these countries, including Ceylon, mainland China, Taiwan, India, Japan, Pakistan, the Philippines, Thailand, and South Korea. Furthermore, West Germany has been successful in gaining increasing shares of the imports of Asian countries. Its shares in 1962 in many Asian countries were larger than in 1948, and in some cases larger than 1938.

West Germany's imports from Asia have been increasing in value in the postwar years. This increase is most apparent in its trade with mainland China, Taiwan, Hong Kong, and Thailand. In other Asian countries there had also been an increase, but a peak was reached in 1957, and a downward adjustment appeared in 1958. This was true in the case of Japan, India, Indonesia, Pakistan, the Philippines, Australia, and New Zealand.

From the point of view of Asian countries, West Germany has become an increasingly important market. West Germany's shares have increased in the exports of Hong Kong, India, Indonesia, Malaya, and Singapore, up to 1959.

The rapid growth of the trade of West Germany is mainly an outcome of its fast economic development in the postwar period. The achievement attests to the energetic character of the German people, their highly developed technical skill, the advance business organizations, and their keen interests in foreign trade. In recent years, from 1959-62, there has been a slight decline in West Germany's shares in the trade of some Far Eastern countries, and this is largely due to the establishment of the Common Market, which requires the upward adjustments of the tariffs of West Germany on some commodities.

Table 16

West Germany's Trade with some Far Eastern Countries

	1938	1948	1952	1956	1959	1962
Share in the Imports (in percentages of total)						
Hong Kong	6.3	0.2	...	2.6	2.9	2.1
India	8.5	0.4	3.1	10.0	13.3	9.4
Indonesia	10.0	1.5	6.6	8.9	11.6	9.7
Malaya & Singapore	2.1	0.1	1.5	2.2	...	3.3
Pakistan	0.3	...	2.9	6.3	10.9	9.4
Philippines	3.1	---	...	3.4	4.7	5.6
Australia	4.0	0.2	2.7	3.9	4.9	5.7
Share in the Exports (in percentages of total)						
Hong Kong	...	...	...	1.1	2.2	3.4
India	5.1	0.6	2.0	2.4	3.2	2.3
Indonesia	3.7	2.1	3.6	4.0	5.9	3.9
Malaya & Singapore	3.1	2.7	3.4	4.7	5.0	4.0
Pakistan	2.4	...	5.1	7.4	6.9	4.9
Philippines	1.0	1.7	...	3.1	2.8	5.4
Australia	...	...	2.8	5.0	3.9	3.5

Source:　Direction of International Trade.

The Common Market and its Effects on the Far Eastern Trade

　　After two years of negotiations, the Treaty of Rome was signed in 1957 to create the European Economic Community (EEC), or the Common Market, by six European nations, namely, Belgium, France, West Germany, Italy, Luxemburg, and the Netherlands. It aims to establish, among other things, a customs union in which internal tariffs on industrial products are gradually abolished and external tariffs unified.

The rates of the common external tariff, when it is fully established, will be the arithmetic averages of the duties of the six nations on January 1, 1957. [13] The common external tariff will retain some protectionistic features. Primary products not competing with the six and their overseas territories will be admitted free or subject to low duties. Processed materials will be subject to high duties, and finished products even higher duties. [14] This is to protect the processing and manufacturing industries of the six nations. This certainly is to the disadvantage of the Far Eastern countries as they are now trying very hard to promote their export trade of processed and manufactured products.

Recently the United Kingdom applied for membership in the Common Market. In the event that the United Kingdom is admitted, the future of the trade of the Far East in western Europe will be further complicated.

Some of the members of the Common Market have overseas territories, for instance in East Africa and West Africa. These territories are brought into this system. Provisions have been made for the exports of the overseas territories to come to the Common Market duty free, and for the exports of the Common Market members to go into the territories either duty free or under favorable rates. The former colonies of the members nations, now independent, are treated with special considerations: for instance, the trade between France on the one hand and South Vietnam, Cambodia, and Laos on the other is subject to favorable rates. However, goods from these three nations are not to be re-exported from France to other members without payments of the common tariffs. [15]

With the establishment of the external tariff on industrial products by the Common Market, Japan could be hurt in its trade with the Common Market because about 90 per cent of Japan's exports consists of manufactures. However, because of the fast economic growth in Japan and the Common Market, the trade between the two has expanded in recent years.

On India and Pakistan, whose exports to the Common

Market are mainly manganese ore, coffee, coir yarn, hides, skins, raw cotton, raw jute, raw wool, and jute manufactures, the establishment of the Common Market will have little effect. This is because most of their exports are raw materials on which the Common Market has no tariff and which will continue to be allowed free entry. The only commodities that will face difficulities are jute manufactures. If the United Kingdom should join the Common Market, this will present more problems. India and Pakistan export sizeable amounts of cotton textile, jute manufactures, tea, hides, and skins to the United Kingdom under preferential tariffs. The question is whether the United Kingdom would have to abolish these preferential tariffs and take up the uniform common tariff of the Common Markets on these products. If so, India and Pakistan would lose their United Kingdom market because they would have to compete with other nations: for instance, the cotton textiles of mainland China and Japan. However, there would be no adverse effect if the United Kingdom were allowed to keep her preferential tariffs to protect the interests of India and Pakistan. [16]

Ceylon, Malaya, Singapore, Indonesia, and the Philippines export to the Common Market mainly tin, rubber, coconut oil, coir fibre, spices, coffee, sugar, pineapples, and tea. Raw materials such as tin, rubber, and coir fibre would enter the Common Market free of duty, and, therefore, there would be no difficulties. The other exports are tropical foodstuffs and probably would suffer. The Common Market allows coffee, tea, spices, vegetable oils, oilseeds from the dependent territories of France, Belgium, Italy, Africa, and elsewhere to enter under preferential tariffs, but will apply external common tariffs on these products from Asia. Therefore, in the trade of these products Asia would lose out to those dependent territories. If the United Kingdom joins the Common Market the same arrangement is applied, Asia would lose the British market for tropical foodstuffs, too. But there is no reason to doubt that the United Kingdom would negotiate with the Common Market about keeping its preferential tariffs on Asian tropical foodstuffs. [17]

Australia and New Zealand export to the Common Market wool, hides, skins, lead, zinc, butter, wheat, barley, beef, and veal. Raw materials such as wool, zinc, lead, hides, and skins would not be affected, as the Common Market either allows them free entry or applies only minimum duties. Temperate foodstuffs would face some competition from Common Market members. Foodstuffs of Common Market origin may go from one country to another under the internal tariffs which eventually will be reduced to nil, while foodstuffs from Australia and New Zealand would be admitted under the higher external tariffs. Furthermore, the Common Market countries are now striving to gain self-sufficiency in foodstuffs by improving their production efficiency. All these tend to create difficulties for Australia and New Zealand. However, the picture is not entirely desperate because labor shortage in the Common Market countries may present obstacles in their foodstuff production, and as standards of living rise in these countries, there may even be an increasing demand for meat and dairy products. Australia and New Zealand export to the United Kingdom the same group of commodities as they do to the Common Market. The United Kingdom now gives them preferential tariffs on these products. In case the United Kingdom joins the Common Market, the question would rise again as to whether the United Kingdom would be able to maintain these preferential tariffs. If Australia and New Zealand should lose their preferential tariffs in the United Kingdom, they would suffer some loss of the British market, because they would have to face the competition of the foodstuffs from both the Common Market members and the Free Trade Association members. Of course, there is reason to believe that some preferential tariffs of the United Kingdom would be maintained. [18]

Burma and Thailand have little trade with Europe. Their foodstuffs exports go mainly to Asian countries; therefore, they have not been affected by the establishment of the Common Market.

To summarize, with the establishment of the Common Market, we do not expect much adverse effect on the exports of raw materials of the Far East. It is hoped that free trade in the Common Market would foster economic growth, and possibly bring about larger demands on the raw materials of the Far East. However there are problems for the foodstuffs exports and manufactures exports of the Far East. The Far East will have to look elsewhere for a better market for their

manufactures. Should the United Kingdom join the Common
Market, the Commonwealth nations would suffer considerable
loss of market in England unless the preferential tariffs
heretofore accorded them can be, to some extent, preserved.

Notes to Chapter 3

1.   The Economist Intelligence Unit, The Commonwealth and
     Europe (London: The Whitefriars Press, 1960), p. 33.

2.   ibid. , p. 34.

3.   ibid. , p. 21.

4.   ibid. , p. 21.

5.   ibid. , p. 11.

6.   ibid. , p. 11.

7.   Elliot Zupnick, Britain's Postwar Dollar Problem (New
     York: Columbia University Press, 1957), pp. 121-25,
     148-49.

8.   U.S. Department of Commerce, Bureau of Foreign
     Commerce, World Trade Information Service, Eco-
     nomic Reports, Part 1, No. 61-47, p. 5; The Common-
     wealth and Europe, pp. 461-62.

9.   U.S., Department of Commerce, Bureau of Foreign
     Commerce, World Trade Information Service, Statistical
     Reports, Part 3, No. 60-19, pp. 3-7.

10. Federation of British Industries, A Trade in Transition,
     London, 1961, pp. 1-4.

11. Lennox A. Mills, Southeast Asia (Minneapolis: University
     of Minnesota Press, 1964), pp. 318-19; The Consultative
     Committee of the Colombo Plan, The Tenth Annual Report,
     Kuala Lumpur, 1962.

12. World Trade Information Service, Economic Reports, Part 1,
     No. 58-84, pp. 15-17.

13. National Industrial Conference Board, Inc., Economic Unity in Europe, Progress and Problems, New York, 1960, pp. 37-38 and p. 44.

14. United Nations, Economic Survey of Asia and the Far East, 1962, New York, 1963, p. 41.

15. The Commonwealth and Europe, ibid., pp. 51-52.

16. The Commonwealth and Europe, ibid., pp. 354-56, p. 369.

17. The Commonwealth and Europe, ibid., p. 384, pp. 398-99.

18. The Commonwealth and Europe, ibid., pp. 298-99.

CHAPTER 4   THE SINO-SOVIET BLOC'S TRADE WITH THE FAR EAST

ECONOMIC EMBARGO

In the postwar period, the two events having great bearing on the Soviet Bloc's trade with the Far East are the United Nation's economic embargo and the Sino-Soviet aid to the Far East. The United States initiated economic embargo against the Sino-Soviet bloc in Europe in 1947.

The fifteen-nation consultative group at Paris and its Co-ordinating Committee (COCOM) were organized in January, 1950, to exercise international export controls. The Mutual Defence Assistance Control Act, often referred to as the Battle Act, was enacted in 1951, and the actual control was put into full effect in 1952.

The United Nations' decision to impose an economic embargo on Communist China and North Korea was reduced in May, 1951, and the China Committee (CHINCOM) of the consultative group was established in September, 1952.

United States economic and military aid started to flow to the Far Eastern countries almost immediately after the war, with large amounts of capital in the form of goods and services continuously pouring into the economies of these nations to help them to rebuild and develop.

The Soviet Union responded to the American aid with an economic aid program of its own. During the years since Stalin's death, the Soviet Union has shifted the challenge to the West from one of overt aggression to a purposely elusive economic offensive.[1]

SINO-SOVIET AID TO THE FAR EAST

Sino-Soviet aid to the Far East came much later than American aid. The Sino-Soviet bloc's aid did not really start until 1954. After years of denouncing foreign aid as an instrument of imperialism, the Sino-Soviet bloc, in the period from July 1, 1954 to June 30, 1960, concluded agreements with 21 underdeveloped countries in Asia, Africa, and the Middle East. These agreements provided for the extension of an estimated $4 billion in intermediate and long-term credits and grants. The portion designated as grants was comparatively small. The greater part of the aid was in the form of interest-paying credits. Of the total, more than $820 million consisted of credits for the purchase of Soviet bloc arms extended to such countries as Egypt, Syria, Iraq, Yemen, Guinea, Indonesia, and Afghanistan. Most of the major Soviet nonmilitary credits carried a low interest rate of 2.5 per cent and were payable over a period of twelve years, with the first installment not due until after the completion of deliveries for a project. The credit agreements usually provided for repayment in commodities and/or convertible currencies with the proportions of the two items, as well as the type, amount,and prices of acceptable commodities subject to annual negotiations. 2

The Sino-Soviet aid of $4 billion is much smaller than the United States aid to the world which in the postwar period from 1945-60 amounted to $85 billion. Of the U. S. aid, $28.5 billion was for military aid and $56.5 billion for economic aid. United States aid to the Near East and Asia alone amounted to a total of $33.1 billion with $20.1 billion for military aid and $13.0 billion for economic aid. 3

Soviet credits to the Far East have largely been concentrated in the neutral countries of India, Indonesia, and Ceylon. For the period 1955-60, India was given a total of 3,200 million rubles of credits to finance such projects as iron and steel works, mining equipment, manufacturing, heavy machinery manufacturing, thermal electric stations, and oil refineries. Indonesia was given a total of 1,470 million rubles of credits to finance iron and steel, nonferrous metals, chemical and textile industries. Ceylon was given a total of 120 million rubles of credit to finance irrigation, hydroelectric projects, iron and steel plants, building material factories, and automobile tire plants. [4]

In general, the Sino-Soviet bloc was not completely successful in carrying out its aid agreements. Deliveries often lagged considerably behind the commitments. This was because the Sino-Soviet bloc constantly injected a variety of noneconomic factors in the operation of its aid program. The delivery of arms has been very prompt because they come from stocks, while delivery of economic goods hinges on current output. [5]

The Soviet Union has assumed the central role in the bloc's aid system. While no strict organization is in evidence, it may be presumed that some coordination and supervision are exercised by the Soviet Union over the extending of aid to its satellites. Of the $4 billion aid extended during the period 1954-60, the Soviet Union itself provided 75 per cent, the European satellites about 20 per cent, and Communist China about 5 per cent of the total. [6]

Between 1955 and 1959, the Soviet Union supplied underdeveloped countries with technical assistance in the construction of more than 100 manufacturing enterprises and 110 other projects in the fields of mining, metalurgical, chemical, power, oil refining, and machine building enterprises. In connection with the construction of capital projects, technicians came to the underdeveloped countries to perform the installations themselves and at times remained to furnish operating assistance during the first few years. In 1959 there were about 6, 100 technicians operating in Asia, the Middle East, and Africa. Of this total, 4, 700 were engaged in nonmilitary activities and 1, 400 in military activities. The Soviet Union furnished 61 per cent of the technicians, the European satellites 27 per cent, and Communist China 12 per cent. [7]

Communist China has made a particular effort to expand her economic aid to countries in Southeast Asia. The role of Communist China is obviously much limited since its economic capabilities are still at a low level. The total credits granted by Communist China, in the period 1955-58, were estimated at $56 million. [8]

In comparing the aid granted by the Sino-Soviet bloc with American aid, a few general observations may be made:

1.   While agricultural products occupy an important share of American aid, they are usually absent from the Sino-Soviet bloc aid program. American agricultural surplus has been sent to underdeveloped countries and sold for local currency which is, in turn, used to subsidize the local economy.

2.   While American aid has been granted a large number of countries with which the United States maintains military alliances, the Sino-Soviet bloc aid tends to be concentrated in a few countries such as Yugoslavia, Afghanistan, India, Indonesia, Egypt, and Syria, with these few countries receiving about 95 per cent of the total aid.

3.   The purpose of American aid has been general in nature, including military and economic projects, and subsidy to the recipient governments; the Sino-Soviet bloc aid has been very specific with some special projects as the goal.

4.   While the interest rates of American credits usually range from 3 per cent for mutual security loans to 6 per cent for Export Import Bank loans, the interest rates of the Sino-Soviet bloc credits range from 2 per cent to 2.5 per cent.

5.   While the length of time for repayment of American credits is up to 40 years, that of the Sino-Soviet bloc credits is usually about 12 years.

6.   While the repayment of interest for American credits may begin within the year or be deferred for 3 years, that for the Sino-Soviet bloc credits may be deferred for one year. While the repayment of prinicipal for American credits may be deferred for 4 years, that for the Sino-Soviet bloc credits may be deferred for 8 years. [9]

Although there are differences in the manner in which the aid has been extended by the two sides, the aim has been the same: that is, to promote better economic and political relations with these countries. The aid programs of both sides have been effective. In countries where the Sino-Soviet bloc concentrates its aid efforts, there has been a definite gain in

the bloc's share of trade, but in other countries the advantages are on the side of the United States.

DEVELOPMENT OF THE SINO-SOVIET BLOC'S TRADE WITH THE FREE FAR EAST

In 1959, the volume of trade of Soviet Russia was much
larger than that of 1938. In 1959 Soviet Russia exported almost $5. 5 billion's worth of goods, or more than 16 times the
value of her 1938 exports at current prices. The physical
volume of goods exported in 1959 was more than 8. 5 times
larger than that in 1938. As a trading nation, Soviet Russia
ranked 6th in 1959 as compared to 16th place in 1938. In
relation to world trade, Soviet Russia's exports in 1959 accounted for almost 4. 5 per cent of world exports, whereas in
1938 it accounted for a little more than 1 per cent of world
exports. However, as compared to the trade of Czarist days,
Soviet Russia's record is not particularly impressive. The
Russia of the period 1911-13 accounted for about 4. 2 per cent
of world exports, not far below the 4. 5 per cent for Soviet
Russia in 1959.

The trade of Soviet Russia since the end of World War II
has been predominantly an exchange of goods with countries of
the Sino-Soviet bloc. In 1959, almost three quarters of Soviet
Russia's trade was within the Soviet bloc. Actually, in 1959,
Soviet Russia's exports to countries outside the Sino-Soviet
bloc were only on a level with those of Denmark (approximately $1. 4 billion) and amounted to little more than 1. 5 per
cent of the total imports of the free world. [10] Soviet Russia's
trade with the Far East has been small. The Sino-Soviet
bloc's trade with the Far East has largely consisted of the
trade between Communist China and the rest of the Far East. [11]

The free Far East countries can roughly be divided into
two groups: the pro-West group and the neutral group. The
pro-West group is commercially as well as politically orien-
tated toward the West. The Sino-Soviet bloc's shares in the
imports and exports of these countries have been less than
5 per cent. These countries are Laos, Japan, Pakistan,
Formosa, South Korea, South Vietnam, the Philippines, Thailand, Australia, and New Zealand. These countries receive

large amounts of U. S. aid, and have been applying the embargo faithfully against the Sino-Soviet bloc. The economic offensive of the Sino-Soviet bloc has not made any inroad on this
group. In fact, the Sino-Soviet bloc's shares in the imports
of Australia and New Zealand declined in the period 1953-59.
The Sino-Soviet bloc took only 4. 0 per cent of the exports of
Japan and supplied only 3. 5 per cent of the imports of Japan
in 1962.

The neutral group is where the Sino-Soviet bloc has been
concentrating its economic activities, and where the Sino-Soviet bloc aid has been spent. These countries are Burma,
Cambodia, Ceylon, India, Indonesia, Malaya, and Singapore.
This is the area where the Sino-Soviet bloc's shares in imports
and exports of these countries have exceeded 5 per cent.

A very impressive gain in trade made by the Sino-Soviet
bloc has been in Indonesia. In the period 1952-62, the Sino-
Soviet bloc's share in the imports of Indonesia has increased
from 0. 5 per cent to 9. 8 per cent, and the bloc's share in the
exports of Indonesia has increased from 1. 1 per cent to 4. 6
per cent. In absolute figures, the Sino-Soviet bloc's imports
from Indonesia amounted to $42. 7 million in 1962, and the
bloc's exports to Indonesia amounted to $73. 1 million. With
this rate of progress going on, before long the Sino-Soviet
bloc may begin to occupy an important position in the trade of
Indonesia. The Sino-Soviet bloc aid, of course, has contributed to this development. For the period 1955-58, Indonesia
was promised a total of $109 million credits, mainly for the
construction of a sugar mill with equipment and technicians
from East Germany, and the construction of an automobile tire
factory and an irrigation project with equipment and technicians
from Czechoslovakia. [12]

Another country where the Sino-Soviet bloc has made a
substantial commercial gain is Ceylon. For the period 1952-62,
the bloc's share in the exports of Ceylon increased from 0. 9
per cent to 12. 5 per cent, and its share in the imports of Ceylon increased from 0. 3 per cent to 7. 6 per cent. In absolute
figures, the bloc's exports to Ceylon in 1959 amounted to $24. 6
million, and its imports from Ceylon $44. 0 million. This in-
crease is partly due to the trade agreements with Communist
China for the exchange of Ceylon's rubber for Communist

China's rice, soybeans and other items for the period from
1952-59. Ceylon received, in the period 1955-58, $50 million
credit from the Sino-Soviet bloc. Of this total, $16 million
was from Communist China. The aid was to be used for the
construction of a sugar refinery and a cement factory with
equipment and technicians from Czechoslovakia, and for land
clearing, irrigation and hydroelectric projects, and industrial plants with Russian equipment and technicians. [13]

India has also increased her trade with the Sino-Soviet
bloc. For the period 1952-62, the bloc's share in the exports
of India increased from 1.0 per cent to 11.7 per cent, and
the bloc's share in the imports of India increased from 2.3
per cent to 9.6 per cent. In absolute figures, the bloc's exports to India amounted to $179.8 million in 1962, and its im-
ports from India, $134.4 million. India has been the prime
target for Sino-Soviet bloc aid. For the period 1955-60, India
was promised a total of $300 million. Of the total, a very
small part was given as a grant requiring no repayment, and
the rest were credits of usually 12 year terms at 2.5 per cent
interest. The aid was earmarked for the construction of the
Bhilai Steel Mill, a heavy machinery plant, a plant for manufacturing coal mining equipment, an optical and opthalmologi-
cal lens factory, and a 250,000 kilowatt power station with
Russian material and technical help. The aid also provided
for coal mine drilling rigs and oil drilling rigs. It also included the delivery of some laboratory equipment for the Technological Institute of Bombay. There were provisions for the
training of Indian technicians by Russian personnel for taking
over the operation of the aid projects. [14]

There was some gain made by the Sino-Soviet bloc in its
trade with Malaya and Singapore. For the period 1952-62, the
bloc's share in the exports of Malaya and Singapore increased
from 1.7 per cent to 9.1 per cent, and the bloc's share in the
imports of Malaya and Singapore increased from 2.4 per cent
to 6.2 per cent. In absolute figures, the bloc's imports from
Malaya and Singapore reached $165.6 million in 1959, and the
bloc's export to Malaya and Singapore reached $83.1 million.

The Sino-Soviet bloc also made gains in the trade of Burma.
For the period 1952-62, the bloc's share in the exports of Burma increased from 0.5 per cent to 12.1 per cent, and the

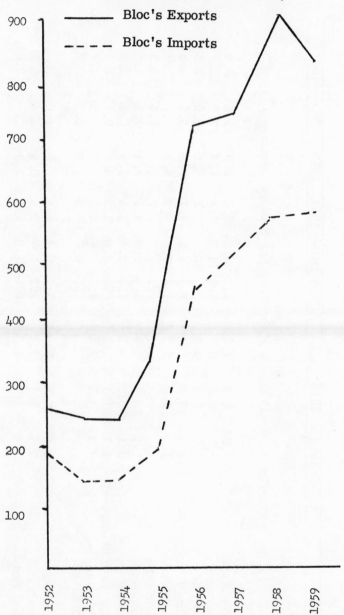

FIGURE 3
TRADE OF SINO-SOVIET BLOC WITH FREE ASIA
(in millions of U.S. dollars)

——— Bloc's Exports

– – – – Bloc's Imports

Source: International Monetary Fund and International Bank for
Reconstruction and Development, Direction of International
Trade (New York: United Nations), V. 7, N. 6, P. 74,
pp. 236-37; V. 7, N. 9, p. 117; and V. 11, N. 9, pp. 327-28.

107

Table 17

Sino-Soviet Bloc's Trade with Free Far Eastern Countries

Share in the Exports

(in percentage of the total exports of the Free Far Eastern Countries)

	1952	1953	1954	1955	1956	1957	1958	1959	1962
Free Asia	2.2	2.0	1.8	2.0	4.8	5.1	6.0	5.5	4.9
Burma	..	0.5	0.3	18.5	12.6	9.4	1.6	2.0	12.1
Ceylon	0.9	0.2	0.1	..	10.5	10.2	6.1	6.0	12.5
Hong Kong	18.0	19.8	16.1	7.1	4.2	4.1	5.2	3.5	1.8
India	1.0	0.8	1.2	1.8	2.5	4.6	5.7	7.5	11.7
Cambodia	..	..	..	..	..	..	..	2.5	12.3
Indonesia	1.1	0.5	1.1	3.6	2.9	4.8	7.4	7.3	4.6
Japan	0.1	0.3	1.5	1.9	2.9	2.5	2.6	0.8	4.0
Malaya & Singapore	1.7	1.1	1.2	0.9	4.9	3.9	9.6	9.1	9.1
Pakistan	6.7	2.8	2.1	1.3	1.4	5.3	6.5	2.5	3.3
Thailand	..	..	..	..	0.4	0.9	1.0	0.8	..
Oceania	0.8	2.6	2.9	1.7	2.1	2.5	0.9	1.0	..
Australia	0.5	3.1	3.4	2.2	2.7	2.9	0.9	1.4	6.5
New Zealand	1.4	1.7	2.3	0.9	1.2	2.3	1.2	..	0.03

Share in the Imports

(in percentage of the total imports of the Free Far Eastern Countries)

Free Asia	2.5	2.6	2.6	3.6	6.2	5.3	7.5	5.8	5.4
Burma	1.9	1.1	1.6	1.9	16.6	7.3	10.6	8.0	18.3
Ceylon	0.3	0.4	0.4	...	8.3	4.7	9.1	7.6	7.6
Hong Kong	22.0	22.1	20.1	24.2	22.8	21.9	30.4	20.9	20.2
India	2.3	0.5	1.2	1.6	4.6	5.1	8.8	5.1	9.6
Cambodia	...	...	...	...	...	2.6	6.7	8.2	11.6
Laos	...	...	...	...	...	0.5	0.4	...	...
Vietnam	...	...	...	0.1	...	...	...	...	9.5
Indonesia	0.5	0.9	2.4	6.5	4.5	4.3	13.5	17.1	9.8
Japan	0.8	1.6	2.2	3.6	2.8	2.1	2.5	1.5	3.5
Malaya & Singapore	2.4	2.7	2.3	2.4	2.3	2.8	4.6	3.7	6.2
Pakistan	0.9	0.3	0.4	0.2	0.1	2.4	3.4	1.8	2.2
Philippines	--	...	--	...	...	...	...	...	0.1
Thailand	...	...	0.5	...	0.1	0.1	--	0.2	0.8
Oceania	0.6	0.6	0.5	0.5	0.4	0.4	0.5	0.6	...
Australia	0.7	0.8	0.8	0.7	0.6	0.7	0.7	0.7	1.0
New Zealand	0.3	0.3	0.1	0.1	0.1	0.1	0.2	...	...

Source: The percentage figures are calculated by dividing the exports (imports) from the Sino-Soviet bloc by the total exports (imports) of the Free Far Eastern countries.   This is to show how much of the exports and imports of the Free Far Eastern countries is provided by the Sino-Soviet bloc.   The total imports figures for the Free Far Eastern countries are given by the International Monetary Fund, <u>International Financial Statistics,</u> Washington, D.C., V. 14, No. 6, June, 1961, pp. 36-39.

bloc's share in the imports of Burma increased from 1.9 per
cent to 18.3 per cent. The Sino-Soviet bloc aid granted to
Burma for the period 1955-58 included: expansion of textile
mills; construction of four scientific libraries, a technical institute, a hospital, a sports arena; and the provision of some
books and equipment for the University of Rangoon. [15] The decline of the bloc's trade with Burma from 1957-59 was probably due to political conditions in Southeast Asia and the limited
trade of Communist China.

The Sino-Soviet bloc has made a modest beginning in its
trade with Cambodia. In 1962, the bloc's share in the exports
of Cambodia was 12.3 per cent, and in the imports of Cambodia
11.6 per cent. In absolute figures, the bloc imported from
Cambodia $10.6 million and exported to Cambodia $8.6 million.
Cambodia has received some aid from Communist China in the
form of goods from China, which are sold in Cambodia, and the
proceeds in local currency are used for economic development. [16]

As the free world has strengthened its commercial ties
with the pro-West Asian countries, the Sino-Soviet bloc has
made some gain in the neutral countries. What is the over-all
picture in the struggle of the two camps for the trade of free
Asia as a whole? The Sino-Soviet bloc expanded its exports
to free Asia for the period 1952-62 from $261.8 million
to $967.4 million and its imports from free Asia from $183.0
million to $728.2 million. This is not impressive. The Sino-
Soviet bloc's share in the exports of free Asia as a whole increased from 2.2 per cent to 6.0 per cent for the period 1952-
58, and its share in the imports of free Asia from 2.5 per cent
to 7.5 per cent. From 1958-62, there was a decline in the
bloc's share in free Asia's trade. The bloc's share of free
Asian exports for 1962 was 4.9 per cent and of free Asian imports, 5.4 per cent. That is, the Sino-Soviet bloc's share of
free Asian trade as a whole has seldom exceeded 8 per cent at
any time. In other words, free Asia in the 1950's was closely
linked commercially to the free world, doing more than 92 per
cent of its trade with the free world. This is an immensely
significant phenomenon vastly encouraging to the free world.
Free Asia is far from being lost to the economic offensive of the
Sino-Soviet bloc.

COMPOSITION OF THE SINO-SOVIET BLOC'S TRADE

Based on the commodity composition of the trade of Soviet Russia, it is evident that Russia has undergone a transition: from an agricultural country in 1938 to an industrial country in 1959. The relative share of manufactured goods in Soviet Russia's exports has changed from 39 per cent of the total exports in 1938 to 63 per cent in 1959. The share of machinery and equipment in Soviet Russia's exports has shown an increase from 5 per cent in 1938 to 21 per cent in 1959. In recent years, Soviet Russia has been a net importer of foodstuffs. [17]

Soviet Russia's exports to free Far Eastern countries consist primarily of petroleum and petroleum products, rolled steel, lumber, cement, cotton cloth, wheat, machinery, and equipment. Soviet Russia's exports of machinery and equipment have increased thirtyfold since 1955, and now account for more than 30 per cent of Soviet Russia's total exports to the underdeveloped countries. Soviet Russia's imports from these countries consist mostly of food and raw materials such as rubber from Malaya and Indonesia wool, hides, and skins from India. [18]

Communist China's exports consist largely of agricultural products such as soybeans, vegetable oils, eggs, bristle, and wool. These agricultural products amounted to 54.4 per cent of her total exports in 1959. Communist China also exports some nonferrous metals and coal. Since 1954, there have been some items for export such as structural steel sent to Burma and machine tools, textile machinery, and other equipment sent to Indonesia. Communist China imports from the free Asian and Oceanic countries mainly raw materials, fuels, and consumer goods such as jute, tin, cotton, rubber, petroleum and petroleum products, rice, and sugar. [19]

STATE TRADING

The trade of Soviet Russia is not handled by private business, but is assigned to state agencies. After a period of experiment in the early days, there were such establishments as the foreign trade corporations (Vneshtorgovoe Obyedinenie)

in charge of exports and imports, under the general control of
the Ministry of Foreign Trade. There are roughly two dozen
such corporations, with each having a monopolistic control
over a group of commodities. Import requirements and exportable surpluses are made known to these corporations by
the Gosplan (the State Planning Commission of the Council of
Labor and Defense). All trade transactions with the West are
made by negotiations through these corporations. The agreements entered into by these corporations would include the kinds
of commodities traded, the prices, the quantities, the terms of
payment, and credit arrangements, if any. It is difficult to
compare prices and costs, as the market of commodities in
Soviet Russia is of an entirely different nature than that of the
West. These corporations are to try to exchange exportable
surpluses for needed imports at the best possible bargain they
can arrange. Of course, the world market prices are generally used as a reference. There is also a state corporation for
foreign tourists. This corporation combines its function with
the responsibility for licensing of companies that package and
ship goods from the United States to individuals in Soviet
Russia. In the United States these trade corporations are represented by Amtorg, the official Soviet Russia trading agency,
located in New York. [20]

Since 1935, the trade of Communist China has been similarly handled by state trade corporations. There are about
sixteen of them, with each specializing in the trade of a group
of commodities. There are three trading agencies of Communist
China in Hong Kong, through which the trade with the Asian
countries is conducted. [21]

PROSPECTS

What will become of the trade of the free countries of the
Far East? Barring any major Communist military conquest in
this area, the West should be confident that free Asia is a dependable commercial partner because free Asia is directing the
major share of her total trade to the West. There are reasons
to believe that this pattern will continue for years to come.

For centuries the United Kingdom, France, the Netherlands,
and other European countries have had trade relations with the
free Far East. China also has long had trade relations with

this area, but Communist China's trade capability is limited by her low income level. Soviet Russia is a newcomer in trade with this area. While European products have already established their markets in free Asian countries, it will be some time before Soviet Russia can establish markets for her products.

Economic and military aid from the United States came to this area earlier and in larger quantities than the aid from the Sino-Soviet bloc. The actual delivery of goods and services by the United States has been more dependable than that by the Sino-Soviet bloc.

Trade in the free Far Eastern countries has been in the hands of European import-export firms, American business-men, and local agents who have had long association with the West. Shipping facilities, warehouse space, communication channels, and trade information sources are all in the hands of these groups. This has been long established tradition and will facilitate the trade between the free Far East and the West.

Basically, the Sino-Soviet bloc directs its trade among members of the bloc. Its trade with the free Far East is supplementary to its trade within the bloc. The bloc has a favorable balance with the free Far East, and it is using the region as a source of foreign exchange.

Notes to Chapter 4

1.   Dumond Peck Hill, Staff Memorandum of the Communist Economic Offensive, U.S. Congress, 85th Cong. , 2d Sess. (Washington: U.S. Government Printing Office, 1958), p. 1.

2.   Milton Kovner, The Challenge of Coexistence a Study of Soviet Economic Diplomacy (Washington: Public Affairs Press, 1961), p. 97.

3.   "Is the Dollar Headed for New Trouble?" U.S. News and World Report, October, 6, 1961, p. 56.

4. V. Rimalov, Economic Co-operation Between U.S.S.R. and Underdeveloped Countries, Moscow, 1962.

5. Robert L. Allen, Communist Economic Warfare, House of Representatives, U.S. 86th Cong., 2d Sess. (Washington: U.S. Government Printing Office, 1960), pp. 11-12.

6. Kovner, op. cit., p. 98.

7. Kovner, loc. cit.

8. Hill, op. cit., pp. 6-10.

9. Hill, loc. cit.

10. Kovner, op. cit., p. 27.

11. Robert J. Barr, American Trade with Asia and the Far East (Milwaukee, Wis.: Marquette University Press, 1959), pp. 293-301.

12. Hill, op. cit., pp. 11-12.

13. Hill, loc. cit.

14. Hill, loc. cit.; Celia I. Herman, Investment in India, U.S. Department of Commerce, Bureau of Foreign Commerce, 1961, Washington, D.C., pp. 131-32.

15. Hill, op. cit., p. 11.

16. Hill, loc. cit.

17. Kovner, op. cit., pp. 98-99.

18. Kovner, loc. cit.

19. T.J. Hughes and D.E.T. Luard, The Economic Development of Communist China (London: Oxford University Press, 1959), p. 129.

20. Alec Nove, The Soviet Economy, an Introduction (New

York: Frederick A. Praeger, 1961), pp. 42-43,
pp. 190-91.

21.   For details, see Chapter 7.

DEVELOPMENT

Trade between the United States and Asia predated the establishment of the Federal Constitution in 1787. It was in 1785 that the vessel Express of China entered New York from Canton, and in 1787 the Grand Turk sailed into Salem from Canton. In 1789, of the forty-six foreign vessels entering Canton, eighteen were American. It was also during these years that the first New England mariners reached the West coast in search of furs. Captain Gray's famous voyage to Oregon and China in the period 1787-90 opened the New England-Northwest-China trade, a lucrative traffic whereby the New Englander traded manufactured products with the northwest Indians for furs, and then sailed for China to trade the furs for oriental goods. [1]

The trade of the United States with the Far East grew rapidly after the industrialization of the United States, and has been in full swing since 1870. World War I helped to promote this trade because of the absence of competition from Europe, but the great depression of 1929 temporarily reduced this trade. By 1938, the United States exported $574.8 million to the Far East, and imported $556.5 million. These amounted to 19.7 per cent of the total exports of the United States in that year and 26.0 per cent of the total imports. [2]

In trading with the Far East, the United States has been contending with competition from European countries from the very beginning and competition from Japan since 1920. During World War II and the immediate postwar period, the export capacities of Western Europe and Japan were greatly reduced, and the United States was able to fill their places with increased trade. In 1948, United States exports to the Far East reached 1.9 billion, and her imports from these areas $1.4 billion.

United States trade with the Far East increased further up
to 1951, stimulated by the demands of the Korean War. In
that year, United States exports to the Far East increased to
$2.1 billion; her imports from these areas reached a peak of
$2.3 billion. From 1952-54, the United States trade with these
areas declined slightly due to the ending of the Korean War and
the increasing competition from Japan and other European
countries as these countries progressed on the road to economic recovery.

From 1955-57, United States trade with the Far East
was improving. In 1958, there was a drop in both the export of the United States to the region and the imports of the
United States from the region. This was mainly due to the recession in the United States and import controls by countries in
the region. In 1962, United States exports to these areas
reached $4.0 billion, and United States imports from these
areas reached $3.1 billion. These accounted for 18.5 per cent
of the total exports of the United States and 18.8 per cent of
her total imports. Trade with the Far East is important to the
United States not only because of the dollar value involved, and the
large percentage in total trade, but also because of the imported
essential raw materials which we need for our industries.[3]

The United States, throughout the postwar period, has enjoyed a favorable balance of trade with the Far East, with the
exception of 1950 and 1951 when a surplus import occurred
because of the Korean War. There was a balance of trade in
1959 due to the large increase of exports to the Far East.

DIRECTION OF TRADE

If one were to compare the various major areas of the
world in their trade with the United States, they would rank
(in order of importance), as follows: Europe, Central and
South America, Canada, Asia, Africa, and Oceania. Europe

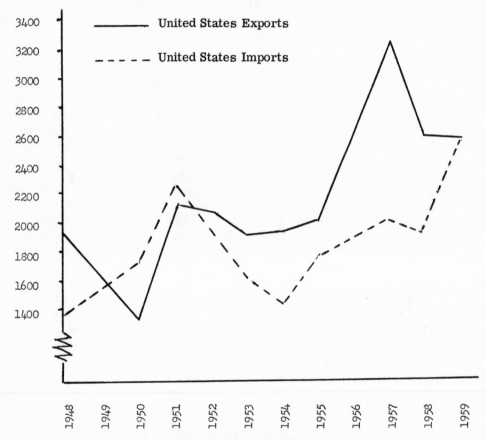

FIGURE 4
TRADE OF THE UNITED STATES WITH
THE FAR EAST
(in millions of U.S. dollars)

————— United States Exports

– – – – – United States Imports

Source: International Monetary Fund and International Bank for
Reconstruction and Development, Direction of International Trade (New York: United Nations), V. 4, N. 1/2,
p. 8; V. 7, N. 6, p. 82; V. 9, N. 10, p. 56; V. 11, N. 8,
p. 60; and V. 11, N. 9, p. 115.

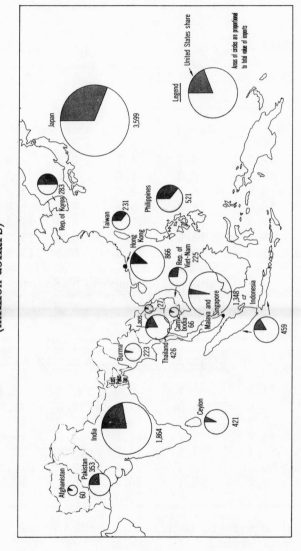

FIGURE 5

UNITED STATES SHARES OF IMPORTS
INTO FAR EASTERN COUNTRIES, 1959

(million dollars)

Source: Taken from U.S. Department of Commerce, Bureau of Foreign Commerce,
World Trade Information Service, Statistical Reports, Part 3, No. 61-3.

Table 18

Direction of United States' Trade

United States Exports by Destination
(percentages of U.S. Exports)

	Europe	Canada	South America	Central America	Asia	Africa and Oceania
1860	74.8	6.9	4.7	8.8	2.4	2.5
1871-75	80.2	6.4	4.0	7.2	1.0	1.2
1891-95	79.5	5.5	3.7	6.8	2.3	2.2
1911-15	64.0	14.2	5.2	7.7	5.6	3.3
1931-35	47.4	14.8	7.0	8.0	17.3	5.5
1951-55	23.4	18.8	15.1	10.9	13.7	5.3
1959-61	32.4	20.4	11.8	9.2	19.4	6.4

United States Imports by Source
(percentages of U. S. Exports)

	Europe	Canada	South America	Central America	Asia	Africa and Oceania
1860	61.3	6.7	9.9	12.5	8.3	1.3
1871-75	55.6	5.9	11.0	16.6	9.7	1.3
1891-95	50.6	4.6	14.9	16.3	10.8	2.7
1911-15	46.6	7.7	12.8	14.5	15.8	2.5
1931-35	30.1	13.8	14.3	10.3	28.7	2.8
1951-55	20.2	22.5	21.2	12.0	16.3	7.7
1959-61	29.2	20.7	16.2	10.1	17.7	6.1

Source: Historical Statistics of the United States, Survey of Current Business, July, 1962.

has always been the first in the mind of the American public, not only concerning commercial interests but interests in general. There is also great emphasis on Canada and Central and South America as trade partners of the United States, but a tendency to neglect Asia, Africa and Oceania. However, in examining the long run development of the trade of these major areas with the United States, these traditional concepts have to be greatly modified. In 1860, Europe bought 74.8 per cent of United States exports, but only 32.4 per cent in 1959-61. In 1860 Europe supplied 61.3 per cent of United States imports, but only 29.2 per cent in 1959-61. Central America has not gained much in its shares in the trade of the United States for the period 1860-1960. Canada, South America, Asia, Africa, and Oceania are the areas whose shares in the trade of the United States have greatly improved. The fastest gain has been made by Asia in its share in the export trade of the United States, taking 2.4 per cent in 1860, but 19.4 per cent in 1959-61. Tremendous gain has also been made by Africa and Oceania as a source of the import trade of the United States, supplying 1.3 per cent in 1860, but 6.1 per cent in 1959-61. If this pattern should continue, then there is reason to expect further gain in the importance of Asia in the trade of the United States at the expense of Europe and Central America.

In 1962, the major nations in Asia and Oceania receiving exports of the United States, in the order of their importance, were Japan, India, Australia, Pakistan, the Philippines, South Korea, Taiwan, Hong Kong, Indonesia, and Indochina.

In 1962 the major countries supplying the imports of the United States, in their order of importance, were Japan, Australia, the Philippines, India, Malaya and Singapore, Hong Kong, New Zealand, Indonesia, and Taiwan.

The United States enjoys a favorable balance of trade with most countries in the Far East because of the enormous requirements for American equipment and materials for reconstruction and industrialization in such countries as Burma, Taiwan, Hong Kong, Indochina, Japan, Pakistan, the Philippines, South Korea, and Australia. In these countries there is the traditional shortage of American dollars and difficulties in balancing international payments. However, in 1962, Hong Kong and Australia had a favorable balance of trade with the United States.

There are also other countries which have had a favorable balance of trade with the United States in the postwar period: for instance Ceylon, Indonesia, Malaya and Singapore, and Thailand. New Zealand, since 1956, has had a favorable balance of trade with the United States. In these countries there is a dollar shortage and no adverse payments difficulties. Consequently, their currencies have been strong and their foreign exchange rates rather stable.

United States Trade with Japan

Trade between the United States and Japan is more important to Japan than it is to the United States. In 1938, the United States share in Japan's trade was 34.4 per cent. This increased greatly in the immediate postwar period, with the United States share reaching 62.9 per cent in 1948. Gradually, as Japan regained her trade with the world, the United States share declined to 31.3 per cent in 1955, but by 1960, it reached 34.4 per cent, the prewar level. Roughly speaking, one third of the trade of Japan has been with the United States.

Japan's share in the trade of the United States in 1938 was only 7.8 per cent. In the immediate postwar period, due to low export capability, Japan's share declined to 2.6 per cent. From 1956-60, Japan's share in the trade of the United States gradually improved, and Japan's share in 1960 was 6.5 per cent, still below the prewar level.[5]

Japan's imports from the United States consist mainly of raw cotton, wheat, corn, soybean, coking coal, iron and steel scrap, machinery, transport equipment, chemicals, and petroleum products. In return, Japan exports to the United States clothing, plywood, radio receivers, raw silk, silk and woolen fabrics, toys, pottery, sewing machines, tuna, photographic equipment, metal products, and ships.[6]

All through the postwar period, Japan has had a trade deficit with the United States. Japan has been able to meet her international payments partly because of United States and

FIGURE 6
UNITED STATES TRADE WITH MAJOR
COUNTRIES IN THE FAR EAST IN 1962
(in millions of U.S. dollars)

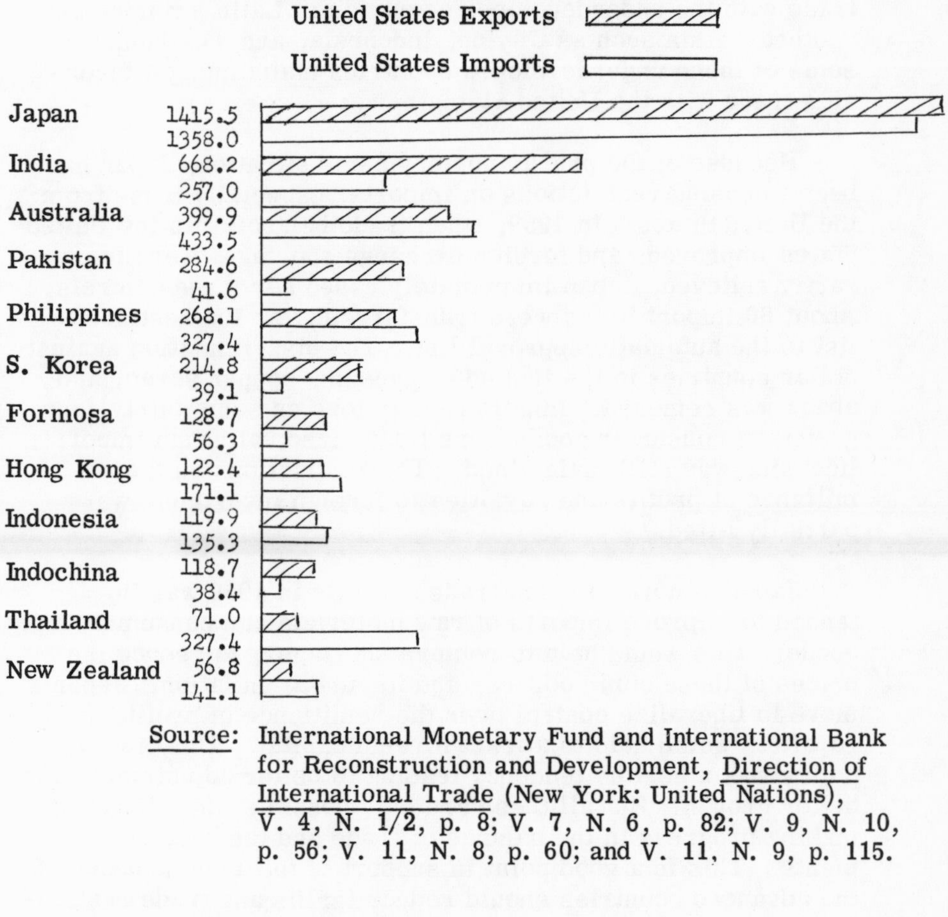

United States Exports

United States Imports

Country	Exports	Imports
Japan	1415.5	1358.0
India	668.2	257.0
Australia	399.9	433.5
Pakistan	284.6	41.6
Philippines	268.1	327.4
S. Korea	214.8	39.1
Formosa	128.7	56.3
Hong Kong	122.4	171.1
Indonesia	119.9	135.3
Indochina	118.7	38.4
Thailand	71.0	327.4
New Zealand	56.8	141.1

Source: International Monetary Fund and International Bank
for Reconstruction and Development, Direction of
International Trade (New York: United Nations),
V. 4, N. 1/2, p. 8; V. 7, N. 6, p. 82; V. 9, N. 10,
p. 56; V. 11, N. 8, p. 60; and V. 11, N. 9, p. 115.

United Nations aid and military expenditures, and partly because of the foreign-exchange proceeds earned through her
trade with Southeast Asia and Latin America. There is the
possibility of a triangle trade: the United States maintaining
a favorable trade with Japan; Japan maintaining a favorable
trade with the underdeveloped countries in Latin America and
Southeast Asia such as Ceylon, Indonesia, and Thailand;
some of these underdeveloped countries maintaining a favorable trade with the United States.

Because of the precarious payments situation, Japan has
been imposing restrictions on imports, especially those from
the United States. In 1959, when trade balance with the United
States improved, and foreign-exchange shortages were temporarily relieved, Japan immediately eased her trade controls.
About 80 import items were transferred from the restrictive
list to the automatic approval list. The discrimination against
dollar countries in the import of gypsum, copper scrap, and
abaca was removed. Import restrictions on some thirty-four
groups of consumer goods were liberalized, although import
licensing was still maintained. The restrictions on the remittance of profits and royalties to foreign investment were
partially lifted. [7]

Japan's move to relax trade controls in 1959 was intended to improve imports of raw materials and consumer
goods. This would help to remove shortages, to reduce the
prices of these commodities, and to curtail inflation. Japan's
move to liberalize control over the remittance of profits and
royalties would help to attract foreign capital. This liberal
policy was a healthy tendency leading to better adjustments and
better growth. But all these are only possible when Japan is
making progress in the balance of trade and the balance of payments. This is a good point in support of the argument that if
the advanced countries should reduce tariffs and trade restrictions on the imports from less-developed countries, then the
less-developed countries could sell more, and thereby improve
their balance of trade and balance of payments. They could
then be in a position to reduce their tariffs and trade controls
in order to improve their imports, thus curtailing inflation in
their domestic markets. The result could be free trade for all
concerned and better economic growth for the less developed
countries. [8]

United States Trade with the Philippines

The United States imported $311.8 million worth of goods from the Philippines in 1959, and exported $275.2 million worth to that country.[9] This trade, of course, is important to the United States, but it is far more important to the Philippines. The United States is the leading market for Philippine exports and the leading supplier of Philippine imports. From 1951-58, the United States had a favorable balance of trade with the Philippines, but from 1956-60, there had been a decline in the United States exports to the Philippines, and an increase of United States imports from the Philippines. This resulted in an unfavorable balance of trade with the Philippines in 1959 and 1960.[10] This decline of United States exports to the Philippines was probably due to the increase of Philippine tariff rates. By the trade agreement of 1959, the two countries are gradually applying tariffs to each other according to a schedule as follows:

Table 19

U. S.--Philippines Tariffs

	Percentage of U. S. tariff rates on Philippine goods	Percentage of Philippine tariff rates on U. S. goods
1956-58	5	25
1959-61	10	50
1962-64	20	75
1965-67	40	90
1968-70	60	90
1971-73	80	90
1974	100	100

Sources: Robert J. Barr, American Trade with Asia and the Far East, The Marquette University Press, Milwaukee, Wisconsin, 1959, p. 178.

This means that before 1955 there had been free trade between the two countries, and from 1956-73 tariff rates will be
gradually added by the countries, and in 1974 the two countries
will apply their full tariff rates to each other. The United
States has been restricting, by the use of quotas, the imports
of sugar, cordage, rice, cigars, tobacco, coconuts, and buttons
from the Philippines. As tariffs are gradually added to these
items, the quotas will be reduced. [11]

Because of the application of tariffs by the two countries,
the United States share in the trade of the Philippines has declined in the postwar years, with Japan and European countries
gaining in their shares. [12]

Because the Philippines had a favorable balance of trade
in 1959 and 1960, the shortage of the United States dollars
was relieved, and the government immediately started a de-
control program in 1960 with the aim of gradually eliminating
the exchange controls. [13]

United States exports to the Philippines consist mainly of
machinery, equipment, vehicles, textile fibers, textile
manufactures, food, chemicals, and paper. United States
imports from the Philippines consist mainly of food, coconut
products, textile manufactures, paper, plywood, and metal
and metal products.

In the process of industrialization, the Philippines require foreign capital, but nationalistic feeling is still strong.
For the development of natural resources and public utilities,
the Philippine constitution guarantees 60 per cent Filipino
ownership. In 1959, the National Economic Council applied
this principle of 60 per cent Filipino ownership to all co-
operations. However, the provisions of the Bell Trade Agreement granted Filipino status to United States citizens. Therefore, there is no restriction on American investment. This
agreement will expire in 1974. [14]

Table 20

Major Commodities of U. S. --Philippine Trade
(in millions of U. S. dollars)

	United States Imports from the Philippines	
	1959	1960
Total	311. 8	306. 4
Food	137. 6	149. 6
Coconut meat	18. 3	17. 1
Sugar	109. 8	122. 6
Vegetable products	93. 4	80. 1
Copra	66. 0	60. 9
Coconut oil	24. 7	15. 0
Textile fibre and manufactures	31. 4	32. 1
Cotton manufactures	12. 0	13. 3
Manila, abaca	11. 2	9. 9
Wood and paper	26. 9	18. 8
Plywood	14. 7	8. 0
Metals & manufactures	9. 2	18. 7
Chrome	6. 7	7. 4

	United States Exports to the Philippines	
	1959	1960
Total	275. 2	293. 4
Food	36. 1	40. 0
Dairy products	14. 9	17. 6
Grains	9. 0	
Textile fiber & manufactures	48. 3	58. 1
Raw cotton	13. 4	21. 3
Cotton manufactures	23. 7	26. 2
Paper & products	14. 5	13. 9
Non-metallic minerals	12. 1	10. 8
Machinery & vehicles	75. 9	78. 8
Electric machinery	19. 5	15. 3
Industrial machinery	34. 6	37. 3
Tractors & parts	2. 8	5. 1
Cars & parts	15. 4	16. 6
Chemicals & products	31. 2	30. 4

Source: Bureau of Foreign Commerce, U. S. Department
           of Commerce, World Trade Information Service,
           Economic Reports.

United States Trade with India

    Before World War II, India was a net exporter to the
United States, but after the partition of India and Pakistan,
India had a deficit in trade with the United States, except for
the three years 1953-55.

    In the postwar period, trade between the United States
and India has grown very fast. The United States in 1959
occupied a position in the trade of India second only to that
of the United Kingdom.

    The United States imports from India mainly jute, tea,
cashew nuts, and manganese ore. Jute is the important
item, but both the price and the volume have gradually dropped
during the postwar period, with only a temporary recovery
during the Korean War years. Tea was the second item whose
volume reached a peak in 1955, but since then both the volume
and price have dropped, and lately it has usually ranked below cashew nuts and manganese ore. The import of cashew
nuts from India has doubled in value in the period from
1948-57. The import of manganese ore rose in the period
1948-53 threefold in volume and ninefold in value, but since
1953 there has been a steady decline in price and volume. [15]

    The United States exports to India largely food, raw
cotton, machinery, vehicles, iron and steel, and petroleum.
The export of food increased from 1950-57 due to acute
food shortage in India. The export of cotton increased in
1950-52, but from 1953 on it declined due to better domestic supply. Machinery exported to India included a variety
of types such as construction, mining, agricultural, and
office equipment. Vehicles exported to India included cars,
commercial vehicles, and railway cars. Iron and steel exports to India increased rapidly in the period from 1948-57.
Petroleum exports to India have declined in this period due
to the construction of three large oil refineries in India. [16]

United States Trade with Australia

The United States has a growing trade with Australia: from
$77.6 million in 1938 to $692.3 million in 1962--a growth of
ninefold. During the Korean War years, the United States had a
deficit with Australia, but from 1952 on, the United States has
been a net exporter to Australia.

The United States imports from Australia mainly wool and
nonferrous metals, such as lead, zinc, copper, and tungsten.
Because of this high concentration on a few items, the exports
of Australia are susceptible to the fluctuations of prices of
these items. In 1949, wool price was five times that before
the war, and in 1950, it rose to ten times that before the war.
Wool exports sharply increased, and in 1951 they amounted to
85 per cent of Australia's exports in value. Thereafter, the
United States stopped the stockpiling of wool, and the price of
wool dropped. Wool exports to the United States in 1956 a-
mounted to only 30 per cent of Australia's exports to the
United States in value. Australia's exports of nonferrous
metals to the United States expanded from 1948-56. Their
share in Australia's export to the United States was 10 per
cent in 1948 and 50 per cent in 1956. Copper was the prominent item among these metals. From 1957 the price of copper started to decline.

Australia's imports from the United States consist largely
of machinery, vehicles, aircraft, tobacco, and petroleum.
The volume of petroleum imported has dropped since 1952 due
to the development of the refining industry in Australia. [17]

United States Trade with New Zealand

The postwar period witnessed a fast growth of trade between the United States and New Zealand. The trade expanded
sixfold from $34.9 million in 1949 to $197.9 million in 1962.
If we consider only United States imports from New Zealand,
the expansion is spectacular: from $0.8 million in 1948 to
$135.9 million in 1959, showing an increase of 150 fold. The
United States position in New Zealand's trade is second only
to that of United Kingdom. Until 1955 the United States had a

favorable trade with New Zealand, but since then the United
States has had a trade deficit.

Imports of the United States from New Zealand consist
mainly of wool, hides and skins, dairy products, and fish.
Their relative positions in the imports of the United States
are: 60 per cent for wool, 20-30 per cent for hides and skins,
and the balance for dairy products and fish. Since 1957, due
to the lowering of the prices of hides and skins, the value of
these items has declined, although the volume has remained
constant.

Two thirds of the exports of the United States to New Zea-
land consist of machinery, vehicles, and petroleum products.
The balance included tobacco and sulphur for fertilizers.
Machinery exported is of a variety of types including construc-
tion, mining, agricultural, textile, and electric equipment.
Vehicles exported are mainly cars and railway cars. [18]

United States Trade with Malaya and Singapore

United States trade with Malaya and Singapore increased
fairly fast in the early postwar years, reaching $483.6 million
in 1951, and the United States became the leading buyer nation in that year. From 1952-59, the trade gradually declined
to $227.2 million in 1959. This was due to competition from
the United Kingdom, Japan, and European countries.

The United States has had a traditional unfavorable balance
of trade with Malaya and Singapore which should be considered
a valuable asset of the British Commonwealth of Nations in
earning American dollars.

The United States imports from Malaya and Singapore
largely rubber and tin and also a small quantity of pepper.
Because of the Korean War, the imports of rubber reached a
peak in value in 1951 and that of tin in 1952. As the Korean
War ended, the imports of these items gradually declined.

The exports of the United States to Malaya and Singapore
have been small, and they consist largely of machinery.
There were textile exports to Malaya and Singapore in the
early postwar years, but the United States in recent years
has lost this market to Japan. [19]

United States Trade with Indonesia

There has been an expansion of United States trade with
Indonesia in the postwar period: from $78.8 million in 1948 to
$259.2 million in 1962. This trade reached a peak of $428.1
million in 1951 due to the Korean War, but since then it has declined. The end of the Korean War was a factor in the trade
decline, and there has been increasing competition from Japan,
West Germany, mainland China, Malaya and Singapore. The
United States, throughout the entire period of 1950-59 had an
unfavorable trade with Indonesia.

The content of this trade follows the usual pattern, with
the United States importing rubber, tin, and copra, and exporting machinery, vehicles, and manufactured products.

Indonesia's capacity to export has remained relatively constant, but the total export earnings have risen or fallen mainly
in response to fluctuations in the prices received for basic exports. Indonesia's imports have shown a strong response to the
amount of foreign exchange made available to Indonesian imports.[20]

United States Trade with Hong Kong

Hong Kong, though a British colony, has never been so
British-oriented in its trade concepts as have Malaya and Singapore. This is partly because of the long tradition of American
trade with China through Hong Kong. In the postwar period
this trade expanded from $87.6 million in 1948 to $293.5 million in 1962. United States imports from Hong Kong have
steadily increased, but United States exports first rose to a
peak of $102.7 million in 1950. The exports abruptly dropped
to $26.5 million in 1952 due to the embargo on mainland China.
From 1953 on, United States exports gradually recovered because of the liberalization of the embargo.

The United States has traditionally maintained a favorable
balance of trade with Hong Kong throughout the entire postwar
period, and it was only in 1959 that the trade turned in favor of
Hong Kong for the first time.

The United States imports from Hong Kong cotton garments, hardwood and rattan furniture, artificial flowers, toys, and costume jewelery. The United States exports to Hong Kong food, cigarettes, antibiotics, plastic materials, sewing machines, aircrafts and parts, film, refrigerators, air conditioning units, electric appliances, office equipment, lubricants, building materials, and synthetic textile products.

In Hong Kong, the United States faces competition from Japan. In the fields of machinery, equipment, appliances, and chemical products, the United States enjoys some advantage.[21]

United States Trade with Pakistan

United States exports to Pakistan have shown very rapid growth in the postwar years, reaching $326.2 million in 1962, seventeen times that of $16.9 million in 1949. United States imports from Pakistan have also grown in the postwar years, but at a much slower pace, with $41.6 million in 1962 and $26.1 million in 1948--an increase of 55 per cent.

Immediately after the partition from India, Pakistan had a brief period of favorable trade with the United States, but from 1952 on, the trade has been unfavorable. This continued unfavorable balance is possible because of foreign aid from the United States. The aid in 1959 amounted to $283.6 million, of which $95 million was for defense and the balance for economic activities.[22]

United States imports from Pakistan consist largely of raw jute, jute products, and wool, with the three accounting for 80 per cent of the total. The remainder includes hides, skins, raw cotton, gums and resins. After India imposed an embargo on the exports of raw jute in 1950, Pakistan became the only source for the United States, and Pakistan has been able to meet the United States requirements adequately. Wool is the second most important item, accounting for one third of total United States imports from Pakistan. The high point in the price of wool came in 1951, followed by a decline. Recently, there has been a recovery.[23] There is a promising new market in the United States for Pakistan's goat skin and kidskin.

Among United States exports to Pakistan, there have been large quantities of food to meet the shortages which occurred from time to time, for instance in 1953, 1956, and 1957. United States exports of machinery and equipment to Pakistan have been constantly on the increase. Construction and mining equipment are the dominant types. Cars and railroad equipment are also gaining importance. [24]

United States Trade with Ceylon

United States exports to Ceylon have been quite small in the postwar years, with $23.1 million for 1959, showing an increase of 20 per cent over the 1948 amount. United States imports from Ceylon rose to a peak in 1950 at $66.2 million, and then there was a decline. The 1959 imports were only half of 1950 imports in value.

The United States imports rubber and tea from Ceylon. Since 1952, the imports of rubber declined due to the cutback of rubber requirements.

The United States exports to Ceylon consist largely of machinery, vehicles, and tobacco. Ceylon used to buy cotton manufactures from the United States, but now it buys from Japan. [25]

Ceylon has always enjoyed a favorable balance of trade with the United States in the postwar period.

COMPOSITION OF UNITED STATES TRADE
WITH THE FAR EAST

To the United States, the Far East is mainly a source of raw materials. United States imports from this area are mainly, in the order of their importance: rubber, wood, sugar, wool, vegetable oil, oilseeds, tin, and petroleum. There is a small amount of manufactures of light industries such as textiles, electric appliances, sewing machines, toys, and photographic supplies, largely from Japan and Hong Kong.

Generally speaking, for the period 1938-57, there was a net diversion of origin of U. S. imports away from Asian countries for all commodities.

Comparing 1955-57 with 1938, there was a decline in the proportion of rubber and tin originating in Asian countries imported by the United States due to the improvement of the domesti supply of synthetic rubber and a better supply of tin from other areas. On the other hand, other commodities assumed increasing importance. While the total United States imports from Asian countries increased more than six times in value between 1938 and 1955-57, imports of ferroalloys increased more than 15 times, lead 260 times, and wool more than 10 times.

The United States imports from Asia have followed broadly, but with some time lag, the movement in the quantum index of the United States imports of crude and semimanufactured items. [26] In times of recession in the United States (for instance 1949, 1954, and 1958), the requirements for raw materials and semimanufactures have been reduced and consequently imports from the Far East decreased. Because countries in the Far East depend on their exports to a great degree for their income, any drop in prices and/or quantities of their exports will definitely affect their economy. A decline in their exports will be sure to affect their economy adversely because it will mean a reduction of their foreign-exchange earnings, which in turn limits their imports of capital equipment and essential materials from the United States. This will retard their economic growth. Therefore, periods of recession in the United States will have definite repercussions in the Far East.

In times of war or prosperity in the United States (for instance 1950, 1951, and 1957), requirements for raw materials and semimanufactures have been high and, therefore, prices and quantities of imports from countries of the Far East were high. This helped to bring about prosperity in those countries. With larger earnings in foreign exchange, they could buy larger volumes of capital goods and essential materials and, thus, their income grew. In 1951, because of United States stockpiling, prices of raw materials soared to tremendous heights. This caused great dissatisfaction in the United States and there was a revision of United States procurement, with the rate of purchase and the price ceiling established. [27]

To the United States, the Far East also means markets
for capital goods, manufactures, grains, and cotton. Capital
goods amounted to 31 per cent of the United States exports in
1959. They are mainly machinery, equipment, cars and parts, and
iron and steel products. Other manufactures include chemicals, petroleum products, and textiles. There is a constant
demand for United States exports in these areas because the
items are necessities for consumption and for economic development.

As a supplier of capital goods, the United States is facing
competition from the United Kingdom, European countries, and
Japan. Generally speaking, United States equipment tends to
have more labor-saving devices and, therefore, is comparatively
more expensive. As there is no serious labor shortage in the
Far East, it may be an advantage to these countries to buy the
simpler and cheaper equipment of Japan.

Countries in the Far East are not in a position to buy capital equipment with cash; there must be credit terms, if not
grants. They will buy more from countries providing adequate
credit. The large volume of foreign aid funds provided by the
United States has been a factor in promoting exports of capital
equipment. Now, the United Kingdom and France have also
extended aid to their former colonies. Japan also has an Export-Import Bank to provide credits. Therefore, foreign aid
and credit terms have become important factors in the competition for markets for capital goods.

THE UNITED STATES BALANCE OF PAYMENTS WITH THE FAR EAST

Before World War II, the ECAFE countries[28] had a trade
surplus with the United States and a deficit with other parts of
the world. The ECAFE countries used dollar earnings to offset the deficit with other parts of the world. Since the war,
with the exception of the Korean War years, this surplus
trade with the United States has disappeared, and there has
been a severe trade deficit. There have also been payment
difficulties for the area as a whole. [29]

In the early postwar years, Oceania enjoyed a trade surplus with the United States, but from 1954-58, the trade became unfavorable for Oceania. However, the dollar shortage in Australia and New Zealand was not as serious as was the dollar shortage in the Asian countries.

UNITED STATES AID TO ASIA

United States aid to Asia may be discussed in three stages: (1) the relief and rehabilitation program of 1945-47; (2) the technical cooperation program of 1948-50; and (3) the mutual security aid program in effect since 1951.

The first stage of the United States aid program, the relief and rehabilitation program of 1945-47, was not a particularly well-planned program but grew out of a number of measures to rescue a few Asian nations from the ravages and disruptions of war. The main objective was to provide civilian relief and rehabilitation for a few productive activities. Four major measures were undertaken:

1. The United Nations Relief and Rehabilitation Administration. It was largely financed by United States contributions. The program distributed relief goods to mainland China, Japan, Taiwan, Korea, and the Philippines totalling $380.5 million in the period 1945-47.

2. The Government and Relief in Occupied Area Program (GARIOA). It was a civilian supply program operated by the United States Department of War. Its activities centered in the occupied areas of Japan and Korea, distributing a total of $1,526 million of civilian supplies in the period of 1946-48.

3. The Philippine War Damage Program (PWDP). It provided $520 million for the preliminary settlements with the Filipinos for war damages for the period 1946-50.

4. The Relief Assistance Act (RAC). It provided $45.7 million for the relief program for mainland China and Taiwan for the period 1945-48.

All these programs were financed by different appropriations and administered by different agencies. There was little coordination. They were emergency measures to meet the urgent postwar needs.

The second stage of the United States aid had as the central philosophy the Truman Doctrine of technical cooperation. It was aimed at helping Asian countries to gain economic reconstruction in order to resist Communism. The technical cooperation program of 1948-50 grew out of the lessons learned from experiences in China. Communism won a major victory in China in 1948-49. This indicated that military aid alone was not enough; economic assistance, especially technical aid, was necessary. There were the Economic Cooperation Act (ECA) in 1948, the Mutual Defense Assistance Act (MDA) in 1949, and the Act for International Development (AID) in 1950 to provide military and economic aid to Asian countries with special emphasis on Taiwan, Korea, the Philippines, and Japan.

In the third stage, United States aid was part of the mutual security program in Asia. Under the Mutual Security Act (MSA) of 1951, military and economic aid was concentrated on the members of Southeast Asia Treaty Organization (SEATO), including South Vietnam, the Philippines, Thailand, and Pakistan. Aid was also given to Taiwan and Japan, partners in military alliances with the United States. Some aid was also given to neutral countries to match the aid from the Sino-Soviet bloc: for instance, India, Indonesia, Burma, Ceylon, Afghanistan, and Nepal. The objectives of military aid were to strengthen the defense of Asian countries and to provide military bases and facilities in Asia for the United States. The objectives of economic aid were to promote political and economic stability, to resist Communistic infiltration, to improve the United States position in trade, and to guarantee the supply of raw materials for the United States.[30]

From July 1, 1945, to December 31, 1960, there had been a total of $85 billion of gross foreign aid provided by the United States. Of this, $28.5 billion was for military aid and the balance, $56.5 billion, for other types of aid. If we consider the net grants and net credits of this period, the net foreign aid would total $75 billion. Net grants are grants after

the reverse grants and returns by the United States have been
taken out, and net credits are credits after the principal col-
lections by the United States have been taken out. The average of the net foreign aid for the first ten and one half years
was $5.1 billion per year, and during the five year period
from 1956-60, the average dropped to $4.2 billion per year.

Of the $85 billion gross foreign aid, about $23.5 had
been given to Asian countries, with $8.5 billion for military
aid and $15 billion for other types of aid. 31

Table 21

United States Aid to Asian Countries, 1945-60
(in billions of dollars)

	Military Aid	Other Types of Aid	Total
Total	8.5	15.0	23.5
Taiwan (Formosa)	3.0	1.9	4.9
South Korea	1.4	3.1	4.5
Japan	1.4	2.6	4.0
India	---	2.1	2.1
South Vietnam	0.5	1.3	1.8
Cambodia	0.1	0.2	0.3
Pakistan	---	1.1	1.1
Laos	0.1	0.2	0.3
Indo-China (before partition)	0.6	0.2	0.8
Thailand	0.3	0.3	0.6
Indonesia	---	0.5	0.5
Others	1.1	1.5	2.6

THE UNITED STATES INVESTMENT

The United States investment in Asia and Oceania is very
small. In 1959, the total United States investment abroad
amounted to about $50 billion, of which direct investment by in-
dividuals and corporations was about $29.7 billion. 32 The total
United States direct investment in Asia and Oceania in 1959 was
only $1.9 billion. Of this, about $1 billion was invested in Asia

and the balance in Oceania. The United States direct investment in Oceania was concentrated in Australia, with about $0.7
billion in that country. The United States direct investment in
Asia was widely distributed to these countries in the order of
their importance: the Philippines, Japan, Indonesia, India
Malaya, Pakistan, Hong Kong, and Thailand. The United
States direct investment in Asia grew at the rate of threefold
in the nine years 1950-59. The fastest growth of the United
States direct investment was in Japan--almost elevenfold in
the nine years 1950-59.

Table 22

United States Direct Investment in Asia by Country
(in million of U. S. dollars)

	1950	1957	1958	1959
Total	309	881	954	1028
Ceylon	4	4	5	6
Hong Kong	7	12	13	15
India	38	113	120	136
Indonesia	58	109	196	163
Japan	19	185	181	210
Malaya	18	35	38	45
Pakistan	8	29	30	36
Philippines	149	306	341	385
Taiwan (Formosa)	---	4	4	4
Thailand	3	13	14	14
Others	5	12	12	14

Source: Bureau of Foreign Commerce, U. S. Department of
Commerce, World Trade Information Service, Statistical Report, Part 3, No. 61-3, p. 4.

The United States direct investment in Asia is largely in
the fields of petroleum, manufacturing, public utilities, and
trade.

Table 23

Areas of United States Direct Investment in Asia
(in millions of U. S. dollars)

	1958	1959
Total	954	1028
Mining and smelting	18	20
Petroleum	482	492
Manufacturing	199	225
Public utilities	85	92
Trade	88	107
Others	58	59

Source: Bureau of Foreign Commerce, U. S. Department of
         Commerce, World Trade Information Service, Statis-
         tical Report.

Countries in Asia and Oceania are not financially self-
sufficient. With the urgent need of capital for development
and the slow rate of capital formation, foreign capital should be
welcome as new blood to boost the progress in these areas. The
shortage of capital has caused interest, profits, and dividends
to be high, but the United States investment has been small.

To encourage United States investment, there must be a
favorable climate in these countries. To achieve such a climate,
the United Nations Economic Commission for Asia and the Far
East has summarized very well the following requirements. [33]

1. Political stability and freedom from external agression.

2. Security of life and property.

3. Availability of opportunities for earning profits.

4. Prompt payment of fair compensation and its
    remittance to the country of origin in the event of com-

pulsory acquisition of a foreign enterprise.

5. Facilities for the remittance of profits, dividends, interests, etc.

6. Facilities for the immigration and employment of foreign technical and administrative personnel.

7. A system of taxation that does not impose a crushing burden on private enterprise.

8. Freedom from double taxation.

9. Absence of vexatious controls.

10. Nondiscriminatory treatment of foreigners in the administration of controls.

11. Absence of competition of state-owned enterprises with private capital.

12. A general spirit of friendliness for foreign investors.

With the exception of Japan, Australia, and New Zealand, the investment climate in the Far East is not ideal. Some of the obstacles may be due to the circumstances under which these nations have to function. For instance, high tax rates may be caused by the need of governments for revenues and restrictions on the repatriation of foreign capital and remittance of profits, interest, and dividends may be caused by the unfavorable balance of payments. But there are always the irrational factors underlying the restrictive measure on foreign investment. In the minds of the general public of countries recently emerged from colonial status, foreign investment is still associated with the fear of economic exploittation and political domination. Actually, nothing is further from the intentions of the United States. Certainly, the economic policy of the United States is not to reduce the Asian countries to primitive economies, but rather to help them to make progress. Nor does the United States have political domination in mind, as evidenced by the independence of the Philippines.

THE UNITED STATES TRADE CONTROLS

Because of the repeated lowering of rates, duties collected in 1957 were 5.8 per cent of the value of imports as
compared to 18.5 per cent for the period 1931-35.[34] In
1957 duties collected were 10.8 per cent of the value of
dutiable imports, as compared to 50 per cent for the period
1931-35.[35]

Most of the Asian countries have been reducing tariff
rates. Japan's tariff rates are the lowest, and Australia
has been making big reductions; other Asian countries have
been slower in reducing their rates.

Compared to those of West Germany, France, Italy, and the
United Kingdom, the ratio between custom duties collected
and the total value of imports is lower for the United States.
The United States has made a more earnest effort than those
nations in putting to practice the policy of free trade.[36]

Table 24

Ratio of Duties Collected to Total Imports in Value
(in percentage of value of total imports)

	1935	1955	1961
India	32.5	26.3	17.6
Thailand	29.4	17.9	17.5
Australia	25.9	9.5	9.4
New Zealand	19.1	12.7	8.0
Japan	4.6	2.8	...
United States	15.8	5.4	...

Source: American Tariff League, Inc., The United States in
World Trade, A Contempary Analysis and a Program
for the Future, New York, 1958, p. 34.

The United States has import quotas on grains, cotton, and dairy products because of the surplus in domestic supplies. In 1958, there were quotas on lead and zinc to reduce the large stockpile of these materials. For the two years 1951 and 1952, there were import quotas and price ceilings on tin and rubber to correct the extremely high prices caused by the Korean War. [37]

The United States controls exports by the following: the Export Control Act provisions on the general controls by the Department of Commerce, the Foreign Assets Control Regulations on the assets of Communist countries by the Department of Treasury, and the Mutual Defense Assistance Control Act (often referred to as the Battle Act), on the control of foreign aid. United States aid will not be given to any country which exports strategic materials to the Communist bloc. These controls, other than the general supervision, are mainly aimed at the curtailment of trade with the Communist bloc: more specifically, Communist China, North Korea, and North Vietnam. The United States trade with Hong Kong is carefully supervised, as Hong Kong has been, and still is, a commercial gate of Communist China. These controls are dealt with in more detail in the chapters on the trade of Communist China and Hong Knog.

PROSPECTS OF UNITED STATES TRADE
WITH THE FAR EAST

The United States, in the postwar period, has had a fast growing trade with Asia and Oceania, and there is reason to believe that this trade will continue to grow. A number of favorable factors are mentioned here in support of this optimistic outlook.

Asia, from time to time, has acute shortages of food, and the United States has surpluses. There is a natural basis for trade between the two in this respect.

Asia, in the period of reconstruction and industrialization has large requirements of capital goods and essential materials, which are important components of exports of the United States. Of course, in this area the United States faces competition from other countries exporting capital goods and essential materials, such as the United Kingdom, European countries and Japan.

Asian countries have had payments difficulties which have restricted their imports. The United States is in a position to provide foreign aid of a larger amount than that of the Sino-Soviet bloc or any other Western powers. This is a factor which has proved to be effective in keeping Asia from Communist domination, in addition to promoting the trade of the United States.

The United States has a lower tariff than that of the United Kingdom and other European countries. For Asian countries such as Japan, the Philippines, Thailand, and Taiwan (which do not enjoy preferential tariff benefits in their trade with the British Commonwealth of Nations, France, or the Netherlands) there is in the United States a low tariff market for their exports.

In order to promote United States trade with the Far East, certain difficulties must be overcome and certain obstacles removed. Among them are a few outstanding ones mentioned here.

Direct investment by the United States nationals and corporations in the Far East has been very small. Military and political instability are among the major causes of this situation. To promote the confidence of private business in the Far East, it is necessary for the United States to maintain a positive foreign and military policy. Any suggestion of abandoning interest in the Far East on the part of the United States government will keep off potential investors. It is only when private capital starts to come in large quantities that we can expect good progress to be made in the economic development of the Far Eastern countries.

In the Far Eastern countries there is still a fear of economic exploitation and domination by outside business interests--a legacy of their colonial days. There may be an advantage in channeling United States investment through international financial institutions, such as the International Bank for Reconstruction and Development and its affiliated International Development Association, because there is

probably less fear and resistance toward these agencies.
Meanwhile, negotiations can be conducted to create a better investment climate for private capital from the United States,
with favorable provisions on the repatriation of capital, remittance of profits, dividends and interests, employment of
United States personnel, protection of property and private
enterprise, and fair taxation.

While there are, in some Asian countries, high tariff rates
on United States exports, there are also quantitative restrictions imposed by the United States on Asian products, such as
lead, zinc, petroleum, sugar, cordage, rice, cigars, tobacco,
coconuts, and other items. It would be wise, in due course,
for the United States to remove these quotas and, in return, for
those Asian countries to lower their tariffs.   There is the need
for a Pacific regional establishment for the United States and
the Far Eastern countries to work together to promote the free
flow of goods and services among them.

The exports of capital goods from the United States should
be studied with the aim of improving their position in competing
with European and Japanese products. Because of the high cost
of labor here, American capital goods tend to embody many
automation devices, and therefore are quite expensive. There
is no compelling need for these automation devices in the Far
East because labor cost there is low. United States capital goods,
as they are now, may lose out to the cheaper and simpler
European and Japanese products. It is taking too much for
granted to assume that the types of capital goods which have
good markets in the United States will also enjoy good markets
in the Far East. American capital goods for export may have
to be modified or specially designed so that they will sell
better in foreign markets.

While the British Commonwealth of Nations is maintaining their preferential tariff and France is also maintaining some
types of special tariff with its former colonies, the United
States is gradually removing its preferential tariff with the
Philippines. While among nations in the Western world there
is the tendency to lower tariffs, the tariffs between the United
States and the Philippines are being raised. Consequently, the
United States stands to suffer some loss of her share in the
trade of the Philippines. This situation warrants careful in-

vestigation. Of course, it is understandable for the Philippines to desire to reduce her dependence on the United States markets.

Many Far Eastern countries have an unfavorable trade with the United States, and this generally tends to cause these countries to reduce their purchases from the United States unless they have a favorable trade balance with the rest of the world. Any measures that the United States can take to help the Far Eastern countries to promote their exports to the Middle East, Africa, and other areas will improve the international payments position of the Far Eastern countries and will make it easier for them to carry on the unfavorable trade with the United States.

The United Kingdom and other European countries, because of their long association with the Far Eastern countries, enjoy the advantage of having a well-developed network of commercial institutions in the Far East. These institutions help to channel trade to England and continental Europe. The United States has a long way to to improve its commercial institutions in the Far East. But before there can be better commercial institutions in the Far East, there must be more qualified commercial agents. The Far East is usually considered by American businessmen a hardship post. Most are willing to stay for only short periods, and there is a lack of businessmen choosing the Far East as their long term place of activity. American commercial interest will suffer due to the shortage of career personnel and commercial institutions. In this respect our educational institutions can be of great service to the nation. If our universities can strengthen their Far East program, students' interest in the Far East can be stimulated, and the supply of qualified career commercial agents can be improved.

To promote American business in the Far East, it is necessary to provide our business representatives with the right kind of training. It is advisable for them to learn the language of the country in which they reside so that they can develop more intimate contact with the local people. It is necessary for them to learn something of the history of that country and to be familiar with its economic and legal system. It is necessary for them to understand the policy of that

Table 25

United States Trade with the Far East
(in millions of U. S. dollars)

	U. S. Exports	U. S. Exports to the Far East	Percentage of U. S. Exports	U. S. Imports	U. S. Imports from the Far East	Percentage of U. S Imports
1948	12,653	1,927.4	15.2	7,124	1,374.9	19.3
1950	10,275	1,364.7	13.3	8,852	1,714.9	19.4
1951	15,032	2,133.8	14.2	10,967	2,266.4	20.6
1952	15,201	2,047.8	13.5	10,717	1,902.2	17.1
1953	15,774	1,907.9	12.1	10,873	1,626.2	14.9
1954	15,110	1,927.6	12.7	10,215	1,434.1	14.0
1955	15,550	2,038.2	13.1	11,384	1,779.1	15.6
1956	19,090	2,623.8	13.8	12,615	1,900.3	15.1
1957	20,850	3,248.8	15.5	12,982	2,025.1	15.6
1958	17,893	2,599.9	14.5	12,834	1,919.3	14.9
1959	17,566	2,599.9	14.8	15,212	2,599.8	17.1
1960	20,587	3,632.2	17.6	15,065	2,671.0	17.6
1961	20,998	3,686.1	17.5	14,756	2,574.3	17.4
1962	21,568	4,003.2	18.5	16,478	3,104.2	18.8

Sources: The figure for U. S. exports and imports are taken from the Bureau of Foreign Commerce, U. S. Department of Commerce, World Trade Information Service, Statistical Reports, Part 3, No. 60-6, Washington, D. C., 1960, p. 3. The figures for U. S. exports and imports to the Far East are taken from United Nations, International Monetary Fund, and International Bank for Reconstruction and Development, Direction of Internationotional Trade, New York, v. 4, N. 1/2, p. 8; v. 7, N. 6, p. 82, v. 9, N. 10, p. 56, v. 10, N. 8, p. 60, and v. 11, N. 9, p. 115; Annual 1958-62, p. 129-30.

country regarding business and industry (for instance, its plan
for economic development), so that American business can com-
plement local business instead of competing against it. Thus
conflicts of interests can be avoided. To avoid misunderstandings
and blunders, it is important for these representatives to know
the differences between Eastern and Western ways of life and to
try to live with the differences. Good public relations is as
necessary for business success abroad as it is in domestic commerce. It may be more important abroad because of the numerous situations where misunderstandings may arise. It is
always a good policy for our commercial representatives to
take interest in the well being of the local community and to
render assistance to its civic activities, whether welfare,
cultural, recreational, or social. However, it is necessary
for them to keep out of local politics as much as possible to
avoid being charged with seeking special advantage (although
sometimes a certain amount of political pressure is necessary
to counterbalance the advantages obtained by local business).
The proper training of American businessmen to be sent
abroad is a crucial factor to the success of American business
abroad. Unscrupulous practice in business abroad may bring
about short-run profits, but in the long run will jeopardize
the interest of the nation.

To launch an all out economic offensive in the Far East
will take the team work of the three parties: the United States
government, private business, and educational institutions.
The first will afford the protection of interests; the second
will provide the financial and manpower resources; and the
third will contribute the training and preparation of personnel.

Notes to Chapter 5

1.   Harold U. Faulkner, American Economic History (New York:
     Harper & Row, Publishers, Inc., 1954), p. 145.

2.   American Tariff League, Inc., The United States in World
     Trade, New York, 1958, p. 3; Robert J. Barr, American
     Trade with Asia and the Far East (Milwaukee: Marquette
     University Press, 1959), pp. 215-20.

3. Barr, op. cit., p. 5.

4. U.S. Department of Commerce, Bureau of Foreign Commerce, World Trade Information Service, Statistical Reports, Part 3, No. 61-3.

5. World Trade Information Service, Statistical Reports, Part 3, No. 61-39, p. 1.

6. World Trade Information Service, Economic Reports, Part 1, No. 60-7, pp. 1-4.

7. World Trade Information Service, Economic Reports, loc. cit.

8. Louis Banks, "What Kennedy's Free Trade Program Means to Business?" Fortune, March, 1962, p. 218.

9. The figures here do not agree with figures given in Chapter 8 on the trade of the Philippines. The United States imports from the Philippines in 1959, as given here, were $311.8 million, but the Philippine exports to the U.S. in 1959, as given in Chapter 8, were $274.6 million. The reason for this discrepancy is mainly that import figures are c.i.f. figures, including charges, insurance, and freight for ocean transportation, while export figures here are f.o.b. figures without these items. Another reason is that figures here are from U.S. sources, while figures in Chapter 8 are from Philippine sources. The same type of discrepancies exist in the book where similar statistics are given.

10. World Trade Information Service, Economic Reports, Part 1, No. 61-52, p. 3.

11. World Trade Information Service, Economic Report, No. 55-3, p. 1.

12. World Trade Information Service, Economic Report, No. 61-52, p. 3.

13. loc. cit.

14. World Trade Information Service, Economic Report, No. 60-7, pp. 7-8.

15. Intelligence Branch of the Commonwealth Economic Committee, Commonwealth Trade with the United States (London: Her Majesty's Stationery Office), pp. 34-36.

16. loc. cit.

17. Commonwealth Trade with the United States, op. cit. pp. 23-25.

18. Commonwealth Trade with the United States, op. cit. pp. 28-29

19. Commonwealth Trade with the United States, op. cit. , pp. 44-45; Barr, op. cit. , pp. 34-35; World Trade Information Service, Economic Reports, Part 1, No. 61-6, p. 31.

20. Barr, op. cit. , pp. 186-204.

21. Barr, op. cit. , pp. 44-45; World Trade Information Service, Economic Reports, Part 1, No. 60-7, p. 13.

22. World Trade Information Service, Economic Reports, No. 60-7, p. 13.

23. Commonwealth Trade with the United States, op. cit. , p. 38.

24. Commonwealth Trade with the United States, op. cit. , p. 39.

25. Commonwealth Trade with the United States, op. cit. , pp. 39-41; Barr, op. cit. , pp. 155-62.

26. Economic Commission for Asia and the Far East, United Nations (Bangkok, Thailand, Economic Survey of Asia and the Far East, 1958), p. 30.

27. ibid. , 1951, pp. 84-93; 1958, pp. 20-30.

28. ECAFE (Economic Commission for Asia and the Far East) countries include Burma, Brunei, Cambodia, Ceylon, Taiwan, Federation of Malaya, Singapore, Hong Kong, India, Indonesia, Japan, South Korea, Laos, Nepal, North Borneo, Pakistan, the Philippines, Sarawak, Thailand, and South Vietnam.

29. Economic Survey of Asia and the Far East, 1948, p. 207.

30. Charles Wolf, Jr., Foreign Aid: Theory and Practice in Southern Asia (Princeton, N.J.: Princeton University Press, 1960), p. 16, p. 69, p. 90, p. 102, pp. 121-22, p. 404, pp. 406-7; Economic Survey of Asia and the Far East, 1954, p. 28; 1956, pp. 32-33.

31. "Is the Dollar Headed for New Trouble?" U.S. News and World Report, Oct. 6, 1961, p. 56; Robert E. Asher, Grants, Loans and Local Currencies, Their Roles in Foreign Aid (Washington: Brookings Institution, 1961).

32. Bureau of National Affairs, International Trade Reporter's Survey and Analysis, Washington, August 25, 1961, p. 1.

33. United Nations, Economic Commission for Asia and the Far East, Committee on Industry and Trade, Second Session, Foreign Investment Laws and Regulations in the ECAFE Region, Bangkok, March, 1950, pp. 4-5.

34. American Tariff League, Inc., The United States in World Trade, A Contempary Analysis and a Program for the Future, New York, 1958, pp. 32-33.

35. U.S. Department of Commerce, Bureau of Census, Statistical Abstract of the United States (Washington, D.C.: Government Printing Office, 1958), p. 900.

36. The United States in World Trade, A Contemporary Analysis and a Problem for the Future, op. cit., p. 66.

37. Commonwealth Trade with the United States, op. cit., pp. 57-62.

CHAPTER **6** THE TRADE OF JAPAN

Japan is a country of 143,000 square miles (smaller than California), yet its population exceeds 94 million, which is about half the population of the United States. The density of population is 650 persons per square mile, more than ten times that of the United States. The terrain is mostly mountainous; only about 16 per cent of the area is suitable for agriculture. Farms are tiny, averaging less than 2.5 acres, as compared with more than 200 acres in the United States.

Besides suffering a scarcity of productive land, Japan is also poor in natural resources for industry. As compared to the prewar years, Japan is much less dependent on foreign natural resources, due to the improvement of domestic supplies. However, it still lacks adequate supplies of coking coal, having to import about half of its requirements, and the present production of petroleum amounts to less than two per cent of the country's consumption. Japan is also deficient in almost all metals and must import part of all of its needs from foreign sources. It must, for example, import 90 per cent of its iron ore requirements, all of its bauxite, and most of its ferroalloys. Japan must also depend on imports for part of its agricultural needs, including all of its raw cotton and raw wool requirements and 15 to 20 per cent of its food.

Life in Japan is hard. However, through diligence, thrift, and drive, the Japanese people have built a prosperous nation with a per capita income of U.S. $400 a year in the early 1960's, though living standards are still well below those of the W

Japanese steelmakers surpassed the United Kingdom in steel output in 1961, to make Japan the world's fourth largest producer. Japan leads the world in shipbuilding, and possesses one of the world's largest and most modern merchant marines. Japan is the world's leading exporter of cotton textiles, and is second only to the United States in the production

of synthetic fibers. Japan is second to the United States in
the production of radios and television sets. Japanese tran-
sistor radios and portable television sets are now widely
marketed in the United States. Other growing industries include optical equipment, sewing machines, automobiles,
buses, and trucks. In these fields, Japan competes with the
West in the world market.

Credit must be given to the Japanese government for
its leadership in promoting economic development of the
country. Japan's economic planning has involved thorough
programming of the public sector, but has given it little
scope and direct control over the private sector. Nevertheless, targets have been set for all branches of the economy
on the basis of careful analysis and projection. The work
goes back to the immediate postwar period, when an Economic
Stabilization Board, comprising representatives of government and private interests, began to publish long-term pro-
jections for the most important types of economic activities.
Various ministries soon made plans for their work, project-
ing some time ahead, and an Economic Self Support Council,
attached to the Board, began to make policy recommendations
in 1950. A six-year plan was adopted in 1956, and an Economic
Planning Agency established. It was soon apparent that target rates had been set too low, and dangers of expansion to
the balance of payments inadequately considered, so that a revised plan was adopted in 1958, for the remaining four years.
This, however, again underestimated the Japanese economy's
capacity for growth. The new Long-Range Economic Plan is
for the ten year period 1961-70, with double the national income as its goal.

TRADE EXPANSION AND ECONOMIC DEVELOPMENT

During the postwar period, Japan's economy grew
spectacularly. It has become the envy of its neighbors in the
Far East and has caused some alarm among the industrial nations in the West because of the stiff competition it has given
them. The Economic Commission for Asia and the Far East
reports that the average annual rate of growth in real gross
national product for Japan for the period 1950-59 was 9.1
per cent, while that for West Germany was 7.5 per cent,

Italy 5. 7 per cent, France 4. 0 per cent, the United States 3. 3
per cent, and the United Kingdom 2. 5 per cent. [1] The average
annual rate of growth in real per capita production for the
same period for Japan was 7. 9 per cent, signifying that there
has been much improvement in the standard of living for the
people. [2] Japan is boasting that by 1970 she will have doubled her
income.   It is generally recognized that this phenomenal economic development of Japan has been largely induced by its trade
expansion.   Do we have in Japan a practical application of the
theory of Sir Denis Robertson and Ragnar Nurkse that trade is
an engine growth?   The purpose of this chapter is to ascertain
whether there is a mathematical basis, a theoretical explanation,
and a statistical analysis for the relationship between the trade
expansion and the economic development of Japan.

FIGURE 7
PROSPERITY CYCLE OF JAPAN

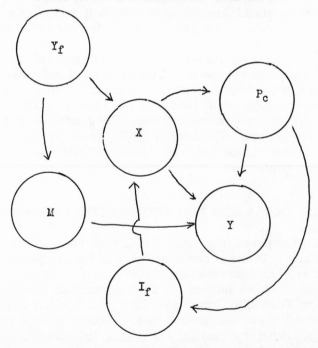

Source: Joseph E. Haring, "Export Industrialism and Economic
         Growth," Western Economic Journal, Spring, 1963.

Theoretical Explanation

From the findings of an econometric mode, Professor Haring comes to the conclusion that a prosperity cycle is generated in the economy of Japan, in that income is elastic in response to the change in exports. An increase in exports will stimulate investments, first in the export industries, and then in other industries in higher level of income. The higher level of income will increase the capacity for producing more export goods. To illustrate this chain reaction of factors, Professor Haring presents the above chart[4] (which is modified in only one aspect, by adding an arrow connecting M to Y), where Y stands for the current income, Y_f an index of the gross national product in the United States, X the value of exports, M the value of imports, P_c corporate profits and I_f the fixed investment.

The Role Played by Imports

What is the part played by imports in a country's economic development? The expansion of imports is often said to have devastating effects on a country's production, as imports tend to compete with domestic industries and take away their markets. The expansion of imports may cause unemployment due to reduced domestic production. The expansion of imports may result in deficits of international payments and reduce the country's gold and dollar reserves. Thus, it may weaken the country's currency. Expansion of imports is said to retard the nation's capital formation if imports consist largely of consumer goods, especially of the luxury type.

But this was not the case with Japan. Since 1949, due to the precarious position of payments, the Japanese government has practiced rigid foreign-exchange control and import licensing. The practice requires that all the private earnings of foreign exchange, through trade or other sources, be surrendered to the government for yen at the official rate, and the government is the sole seller of foreign exchange to all users who have to apply for the amounts of foreign exchange they need. Semiannually the government has a budget of foreign exchange. The estimated amount of foreign exchange earned through trade or other private or government sources is carefully allocated to business for imports

of food for consumption and for essential materials and equipment needed for production activities. The traditional trade
policy of the Japanese government has been to ascertain a
target figure for the minimum imports needed to sustain and
promote economic growth, and then to try to promote exports
and other sources of foreign exchange to pay for these imports. Because of this practice, imports that tend to compete
with domestic production are prohibited from coming in, luxury consumer goods are not allowed to be imported, international payments are more or less balanced, and those imports
that are allowed to come in have a large investment content.
As shown in the model, the inventory investment is largely
determined by imports. The evils of imports are removed
and the beneficial effects of imports are accentuated, so that
the expansion of imports positively promote the economic
growth of Japan.

Historical Background

Having delineated the relationship between trade expansion
and economic development in Japan, we can turn to the historical development to find out what has really happened.

For Japan, World War II lasted from 1937-45, when
finally Japan's economy was brought to ruin at the defeat. In
the early postwar years, the relation between industrial
growth and trade expansion was not obvious. The export trade
was slow to recover, and its expansion was unfavorably compared to industrial growth. This was largely due to the loss
of markets and the decline of the traditional trade commodities.
In the prewar years, Japan had two major markets: North
America and East Asia; but in the postwar years, mainland
China and North Korea were engulfed by the Communist Bloc.
This certainly presented problems, and it took time for Japan
to develop new markets. In the prewar years, Japan made
good profits in silk and cotton textiles, but in the postwar
years, the silk market collapsed and the cotton textile market faced fast decline. Japan had to develop new contents for
her export trade. The period 1945-50 was a period of confu-
sion. As the economy began its hard road to recovery, there
was serious inflation. Industrial rehabilitation was slow and
export trade hardly existed. Only agriculture was doing better,

and by 1950 its output regained the prewar level of 1937. [5] The
economic development of Japan in the early postwar years certainly cannot be attributed to exports.

The aid from the United States was a major factor in keeping Japan's international payments balanced and its domestic economy going. From 1946-50, there was an import surplus of $2
billion, amounting to about 57 per cent of the total imports of
the period, and this was entirely covered by United States aid. [6]
The United States foreign aid program ceased in 1950.

From 1950 on, the Japanese economy began to recuper-
ate, and gradually it gained speed in fast growth. It is in this
period that trade expansion and economic growth came hand
in hand. To describe the relationship of the two, the Economic Commission of Asia and the Far East uses Figure 8
and its findings can be summarized as follows:

1. The clear implication of the curves of Figure 8 is
that it was the foreign trade sector which initiated and subsequently maintained the whole process of economic expansion.

2. The period from 1950 to now can again be divided into
two stages: From 1950-53, and from 1953 to now. The relationship between trade expansion and economic growth during
the two stages was not the same. In the early period, as
shown in Figure 8, the rate of increase for imports continuously exceeded that for exports. The economic growth of the
country was largely due to the expansion of imports which provided the necessary supplies of raw materials and equipment.
Before 1953, there had been continuous adverse balance of
payments with the deficits paid by the earnings from the
United States special procurement program.

3. After 1953 the recovery period was over. The
growth of exports became a factor of effect demand--the main
propellent of economic expansion. [7]

To describe the spectacular growth in the Japanese economy, the Economic Planning Agency of the Japanese government has this to say: "The recent high rate of growth of the
Japanese economy has been bolstered by the swift build-up of

exports and imports." [8]

In the period 1950-56, the average rate of growth was 19.5 per cent for exports, 16.4 per cent for imports, 14.1 per cent for industrial production, and 7.9 per cent for real national income. [9]

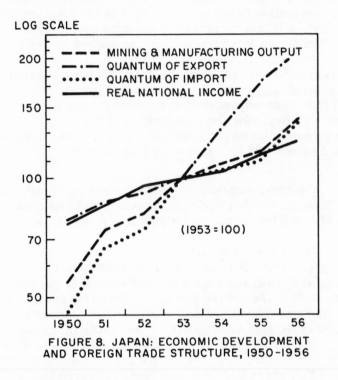

FIGURE 8. JAPAN: ECONOMIC DEVELOPMENT
AND FOREIGN TRADE STRUCTURE, 1950-1956

Source: Economic Survey of Asia and the Far East, 1957, p. 49.

Of course the Korean War gave the Japanese economy a very strong stimulus and helped its trade and economic growth to reach high rates of growth. The United States not only bought large amounts of supplies from Japan for fighting the war in Korea, but also paid the expenses for maintaining bases and forces in Japan--yielding altogether a total of $3 billion under the special procurement program for the period of

1950-54.

Interindustry Analysis

To find out, in reality, how the trade sector has helped
Japan's economy calls for a study of the interindustry relations,
or in other words, the input-output analysis of the different
sectors of the economy. Professor Isamu Yamada of
Hitotsubaschi University, in his book The Theory and Application of Interindustry Analysis, published in 1961, presents
a very valuable summary of his findings after some fifteen
years of study of this subject. Yamada in his book discusses
the findings of different agencies and research institutions.
The part that concerns this discussion contains, largely,
three input-output tables constructed by the Economic Planning Agency of the Japanese government for 1951, 1953, and
1955. These, of course, are far from being broad enough to
warrant any general conclusions, but they represent serious
attempts to examine the role of the trade sector in Japan's
economy.

Table 26 is the input-output table for Japan for 1951.
The economy is divided into five endogenous sectors and four
exogenous sectors. The first five are: (1) Agriculture including forestry and fishery, (2) Mining and Industry including construction, (3) Commerce including services, (4) Transportation including communications and public utilities, and
(5) Industries not elsewhere specified (n. e. s.). The other
four are: (1) Private capital formation, or depreciation, (2)
Trade including imports as the input of various sectors and
exports as their output, (3) Government, and (4) Households.

The table is constructed with each row indicating the
output, or money receipts, of a sector. The output can be
largely divided into intermediate goods and final goods. Intermediate goods are distributed to the various production
sectors, or used by the sector itself, and the final goods are
sold to the government and households for consumption or export. The balance is the capital formation for that sector.
Each column indicates the input, or money expenditures, of a
sector. This includes supplies and services from other sec-

tors or from the sector itself, supplies and services imported,
supplies and services from the government, supplies and services from households, and depreciation on the capital account.
The total output of a sector is given at the end of a row, and
the total input at the bottom of a column. Generally, the total
output of a sector would equal its total input, with the capital
formation as the balancing item: that is, a larger output than
input for a sector would yield a positive capital formation for
that sector.

From the input-output table, we can single out the role
played by the trade sector in the economy. When a production sector received imports, goods and services go into that
production sector. But from the money-flow viewpoint, money
is received by the trade sector from that production sector. On
the other hand, when a production sector produces exports,
goods and services go to the trade sector. But from the money-
flow viewpoint, money is paid out by the trade sector to the production factor. With this information, we can construct a social
account table of the trade sector, which is Table 27. There are
two sides of the table: receipts of the trade sector and payments of the trade sector. The trade sector's receipts are
gained from the various sectors, for their imports, and the
trade sector's payments are made to the various sectors, for
their exports. Since there is no necessary balance between
imports and exports of each of these sectors, it is possible for
the trade sector to receive from a sector more money than it
pays to that sector, or vice versa. For instance, the agriculture sector imported 1,334 hundred million yen of supplies
in 1951, but exported only 55 hundred million yen of goods.
From the flow of goods and services viewpoint, the agriculture sector gained in supplies. But from the money-flow
viewpoint, the trade sector received the balance of 1,279
hundred million yen from the agriculture sector, as indicated by the first line of Table 27.

The mining and industry sector exported 5,215 hundred
million yen of supplies in 1951, but imported 3,680 hundred
million yen to the mining and industry sector, as indicated
by line two of Table 27. Similarly, the trade sector paid
out the balance of 290 hundred million yen to the commerce
sector, 512 hundred million yen to the unspecified industries

Input-Output Table of the Japanese Economy, 1951
(100 million yen)

	Agriculture	Mining & Industry	Commerce	Transportation	Industries n.e.s	Capital	Export	Government	Household	Total
Agriculture	2,237	5,255	323	35	308	1,167	55	331	7,675	17,386
Mining & Industry	1,320	27,209	1,412	2,269	914	10,979	5,215	2,751	10,281	63,350
Commerce	866	3,788	1,589	743	1,117	562	386	1,299	8,955	19,305
Transportation	339	3,541	1,158	593	1,006	233	556	392	1,331	9,149
Industries n.e.s.	149	2,476	216	197	---	0	635	216	296	4,185
Capital	408	939	188	631	80	---	---	---	595	2,811
Import	1,334	3,680	96	949	123	1,038	---	8	46	7,274
Government	414	788	986	285	547	---	559	---	8,016	11,595
Household	10,319	14,674	13,337	3,417	90	---	829	2,902	105	45,703
Total	17,386	62,350	19,305	9,149	4,185	13,979	8,235	7,899	37,300	179,788

Source: Isamu Yamada, Theory and Application of Interindustry Analysis, Kinokuniya Bookstore Co. Tokyo, 1961, p. 113.

Table 27

Interindustry Relations Trade Sector, Japan, 1951
(100 million yen)

	Receipt	Balance
Agriculture	1, 334	1, 279
Mining & Industry	3, 680	
Commerce	96	
Transportation	949	393
Industries, n. e. s.	123	
Capital	1, 038	1, 038
Government	8	
Household	46	
Excess of exports	961	961
	8, 235	3, 671
	Payment	Balance
Agriculture	55	
Mining & Industry	5, 215	1, 535
Commerce	386	290
Transportation	556	
Industries, n. e. s.	635	512
Capital	---	
Government	559	551
Household	829	783
	8, 235	3, 671

Source: Isamu Yamada, Theory and Application of Interindustry
　　　　Analysis, Kinokuniya Bookstore Co. Tokyo, 1961, p. 121

sector, and also yielded some revenues for the government and
households. In other words, the trade sector functioned as a
channel of funds from some sectors to other sectors. This flow
of funds to the mining and industry and the commerce sectors
represents the contribution made by trade in promoting the
growth of the two sectors.

From the flow of funds among the different sectors, an Eco-circ graph can be constructed to show the net flows of funds among the different sectors. To single out the role played by the trade sector, the part of the Eco-circ graph concerning only the trade sector is given in Figure 9.

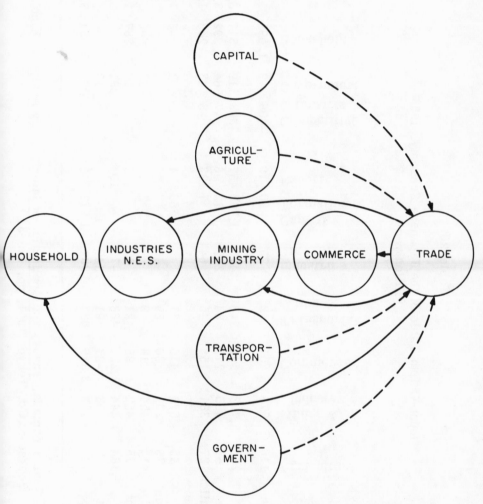

FIGURE 9. ECO-CIRC GRAPH OF TRADE SECTOR, JAPAN, 1951

Source: Isamu Yamada, Theory and Application of Interindustry Analysis (Tokyo: Kinokuniya Bookstore Co. , 1961), p. 121.

Table 28

Input-Output Table of the Japanese Economy, 1953
(billion yen)

	Agriculture	Mining & Industry	Commerce	Transportation	Industries n.e.s.	Capital Formation	Export	Competitive Imports	Government	Household	Total
Agriculture	116	878	51	2	75	-90	19	-408	9	1,092	1,744
Mining & Industry	228	3,783	542	248	470	1,763	457	-393	119	1,517	8,733
Commerce	57	485	279	84	242	72	46	-7	564	1,992	3,815
Transportation	27	381	156	45	64	7	123	-5	43	243	1,083
Industries n.e.s.	45	672	410	31	-40	168	1		62	-6	1,382
Depreciation	75	231	86	89							422
Imports	413	454	18	9		2			13	6	102
Government	15	452	85	21	42		5			787	1,407
Household	1,184	1,844	2,221	468	-19		194		231		6,124
Adjustment	-7	-53	-27	91	547				19		570
Total	1,744	8,733	3,815	1,083	1,382	1,922	845	-814	1,061	5,631	25,403

Source: Isamu Yamada, Theory and Application of Interindustry Analysis, Kinokuniya
Bookstore Co. Tokyo, 1961, pp. 130-31

Table 29

Interindustry Relations Trade Sector, Japan, 1953
(billion yen)

	Receipt	Balance
Agriculture	413	393
Mining & Industry	454	
Commerce	18	
Transportation	9	
Industries, n.e.s.		
Capital	2	2
Government	13	9
Household	6	
	915	404

	Payment	Balance
Agriculture	20	
Mining & Industry	456	2
Commerce	46	28
Transportation	123	114
Industries, n.e.s.		
Capital		
Government	4	
Household	194	188
Balance	72	72
	915	404

Source: Isamu Yamada, Theory and Application of Interindustry
Analysis, Kinokuniya Bookstore Co. Tokyo, 1961, p. 139.

Table 28 is the Input-Output Table for Japan in 1953. Again,
Table 29 can be constructed for the social account of the trade
sector in 1953. Here the pattern is similar to that of 1951. The
trade sector in 1953 pumped the balance of 2,167 million yen into
the mining and industry sector, the balance of 28,270 million yen
into the commerce sector, the balance of 114, 160 million yen into the transportation sector, the balance of 351 million yen into
unspecified industries sector, and yielded some 187,876 million

Table 30

Input-Out Table of the Japanese Economy, 1955
(billion yen)

	Agriculture	Mining & Industry	Commerce	Transportation	Industries n.e.s.	Capital Formation	Export	Competitive Imports	Government	Household	Total
Agriculture	132	893	56	2	58	78	9	414	6	1,341	2,160
Mining & Industry	277	4,078	661	288	776	1,653	681	-411	84	1,924	10,011
Commerce	71	537	343	120	225	57	102	-12	689	2,391	4,522
Transportation	33	436	187	62	105	7	202	-11	34	283	1,337
Industries, n.e.s.	49	1,143	327	42	-82	209	8		45		1,823
Depreciation	77	321	186	121							623
Imports	417	477	26	12		2			24	9	119
Government	18	1,255	104	28	51						1,456
Household	1,507	1,320	2,675	566	-47		6		347	705	7,079
Adjustment	-7	-38	-31	108	737				56		826
Total	2,160	10,011	4,522	1,337	1,823	2,006	1,007	848	1,285	6,653	29,908

Source: Isamu Yamada, Theory and Application of Interindustry Analysis, Kinokuniya
Bookstore Co. Tokyo, 1961, pp. 148-49.

Table 31

Interindustry Relations Trade Sector, Japan, 1955
(billion yen)

	Receipt	Balance
Agriculture	417	408
Mining & Industry	477	
Commerce	26	
Transportation	12	
Industries, n.e.s.	---	
Household	9	3
Capital	2	2
Government	24	24
	967	437

	Payment	Balance
Agriculture	9	
Mining & Industry	681	204
Commerce	102	76
Transportation	202	190
Industries, n.e.s.	8	8
Household	6	
Capital	---	
Government	---	
Balance	-41	-41
	967	437

Source: Isamu Yamada, Theory and Application of Interindustry Analysis, Kinokuniya Bookstore Co. Toyko, 1961, pp. 148-49.

yen for households.

The only difference between 1953 and 1951 was that in 1951 the mining and industry sectors received the largest flow of funds from the trade sector, while in 1953 the transportation sector was the major beneficiary. In Colin Clark's terms, the emphasis of the Japanese government policies began

to shift from secondary industries to tertiary industries, indicating that the economy is moving to a higher stage of
development.

Table 30 is the Input-Output Table of Japan in 1955, and
from it we can again derive Table 31, the social account table
of the trade sector. Again we have the same pattern in that
the trade sector supported the mining and industry sector, the
commerce sector, and the transportation sector.

The Role Played by Capital

Now let us look into the part played by capital in the economic growth of Japan. In 1951, capital formation was insignificant; investments were concentrated on mining and in
industry. Funds came largely from savings of previous years.
In 1953 significant amounts of capital were derived from agriculture, commerce, and transportation sectors; investments
were poured into the mining and industry sector and the unspecified industries sector. In 1955 the pattern changed.
After years of heavy investments in mining and industries, the
fast progress made enabled it not only to be financially self-
sufficient, but furthermore to become a source of capital formation. In 1955 investments began to go into commerce and
transportation sectors.

The Role Played by Government

From the input-output tables of these years, we can also
find out the part played by the government in the economic
growth of Japan. In 1951, the government favored the mining
and industry sector and the commerce sector. Funds came
from tax revenues. In 1953 the government began to favor
the commerce and transportation sectors. Government
revenues came from agriculture, mining and industry, and
households. The 1953 pattern was repeated in 1955. Here
there is a clear division of labor, with the government concentrating on services and utilities and private enterprises on
productive activities.

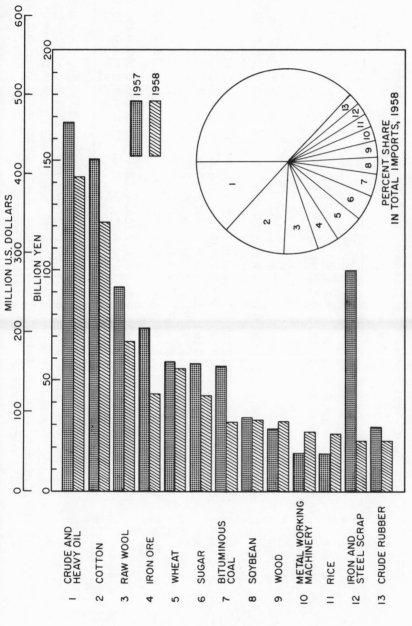

FIGURE 10. IMPORTS: PRINCIPAL COMMODITIES, JAPAN

Source: Ministry of Foreign Affairs, Japanese Government, Statistical Survey of Economy of Japan, Tokyo, 1959, p. 37.

169

Table 32

Dependency of Industries on Imports, Japan
(imports as percentages of consumption)

	1934-1936	1950	1951	1952	1953	1954	1955	1956	1957	1958	1959	1960	1961
Food													
Wheat	24.5	52.9	52.6	55.0	55.7	60.6	60.9	62.3	66.1	64.0	63.0	63.4	59.6
Sugar	87.5	95.2	93.4	95.0	95.3	95.2	96.0	93.6	91.7	89.0	...	...	...
Industrial Materials													
Phosphate rock	100.0	100.0	100.0	100.0	100.0	100.0	100.0	100.0	100.0	100.0	100.0	100.0	100.0
Raw cotton	100.0	100.0	100.0	100.0	100.0	100.0	100.0	100.0	100.0	100.0	100.0	100.0	100.0
Raw wool	100.0	100.0	100.0	100.0	100.0	100.0	100.0	100.0	100.0	100.0	100.0	100.0	100.0
Bauxite	---	100.0	100.0	100.0	100.0	100.0	100.0	100.0	100.0	100.0	100.0	100.0	100.0
Iron ore	93.4	64.0	77.7	82.5	79.7	81.0	78.9	88.2	89.2	86.7	89.9	92.1	94.8
Coal	11.1	2.1	4.3	7.2	9.6	7.4	6.5	7.6	11.1	8.5	9.5	14.0	17.0
Crude oil	93.5	81.0	88.6	98.1	94.7	95.2	96.0	97.1	97.6	97.5	98.1	98.1	98.1
Crude rubber	100.0	100.0	100.0	100.0	100.0	100.0	100.0	100.0	100.0	100.0	100.0	100.0	100.0
Salt	65.0	60.6	80.4	77.2	75.0	80.2	78.6	78.2	70.6	61.6	62.2	73.9	73.9

Sources: J. B. Cohen, Japan's Postwar Economy, 1958, p. 123 for 1934-36, 1950 and 1951 figures; Ryokichi Minobe, Japan's Foreign Trade, Ministry of Foreign Affairs, Japanese Government, 1958, p. 47, for 1952-58 figures; Bureau of Statistics, Office of Prime Minister, Japan, Japan's Statistical Yearbook, 1963, Tokyo, 1964, p. 254 for 1959-61 figures.

The Content of Imports

Now, to examine what particular fields of mining and industry have been helped by trade, we need to go into the content of imports and exports. By quantity, imports amounted to only 15.6 per cent of national income in 1956, but they are important to Japan's economy because of their essential content. The content of imports in 1958 is given in Figure 9.[10] It includes crude oil, cotton, raw wool, iron ore, wheat, sugar, bituminous coal, soybean, wood, metal working machinery, rice, iron and steel scrap, and crude rubber. Without these supplies, there will immediately be difficulties in the cotton and woolen textiles, iron and steel, and machinery industries. Since the content of imports is completely under the control of the government through import licensing, the fact that these supplies are allowed to come in indicates that the government favored these industries.

Dependency of Industries on Imports

Some of Japan's industries depend on imports to the degree that these imports sometimes constitute the major shares or even 100 per cent of the needed supplies. The dependency ratio is the quantity of imports compared to the combined quantities of domestic production and imports.

Any decline in the imports of supplies in Table 32 would certainly slow down economic progress. As in the case of phosphate rock, raw cotton, raw wool, and crude rubber, there are no domestic supplies to fall back on. The Japanese government realizes this precarious position and has tried to reduce the degree of dependency on imports by encouraging the use of substitutes or by promoting production processes where the production coefficients of imported materials are low. But, as indicated in Table 32, no significant success has been made in the materials listed.

The Content of Exports

The content of exports of Japan in 1958 is given in Figure 10.

It includes the following items, listed in the order of their importance: ships, cotton fabrics, iron and steel, fish products, clothing, spun rayon fabrics, nitrogenous fertilizers, rayon filament fabrics, plywood, ceramics, and optical instruments. [11] The export trade helps the economy to grow by providing markets for related industries. Any expansion of the export trade would stimulate the production of these industries. However the export effects on industries are not uniform.

Table 33 lists the industries making the fastest gains in the value of their exports. Generally, the fastest gains in export value were made in machinery, chemical, and basic industries.

A reappraisal of the pattern of Japan's economic growth is in order. The reason that Japan has had income growth is due to the growth in industrial production. Upon closer examination of industrial production, Table 34 shows that for the period 1955-58 mining, with the index of 117.6, did not do as well as manufacturing, with the index of 147.8. Among the different manufacturing industries, ferrous metals, textiles, food, and allied products did not do as well as the machinery industry, with the index of 218.1, and the chemical industry, with the index of 148.0. The pattern of economic growth of Japan is thus revealed. It has been the extremely rapid growth in the machinery and chemical industries that has led the industrial production to a high rate of growth, and it has been the industrial production that has led the general economy of Japan to a high rate of growth. And it has been the export trade that has provided for the machinery and chemical industries the very favorable world markets they enjoy, so they have been able to earn the high rates of profits that have made the very fast growth of these industries possible. Here we see the link between trade expansion and economic growth of Japan. Here is the "carry-over" effect of trade on the economy of Japan. The principal industries making the fastest growth of production happen to be the same industries which have made the biggest gains in the export trade.

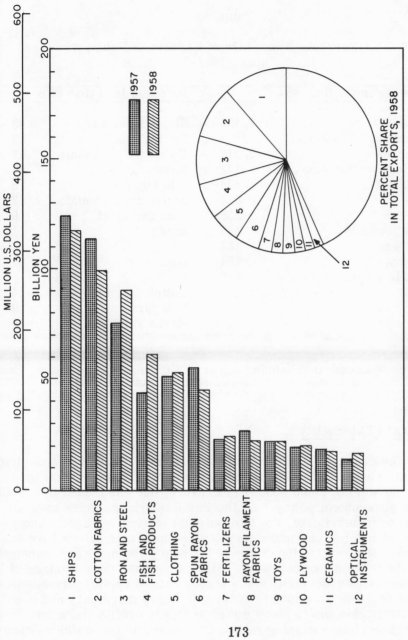

FIGURE II. EXPORTS: PRINCIPAL COMMODITIES, JAPAN

Source: Ministry of Foreign Affairs, Japanese Government, Statistical Survey of Economy of Japan, Tokyo, 1959, p. 37.

173

Table 33

Percentage Increase of Exports in Value,
Japan, 1951-56

Increase more than 85%		Increase less than 85%	
Ships	1, 497	Staple fiber yarn	63
Chemical fertilizers	1, 174	Sewing machines	59
Cameras	1, 018	Pottery & porcelain	49
Staple fiber fabrics	522	Rayon fabrics	32
Plywood	404	Silk fabrics	25
Toys	343	Non-ferrous metals	12
Clothing	255	Iron and steel	9
Fish products	243	Raw silk	1
Lumber	223		
Cement	154	Decrease	
Textile machinery	146		
		Cotton fabrics	-14
		Silk yarn	-20
		Rayon yarn	-46

Source: Economic Planning Agency, Japanese Government, Economic Survey of Japan, 1957, p. 53.

Forward Externality

The change of content of the export trade from light industries of cotton and silk textiles to heavy machinery and chemical industries did not come about haphazardly, but was guided by a deliberate government policy. As the Far Eastern countries have all begun to industrialize, the international market for light manufactures has become more competitive, and their prices have declined. Meanwhile, the demands for heavy chemical and machinery manufactures have increased. Since Japan had the advantage of technological superiority and a higher rate of capital formation, it was feasible for Japan to convert to heavy machinery and chemical industries where there would be higher profits and a better foreign-exchange earning ratio. Of course, in these fields Japan would come into competition with the industrial countries of

North America and Europe, but that was the risk it chose to take. In 1953 the Japanese government limited the exports of textiles and provided ample funds for the chemical and machinery industries, when the productivity in the textile industry was high and that for the chemical and machinery industries low. There the Japanese government, in implementing the change to heavy industries, deliberately took a lower short-run return for its capital. [12]

Industries are mutually dependent, with the output of one going into the input of another. Any improvement of productivity in one industry may improve the margin of profit for another. There are two types of externality effects: forward and backward. Forward externality refers to the type of effect that the improved efficiency of basic industries has on the light industries and service industries, whereas the backward externality is the effect in the reversed direction. Hirschman considers generally the forward externality is more effective than the backward externality, and therefore he advocates the type of development policy to place emphasis on basic industries. In Japan, Hirschman's theory has a successful application. It is only when the cement industry produces cheaper and better cement that the construction industry will receive a higher rate of profits, and then it would be cheaper for factories to expand their buildings and plants. It is when the machinery industry produces cheaper and better equipment and tools that industries in general will find it more profitable to improve their capital goods, and then they can improve their productivity. Thus, the entire economy will have a better chance to come to a higher level of income and to become more competitive in the international market. However, this pattern of development is more likely in a country like Japan where there is a high level of technological attainment and a high rate of capital formation.

Because of the growth in the machinery industry, equipment investment for the entire economy increased very fast: for instance, 80 per cent in 1956. There was in that year heavy equipment investment in a large number of industries including consumer goods, iron and steel, electric power, textile machinery, petro-chemical, synthetic fibers, and plastics. [13]

Table 34

Index Numbers of Industrial Activity and Production of JAPAN

(1955=100)

		Industrial Activity								
			Industrial Production							
						of which:				
	Total	Public Utilities	Total	Mining	Manufacturing	Ferrous Metals	Machinery	Chemicals	Textiles	Food and Allied Products
No.of Items	328	2	326	14	312	18	104	66	32	14
Value Added Wts.	10,000.0	719.6	9280.4	716.9	8563.5	897.5	1703.2	1075.0	1504.3	1153.4
1930	31.0	27.2	30.9	66.0	28.0	22.2	--	--	55.3	--
1931	31.1	28.0	31.0	62.0	28.3	20.0	--	--	62.3	--
1932	33.0	29.7	32.9	63.0	30.2	24.9	--	--	66.1	--
1933	38.6	32.8	38.9	72.4	35.7	33.3	--	--	71.7	53.9
1934	44.5	36.1	44.8	80.0	41.3	40.4	--	--	81.7	57.8
1935	48.6	40.4	48.8	86.2	45.0	47.8	--	--	87.0	59.9
1936	54.9	44.0	55.3	95.8	51.1	53.4	--	--	91.9	59.9
1937	63.6	48.8	64.3	104.4	59.7	60.5	--	--	108.2	63.8
1938	68.1	53.1	68.8	110.9	63.9	68.0	--	--	95.7	65.8
1939	73.1	55.8	73.9	116.1	68.8	72.6	--	--	90.7	75.1

176

1940	73.3	57.1	74.0	120.2	68.7	72.7	---	---	82.5	65.5
1941	74.1	61.8	74.4	124.6	68.9	70.6	---	---	69.4	56.2
1942	71.2	61.8	71.2	121.8	65.9	76.2	---	---	49.5	51.5
1943	73.8	63.0	74.0	120.5	68.3	82.1	---	---	33.7	44.8
1944	76.2	61.9	75.7	111.8	71.8	80.7	---	---	20.1	33.8
1945	31.4	35.1	30.7	60.6	30.3	30.0	---	---	6.5	16.9
1946	19.3	48.0	17.9	42.5	15.0	8.9	---	---	11.1	21.2
1947	24.2	54.2	22.8	56.0	18.9	11.9	---	---	14.5	20.4
1948	31.4	57.8	30.1	68.4	25.7	19.4	---	---	19.9	22.4
1949	40.0	65.6	38.8	78.1	34.2	34.8	---	---	26.1	34.8
1950	50.5	70.6	49.5	81.5	45.7	51.0	---	---	40.6	39.5
1951	67.2	75.4	66.7	93.2	63.5	68.5	---	---	58.1	51.6
1952	73.0	81.2	72.5	96.3	69.5	72.2	---	---	66.9	57.7
1953	84.4	87.7	84.2	103.0	81.7	83.6	---	---	79.7	75.4
1954	92.1	93.4	91.9	99.1	90.6	86.2	---	---	89.0	82.2
1955	100.0	100.0	100.0	100.0	100.0	100.0	100.0	100.0	100.0	100.0
1956	123.3	115.0	122.4	110.5	123.5	121.8	145.2	120.8	118.8	105.7
1957	143.3	128.2	144.5	121.8	146.4	138.7	202.1	142.0	131.2	111.0
1958	144.8	136.1	145.5	117.6	147.8	130.2	218.1	148.0	117.7	117.5
1959 J	148.9	145.9	149.1	117.0	151.8	136.9	221.5	154.7	116.5	118.2
F	163.9	137.1	166.0	118.1	170.0	141.5	250.8	154.7	126.3	191.1
M	176.8	154.0	178.6	101.7	185.0	146.5	273.7	169.1	128.0	218.3
A	167.3	152.5	168.4	109.7	173.3	158.7	279.1	184.2	131.9	100.9
M	171.4	156.9	172.5	117.4	177.1	173.5	289.7	174.9	131.4	103.1

Source: Ministry of International Trade and Industry

177

Development of Financial Institutions due to Trade

The fast growth in the chemical and machinery industries calls for a developed financial system to take care of the large capital requirements for production and for distribution. Beginning in the second half of the 1950's, Japan began to export machinery to Central and South America, and Asian countries: first in individual units and gradually in sets of equipment for an entire plant. Originally, agricultural machinery and implements and textile machinery were exported, and then boilers, turbines, generators, mining machinery, printing machinery, and machine tools in general were added. [14]

To sell plants in a foreign country, long-term credits will have to be granted. In the period from 1951-58, a total of U. S. $131 million was invested abroad: for establishing shipyards, steel works and auto plants in Brazil; for sending out mining machinery to Chile, Thailand, and the Philippines; and to construct fishery concerns in Mexico. To handle the financial arrangement for capital exports, government banks have been established to assist private banks. Among the government banks established there are: Japan Development Bank, the Export-Import Bank of Japan, People's Finance Corporation, Small Business Finance Corporation, and the Hokkaido and Tohoku Development Finance Corporation. The Export and Import Bank of Japan has been concentrating on the long-term financing of the exports of ships and rolling stocks. [15]

Capital formation, of course, is stimulated in Japan by the needs of capital for the export trade and by the fast development of financial agencies. Professor F. D. Graham believed that the group of entrepreneurs who needed capital to invest for high rates of return saved the most. This also agrees with Bertil Ohlin's concept that when a country's comparative advantage lies in capital intensive commodities, extension of international trade raises the real reward to capital. If the supply function for saving is positively sloped, the rate of capital formation is speeded up. [16]

When the export trade can induce a higher rate of capital formation, then the increase in investment certainly will push the economy to a higher level of production.

Technological Improvement through Trade

As Japan has committed itself to a policy of concentrating
on capital goods for exports, the die is cast. Japan has em-
barked on the course of long-term competition with the industrial West. Its well-being depends on whether it can keep up
with the industrial West in the technological race.

In shipbuilding, Japan leads the world in the construction of merchant vessels. In 1953 the Kawasaki Dockyard
Company constructed the largest floating dock in the orient,
and in 1957 it devised a unique "transverse shifting construction method" by which mammoth tankers have been produced
in rapid succession. Now the company is conducting intensive
research on nuclear-powered vessels. [17]

The Maruzen Oil Company imports oil from the Persian
Gulf area, Southeast Asia, and the United States, and exports
petroleum products back to Southeast Asia and the United
States. In 1958 it went into the production of petrochemical
field in full scale. Its high technical level has been widely
recognized throughout the world. In 1959 part of its production techniques were adopted by an American firm under a
special contract. [18]

Toyo Rayon Company's nylon synthesizing method is
highly evaluated by the Du Pont Company of the United States,
which originally started the company on its manufacturing of
nylon. Kawashiki Rayon Company's vinylon process is in-
ternationally recognized. [19]

Japan has made fast progress in the technology of optical
and precision instruments.

The road to technological advancement is not easy.
Again, it has been guided by the encouragement of the government and the initiative of private business. When the war
ended, the United States emerged as the leader of scientific
and industrial technology of the world. To expedite economic

recovery, Japan had to import technical knowledge from the
United States. The Japanese government enacted the Foreign
Capital Law that guaranteed the remittance of royalties for the
techniques imported. In the 1950's private businesses competed
with one another in buying up patent rights and blueprints
from the United States. Business executives and engineers
lost no time in studying American techniques and in incorpor-
ating these techniques into their production process, and the
result was that in a large number of fields the Japanese products were the exact copies of the American counterparts.
Japan had to catch up with the West quickly and time was of
primary importance. By the 1960's Japan began to develop, in
some fields, techniques of its own, with new ideas and new approaches invented to modify the imported techniques to meet
local conditions. Japan is now moving into new fields without
having to depend on any imported techniques. [20]

The export trade requires speedy advancement of technology to remain competitive in the international market, and,
of course, the technological progress will definitely improve
national income.

The Industrial-Financial-Trading Combines

Since manufacturing requires trading firms to promote
exports, and the export trade requires financing, it is natural
for the three sectors--the manufacturing, the trading and the
banking institutions--to come together to form combines. In
Japan, these take the form of zaibatsu, a combine with added
oriental refinements. A zaibatsu usually has a bank and a trading
firm as its nucleus. As it grows stronger, its investment will go
to the different manufacturing fields. The bigger it is, the
larger number of affiliated industries it will have. There is
usually the interlocking directorate, or the interlocking stock
acquisition, for the combine, although each affiliated firm
may be independent in name. During World War II, the
zaibatsu supported the military group in waging war against
the Allied nations. During the occupation, a number of the
combines were dissolved: among them, Mitsui, Mitsubishi,
National Policy Companies, Japan Iron and Steel Company,
and Japan Electricity Generation and Transmission Company.

The antitrust laws and institutions of the United States were
transplanted to Japan under the occupation authorities to introduce competition in the Japanese economy. However, most
of the banks and trading firms of these combines were left
alone because they were considered necessary for the recovery
of the economy. After political sovereignty had been restored
to the Japanese, the zaibatsu began to reorganize their empires
in 1952, using their banks and trading firms as nuclei. Mitsui,
Mitsubishi, and Sumitono again assumed leadership in the economy due to their financial power and their technical knowledge.
By 1960, the giant zaibatsu had recovered their prewar position
of domination. In the '60s, Mitusi Bussan has increased its
holding of shares of Nippon Metal Industry, Kawakami Paint
Manufacturing Co. , and Nippon Synthetic Chemical Industry.
Mitsubishi Shoji has increased its holding in Nippon Kokan
Steel Manufacturing Co. , Nippon Suisan Steel Manufacturing Co. ,
and Saka Steel Manufacturing Co. Marubeni Iida has increased
its holding in Hitachi Shipbuilding and Engineering Co. and
Sekisui Chemical Co. C. Itoh and Co. has increased its holding in Sumitomo Metal Industry and Matsuchi Electric Industry. [21]
The Kawasaki Dockyard Co. , before World War II, had branched
out into rolling stock, aircraft, shipping service, and steel industries, but the combine was dissolved under the occupation.
Now all these subsidiary industries have been re-established and
an additional company, the Kawasaki Electric Manufacturing
Company, has been added.

    The zaibatsu is a typical Japanese institution which adds
vitality, boldness, and resourcefulness to the business world
of Japan. Any new discovery of international market possibilities will be immediately passed on to the manufacturing
branches; any new products developed will become new chal-
lenges for the trading branches to develop new market channels; financial branches will work together with the trading
branches to facilitate the sale of capital goods abroad.
Through the zaibatsu there can be coordination and synchro-
nization of activities. Trade expansion and economic growth
are brought together. Monopoly is seemingly an efficient and
orderly way of promoting economic recovery; however, there
is always the possibility that after it has established itself in the
market, it will stifle further growth, due to the absence of
competition.

The findings of this section can be summarized as follows:

1.   Because of import restrictions and foreign-exchange controls, the imports of Japan have a large investment content. An increase of imports will promote economic growth.

2.   The economic growth of Japan in the postwar period can be divided into two stages: From 1950-53 economic growth was largely due to the expansion of imports, and from 1953 on, due to the expansion of exports.

3.   In 1951 the trade, government, and capital sectors concentrated their efforts in building up the mining and industry sectors. By 1953 the mining and industry sector was becoming self-sufficient in funds, and therefore the emphasis began to shift gradually to commerce and transportation sectors.

4.   Within the mining and industry sector, trade has helped to build up textile, iron and steel, machinery and chemical industries. These industries produce the major trade items, and their expansion has been the fastest. It is the extremely fast expansion of these industries that has brought about the fast growth of the mining and industry sector which in turn has brought about the growth of the entire economy.

5.   The rationale of promoting especially iron and steel, machinery, and chemical industries through trade, lies in the great forward externality of these basic industries. Here Japan applies Hirschman's concept of unbalanced growth.

6.   Japan has chosen the role of an exporter of capital goods in the Far East and, as an exporter of capital goods, there is the need of capital to finance the sale of capital goods. This need stimulates capital formation and forces the country to develop the Export Import Bank and other financial institutions. Japan is becoming a financial center of the Far East.

7.   As an exporter of capital goods, Japan is constantly in competition with the industrial West. This forces Japan to promote industrial and commercial technology, which in turn will help the economy to grow.

8.   The externality of trade on the general economy
works its way through the operations of the zaibatsu, the in-
dustrial-financial-trading combines, which coordinate economic activities of various phases in the country.

9.   There are other factors contributing to the economic
success of Japan: United States aid to Japan, the special procurement program, the offshore procurement program, the
inflow of foreign capital, political stability, an efficient government friendly to business, diligence of the people, managerial
ability of private enterprise, the technical attainment, the fine
educational system, the savings for the nation due to the
absence of a defense system, the adequate legal system, and
the favorable geographical features for shipping and trade.
Japan's experience warrants careful study. For lack of favorable conditions, it may not be possible for the Far Eastern nations to duplicate the economic growth of Japan, but they may
find in Japan an encouraging example, which they may emulate
with varying degrees of success.

POSTWAR DEVELOPMENT OF TRADE

During the 1930's, Japan became one of the great trading
nations of the world. In 1938, her exports represented 5. 4
per cent of the world exports, and her imports 4. 6 per cent
of the world imports. At the same time, she had become a
great sea carrier. Her merchant marine was the third
largest in the world. Her sale of shipping services to foreign customers brought in receipts sufficient to pay for
nearly one tenth of her imports. It was also during the 1930's
that significant changes occurred. North America declined,
relatively, as a customer as the silk trade declined, but the
Far East was becoming more important to Japan as a market. 22

During the war years, Japan's trade was disrupted. Immediately after the war, under Allied occupation in 1946, her
trade was prohibited, but exports on a restricted basis were
allowed in 1947. In 1949, the Supreme Command for the Allied Powers, SCAP, restored the trade and foreign-exchange
controls to the Japanese government, and in 1949 a single
exchange rate between the Japanese yen and the American

dollar was established to replace the multiple rates. Trade
resumed gradually. [23] In 1950, government trading corporations were abolished and private trading corporations were
organized as trade was returned to private enterprise. From
1947-50 there were little exports, due to the low level of production. Imports were mainly grains and raw materials for
the basic needs of the people. Fifty-seven per cent of the
imports in value was paid by American aid. [24]

From 1950-52, due to the Korean War, there was a boom
in Japan's trade. Both exports and imports expanded. United
Nations special procurements accounted for 65 per cent of
Japan's exports. These helped Japan greatly, as American aid
was being withdrawn.[25] From 1953 on, the trade of Japan,
both exports and imports, has been expanding steadily, as the
economy makes a spectacular recovery.

Table 35

Trade of Japan
(in millions of U. S. dollars)

	Imports	Exports	Balance
1938	1,070	1,109	39
1951	2,044	1,355	-689
1952	2,028	1,273	-755
1953	2,410	1,275	-1,135
1954	2,399	1,629	-770
1955	2,471	2,011	-460
1956	3,229	2,501	-728
1957	4,284	2,858	-1,426
1958	3,033	2,877	-156
1959	3,599	3,456	-143
1960	4,491	4,055	-436
1961	5,810	4,234	-1,596
1962	5,635	4,918	-717
1963	6,737	5,452	-1,284

Sources: Figures for 1938 and 1951-56 are taken from

Jerome B. Cohen, Japan's Post War Economy, Indiana University Press, Bloomington, 1958, p. 111,
and figures for 1957-60 are calculated from statistics given by International Monetary Fund, International Financial Statistics, Washington, D. C.,
June, 1961, pp. 36-69. Throughout the book, unless otherwise indicated, the value of exports is on
the f.o.b. or "free on board" basis, which means
the value is based on the prices on board the ship or
other means of international transport at the port or
place of dispatch at the frontier of the exporting
country, including export duties and internal taxes
of the exporting country. The value of imports is on
the c.i.f. or "cost, insurance, and freight" basis,
which means the value is based on the prices at the
port or place of entry at the frontier of the importing country excluding custom duty and internal taxes
of the importing country.

Any comparison of Japan's prewar trade with her trade of
the postwar years runs into the difficulty of having to account
for changes due to the changing territorial claims of Japan.
Before World War II, statistics of Japan's foreign trade would
not include her trade with Korea, Formosa, and the Mandated
islands, as these were within her boundaries, but after the war,
the trade with these areas is included in statistics. All through
the postwar period, there has been an unfavorable balance of
merchandise trade for Japan, but from 1958 on, exports have
expanded and imports decreased; consequently the unfavorable
balance has been reduced.

Japan is now the nation with the largest value of trade in
the Pacific. However, Japan has not yet regained her prewar share of world trade. Japan's share of world imports
was 4.6 per cent in 1938, but 3.8 per cent in 1960, while her
share of world exports was 5.4 per cent in 1938, but 3.58
per cent in 1960. She has been making very good progress
in regaining her share.

This increase in the value of Japan's trade is not due to
higher prices, as both the prices for her imports and exports

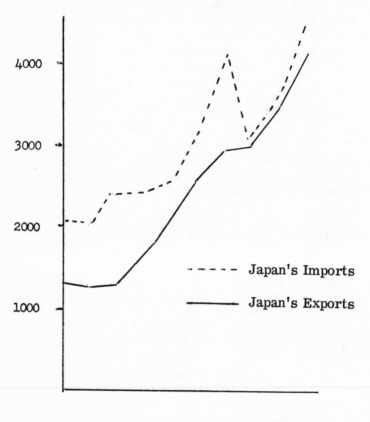

FIGURE 12
TRADE OF JAPAN
(in millions of U.S. dollars)

- - - - Japan's Imports

——— Japan's Exports

4000

3000

2000

1000

1951 1952 1953 1954 1955 1956 1957 1958 1959 1960

Source: Jerome B. Cohen, Japan's Postwar Economy (Blooming-
ton, Indiana: Indiana University Press, 1958), p. 111;
International Monetary Fund, International Financial
Statistics (Washington, D.C.: International Monetary
Fund, June, 1961), pp. 36-39.

186

Table 36

Japan's Share of World Trade

	World Trade (in millions of U. S. dollars)		Japan's Trade as percentage of world trade	
	Imports	Exports	Imports	Exports
1938	23,250	20,650	4.6	5.37
1951	81,840	77,140	2.5	1.75
1952	79,200	72,300	2.6	1.76
1953	75,800	73,300	3.2	1.74
1954	79,000	76,100	3.0	2.14
1955	88,000	82,800	2.8	2.44
1956	96,900	91,900	3.3	2.74
1957	108,210	100,880	4.0	2.83
1958	101,080	96,080	3.0	2.99
1959	106,480	101,780	3.4	3.40
1960	118,600	113,200	3.8	3.58

Sources: Figures for 1938 and 1951-56 are taken from Jerome
B. Cohen, Japan's Post War Economy, Indiana University Press, Bloomington, 1958, and figures for
1957-60 are calculated from statistics given by International Monetary Fund, International Financial Statistics, Washington, D. C., June, 1961.

have been quite stable. It is due to the increase in the volume
of her exports and imports.

Trade is of the utmost importance to Japan, as she now
buys one third of her needs of iron ore from North America;
most of her coking coal from North America; mica and manganese from India; cotton and wheat from Pakistan; oil, tin, coal,
asbestos, and bauxite from Indonesia; rice from Burma and
Thailand; salt from Cambodia, Laos, and Vietnam; copper from
the Philippines; and rubber from Malaya. Japan has to obtain
these materials in order to maintain her economic growth.
Since December, 1955, when the Japanese government announced

the Five Year Plan, trade has become absolutely necessary
for carrying out her program. Japan's imports and exports
were each equivalent to about 17 per cent of her national income in 1934-36. Her exports were 9.0 per cent of her national income in 1952 and 12.1 per cent in 1956. Her imports
were 14.5 per cent of her national income in 1952, and 15.6
per cent in 1956.[26]

TERMS OF TRADE

Japan since World War II has been enjoying a very favorable bargaining position in her foreign trade. Owing to the
wide range of her export and import commodities, covering
capital goods, light industrial manufactures, and agricultural
products, both her export and import prices have been comparatively stable. This is in marked contrast to some of the
Southeast Asian countries, where exports are dominated by one
or two commodities and their prices often fluctuate violently.
The Korean War improved the export prices for Japan in 1951
to an unprecedented high, and Japan's terms of trade became
favorable. The terms of trade improved 106.1 per cent
from 1934-51. Her export prices slowly declined from 1951-
55, rose again in 1956, and then declined from 1957-60. Her
import prices rose in 1951, but declined after 1952 at a faster
pace than her export prices. Thus the terms of trade have
been slightly in favor of Japan all the time. The terms improved 115 per cent from 1950-56, and again improved
to 114 per cent from 1952-60. This means that Japan has
been enjoying a favorable bargaining position all through the
postwar period. She has, in fact, attained a better position
than she had in the prewar period.

The Japanese economist, Shigeru Fujii, worries over
the increasing portion of capital goods in Japanese exports,
which may cause Japan's exports to become more susceptible to the changes in the business cycles of the countries
of destination. The reason is that demands for capital goods
are unstable, and it is only when a country is enjoying prosperity that it will import large quantities of capital goods.
But judging from the statistics on the volume of exports indexes, throughout the postwar period, Japan's exports have

been expanding in volume. Of course, this does not mean that
Japan's exports would not suffer in case of a serious depression in the countries she trades with, but so far no business
fluctuation has affected Japan's exports.

DIRECTION OF TRADE

The most significant factors which have affected the direction of Japan's trade are the loss of her former colonies and
the rise of the Communist regime in China. Formosa, Korea,
and mainland China, before World War II, were the largest
sources of her imports and the largest market for her exports. But now, with Formosa under the Republic of China,
Korea having become independent, and mainland China under
the Communists, Japan's trade with these countries has
greatly declined. For instance, in 1935, Japan shipped to
these three countries 41.1 per cent of her exports, but in 1959
only 4.3 per cent. In 1935, Japan imported from these countries 35.2 per cent of her imports, but in 1959 only 2.8 per
cent. To compensate for this loss, Japan now has to promote
trade with the rest of the world. As a consequence, her trade
with the rest of the world has increased both in absolute and
relative figures. Japan's trade in Asia as a whole declined,
but her trade with South and Southeast Asia expanded.

The leading countries which received the largest volumes
of Japan's exports in 1956 are arranged here according to their
importance: The United States, Liberia, Hong Kong, India,
British West Africa, Malaya and Singapore, Formosa, Indonesia, Communist China, Indochina, and Korea. The United
States in 1959 bought 30.4 per cent of Japan's exports, which
included largely cotton and silk textiles, fish products, lumber
and products, toys, and pottery.[27] Japan's exports are now
widely spread over a large number of countries, with no one
country, the United States excepted, taking more than 10 per
cent.

The leading countries which supplied the largest volumes
of Japan's imports in 1956 are, in the order of their importance: the United States, Australia, Canada, Saudi Arabia,
Malaya and Singapore, Mexico, the Philippines, India, In-

Table 37

Direction of Japan's Trade

Japan's Imports
(in percentages of Japan's total imports)

	1938	1948	1955	1956	1957	1958	1959
Total	100.0	100.0	100.0	100.0	100.0	100.0	100.0
United States	33.0	64.5	31.3	33.0	37.9	34.8	31.0
Canada	3.4	0.6	4.4	4.4	3.9	4.0	...
Latin America	3.5	12.8	9.8	10.8	7.2	8.5	...
Sterling Area	18.0	9.0	23.8	25.3	26.1	26.1	...
Soviet Area	0.3	0.4	0.3	0.3	0.4	0.8	...
W. Europe	13.7	2.8	7.1	7.1	9.1	8.6	...
Africa	0.6	0.7	1.2	1.5	1.5	1.6	1.4
Asia	36.7	14.2	30.1	25.5	20.6	21.4	...
Burma	0.3	0.2	1.9	1.3	0.5	0.4	0.3
Ceylon	0.1	0.03	0.1	0.1	0.1	0.2	0.3
Taiwan	15.7	1.0	3.3	1.4	1.3	2.4	2.0
Mainland China	21.1	2.1	3.2	2.6	1.8	1.4	0.5
Hong Kong	0.04	0.5	0.3	0.6	0.6	0.4	0.8
India	6.4	4.0	3.1	3.2	2.4	2.4	2.5
Pakistan	...	...	1.5	1.5	1.1	1.1	0.9
Indonesia	3.0	1.7	3.3	2.7	1.5	1.1	1.6
Korea	26.6	1.2	0.4	0.3	0.3	0.3	0.3
Malaya & Singapore	3.6	1.5	4.4	4.3	4.5	4.1	4.9
Philippines	1.3	1.4	3.6	3.6	2.6	3.2	3.7
Thailand	0.2	0.01	2.5	1.1	0.7	0.7	1.0
Australia	3.0	1.1	7.1	7.7	8.4	7.4	8.1
New Zealand	0.3	...	0.3	0.3	0.6	0.6	...

Japan's Exports
(in percentages of Japan's total exports)

Total	100.0	100.0	100.0	100.0	100.0	100.0	100.0
United States	16.2	25.4	22.7	22.0	21.2	24.0	30.4
Canada	0.5	0.7	2.2	2.7	2.2	2.5	...
Latin America	3.0	0.6	8.9	6.5	5.2	6.1	...
Sterling Area	21.6	27.0	31.8	27.3	28.2	26.0	...
Soviet Area	0.2	1.7	0.5	0.2	0.5	0.8	...
Western Europe	9.9	10.5	9.7	10.1	11.1	11.4	...
Africa	4.0	5.0	9.0	10.9	16.0	13.2	9.6
Asia	60.0	48.6	37.5	37.4	36.0	32.2	...
Burma	0.6	0.5	1.9	1.5	2.7	1.6	1.5
Ceylon	0.5	0.5	1.0	1.0	0.9	1.2	0.8
Taiwan	12.2	0.1	3.2	3.1	2.9	3.1	2.5
Mainland China	43.0	0.5	1.4	2.7	2.1	1.7	0.01
Hong Kong	0.6	6.7	4.4	5.3	4.5	3.4	3.7
India	7.0	3.5	4.2	4.2	4.5	2.9	2.2
Pakistan	...	...	2.1	0.7	0.6	0.7	0.7
Indonesia	3.8	21.9	3.2	3.0	2.3	1.7	2.1
Korea	34.0	9.2	1.9	2.5	2.0	2.0	1.8
Malaya & Singapore	0.8	2.4	3.6	3.0	2.9	3.1	2.7
Philippines	1.2	1.6	2.6	2.2	3.1	3.1	3.2
Thailand	1.4	2.1	3.1	2.4	2.8	2.9	3.0
Australia	2.6	0.9	2.7	1.2	1.4	2.2	2.3
New Zealand	0.5	0.2	0.3	0.2	0.2	0.2	...

Source: United Nations, International Monetary Fund and International Bank for Reconstruction and Development jointly, Direction of International Trade, New York, 1959, p. 285; the 1959 figures are taken from the United Nations Statistical Office, Yearbook of International Trade Statistics, New York, 1959, p. 158, 1954, p. 313, and 1959, p. 325; the figures for Korea, Taiwan, and China for 1938 are not included in foreign trade figures.

donesia, and Communist China. The United States sold to
Japan foodstuffs, fuel, capital equipment, and raw materials.[28]

Trade with the United States

Since World War II, the United States has become the
most important nation for Japan's trade. In 1938, the United
States took 16.2 per cent of Japan's exports, but in 1959,
30.4 per cent. In 1938 the United States provided 33 per cent
of Japan's imports, and in 1959, the figure was 31 per cent.
Meanwhile, Japan also ranks high among the leading nations
in trading with the United States. Japan has become the second
most important market for the exports of the United States and
the fourth ranking supplier of the imports of the United States.[29]

Trade between Japan and the United States has risen
sharply in recent years, its value reaching more than $1 billion
each way by 1959. Every year from 1946-60, Japan has been
buying more from the United States than she has been selling
to the United States. The yearly unfavorable balance of trade
for 1953 and 1954 amounted to more than $400 million U. S.[30]
Japan has been able to bridge the gap because of American aid
and the special procurement expenditures. The United States
sold Japan large quantities of cotton and wheat. The price of
wheat was sometimes lower than the domestic price in the
United States, because surplus wheat was involved.[31] Among
Japan's exports to the United States, 15 per cent was cotton
textiles in 1956. Although Japanese cotton textiles amounted
to only 2 per cent of the total cotton textile production in the
United States, there has been an outcry from the textile producers in the United States against Japanese products, on the
grounds that they have had to contend with the unfair competition
of low Japanese labor costs. In 1957 the Tariff Commission
of the United States made a recommendation to double the
tariff rates on some cotton textile products, for instance vel-
veteens. However, this was turned down by President Eisen-
hower, as the Japanese government had agreed to put voluntary quotas on shipments of cotton textiles to the United
States. There are now similar quantity quotas on Japan's exports of sewing machines, tuna fish products, plywood, and
several other items. As a consequence, in 1956, while the
cotton textile mills in the United States were in full operation,

some Japanese mills were partially idle. [32]

Japan's exports to the United States are subject to higher
tariffs than in the 1930's. This is not due to any changes in
the tariff rates of the United States, but rather to the changes
in the types of Japanese exports. In 1934-36, only 30 per
cent of Japan's exports were subject to duty because they
were mainly raw silk and a few other items of raw materials
on which the duties were low or nonexistent. The raw silk
market in the United States has since declined due to the
competition of rayon and other synthetics. Now Japan's exports to the United States include, largely, manufactures on
which the tariff rates are high. In 1956, about 87 per cent
of the value of Japan's exports to the United States was
dutiable. [33]

Trade between Japan and the United States will continue
to grow because there will continue to be a good market in
the United States for low cost Japanese products and Japan's
need of capital goods, foodstuffs, and certain industrial raw
materials from the United States will also persist. However,
Japan's ability to import from the United States is limited by
the shortage of American dollars. This lack has already
caused Japan to try to buy from the sterling area. Japan's
exports to the United States will grow, but there are also
limiting factors, such as tariffs and the voluntary quotas.
It is very likely that the unfavorable balance of trade will continue for Japan.

As Japan has become increasingly industrialized, and her
exports of manufactures began to increase, Japan has come
into competition with the United States in certain kinds of
commodities in the third country markets--for instance in
Asia. The Tariff Commission of the United States made a
study of this in 1958 by comparing the 1935-36 share of the
United States in the total exports of the United States and
Japan with the 1954-55 share of the United States in the combined exports of the two countries. For commodities such as
cotton cloth, iron and steel products, internal combustion engines, and toys, the United States has either maintained her
share or has improved her share in the total exports of the
two countries. But for commodities such as rayon fabrics,

textile machinery, sewing machines, and cameras, the United
States has lost ground, with Japan taking an increasing share
of the total exports of the two countries. [34] It is safe to say
that with lower labor costs and certain geographical advantages, Japan will continue to be a formidable competitor of
the United States in certain fields.

Trade with South and Southeast Asia

While Japan has suffered losses in the trade with mainland China, Korea, and Formosa, and her trade with Asia as
a whole has declined, her trade with South and Southeast Asia
has expanded in the postwar period. In 1938, South and Southeast Asia supplied 14. 9 per cent of Japan's imports, but in
1959, the amount was 16 per cent. In 1938, South and Southeast Asia took 15. 9 per cent of Japan's exports, but in 1959,
20. 3 per cent. Japan now considers this area as an increasingly important market for her goods and a source of supply
for her foodstuffs and raw materials. For instance, Japan's
exports to Hong Kong, Malaya, and Singapore, the Philippines,
and Thailand, and her imports from these countries in 1959, were
larger than those in 1938, both in absolute and relative
figures. In the 1930's, Japan's exports to this area were
mainly agricultural products and light industrial manufactures, but now capital goods are included. Of course here,
Japan faces the competition of the United States, Great Britain, and European countries, as well as Communist China.
Japan has done very well in this area, selling sewing machines,
cameras, binoculars, bicycles, toys, pencils, pottery, and
other commodities which can be produced efficiently in small
size factories. There are also limiting factors in Japan's
trade in South and Southeast Asia. Although this area has
gained political independence, it is still not yet entirely economically independent. Countries in this area still receive
large amounts of grants and aid from their former mother
countries, and therefore their trade still follows the traditional direction with their former protectors. For instance,
the Philippines in 1954 sold 72. 7 per cent of her exports to
the United States, and bought 67. 6 per cent of her imports
from the United States, as compared with 82. 7 per cent and
68. 4 per cent, respectively, in 1938. India, in 1954, still sold

33 per cent of her exports to Great Britain and bought 25 per cent of her imports from Great Britain, and the corresponding figures for 1938 were 34. 4 per cent and 31. 0 per cent. Burma, in 1954, still sold 6. 4 per cent of her exports to Great Britain and bought 25 per cent of her imports from Great Britain, and the corresponding figures were 14 per cent and 28 per cent for 1938. [35] Countries in this area often have difficulities making payment for their imports, and they have been buying from the countries where they can obtain grants and aid. Japan has made some loans and investments in this area, but she is still not in a position to make grants and give aid to these countries.

In competing with the United States, Great Britain, and European countries for the market of capital goods of heavy industries in South and Southeast Asia, Japan has not made too much progress. This is mainly because of Japan's high cost of production for these commodities. Japan is still behind the West in production techniques for most of the capital goods of heavy industries. Material costs may be high for Japan, as materials have to be shipped in from far away sources, and the skill of labor in terms of output per man-hour is still low. Consequently, the market of capital goods of heavy industries in the countries associated with the Economic Commission for Asia and the Far East was divided among the four major sources in the following proportions: 53 per cent for Great Britain, 32 per cent for the United States, 9 per cent for West Germany, and 6 per cent for Japan. It will probably be some years before Japan can command a more impressive share of the market of capital goods of heavy industries in this area. [36]

Japanese businessmen are looking longingly toward the nations of Southeast Asia as ripe targets for their country's export drive. Already, Asia is the largest continental customer for Japanese goods. Asian countries bought 32 per cent of Japan's exports in 1961. North America bought 30 per cent. The proximity of industrialized Japan to the Asian continent, and the fact that she uses much of the raw materials exported by Southeast Asian lands, give Japan a marked advantage over trade competitors for Asian markets.

Among the Southeast Asian countries, Hong Kong is the leading importer of Japanese goods, followed by the Philippines, Thailand, Indonesia, India, Formosa, and South Korea. Each of these nations bought more than $100 million of Japanese goods in 1961. Of the Southeast Asian nations selling goods to Japan, Malaya leads the list,followed by the Philippines, India, Formosa, Thailand, and Indonesia. During his trip to India, Pakistan, Burma, and Thailand in November, 1961, Japanese Premier Ikeda repeatedly emphasized to the leaders of these countries that Japan's economic future depended on the prosperity of Southeast Asia. He said Japan must increase her exports to the area if she is to meet her economic goal of doubling the national income within ten years.

Japan now uses direct loans, yen credit, deferred payments, and private investments to help develop its markets. A United States businessman, Joseph Reday, in a recent article, claims that much of Asian bulk buying from Japan is being done with United States funds, in spite of "Buy American" restrictions. He also points out that Japan finances some Southeast Asian buying with wartime reparations payments. According to Reday, cheap freight charges and fast and frequent sailing help Japan as an exporter to the countries of Southeast Asia.

Goods bought by the Southeast Asian countries from Japan consisted mainly of machinery, textiles, steel and other metals, chemicals, and foodstuffs in 1961. Sales of trucks, motorcycles, and cars to India, Thailand, and South Vietnam increased in 1961, as did sales of ships to the Philippines, railroad equipment to Formosa and Burma, and machinery to Hong Kong and Pakistan.[37] The exports from Southeast Asian nations to Japan consisted mainly of iron ore, timber, sugar, and mineral fuels.

Trade with Latin America, Africa, and Australia

The increase of Japan's trade with Latin America has occurred mainly in Argentina and Brazil, where Japan has established a bilateral clearing system to facilitate payments

for international trade. The increase of trade with Africa was
due to the trade activities in Liberia, which took about 50 per
cent of Japan's exports to Africa. The increase of trade with
Australia was due largely to Japan's increased purchases of
wool and wheat there. [38]

Trade with the Communist Bloc

Japan is now carrying on a small volume of trade with the
countries of the Communist Bloc. The total value of this trade
with the Soviet Union, mainland China, and eastern Europe
came to about $300 million in 1960, a relatively small part of
Japan's total trade of over $10 billion.

The largest part of this trade is with the Soviet Union and
is composed mostly of Japanese machinery, metals and metal
products, in exchange for Russian petroleum, wood, and other
raw materials. A large increase in trade with the Soviet
Union seems unlikely at this time, although recently the Soviet
Union has been pressing for major increases in Japan's imports of petroleum.

Trade with Mainland China

In the postwar period, there has been a great decline of
Japan's trade with mainland China. In 1938, Japan sold 43.0
per cent of her exports to mainland China, and bought 21.1
per cent of her imports from China. In 1959, the corresponding figures were 0.01 per cent and 0.5 per cent. This loss has
been detrimental to the economy of Japan, as it is viewed not
only as a loss of the market for her exports, but also as a loss
of a source of essential supplies such as cotton yarn from
Shanghai, iron, coal, soybeans, and foodstuffs from Manchuria.
What Japan cannot obtain from mainland China, she will have
to buy from elsewhere. The United States has replaced mainland China as the supplier of these commodities. Of course,
this has caused an increase in the transportation costs for
Japan.

This loss of trade with mainland China was mainly due to

Table 38

The United States and Mainland China
as Sources of Supplies to Japan
(in percentage of Japan's total imports of commodities)

		Soybeans Mainland	Coal	Mainland	Iron Ore	Mainland	Salt	Mainl
	U.S.	China	U.S.	China	U.S.	China	U.S.	Chi
1934-36	....	71.3	...	68.4	...	26.0	...	2
1950	43.4	56.5	13.9	58.8	...	18.7	2.3	
1951	93.7	2.6	70.9	1.1	53.6	1.3	10.6	
1952	85.5	0.4	70.2	0.9	35.8	0.8	7.0	
1953	91.1	3.6	82.7	3.8	10.8	0.9	...	

Source: Shigeru Fujii, Japan's Trade and her Level of Living, T
          1955, pp. 46-57.

two factors: Communist occupation of mainland China and the Uni
Nations embargo against China. Japan is one of the fifteen memb
of the committee in charge of embargo measures. There are am
Japanese merchants some who are very active in trying to re-
establish trade with mainland China. Political organizations wer
formed with this end in view: for instance, the Japan-China Expo
Import Association and the Diet Members League for Promotion o
Japan-China Trade. Japanese merchants visited Communist Chin
and in 1952, 1953, and 1955, unofficial trade agreements were
signed between Japanese merchant groups with the state trade cor
porations of Communist China. Sino-Japanese trade was broken
off in 1958 over Japan's refusal to grant official status and guaran
tees to Red China's trade missions. Toyko has maintained the
position that Peking's insistence upon an intergovernmental agree
ment is unreasonable and that trade can only be resumed if it is
free of political strings: that is, without de facto recognition of
Red China. Trade reopened in 1960 in the value of less than $25
million and increased to about $50 million in 1961, which is
trifling compared to the prewar trade. There have been some
attempts by the two countries to develop trade since December, 1
The West Japan Federation of Trading Cooperation Unions con-

cluded a substantial contract with China for importing pig iron, magnesium, and cashmere wool, in return for exporting maleicanhydride. The Nippon Steel and Tubing Company, one of Japan's big three, will export 28. 5 tons of ferrochrome alloy in the first such deal by a major steel company since 1958. Kanichi Inayama of Yawata Steel, a prime leader in the steel industry, said recently his firm was ready to sell to Red China under existing conditions. In February, 1961, the Nisshin Trading Company signed a contract with the Red Chinese for 1, 000 tons each of pig iron and fluorspar. In addition, the cast metal industry has received permission to import 2, 000 tons of iron ore in exchange for galvanized sheet, ferro-alloy, and crude steel. The steel industry was said to have hopes of selling 200, 000 tons of iron and steel to Red China in 1961. The industry is also considering importing coal and iron ore from China instead of from the United States because of the substantial difference in price. At a time when the Japanese ammonium sulphate industry was hard hit by the United States decision to cut in half her purchases in Japan, Red China offered to buy 150, 000 tons of fertilizer. The deal did not go through, but the industry, which at one time sent 80 per cent of its exports to mainland China, still looks to that country as a principal market. Japanese shipbuilders are interested in meeting Red China's requirements of two to three million tons of new ships because Japan has been suffering from its worst postwar depression, despite the fact that Japan led the world in tonnage in 1960. The prospect of fat contracts from any quarter naturally arouses interest. [39]

Businessmen in many parts of the Far East think that Japan is inching closer and closer toward resuming commercial relations with Red China. Ever since Sino-Japanese trade was suspended by Peking in the Spring of 1958, its resumption has been a hot issue. The problem is now urgent because, under Japan's new plan for doubling her gross national product by 1970, exports will have to increase from the present $4 billion to $9 billion a year. This is at a time when Japan's best market, the United States, is becoming less hospitable, and competition for other available markets is becoming keener. [40] In Toyko, pressure for resuming full scale trade with China is becoming formidable.

Japanese merchants hope to regain the trade of China in volume similar to the prewar level. There are some doubts as to the possibility of restoration of Japan-China trade to the prewar level. First, China has become gradually self-sufficient in certain items which she used to buy from Japan: for instance, cotton textiles. China may want to protect her own textile industry, and therefore she may not want to buy such large quantities as she did before the war. Second, China's ability to increase exports to Japan is limited. China's exports are still largely agricultural and industrial raw materials. Because of her huge population and her needs for industrialization, she does not have a large surplus of materials to export. Whatever materials surplus she has, she will export to Russia and the Communist Bloc countries for capital goods and equipment. China's exports to Japan will be limited; therefore, her capacity to import from Japan will also be limited. Japan can still export large amounts of supplies to Communist China if Japan is willing to grant long term credits. This, at the moment, is difficult for Japan to do. Third, Communist China has reoriented her trade so that 75 per cent to 80 per cent of her trade goes to the Communist bloc.

Communist China would look for sources of capital goods and supplies first from the Communist bloc and then from the West. Even if Communist China decides to buy from the West, capital goods from Great Britain and Western Germany are preferred because their prices are usually lower than Japanese products. Therefore, even if the embargo is lifted, the future of trade between Japan and Communist China will be limited. Without restrictions, the trade of the two countries will be moderately improved, of course. [41]

Communist China, being fully aware of the potentiality of its trade with Japan, has vigorously been using the trade issue as a propaganda tool, and much has been made of Japan's ties with the United States as an obstacle to the trade with China. As long as Japan remains able to obtain adequate sources of raw materials and good markets for its expanding industries, the present pattern of close relations with the West will not be disrupted. The Japanese government, however, would want to encourage trade with Com-

munist China when and where it is possible to do so without en-
dangering Japan's position with its Western allies and trading
partners.

COMPOSITION OF TRADE

Composition of Japan's Exports

The different classifications of commodities comprising
the exports of Japan are arranged here according to their importance: manufactured goods and articles, machinery, transportation equipment, foodstuffs, chemicals, and inedible
crude materials. If all the industrial products, such as manufactured goods and articles, machinery, transportation equipment, and chemicals, are put together, they occupy about 90
per cent of Japan's exports. It is a clear indication of the
high degree of industrialization that has been achieved in
Japan. Unlike most of the Pacific countries, her exports of
foodstuffs and crude raw materials have declined in importance when compared with prewar days.

Manufactured goods are still the most important classification of her exports. They include: plywood; textile yarn
and thread; cotton, silk, woolen, and synthetic fabrics;
non-metallic manufactures; iron and steel; and metallic
manufactures. Japan has been remarkably successful in ad-
justing her iron and steel industry to profound changes, including the disruption of former channels of material supply
and the loss of former markets in mainland China, Formosa,
and Korea. Since 1952, she has done much to overcome technical deficiencies. The market conditions for Japan's manufactures goods have been good. Japan has not yet been faced
with stiff price competition from the Western powers, as the
latter have not yet started any serious trade drive in the Far
East. [42] Among the manufactured goods, textile and fabrics
have declined in importance, but plywood, nonmetallic manufactures, iron and steel, and metallic manufactures have gained
in importance. In 1929, textile yarn and fabrics occupied 70
per cent of Japan's exports in value; in 1936, they occupied
52 per cent, and in 1959, only 22 per cent. The latter group
of manufactured goods occupied, in 1929, 4 per cent of Japan's

exports in value; in 1936 they occupied 14 per cent, and in
1959, 21.2 per cent. [43]

Machinery and transportation equipment have made more
progress than any other group and have become the second
most important classification of Japan's exports. In 1934-36,
they occupied only 7.1 per cent of the total exports in value,
and in 1959, 23.4 per cent. As an exporter of capital goods,
Japan is far behind the three main heavy-industry nations:
the United States, the United Kingdom, and West Germany.
The percentage of exports of capital goods for these three nations accounts for about 80 per cent. Capital goods exported
by Japan include sewing machines, electric appliances and
machinery, motor vehicles, and ships. Since 1956, Japan
has become the world's largest producer of ships, substantially exceeding Great Britain in tonnage completed. Some
of her shipyards are equipped to construct the largest tankers in the Pacific (of 100,000 dead weight tonnage). [44] She
certainly has come a long way in becoming a major exporter
of capital goods.

About 16.4 per cent of Japan's exports in 1959 was miscellaneous manufactured articles such as clothing, footwear,
instruments, chinaware, binoculars, cameras, toys, pearls,
jewelery, artificial flowers, and other articles. [45] Her binoculars, cameras, and other precision instruments are low in
price and fairly good in quality. They have found good markets throughout the world. Her pottery and ceramics are
selling well in the Far East. [46]

Foodstuffs still occupied 7.3 per cent of Japan's exports
in value in 1959. They were mainly tuna fish, crab meat, tea,
and other canned goods. A large part of her foodstuffs was exported to the United States. [47]

Japan's chemical industry has made good progress in the
postwar period. In 1949, Japan succeeded in restoring chemical industry to the prewar output level. In 1956, her annual
output of ammonium sulphate was more than twice the annual
output of 1936, and Japan started to export chemical fertilizers at the international market prices (which were lower
than her domestic prices). However, the future of this aspect

of her chemical industry is very bright because production can be based upon domestic supplies of raw materials and electric power. Other branches of her chemical industry are also making progress, but there are raw material problems. For instance, in the case of caustic soda and soda ash, the raw materials came from mainland China in the prewar days. Now they have to be obtained from India, Aden, and North Africa. Consequently, Japan still does not have a chance to compete in the world market, due to high costs. [48]

All in all, Japan has made tremendous progress in her international trade. The composition of her exports is an illustration of this fact. As an exporter of manufactured products and capital goods, she is competing among nations of advanced economy in highly technical fields. She certainly can be expected to improve the living standards of her people through trade.

Composition of Japan's Imports

The different classifications of Japan's imports are arranged here according to their importance: inedible crude materials, mineral fuels and lubricants, foodstuffs, machinery, transportation equipment, chemicals, manufactured goods, beverages, and tobacco. Compared with prewar days, foodstuffs declined in importance, probably because agricultural improvements have enabled Japan to achieve self-sufficiency. Japan's imports concentrate heavily on crude materials, mineral fuels, lubricants, machinery, and transportation equipment because of the rapid industrialization program that has been going on in the postwar period.

In recent years about one half of the value of Japan's imports has been crude raw materials: for instance soybeans,, natural rubber, wool, cotton, iron ore and concentrates, iron and steel scraps. Two thirds of the soybeans imported came from the United States and one third from Communist China. [49] Natural rubber came mainly from Southeast Asian countries; wool mainly from Australia; and cotton, iron ore and concentrates, iron and steel scraps came, largely, from the United States. Cotton, before the war, was a very important import, but now its position has declined due to the development of

synthetic fibers which can be produced at home.[50] Over half
of the imports of crude oil came from the dollar area, and
about two thirds of the machinery came from the United
States.[51] Japan is an importer of coal. Her own coal is of a
low quality not suitable for coking purpose. During the 1930's,
Japan imported one tenth of her home supply from China, but
now she imports from the United States.[52] Although Japan is
importing less foodstuffs than before, she still depends on foreign sources for about one fifth of her supply. The foodstuffs
imports consist mainly of rice, wheat, barley, corn, other
cereals, and sugar. Her imports of sugar have exceeded the
1934-36 level in value.[53] Foodstuffs now come largely from
the United States, Canada, Australia, and some Southeast
Asian countries instead of the prewar sources of mainland
China and Korea.

The fact that Japan's imports of machinery and transportation equipment are still gaining in importance shows that
Japan's industries have not yet attained the level of Western
powers, and that she still depends on imports for her capital goods and equipment.

BALANCE OF PAYMENTS FOR JAPAN

On the whole the picture of the balance of payments for
Japan is encouraging. In the three years 1958-60, Japan received more payments from foreign countries for her goods
and services than she paid out. There was a deficit in 1961
for the goods and services account, but a balance in 1962.
These, plus the special purchases of the United Nations and
the United States for their military and civilian personnel
stationed in Japan and for maintaining bases, and some private donations, have made it possible for Japan to send investments abroad, to pay reparations, to fulfill her official
obligations, and to build up a reserve in pounds sterling,
American dollars, and gold. There is no critical shortage
of foreign exchange, and the foreign-exchange controls have
been gradually liberalized. A brief explanation of Table 42
on the Balance of Payments for Japan, appended at the end
of this chapter, is given item by item as follows:

Goods and Services

These include all the transactions of goods and services performed by governments or private businessmen between Japan and other nations.

Exports, f. o. b, are based on trade returns. However, the figures given here are smaller than the trade returns figures because certain deductions have been taken from the trade figures to account for exports sent out without bringing in payments: for instance, samples, goods for advertising, and goods returned for refunds. This discrepancy between the value of exports given in Table 37 on the direction of trade and the value of exports given in the table on payments exists in all other chapters throughout the book.

Imports, f. o. b, are also based on trade returns, but are smaller because similar deductions have been taken from the trade figures to those for exports. Furthermore, the trade figures for imports are c. i. f. value, which includes the freight and insurance. Imports in this table are f. o. b value with the freight and insurance deducted, because the freight and insurance are treated separately. This accounts for the fact that while trade returns show imports exceeding exports for the entire postwar period, the balance of payments show exports exceeding imports in 1958-60. This discrepancy exists throughout the book.

Freight and Insurance

Japan uses foreign shipping and insurance services, as other nations use Japan's services. Here the table shows net outpayments to foreign nations, indicating Japan still does not have adequate shipping and insurance facilities to handle her trade. In the 1930's, Japan had a strong merchant fleet of over 6 million tons, but it was all destroyed during World War II, with about 1. 3 million tons of obsolete ships left in 1945. Good progress has been made in rebuilding her shipping facilities, and by 1956 she had 3. 8 million tons, of which two fifths was under five years old. [54] As her shipbuilding industry is functioning efficiently, it probably will be only a matter of time before these net payments for transportation and services can be saved.

Government, n.i.e.

This item means government purchases not included elsewhere. It has been most important in balancing international
payments for Japan. It has earned foreign exchange for Japan
to pay for most of the import surplus in the postwar period,
and it was responsible for turning the balance for goods and
services into a favorable one in 1958-60.

This item includes goods and services sold to military personnel and foreign diplomats stationed in Japan, those sold to
the United Nations forces under the special procurement program, and those sold to the United States and Great Britain for
maintaining their forces in Japan. Japan's purchases from
foreign countries to maintain her diplomats abroad are deducted from this item. As long as military bases are maintained by the United States in Japan, this item will continue to
help Japan to earn foreign exchange. [55]

Private Transfers

This item covers all personal and institutional remittances in cash and in kind. It declined greatly in 1950, and
since then there has been a slight increase. It totaled only 20
billion yen in 1962, but it is a source of some foreign exchange.

Private Capital

It includes the sale of securities to foreigners, the pur -
chases of securities from foreigners, incoming and outgoing
contractual payments, long-term loans received by private
companies and foreign companies, and long-term loans extended to them. Private capital has fluctuated in the postwar
period, as Japan has had large amounts of foreign investments
coming in, and also investments going out. During the period
1950-56, the net receipt of foreign private capital averaged
about 25 million U. S. dollars annually. Foreign investments
in Japan as of 1957 totaled about 320 million U. S. dollars,
mainly from the United States. The amount has been small.
A major obstacle is the Japanese Foreign Investment Law

which permits the repatriation of equity capital only over a
seven year period: That is, there is an initial waiting period
of two years, after which one fifth of the capital can be repatriated
each year. [56]

Since the mid-50's Japan has begun investing private capital
in Southeast Asia. The capital formation in Southeast Asia
ranges from 5 per cent to 10 per cent, while it ranges in
Japan from 15 per cent to 20 per cent of the nation's national
income. There has always been a lack of capital in Southeast Asia, and Japan's private capital has begun to move in.
Japan has investments in tin mines in Indonesia; iron ore
mines in India, Goa, and Malaya; copper mines in the Philippines; and hydroelectric power plants in Vietnam. The investments are aimed at developing new sources of raw
materials to provide steady supplies for industries, sometimes at prices lower than the international market.
Premier Kishi, in 1958, proposed a large project of providing capital investments for Southeast Asia, and he hoped to
interest the United States in making capital investments for
the development of this area. [57]

Government Transfers

This item is a balance between the United States aid received by Japan, in the positive, against the reparation payments paid by Japan to other countries, in the negative. This
item was in the positive for the period 1948-52, as Japan received large amounts of United States aid, amounting to U.S.
$2 billion. United States aid stopped in 1952, and Japan since
then has been on a self-sustaining basis. This item has turned
into negative ever since 1955, as Japan began to make reparation payments. [58]

A peace agreement was signed between Japan and Burma,
requiring Japan to pay reparations of $200 million U.S. goods and
services in the next ten years and to provide $50 million U. S.
for joint enterprises. A similar agreement was signed with
Thailand, providing a reparation of $41 million U.S. A peace
agreement was signed with the Philippines in 1956, to provide
for a reparation of $550 million U. S. to be made in capital
goods over a period of twenty years and to offer a loan of $250

million for economic development.   Another agreement was
signed with Indonesia to provide for a reparation of $225 mil-
lion U.S. to be paid in twelve years, to renounce a trade debt
of $175 million U.S. owed by Indonesia, and to advance a
loan of $400 million U.S. over a period of twenty years.   The
total settlement with Asian countries in reparations and
in loans will add up to about $1.5 billion U.S., to be paid in
the next twenty year period in the 1950's and 1960's.[59]   This
will prove to be a burden for Japan for years to come.

Government Capital (net)

This item includes net drawings or repayments on loans
from the International Bank for Reconstruction and Development, Foreign Operations Administrations, and International
Co-operation Administration. Net drawings are in payments,
in the positive, resulting in larger official long-term liabilities
for Japan, while net repayments are in the negative, reducing
the long-term official liabilities. From 1949-53, Japan made
net repayments, but from 1954-60, Japan had net drawings
from these institutions.

Short-Term Liabilities (net)

Commercial bank assets and liabilities include outstanding export and import pre-payments, import credit received
and export credits extended. Monetary authority transactions
include net drawings from, or re-payments to, the International
Monetary Fund, other payment agreement funds and other assets, and the purchases or sales of foreign exchange and gold
by the government. Figures in Table 39 are mostly in the
negative, indicating out-payments made by the government for
the purchase of foreign exchange and gold to increase their
reserves. As a result, Japan has been able to increase her
reserves of pounds and sterling, American dollars, and gold.
The Tariff Commission of the United States gives Japan's
aggregate reserves of foreign exchange and gold, as of the
different years, in Table 39.

Considering all the factors against Japan at the end of
World War II--the loss of shipping facilities, the loss of
foreign investments, and the exhaustion of her holdings of

Table 39

Japan's Holdings of Gold and Foreign Exchange
(millions of U. S. dollars)

Dec. 31	Gold	Foreign Exchange	Total
1950	7	562	569
1951	10	916	926
1952	16	1149	1165
1953	18	999	1017
1954	21	1109	1130
1955	23	1448	1471
1956	23	1623	1646
1957	...	...	...
1958	54	946	1000
1959	...	...	...
1960	247	1577	1824
1961	287	1199	1486
1962	289	1553	1842
1963	289	1589	1878
1964	304	1495	1799

Source: The Tariff Commission of the United States, Postwar
Development in Japanese Foreign Trade, p. 119

foreign exchange--she certainly has come a long way in this
short period of time. She has been able to meet her international obligations, and in addition, she has accumulated holdings
of gold and foreign currencies close to two billion U. S. dollars.

SYSTEM OF TRADE CONTROLS

The commercial policy of Japan aims at the promotion of
exports to balance the merchandise trade, to secure an adequate
supply of necessary foodstuffs and industrial raw materials, to
avoid shortages of American dollars and pounds sterling, and to

foster economic growth at home. There are the usual
measures for these purposes, such as tariffs, foreign-
exchange controls, the supervision of exports, and trade corporations.

Tariffs

The collection of import duties was suspended for several
years after the surrender. The tariffs in effect at the present
time were adopted in 1954, and were modified on a few occasions. The rates are generally more moderate than those before World War II. In recent years, they have provided less
than 5 per cent of government revenues. With a few exceptions,
the import duties are levied on an ad valorem basis. About one
fifth of the items enumerated in the tariff law, largely raw materials, are duty free. The rates of duty on the remaining
items range from 5 per cent to 50 per cent ad valorem. About
a fourth of the dutiable items are subject to 15 per cent
ad valorem. About half of the dutiable items are subject to
rates higher than that and about a fourth to rates lower. Duty-
free treatment or rates of 15 per cent or lower apply to
various raw materials, foodstuffs, medicines, chemicals,
live animals, crude oil, plants, and paper products. Rates
of duty deemed to be protective--for instance, from 20 per cent
to 35 per cent--are common for manufactured goods similar to
the types produced in Japan and for goods whose production
Japan seeks to encourage, such as plastics, synthetic resins,
articles of clothing, watches, cars, and certain types of
machinery. The highest rates, from 40 per cent to 50 per
cent ad valorem, apply to luxury items such as beer, wine,
alcoholic beverages, furs, cosmetics, perfumes, toilet articles,
playing cards, and jewelry.[60]

Sometimes the regular rates of tariffs may be temporarily
exempted by the Japanese Government to facilitate the import-
tation of urgently needed materials and supplies. For instance, in 1956 and 1957, by special authorization of the
government, these commodities were imported free of duty:
aircraft engines and parts, certain types of steel plates,
petroleum, coke, statistical and accounting machines, certain
types of lumber products, rice, barley, wheat, soybeans,
skimmed milk, and carbon black.[61]

Because of the peace treaties with the Allied Powers, bilateral trade agreements providing for the most favored nation treatment, and the General Agreement on Trade and Tariffs (GATT), of which Japan has been a member since 1951, Japan has reduced the tariffs on the commodities of a large number of countries. But there are still a few countries which are not members of the GATT, or which do not have peace agreements or bilateral trade agreements with Japan. To these countries, the regular tariff rates apply. Among these countries are French South Africa, New Zealand, Rhodesia, Nyasaland, Cuba, and Haiti.[62] Among the members of the GATT, there are about fourteen countries which invoked Article 35 of the Agreement to prevent tariffs from being reduced on Japan's trade. To these countries, the regular tariff rates apply. Among this group are Great Britain, Australia, New Zealand, the Union of South Africa, India, Belgium, the Netherlands, Luxemburg, France, and Brazil. Of course, for countries which have high protective tariffs against Japanese goods, Japan also has correspondingly high retaliatory rates.[63]

Foreign-Exchange Controls

In 1953, a single rate of exchange was established--at 360 yen to one American dollar. Foreign exchange is controlled by the government. All export proceeds in foreign currencies must be sold to the government, and all imports are licensed by the government. Licenses for imports not requiring foreign exchange are issued by the Ministry of International Trade and Industry, and licenses for imports needing foreign exchanges are issued by the Foreign Exchange Council. The Council has a foreign-exchange budget for the year and uses it as a basis for making decisions on the use of foreign exchange.[64]

Before 1955, Japan sometimes had a shortage of American dollars, and sometimes a shortage of pounds sterling. Also, there were, at times, difficulties in converting pounds to dollars or vice versa. Consequently, Japan followed a policy of maintaining international payment ballances with the dollar bloc and the sterling bloc separately. Japan does not have to maintain an international payment

balance with any one country of the sterling bloc so long as
the international payments with the sterling bloc as a group
are balanced. The same applies to the dollar bloc. For
countries such as Thailand, Korea, Formosa, and Indonesia,
which do not belong to either the sterling bloc or the dollar
bloc, Japan had open accounts arrangements with them.
These countries are also often referred to as the open
accounts countries. Japan's commercial policy with the open
accounts countries was to maintain a bilateral payment balance with each one of them. With each one of these countries,
Japan will buy only so much from it as she can sell to it.
Bilateral clearing accounts were established with each of
them, and virtually all settlements must be made through the
accounts. Any payments imbalance with the open accounts
countries was to be settled in dollars or in pounds. For the
Communist countries, Japan applied barter trade, which
means that there was not only the yearly balance of payments
with a Communist country but also a balance for each barter
transaction between the imports and exports. Of course, all
these measures helped Japan to achieve a balance of payments
and relieve the shortage of foreign currencies, but they certainly meant restrictions on trade and created material shortages. By 1956, when Japan's foreign-exchange situation was
improved, all these restrictions were gradually removed.
Both the barter system and the open accounts arrangements
were discontinued. There is no longer the need to restrict
trade in order to maintain payment balance for any single
transaction or with any particular country so long as there is
no over-all foreign-exchange shortage. In 1957, about 24 per
cent of the total imports was approved under routine procedures without any formal review or specific quantitative
controls. 65

Before 1955, Japan also practiced a link system of exports and imports. There were two kinds of links: the direct
link and the raw material link. The direct link was to allow
the exporter of certain commodities to import certain commodities. For instance, in 1953, the Ministry of International Trade and Industry authorized the exporters of
ships, rolling stocks, machine tools, sulphur, pencillin,
streptomycin, and whale oil to import sugar, bananas, canned pineapple, and whiskey. This is because sugar, bananas,

canned pineapple, and whiskey are luxury items and are
priced very high in Japan. Merchants wanted to import
them for high profit, but the government would not approve
their applications for foreign exchange for this purpose.
When the government, in 1953, allowed the exporters of ships,
rolling stocks, and the above mentioned commodities to use
their foreign-exchange proceeds to import luxury items, the
government actually gave them the high profit monopoly of
these imports. This should be interpreted as an export
subsidy.

The raw material link was to allow the exporters of manufactures to use part of their foreign-exchange proceeds to
import the parts and materials needed for the production of
their commodities. For instance, exporters of ships may be
allowed certain conveniences in importing ship's engines and
equipment. Both types of the link system originated in the
days when there was a shortage of foreign exchange. That is,
a merchant would have to earn foreign exchange before he
could import certain commodities. By 1956, when the foreign-
exchange situation improved, the link system was gradually
abolished. That is, when the government had enough foreign
exchange to allow most of the merchants to import most of
the commodities of their choice, the link system had lost its
purpose. [66]

Supervision of Exports

In 1960 Japan adopted a plan for trade and exchange liberalization and by 1963, for items making up to about 90 per cent
in value of its imports, permits were granted more or less
automatically. Since April, 1963, foreign-owned funds in
free yen accounts can be withdrawn at any time, and most kinds
of capital can be withdrawn without the waiting period formerly
required. The controls of trade that remain are the requirement of government permission for foreign investment and the
limitation on the extent of foreign ownership. As a result of
the liberalization policy, for the first time since the 1930's
the tariff is to become the principal means of import control.
This reflects Japan's confidence in its industrial productivity
to compete with foreign producers and in its improving balance
of payments position in recent years. [67]

In order to promote exports, the Japanese government
exercises certain degrees of supervision over the exports.
Since 1956, Japan has applied voluntary quantitative limits to
the exports of textiles, tuna fish products, plywood, and a
number of other exports to the United States, in order to prevent the United States from applying special higher tariffs on
these Japanese goods. If the United States had increased
tariffs on these commodities, the Japanese government might
have had to impose retaliatory tariffs on American goods, and
eventually both countries would suffer loss in trade. To promote general trade between the two countries, Japan decided
to apply certain restrictions on specific items. The Japanese
government also exercises spot checking on the quality of exports in order to protect her markets abroad. The Japanese
government, furthermore, inspects prices of exports and
does not allow them to rise too high, for fear of losing out to
foreign competitors for markets, nor does she allow them to
drop too low, for fear of the outcry of dumping from the countries of destination for these exports. On some thirty commodities
Japan faces keen competition from foreign countries, and their
price inspection has been done most carefully.

PROSPECTS

The trade of Japan has undergone a phenomenal rebirth
from the defeat of 1945-60. Through the hard work and in-
genuity of the people, Japan has not only become the leading
nation in trade in the Pacific, but has come into close competition with the industrial powers of the world. This is an
amazing demonstration of the wisdom and business ability of a
physically small country. What is the future prospect of the
rapidly expanding trade of Japan? Will it continue to expand
by leaps and bounds? What are the factors in her favor, and
what are the factors against her? Factors favoring the expansion of Japan's trade are given as follows.

Low Labor Costs

Japan has an adequate labor force with commendable
training and skill. The wages paid to Japanese industrial
workers in recent years have averaged about 25 cents U. S.

currency per hour, or about one seventh of the rate paid in
the United States. Of course, the productivity of Japanese
labor is also lower than that of the United States. In balancing the wage against the productivity, the average unit labor
cost for Japan is still lower than that of the United States. [68]
That is, for most industries, comparing only the labor cost,
Japan enjoys a superior position in competing with the United
States and the major industrial powers in the West. Japan
certainly will continue to exploit this advantage in concentrating on those industrial fields where labor is the major cost
factor. In the postwar years, Japan has witnessed a substantial rise in the money wage; however, its increase in wages
has lagged behind the rise in labor productivity, and this
perhaps explains the strong potentiality still possessed by
Japanese export commodities in competing with the West.

Table 40

Productivity and Wages Indexes, 1956
(1951=100)

	Industrial Production Employment (A)	Wages (B)	B/A
Japan	167	165	99
United States	112	124	111
England	109	138	127
West Germany	126	136	108
France	138	145	107
Italy	134	123	92

Source: Kiyoshi Matsui, Essays on International Trade,
          Science Council of Japan, Economics Series No. 20,
          Tokyo, 1958, p. 79.

Comparing Japan with the United States and England in the
production of steel ingots and cotton yarn: Although Japan's
labor productivity is low, its level of wages is even lower, and
therefore the result is a low per unit labor cost for Japan. This
will give Japanese products a strong competitive position in the

world market.

Table 41

Productivity and Wages in Steel Ingots, 1952

	Production per person per month (tons)	Wages per week (US$)	Wages per ton (US$)
Japan	3.95	12.57	13.71
United States	14.27	74.60	22.40
England	7.08	28.00	16.95

Productivity and Wages in Spinning Industry, 1951

	Production per person per hour (pounds)	Wages per hour (US cents)	Wages per /- (US cents)
Japan	7.3	13.0	1.8
United States	15.2	132.0	8.6
England	5.2	39.0	7.5

Source: Kiyoshi Matsui, Essays on International Trade,
          Science Council of Japan, Economics Series No. 20,
          Tokyo, 1958, p. 77-78.

As the productivity of Japan still has a long way to go to
catch up with the West, especially the United States, and as
the labor unions are not as well developed, there is still the
possibility that in Japan the increase in productivity will continue
to lag behind the increase of wages and, therefore, the cost
of labor per unit of output in certain fields will remain low.
This would mean continued good prospect for Japan's
trade in its competition with the West in certain respects.

The Large United States Market

Japan has become the third or fourth most important market for the exports, and the fourth most important supplier of the imports, of the United States. Japan has been buying more from the United States than she has been selling to the United States. Neither the United States nor Japan can afford to lose each others' market. The two countries will have to live together and work out their commercial problems to their mutual benefit. Japan's capacity to import from the United States is limited, to be sure, by the shortage of dollars. American aid and special procurement helped in the past. American aid has stopped. Special procurements may still play an important role in the future, as Japan now has an important position in the collective security system in the Pacific. In case of military action or peace preservation activities, Japan's supplies will be utilized. This will give Japan the opportunity to earn foreign-exchange reserves and will help in improving Japan's capacity to import.

New Markets in Africa and Southeast Asia
and South America

Japan's trade drives in these areas have borne fruit. The underdeveloped countries in these areas provide ample markets for Japanese goods, whether capital goods or consumer goods. The low purchasing power of these areas works also in Japan's favor because the people may not be able to afford better quality European or American goods. Resentment against Japan still lingers in the minds of some Asian peoples: the legacy of the Japanese occupation during World War II. The bitterness, however, will be erased in time. At the present time, the fear and suspicion of Asians is no longer against Japan, but against Communist China and the Soviet bloc.

The future of Japan's trade is not entirely bright. There are problems, and some of these may prove to be difficult to solve.

High Cost of Materials

There are fields in which Japan's prices are higher than international markets, and there Japan still loses out in competition. Some of these are cotton yarn, pig iron, steel bar, steel plate, steel sheet, electric copper, electric lead, cement, ammonium sulphate, caustic soda, coal, and electric power. [69] The higher prices are mainly due to the high cost of raw materials which have to be shipped from far away places.

High Cost of Capital and the Small Size of Factories

Japan has been building up her economy with tremendous speed during the postwar period. The capital formation process is in full swing: That is, a high percentage of the national income is being reinvested in business. However, capital accumulation is still not fast enough to meet the needs of investments. Interests rates are still high, and industries are still facing the problem of lack of capital. This may help to explain partially, the fact that factories are still small in size and that obsolete equipment is still being used. This results in lower productivity as compared with the West, especially in fields where a large capital is required and where production can achieve efficiency only when operated on a large scale: for instance, heavy industries producing complicated and expensive capital goods. It will be years before Japan can make improvements in these fields to bring them to the standards of the West. [70]

Elastic Demands for Japan's Exports

Prior to World War II, the major part of Japan's exports was raw materials and consumer goods, the demands for which were inelastic. Therefore, there was a high degree of stability of her exports. Now, with capital goods occupying an increasing portion of Japan's exports, Japan's exports may become more susceptible to the booms and depressions of the countries of destination, because it is only in times of boom that these countries will need large supplies of capital goods. So far, no business fluctuations in these countries have actually affected Japan's exports, which have kept on expanding steadily.

Trade Restrictions

In Asia, Africa, and Latin America, where Japan has de-

veloped a growing trade, there is tendency toward economic
nationalism. Japan faces trade restrictions, foreign-exchange
controls, and investment obstructions. Tariffs tend to be
protective in nature, and policies aim at self-sufficiency and
the growth of home industries. There will be increasing obstacles and red tape in the path of Japanese trading corporations in their activities in these areas.

Competition from the West

The United States, Great Britain, and other European
powers still are doing very well in their trade with the Pacific
countries. They are able to grant aid and long term credits
to the Pacific countries. They are also able to provide training facilities and render technical assistance to the Pacific
countries. Japan has done some of these, but is not in a position to compete with the West in these respects. The Pacific
countries will still have to do a great deal of their trading
with the West where they can obtain credits and assistance.

Underdeveloped Trading Corporations

Trade corporations in Japan are still in the process of
reorganization. In 1955, they had only about 50 per cent of
the assets they possessed in the prewar days.[71] They are
going through consolidation and mergers and are getting
stronger, but they are not in a position to take on the scale of
selling efforts and marketing activities they used to have before the war. The Japanese have not developed a strong position in the retail domestic commerce of the Pacific countries
such as that enjoyed by the Chinese or the Hindus.

The Cold War

The future of Japan's trade with the Communist bloc is
not very bright. This is not a simple matter of embargo,
blockade, or political recognition. Even if all these issues
are cleared away, the trade may still not go back to anything
similar to the prewar level. The Communist countries have
reoriented their trade to buy or sell among themselves, and
trade with the free world is given only secondary importance.

Taking into consideration all the factors in favor of Japan and those against Japan, it is still safe to say that Japan is a major source of capital goods and manufactures and a buyer of foodstuffs and materials. Her trade will keep on expanding and her economy will gain more strength. She is a major trading nation to be reckoned with.

Table 42

Balance of Payments for Japan
(billion of yen)

	1956	1957	1958	1959	1960	1961	1962
Goods and Services	-21	-211	166	140	60	-339	-7
Trade Balance, f.o.b	-45	-142	135	131	97	-201	145
Freight & Insurance	-66	-127	-6	-12	-33	-105	-76
Government, n.i.e.	182	169	146	134	146	137	132
Other Services	-92	-111	-109	-113	-150	-170	-208
Transfers: Private	12	11	13	15	20	21	20
Government	-3	-24	-84	-25	-29	-36	-31
Commercial Banks:							
Liabilities	49	-14	-11	78	215	281	36
Capital: Private	-1	24	13	-29	-36	-7	92
Government	9	1	15	19	10	10	1
Monetary Authority:	-20	197	-122	-175	-179	146	-82
Net IMF position	---	45	-45	-22	---	-20	----
Monetary gold	---	---	-11	-43	---	-9	---
Payment agreement	-8	-13	59	2	5	1	6
Other assests	-21	158	-112	-96	-180	136	-127
Other liabilities	9	7	-13	-16	-4	38	39
Error & Omission	5	1	26	20	12	7	2
Commercial Banks:							
Assests	-30	15	-16	-43	-73	-83	-31

Sources: For 1948-53, see International Monetary Fund, Balanc of Payments Yearbook for 1947-53, Washington, D. C. and same title for 1950-56, section on Japan. For

1956-62, see International Monetary Fund, International Financial Statistics, Washington, D.C., January, 1964, p. 172.

Notes to Chapter 6

1. Economic Commission for Asia and the Far East, Economic Survey of Asia and the Far East, 1961, New York, 1962, pp. 11-12.

2. ibid.

3. Shegito Tsuru, Essays on Japanese Economy (Tokyo: Kinokuniya Bookstore Co., 1958), p. 60 and p. 97. The Planning Agency of Japanese Government in working out Five Year Plan 1956-60 uses $b(Y-Y-_1)$ to calculate gross-capital formation.

4. Joseph E. Haring, "Export Industrialism and Economic Growth," Western Economic Journal, Spring, 1963.

5. George C. Allen, A Short Economic History of Modern Japan 1867-1937 (London: Allen and Unwin, Ltd., 1962), p. 171.

6. Economic Survey of Asia and the Far East, 1957, p. 49.

7. Economic Survey of Asia and the Far East, 1957, p. 56.

8. Economic Planning Agency, Japanese Government, Economic Survey of Japan, Tokyo, 1957.

9. ibid.

10. Ministry of Foreign Affairs, Japanese Government, Statistical Survey of Economy of Japan, Tokyo, 1959, p. 37.

11. ibid. p. 36.

12. Economic Commission for Asia and the Far East, Economic Survey of Asia and the Far East, 1963, New York, 1964, pp. 96-99.

13. Economic Planning Agency, Japanese Government, op. cit. , p. 7.

14. Dentsu Advertising Ltd. , Industrial Japan, Tokyo, 1955, pp. 247-48.

15. Economic Survey of Asia and the Far East, 1958, Bangkok, 1959, p. 70.

16. Richard E. Caves, Trade and Economic Structure, Models and Methods (Cambridge: Harvard University Press, 1963), p. 253.

17. Standard Trade Index of Japan, 1964, Tokyo, 1965.

18. Japan Trade Guide, 1960, pp. 164-65.

19. The Mainichi Newspapers, Industries of Japan, Tokyo, 1962, pp. 11-14.

20. ibid.

21. Industries of Japan, op. cit. , p. 15.

22. George C. Allen, Japan's Economic Recovery (London: Oxford University Press, 1958), pp. 163-64.

23. G. N. Ganguli, India's Economic Relations (Bombay: Orient Longmans, 1956), p. 152.

24. Allen, Japan's Economic Recovery, pp. 164-70.

25. loc. cit.

26. United Nations, International Monetary Fund and International Bank for Reconstruction and Development jointly, Direction of International Trade, New York, 1959, p. 285; the 1959 figures are taken from the United Nations Statistical Office, Yearbook of International Trade Statistics, New York, 1951, p. 158, 1954, p.313, and 1959, p. 325; the figures for Korea, Taiwan, and China for 1938 are not included in foreign trade figures.

27. Jerome B. Cohen, Japan's Postwar Economy (Blooming-
    ton: Indiana University Press, 1958), p. 121.

28. Cohen, loc. cit.

29. United States Tariff Commission, Postwar Development in
    Japanese Foreign Trade (Washington: Government Printing
    Office, March, 1958), pp. 127-34.

30. Cohen, op. cit., pp. 137-38.

31. Cohen, op. cit., pp. 140-42.

32. Cohen, op. cit., pp. 146-51.

33. The Tariff Commission of the United States, op. cit.,
    p. 134.

34. ibid., pp. 167-83.

35. Cohen, op. cit., pp. 162-64; Los Angeles Times, March
    11, 1962, Section A, p. 14.

36. Cohen, op. cit., pp. 162-64.

37. Los Angeles Times, December 25, 1961, Part V, p. 1.

38. Cohen, op. cit., p. 121.

39. John Barne, "Red China-Japan Trade Resumption Held
    Likely," Los Angeles Times, Los Angeles, August 9,
    1961, Part 4, p. 12.

40. loc. cit.

41. Allen, Japan's Economic Recovery, pp. 178-79; Cohen,
    op. cit., pp. 179-90.

42. Allen, Japan's Economic Recovery, pp.115-6.

43. Allen, Japan's Economic Recovery, pp. 165-66.

44. The Tariff Commission of the United States, op. cit., pp. 66-68; Los Angeles Times, Los Angeles, March 11, 1962, Section A, p. 18.

45. The Tariff Commission of the United States, op. cit., pp. 127-34.

46. Allen, Japan's Economic Recovery, pp. 122-26.

47. The Tariff Commission of the United States, op. cit., pp. 127-34.

48. Allen, Japan's Economic Recovery, pp. 120-22.

49. Cohen, op. cit., pp. 122-24.

50. The Tariff Commission of the United States, op. cit., pp. 97-98.

51. Cohen, op. cit., pp. 122-24.

52. Allen, Japan's Economic Recovery, p. 118.

53. The Tariff Commission of the United States, op. cit., p. 91.

54. Allen, Japan's Economic Recovery, pp. 179-200.

55. Cohen, op. cit., p. 110, the Tariff Commission of the United States, op. cit., pp. 109-14.

56. Cohen, op. cit., pp. 129-30.

57. Ervin O. Anderson, Japan's Foreign Investment and Joint Ventures Abroad (New York: Columbia University Press, 1959), p. 35.

58. Cohen, op. cit., pp. 110-11.

59. Cohen, op. cit., pp. 164-65.

60. The Tariff Commission of the United States, op. cit., pp. 16-17.

61. loc. cit.

62. The Tariff Commission of the United States, op. cit.,
    pp. 21-22.

63. Cohen, op. cit., pp. 130-33.

64. The Tariff Commission of the United States, op. cit.,
    pp. 30-37.

65. loc. cit.; Cohen, op. cit., pp. 130-33.

66. Allen, Japan's Economic Recovery, pp. 164-72.

67. Warren S. Hunsberger, Japan and the United States in
    World Trade (New York: Harper and Row, 1964), pp.
    374-75.

68. The Tariff Commission of the United States, op. cit.,
    pp. 85-86.

69. Fujii, op. cit., pp. 46-47.

70. loc. cit.

71. Fujii, op. cit., p. 60.

CHAPTER 7 TRADE OF COMMUNIST CHINA

Mainland China's national income figures were first disclosed in 1957, but they have not been made consistently available and cannot be taken at face value. Mainland China, under the Communists, succeeded in stabilizing the economy in the period of 1950-52, and in regaining the prewar level of national product from the low ebb of 1949. Real net growth may be said to have begun in 1953, under the First Five-Year Plan for 1953-57, and the Second Five-Year Plan for 1958-62.

Table 43

The Growth of Domestic Product of Mainland China

	Aggregate Product (billion yuan, at 1952 prices)	Aggregate Product Increase (percent of preceding year)	Per capita Product Increase (per cent of preceding year)
1949	35.8	---	---
1950	42.5	18.7	16.4
1951	49.7	16.9	14.1
1952	60.7	22.1	20.2
1953	69.2	14.0	11.2
1954	73.2	5.8	3.3
1955	77.9	6.4	4.1
1956	88.9	14.1	11.7
1957	92.9	4.5	0.7

Sources: Alexander Eckstein, "Sino-Soviet Economic Relations, a Re-appraisal," in C. D. Cowan, The Economic Development of China and Japan. F. A. Praeger, New

York, 1964; p. 128; United Nations, Economic Survey of Asia and the Far East, 1961, p. 92.

Total industrial production seems to have grown at an annual rate of 20 per cent during the First Five-Year Plan period, rising apparently even higher in 1958-59. At the same time, producer goods output increased even more rapidly, approximating a 30 per cent rate, while consumer goods production seems to have risen by less than 10 per cent a year. Meanwhile, agricultural output was sluggish, increasing about 13 per cent during the entire First Five-Year Plan period.

In 1959, 1960, and 1961, the country suffered severe natural calamities, and the operation of the rural commune system was not successful. There were food parcels coming in through Hong Kong, and the government bought large quantities of food from abroad. The crop failures were reported to have had adverse effects on the industrial sector. In 1960, output of light industries, which rely on agriculture for raw materials, such as cotton textiles, sugar, and vegetable oil, fell short of target. Heavy industries also suffered. The sizable shift to the purchase of food has reduced the import of capital goods and essential raw materials.

POSTWAR DEVELOPMENT

Now, in the 1960's, Communist China's trade is very modest indeed for a country of over 600 million people. If we use the figures given by the Communist Chinese Government for her total trade for 1954--8,487 million yuan, or U. S. $3,625 million--the total trade of Communist China amounted to 2.3 per cent of world trade of that year. It was 1.7 per cent before World War I, and 2.2 per cent in 1930.

The trade of Communist China has been growing steadily from 1949-59. When the Communists achieved complete control of mainland China at the end of 1949, foreign trade was at a very low point, having decreased steadily since 1946. After the Communist Government controlled inflation and began reconstruction, China was able to expand her trade continuously until 1955. By 1954, her trade had reached almost the level of 1930. Her foreign trade of 1955 was high, equivalent to 130 percent of the 1930 level, but still not up to the prewar peak of 1928, which was 150 per cent of the 1930 level.[1] Trade declined somewhat after 1959.

Table 44

Communist China's Trade, 1950-62
(in millions U.S. dollars; exchange rate of 2345 yuan = $1 US)

	Exports U. S. $	Imports U. S. $	Balance of Trade U. S. $
1950	833.0	867.0	-34.0
1951	963.5	1,386.5	-423.0
1952	945.0	1,305.0	-350.0
1953	1,322.25	1,752.75	-430.5
1954	1,740.0	1,885.0	-145.0
1955	2,303.0	2,397.0	-94.0
1956	2,374.2	2,258.6	115.6
1957	2,217.3	2,027.5	189.8
1958	2,658.8	2,265.2	393.6
1959	2,094.2	1,864.9	229.3
1960	1,889.3	1,764.1	125.2
1961	1,316.2	1,141.4	174.8
1962	1,192.0	806.8	385.2

Sources: The only figures for the total trade of China announced by the Chinese Communist Government are
for 1954, 1956, and 1957, but there are records on
the comparison of trade for different years in percentage figures.   From these, reasonable estimates
of the total trade for various years can be calculated.
In these calculations, the figures given by
Robert F. Dernberger (see C. F. Remer, op. cit.,
pp. 132, 150, 209, and 215) are used.   There are
several estimates made by other scholars, for instance, Economic Commission for Asia and the Far
East, Economic Survey of Asia and the Far East, Vol.
XI, No. 4, February, 1956, Bangkok; W. W. Rostow,
The Prospect for Communist China, John Wiley and
Sons, New York, 1954, p. 251; Yuan-li Wu, An Eco-

nomic Survey of Communist China, Bookman Associates, New York, 1956, p. 462; and Choh-ming Li,
Economic Development of Communist China, University of California Press, Berkeley, 1959, p. 177.
Li's figures are very close to those given by Dernberger, and both used up-to-date information which
was not available to the others. Figures for 1958
are taken from the United Nations Economic Commission for Asia and the Far East, Economic Survey of Asia and the Far East, 1958, Bangkok, p. 34.
The United Nations Economic Commission for Asia's
figures for 1950, 1951, 1952, 1953, are largers,
those for 1955 are smaller. The Commission quotes
the New China News Agency Press Dispatch for its
source; International Monetary Fund, International
Bank of Reconstruction and Development, Direction of
Trade Annual, 1958-62, pp. 335-36.

A few general observations can be made at this time by way
of explaining the postwar development. One explanation for the
relatively modest amount of Communist China's trade is that
after eight long years of war against Japan, from 1937-45, and
the two years of civil war, from 1947-49, the economy of China
was in a state of total collapse when the Communists took over
in 1949. The trade then had to be restored from scratch.

From 1951 on, the United Nations imposed an embargo
against Communist China as sanctions for her part in the Korean
War. This virtually stopped the shipment of essential military
and industrial supplies to Communist China. In addition, the
United States froze Communist China's assets in America.

Communist China's trade is practically a state monopoly,
with both the imports and exports handled largely by state
corporations. International payments must be made through
designated banks at the official rate. There are still some
private exporters and importers, but every transaction they
make must be licensed by the government agencies concerned.
This necessarily involves coping with red tape, time delay, un-
certainty, and inefficiency, and explains, in part, the small
size of the trade. The imports and exports fluctuate together
closely. Peaks of exports in 1951, 1956, and 1958, were matched
by peaks of imports in 1951, 1955, and 1958; dips of imports

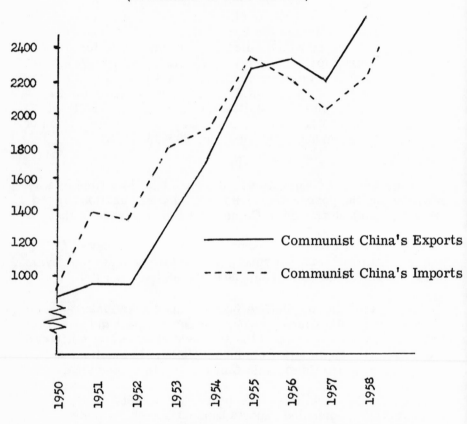

FIGURE 13
TRADE OF COMMUNIST CHINA
(in millions of U.S. dollars)

Communist China's Exports

Communist China's Imports

Source: C. F. Remer, Three Essays on the International Economics of Communist China (Ann Arbor, Michigan:
The University of Michigan Press, 1959), pp. 132,
150, 209, and 215.

in 1952, and 1957 were matched by dips in exports in the
same years. This was because imports were limited by export earnings, and also imports were strictly controlled to
balance the payments.

Communist China is going through a process of recovery
and industrialization. There is urgent need for large volumes
of machinery, equipment, and raw materials. The volume of
imports could be much larger, but there is always the problem
of payments. China has to export in order to import. China's
major exports are agricultural products. Therefore, the development of trade depends to a considerable extent on the outcome of harvests. It must not be forgotten that China has a
large population of over 600 million to feed. Further, the population of China is growing rapidly--at the rate of 12 to 15 million per year. It is difficult for China to find exportable
agricultural surplus commodities to sell abroad. This difficulty limits the volume of imports and, therefore, the total
trade. A bad harvest, as that of 1960, 1961, and 1962 causes
stress within the economy and a decline in trade. [2]

The urgent need for imports of industrial supplies and the
shortage of exportable agricultural commodities resulted in an
unfavorable balance of trade from 1950-55. The excess of
imports was financed by Russian aid. As long as Russian aid
kept coming, the unfavorable balance of trade could continue.
When, in 1956, Russian aid was greatly reduced, this unfavorable balance of trade had to stop also. Communist China had to
cut down on her imports. Consequently, the total trade for
1956 and 1957 declined.

From 1956 on, Communist China has been carrying on a
trade drive directed at the Western countries. The embargo
was gradually relaxed, and her total trade with the West expanded. Because of her use of the barter trade techniques--
that is, not importing unless there is a corresponding export--
Communist China has been able to maintain a favorable balance
of trade with the free world. This helps to explain, in part,
the favorable balance of trade for Communist China for the
years 1956 and 1957.

TERMS OF TRADE

Several factors affect China's terms of trade. The extreme shortage of certain industrial equipment and materials tends to weaken her bargaining position. She has to buy from whatever sources are available and pay whatever prices necessary This shortage of essential industrial equipment and materials was further intensified by the embargo. A situation, then, arises whereby a few neutral countries benefit themselves by exploiting the trade of materials much needed by China through the loopholes of the embargo. It is quite possible that Britain has been making good profits by bringing to Communist China large volumes of an increasing variety of essential supplies, which had originally been included in the banned list. Ceylon has done well, too, in her trade with China. For instance, before 1957, rubber and rubber products were on the banned list. From 1950-52, the United States import of rubber from Ceylon declined in volume, and the price of rubber also dropped. Ceylon had to look for new markets. In 1951, she sent a supply of rubber to Communist China in violation of the United Nations embargo. This act aroused a strong protest from the Western countries against her. In 1952, negotiation between the United States and Ceylon for the trade of rubber broke down because of differences over prices. While the United States was willing to pay the low Singapore market price, Ceylon wanted the higher price which prevailed in her local market. Again Ceylon shipped a supply of rubber to Communist China. Due to the embargo, Communist China could not buy a sufficient amount of rubber, and therefore welcomed this new source from Ceylon with open arms. At the same time, Ceylon was in urgent need of rice. As a result, in 1953, a treaty was concluded between Communist China and Ceylon. Ceylon was to ship 50,000 tons of rubber in exchange for 270,000 tons of rice from Communist China. The terms of trade were completely in favor of Ceylon. Communist China was willing to buy rubber at a price higher than the international market price. Thus, Ceylon was taking full advantage of the embargo to drive a profitable bargain. Communist China granted Ceylon favorable terms of trade in a calculated move to encourage violation of the embargo and to induce other neutral countries to follow suit.[3] Of course, this was an individual case and should not be interpreted as representing the general rule that all neutral countries enjoy favorable terms of trade in their dealings with Communist China.

Communist China's state operated trade corporations are government monopolies with the power to fix prices of imports and exports. So far as China's exports are concerned, these state corporations are monopolies; they are the only suppliers of these exports from China. For imports into China, the state corporations are the sole buyers. This situation tends to strengthen their bargaining position and to improve the terms of trade for China. [4]

In the case of trade between Russia and Communist China, both countries have state corporations to handle their trade. It is a case of bargaining between two monopolists. Communist China is a supplier of raw materials and agricultural supplies to Russia in exchange for Russian industrial equipment and supplies. Communist China's dependence on Russian supplies for her industrialization is far more pressing than Russia's dependence on Chinese supplies. Again, in the matter of ability to pay for each others supplies, Communist China has to buy on credit, and thus she is not in a position to bargain over prices. Therefore, there is the belief, seemingly justified, that Russia must have been enjoying favorable terms of trade in her dealings with Communist China: that is, selling Russian supplies at high prices and buying Chinese supplies at low prices. However, Robert F. Dernberger, in his careful study of the prices that Communist China paid for Russian supplies and the prices that Russia paid for Chinese supplies, as reported by the minister of foreign trade of Communist China, found that for some commodities China suffered a loss, but for others, she gained. [5]

In the trade between Russia and Communist China, prices for Russian capital goods and supplies are quoted in rubles. Communist China presumably did not suffer any losses if the payments in yuan had been converted into rubles also according to a realistic rate of exchange, which according to Robert F. Dernberger, should be about 1.67 yuan to 1 ruble. But Professor Choh-ming Li in his book, Economic Development of Communist China, contends that when China made payments for Russian supplies of capital goods and materials, the official rate was not applied. China had to pay at a higher rate, ranging from 2.177 yuan to 2.5 yuan to 1 ruble. In that case, it appears that the terms of trade favored Russia because of the advantage of the conversion rate. [6]

DIRECTION OF TRADE

The direction of trade of Communist China can be described in two stages. From 1950-55, the trade of Communist
China was oriented toward the Soviet Bloc, whose share increased from 33. 47 per cent to 81. 80 per cent, while the free
world's share decreased from 66. 52 per cent to 18. 20 per
cent. From 1956 on, there was a reversal. Communist
China's trade was reoriented toward the free world. From
1956-62, the Soviet Bloc's share decreased from 75 per cent
to 39. 4 per cent, and the free world's share increased from
25 per cent to 60. 6 per cent.

For the period 1950-55, this reorientation of China's
trade toward the Soviet Bloc was, to a large extent, due to
Russian aid, the coordination of the economy of Communist
countries, and the general atmosphere of the Cold War. The
United Nations embargo imposed on China undoubtedly helped
to facilitate this change.

Ever since the Chinese Communists gained control of
mainland China, Russia has been granting both military and
economic aid to the new regime. Russian economic aid fell
into three categoreis: technical assistance, economic loans,
and trade. It was reported that in 1954, there were from
80, 000 to 100, 000 Russian technicians in Communist China.
With technical help and the loans coming from Moscow, it
became inevitable that trade would expand in that direction.

Russian loans were granted with a certain number of
specific projects in mind. Russian equipment, materials,
and technical assistance were provided for the construction
of these new plants or the renovation of certain old plants.
In this manner, Russian resources could be controlled and
channeled into monumental establishments in Communist China
to show to the people the concrete evidence of Russian help. [7]

The total amount of loans granted by Russia was not received in full by Communist China, because the supplies were
for the planned projects, and the final delivery would not be
completed until the projects were completed. Some of the projects will require ten years to complete and some even longer.
The total loans actually received by China for the period

Table 45

Direction of Trade of Communist China, 1950-62
(1950-56 in million yuan; 1962 in million U. S. dollars)

	1950	1951	1952	1953	1954	1955	1956	1962
Total Value	4,160	5,950	6,490	8,120	8,487	11,024	10,865	1,998.8
A. Communist Bloc	1,393	3,765	5,068	6,130	6,789	9,019	8,149	787.6
1. Russia	1,285	2,899	3,722	4,579	...	6,810	5,800	749.7
2. Eastern Europe	83	788	1,234	1,346	...)	...}2,010	2,349	37.9
3. Rest of Asia	25	78	112	205	...)			...
B. Free World	2,767	2,185	1,422	1,990	1,698	2,005	2,716	1,211.2
1. Africa and Asia	...	...	...	...	1,053	1,247	1,738	622.1
2. The West	...	...	...	...	645	758	978	589.1

(in percentage of total trade of Communist China)

	%	%	%	%	%	%	%	%
A. Communist Bloc	33.47	63.28	78.08	75.49	80.00	81.80	75.00	39.4
1. Russia	30.89	48.72	57.34	56.39	...	61.78	53.40	37.5
2. Eastern Europe	1.99	13.24	19.02	16.58	...)	...}20.02	21.60	1.9
3. Rest of Asia	0.60	1.32	1.72	2.52	...)			
B. Free World	66.52	36.72	21.92	24.51	20.00	18.20	25.00	60.6
1. Africa and Asia	...	...	...	...	12.40	11.30	16.00	31.1
2. The West	...	...	...	...	7.60	6.90	9.00	29.5

Sources: Choh-ming Li, op. cit., p. 186; International Monetary Fund, International Bank of Reconstruction and Development, Direction of Trade, Annual 1958-62, p. 47, pp. 335-36.

235

1953-57 was estimated at about $1, 331 million U. S.

Russian loans to Communist China reached a peak in 1955.
Beginning in 1956, military aid stopped and economic aid dwindled rapidly. As a consequence, Communist China's trade
began to be directed toward the free world.

By 1956, there was an excess of exports from Communist
China to Soviet Russia and this continued through 1958. From
1956-58, the excess exports amounted to U. S. $472 million.
This was due to the fact that in this period Communist China
started to make payments on Russian loans. For 1956, Communist China was to repay Russian loans by excess exports of
about U. S. $30 million. This figure was to increase gradually
to U. S. $250 million for 1958, then it would decrease to U. S.
$150 million for 1959, and about U. S. $50 million for 1960.

Table 46

Estimated Annual Russian Loans Received by Communist China
(in millions)

| | Total Loans | | Economic Loans | | Military and Other Loans | |
	Yuan	US$	Yuan	US$	Yuan	US$
1953	438	187	140. 7	60	297. 8	127
1954	884	377	140. 7	60	743. 4	317
1955	1,657	707	304. 8	130	1,353. 0	577
1956	117	50	117. 4	50	0	0
1957	23	10	23. 3	10	0	0
Total	3, 119	1,331	726. 9	310	2, 394. 2	1,021

Sources: C. F. Remer, op. cit., pp. 78-87, and Choh-ming Li,
           op. cit., pp. 184-85. Figures given by the two sources
           are in agreement. The United Nations Economic Com-
           mission for Asia and the Far East, in its Economic
           Survey for Asia and the Far East, Bangkok, 1957, p.
           103, quotes the same figures for loans received from
           Russia. Alexander Eckstein gives a larger figure of

5, 430 million rubles for the period 1950-57. See
C. D. Cowan, The Economic Development of China
and Japan, p. 152.

Communist China could only buy heavily from Russia if
she was given credits. Whenever credits were no longer extended, China would have to reduce its imports from Russia.
When Communist China was asked to repay Russian loans, she
would have to further curtail imports from Russia to create an
excess in exports to Russia, so that the excess exports could
be used to write off debts. Therefore, trade between Communist China and Russia has depended a great deal on the availability of Russian credits.

Table 47

Communist China's Trade with Soviet Russia

	(in millions of rubles)			(percentage of distribution)		
	1955	1956	1957	1955	1956	1957
Imports from Russia				%	%	%
Machinery & equipment	863	1,167	1,017	29.0	39.8	46.7
Metals & products	282	271	121	9.4	9.2	5.6
Petroleum & products	176	342	361	5.9	11.7	16.6
Paper	29	23	12	1.0	0.8	0.6
Other	1,643	1,129	665	54.7	38.5	30.5
Total	2,993	2,932	2,176	100.0	100.0	100.0
Exports to Russia						
Food & agricultural	1,302	1,511	1,282	50.6	49.4	43.4
Metal ores & con- centrates	249	302	360	9.7	9.9	12.2
Manufactures	773	930	938	30.0	30.4	31.8
Other	250	314	373	9.7	10.2	12.6
Total	2,574	3,057	2,953	100.0	100.0	100.0

Source: United Nations Economic Commission for Asia and the
         Far East, Economic Survey of Asia and the Far East, 1958,
         Bangkok, p. 35.

In the 1950's among China's imports from Russia, machinery, equipment, and industrial materials were steadily increasing, both in absolute and relative terms; among China's exports to Russia, foodstuffs and agricultural supplies have declined but still occupy about half of her total exports. Her exports of industrial raw materials, such as ores and concentrates, are increasing in absolute and relative terms.

Trade with the Free World

The United Nations embargo has been a major factor in restricting China's trade with the United States, Britain, and Japan. The trade of these nations with China started to decline before there was an embargo. The decline can be traced to the end of World War II, to the Communist occupation of China when Western and Japanese business interests were driven out of China, and to the mounting Cold War tension.

The following table, 48, illustrates the decline that has occurred in Communist China's trade with the United States, the United Kingdom, and Japan. These three countries, which in 1927-30 accounted for 50.74 per cent of China's trade, accounted for only 3.44 per cent in 1952-56.

Table 48

Communist China's Trade with Major Free World Countries
(in percentage of China's total trade)

	1927-30 average	1952-56 average
	%	%
United States	15.76	0.14
United Kingdom	7.81	1.28
Japan	27.17	2.02
Total	50.74	3.44

Source: C. F. Remer, Three Essays on the International Economy of Communist China, the University of Michigan Press Ann Arbor, 1959. p. 137.

The United States embargo was imposed in March, 1950, when the Secretary of Commerce of the United States announced the requirement for export licences for shipping of some 600 strategic commodities to the Soviet bloc. In July, 1950, the United States banned shipment of gasoline and other petroleum products to Communist China and North Korea, together with an additional 190 commodities. In September, 1950, Communist China sent troops into Korea, and in May, 1951, the United Nations imposed an embargo against Communist China. Britain and the Commonwealth members, Japan, the Philippines, the Netherlands, and other members of the United Nations gradually applied the embargo on Communist China. The COCOM, Consultative Group Co-ordinating Committee, was established in Paris to coordinate the embargo measures of the United Nations members. Additional items were added to the banned list, which in 1953 contained some 50,000 commodities. There were more items on the banned list for Communist China than those which appeared on the banned list for the Soviet bloc in general. Trade between the United States and Communist China finally dwindled to nothing. Of the pre-embargo U. S. $9 million of Chinese exports to the United States, U. S. $6.7 million happened to be hair, wool, fur, skins, and antiques from outer Mongolia.

Table 49

Communist China's Trade with the United States
(in millions of U. S. dollars)

	Imports from U. S.	Exports to U. S.
1949	82	16
1950	4	146
1951	5	46
1952	–	28
1953	–	9

Source: Hsin Ying, Foreign Trade of Communist China, Union Research Institute, Hong Kong, 1954, p. 125.

The trade between Britain and Communist China is provided by agreements between the two countries. For instance,
in 1952, a treaty was signed in Moscow providing a trade of U.S.
$28 million from each side. China was to export: 25 per cent of
the total in coal, bristles, and sausage casings; 20 per cent in
frozen eggs, eggs and egg products; and 55 per cent in other goods.
Britain was to export 35 per cent of the total in textile goods;
30 per cent in chemicals; and 35 per cent in metals of all kinds,
except copper and aluminum. In 1953, another agreement was
signed between the two countries, establishing a trade of U.S.
$84 million from each side. If there should be any imbalance
of trade, payments were to be made in pounds sterling. Communist China's exports were to be vegetable oils and oil seeds,
animal products, egg products, mineral products, tea, silk,
handicraft products, and other items. Britain's exports were
to include metal products, machine and surgical equipment,
communication and transportation equipment, and other items.
Some of the items given here were banned by the embargo, and
Britain had to stop shipment of these items. After the truce in
Korea, in July, 1953, Britain began to relax the restrictions of
the embargo and started shipping passenger cars, motorcycles,
trucks, and antibiotics and other drugs to Communist China.

From 1956 on, Communist China, despite its constant cas-
tigation of capitalism, has been becoming one of the best customers of capitalist countries. The Peking regime is depending
increasingly on the Western capitalist countries, except the United
States, for goods and for industrial machinery and supplies to
build its own industry. Western trade experts including Stewart
Ross, Secretary of the British Charge d'affaires in Peking, expect
Communist China's trade with the West to increase regardless
of political differences. They agree that the initial reason for
the big switch to the West was the China-Russia split. In 1957,
after discussions in COCOM, the British Government announced that she intended to abandon the differential between
the list for the Soviet Bloc and China. Other COCOM nations
followed suit. It meant freeing the shipment of such goods to
Communist China as locomotives, rolling stock, electric motors,
generators, raw rubber, tires, chemicals, iron and steel products, aluminum products, and copper products. In July, 1958,
Britain, with the support of other COCOM nations, succeeded in
further relaxing the joint list for the Soviet bloc and Communist

China, freeing the export of such goods as: most types of machine tools, motor vehicles, civil aircraft, airplane engines, electrical equipment, petroleum products, ships and lorries not built to military specifications. As a result, the trade between Britain and Communist China recovered a little in 1956, and 1957. [8]

Britain is now emphasizing industrial machinery and supplies. Britain's total sales to Communist China reached $36.4 million in 1963, and final figures for 1964 are expected to reach $56 million. Included in Britain's sales in 1964 were fiber and ammonia plants. Ninety thousand Chinese visited the British Industrial Exhibition at Peking in November, 1964: the biggest ever staged in Communist China. Exhibits were worth $33 million, and the Chinese bought at least three fourths of them on the spot.

Australia occupies first place in Communist China's foreign trade. From 1960-64, its wheat accounted for half of Peking's imports. Since 1960, it has sold 8 million tons of wheat for more than $450 million.

Canada is second, with wheat again the main commodity. In 1963 and 1964, Canada sold to China 85 million bushels at more than $150 million.

France's sales to Communist China included heavy industrial equipment and grains in 1964. France sold about half a million tons of wheat that year. [9]

The trade between Japan and Communist China is also arranged by a series of trade agreements between the two countries. In 1952, the first agreement provided trade of $84 million U. S. for each side. The commodities traded were named and their value in percentages of the total given. Communist China was to export coal, soya beans, manganese ore, iron ore, bristles, salt, wood oil, magnesite ore, bauxite, asbestos, cotton, wool, herb medicine, and lacquer. Japan was to export copper ingots, steel plates, pipes and tubes, structural steel, aluminum ingots, textile machinery and accessories, refrigerator steamers, locomotives, insecticide, medicine, caustic soda, phenol, borax, printing ink, cranes, radio equipment and materials, agricultural

machinery, bicycles, auto parts, typewriters, calculating machines, microscopes, surveying instruments, ball bearings,
ultra short-wave medical apparatus, soda ash, chemical fertilizers, rayon yarn, cotton piece goods, cotton yarn, dye-
stuffs, photo materials, scientific instruments, sea weed,
papers, recording machines, and microphones. The trade
was to proceed on a barter basis, and pound sterling was the
unit of measurement. In 1953 and in 1955, agreements were
signed between the two countries providing trade of the same
amount, $84 million U.S. for each side. The commodities
were for the most part the same as those for the 1952 agreement. Some of the commodities which Japan agreed to export
to Communist China were on the banned list; Japan had to stop
shipment of these items except when she had succeeded in
working among the COCOM nations to have them removed
from the banned list or when she had obtained special permission from the United States government on such shipments.
The United States had the determining voice because she
might withhold economic and military aid from countries
violating the provisions of the embargo. Japan has been successful in gradually relaxing the restrictions of the embargo
on a piecemeal basis. In January, 1953, she succeeded in
taking 93 items off the banned list. They included chemicals,
steel plates, iron ingots, machinery, cotton piece goods, and
others. In July, 1953, another 43 items were taken off the list,
and again in September, 1953, 28 items, including penicillin and
other drugs, rubber products, refrigerators, and automobiles. [10]

Because of the trade agreements and the embargo, the
value of trade between Communist China and Japan has been low
and fluctuating. In 1951, Japan's imports from Communist
China were estimated at U.S. $14.9 million and its exports
U.S. $0.6 million. In 1956, Japan's imports were U.S. $83
million and its exports U.S. $67 million. In 1961, Japan
abolished the compulsory barter-trade practice in favor of a
cash settlement formula. This may induce an expansion of the
trade between these two countries. In the prewar years
of 1930-37, Japan had a trade surplus with mainland China
to the amount of U.S. $47 million annually. But in the post-
war years there has consistently been a trade deficit for Japan
in its trade with Communist China. Japan in the postwar years
has been buying about the same types of commodities from
mainland China as it did in the prewar years: mainly raw

materials such as coal, iron ore, salt, and soybeans. Japan's
exports to Communist China in the postwar years, however, are
quite different from those in the prewar years. They are
largely metal products and machines in the postwar years, but
they included a high percentage of textiles and foodstuffs in
the prewar years. [11]

Red China, a nation of 600 million potential customers,
sits on Japan's doorstep. A segment of Japan's population,
including some businessmen, the opposition Socialists, the
Communists and powerful groups in Prime Minister Hayato
Ikeda's own Liberal Democratic Party, feel the pull of Peking.
They clamor for Japanese recognition of Red China, for official trade links and for greater cultural exchanges. A more
powerful majority advises caution, fearing official involvement with Communist China would cripple the multibillion
dollar U. S.--Japanese trade. Japan's trade with Red China
reached $130 million in the first six months of 1964, as com-
pared with $137 for all of 1963. Ikeda has met the challenge
adroitly. While he approves exchanges of private trade missions, newsmen, and cultural groups, he would not consider
the recognition of Red China until the United States has
changed its policy. [12]

Trade with Southeast Asia

Ever since 1954, Communist China has been trying to develop her trade with Southeast Asia. In 1954, she started to
export industrial as well as agricultural products into this region to build up her market. The motives for this trade drive
are mainly the following: (1) to obtain essential raw materials
and foodstuffs she needs: for instance, rubber, petroleum, nonferrous metals, and rice; (2) to earn more foreign exchange to
pay for her deficit in international payments (and Hong Kong
and Singapore have become Peking's principal sources of
United States dollars and pounds sterling); and (3) to establish
her position in Southeast Asia as a leader and benefactor.
Communist China spends a large amount of money staging international trade fairs in China and participating in trade fairs
in Southeast Asian countries. Communist China signed, altogether, fifty-one trade agreements with these countries
from 1951-58. Communist China also hopes that the twelve
million overseas Chinese, who have established a strong posi-

tion in the domestic trade of these countries, can be won
over to handle her commodities. Due to the unsettled political
and military conditions in Southeast Asia in 1953-55, trade
with Communist China declined, but in 1956 and 1957, it expanded. Furthermore, it is very significant that ever since
1952, Communist China, by the strict regulation of barter
trade with this area, has been able to maintain a favorable
balance. In 1956 and 1957, Communist China sold two and
a half times as much to Southeast Asia as she bought from
this region. [13]

Trade between Burma and Communist China was governed
by an agreement signed in 1954 for a period of three years,
from 1954-57. China was to export coal, silk, silk textiles,
papers, agricultural implements, light industrial products,
handicraft products, enamelware, porcelain, canned goods,
pharmaceutical and medicinal substances, tea, and cigarettes.
Burma was to export rice, rice products, beans, oil cakes,
mineral oils, timber, rubber, and cotton. Based on this
agreement, contracts were signed for China to import from
Burma 150,000 tons of rice in 1955, paying 20 per cent of
the value in sterling and 80 per cent in goods agreed upon. By
a similar arrangement, China was to import from Burma
another 150,000 tons of rice in 1956 and to pay for it in goods.
In 1957, China again, by contract, agreed to import 50,000
tons of rice and pay with sterling. In 1958, a new agreement
was signed between the two countries, but no detailed information regarding this agreement was disclosed. Burma's
trade with Communist China has fallen off drastically in the
two years 1963 and 1964. An 84 million yuan grant was
given to Burma in 1961, but has been used at a snail's pace. [14]

In October, 1952, an agreement was signed between Communist China and Ceylon for China to ship to Ceylon 80,000
tons of rice and use the proceeds to buy rubber from Ceylon.
In December, 1952, a five-year agreement was signed providing a trade of $50 million U.S. each side. China was to send
annually 270,000 tons of rice, 5,000 tons of soya beans, 10,000
tons of newsprint, and 2,000 tons of sulphur, and import from
Ceylon 50,000 tons of rubber. Ceylon took advantage of the
embargo of rubber to obtain a rubber price higher than the international market price and a rice price lower. As a result,
half of Ceylon's rubber output was sent to China during this

period. In 1957, a new agreement covering five years (1958-
62) was signed providing a trade of a similar nature. However,
the rubber price was no longer higher than that of the international market. This was due to the lifting of the embargo on
rubber, and Malaya and Indonesia opened their resources of
rubber to Communist China. [15]

In 1951 and 1952, China exported some 216,500 tons of
rice and 450,000 tons of kaoliang to India in exchange for her
tobacco, gunny bags, cotton cloth, and cotton yarn. In October,
1954, a two-year agreement was signed by which China agreed
to send rice and other cereals, light industrial machinery and
equipment, minerals, silk and silk products, animal products,
chemicals, oils, and foodstuffs in return for Indian tobacco,
mineral ores and concentrates, vegetable oils, cotton and wool,
wood and timber, hides and skins, light industrial machines
and tools, metal manufactures, textiles, and other materials.
As a consequence, there was a tremendous increase of trade
between the two countries in the period from 1954-56. In May,
1956, a new treaty was signed providing a trade of $10.5 mil-
lion U. S. for the first six months. [16] Since the border war
between China and India, trade between the two countries has declined. There was also no trade between them in 1964.

Since the Communists took over mainland China, they have
used Hong Kong as a port of entry for China to obtain the necessary equipment and materials from the free world. Hong Kong's
exports to China steadily increased from 1948-53, but after 1953
they dropped off very sharply. This is probably due partly to
the embargo and partly to the fact that direct barter trade has
been established by China with the free nations. Meanwhile,
Hong Kong's imports from China steadily mounted from 1948-57,
with only the exception of 1954, when there was a slight decline.
Hong Kong was importing an increasing amount of foodstuffs from
Communist China to feed her growing population (caused by the
migration out of China). Hong Kong's trade with Communist China
had become so unfavorable to Hong Kong that, in 1957, Hong Kong
imported from China nine times the value she exported to China.
That is, Hong Kong depends much more on China than China
does on Hong Kong. [17] For Red China, Hong Kong is its biggest
foreign-exchange source. Peking, in 1963, earned an estimated
$500 million from Hong Kong through trade and remittances from
overseas Chinese. This was equivalent to China's grain import from

Canada, Australia, and Europe. For the West, this colony provides a crack in the bamboo curtain through which one can obtain a rough idea of what is going on in Red China. [18]

For the period from 1953-58, there were eight trade contracts between Pakistan and Communist China, but no formal trade agreement has as yet been concluded. The trade consisted mainly of China's coal and grains in exchange for Pakistan's cotton and jute. [19] Pakistan's policy toward Communist China has its peculiar elements. Pakistan is a member of military alliances sponsored by the United States. It has accepted more than one billion U. S. dollars of military aid, along with tremendous amounts of economic assistance. But Chinese goodwill missions, trade delegations, and military groups visit Pakistan, and Pakistan's goal appears to be nonalignment.

Before 1954, trade between Communist China and Indonesia was almost nonexistent. By signing two trade agreements, in 1953 and 1956, trade between these two countries began to grow. It has been mainly an exchange of China's rice, minerals, manufactures and some light machine tools for Indonesia's rubber, copra, coconut oil, sugar, and timber.

Laos has no official trade with China though Chinese goods occasionally slip in through Cambodia.

Cambodia's chief of state, Prince Norodom Sihanouk, made a trip to Peking in 1964. He reported he was offered military and economic aid unconditionally, including establishing textile and cement plants and construction of a new airport along with light and heavy armament sufficient to equip 22, 000 men. In rejecting further United States aid, Cambodia seems to lean over to the Soviet Bloc for support and protection.

Rice-rich Thailand banks heavily on its alliance with the United States to keep the Red Chinese away. Thailand strictly bans trade with Communist China. [20]

After the lifting of the United Nations embargo on rubber in 1956, Malaya and Singapore began exporting rubber to Communist China. In 1958, Communist China sold cement and textiles below the local market prices in Malaya and Singapore, and sent in large quantities of Communist propaganda literature. [21]

The prestige of Communist China has been growing among
the new nations in Africa. In 1956, not a single diplomatic mission of Communist China existed in Africa, but since then
Peking has opened 15 embassies and signed 11 trade agreements.
The economic influence of Communist China is far behind that of the
West and the Soviet Union. The volume of Communist China's
trade with any African country seldom exceeds $20 million yearly.
The trade between Communist China and the staunchly anticom-
munist South Africa is believed to have reached $11 million
yearly. [22]

To summarize, Communist China, during the years 1950-55,
has oriented its trade toward the Communist Bloc. Consequently,
its trade with the West declined drastically. The United Nations
embargo also helped to reduce China's trade with the West. However, in recent years, since 1956, there has been a fast growth
in its trade with the West. This may be explained by the gradual
relaxation of the embargo, the reduction of Russian loans and the
fact that Communist China's needs of capital goods and industrial
materials have not been adequately provided for by the bloc countries. Communist China's trade with Western Europe has grown
the most.

COMPOSITION OF TRADE

As Communist China is undergoing industrialization and urban-
ization, her needs and her products are changing and the composition of her exports and imports will also change. Gradually, there
will be a reduction of the imports of manufactured consumer goods,
especially the products of light industry. When and if she can
attain a high level of industrialization, the imports of capital goods
will be reduced as she will have become more self-sufficient, but the
import of light and heavy industrial raw materials will continue to
grow. The change in composition of her imports should follow
closely her progress in industrialization.

By 1950, Communist China's imports had already changed
in content, as compared to the imports prior to Communist control.
The percentage of total imports for consumer goods dropped, while
that for capital goods increased and the percentage for raw
materials and fuels remained about the same. However, we cannot consider this change as being entirely due to the process of
industrialization. The change may also be due to government

policies restricting the import of consumer goods by tariffs, by
strict import licensing practice, and by not allowing foreign exchange to be used for those goods. The change may also be due
to government policies favoring the import of capital goods, by
reduced tariffs, minimum controls, by provision of generous
bank loans, and by easy payment arrangements.

Table 50

Composition of the Imports of Communist China
(in percentage of total)

	Capital Goods	Raw materials and fuels		Consumer Goods	
1947 total	18.55		62.08		19.37
1959 total	30.72		60.68		8.60
Iron & steel		Cotton	18.04	Sugar	1.99
products	11.34	Rubber	11.52	Rice	1.03
Machinery	8.25	Petroleum			
		products	8.48	Drugs	4.03
Ships, vehicles		Copper	1.76	Others	1.55
tires, tubes	4.39	Ammonium			
		sulphate	1.96		
Cables & wires	1.47	Others	18.92		
Others	5.27				

Source: Yuan-li Wu, An Economic Survey of Communist China,
           Bookman Associates, New York, 1956, pp. 469-70.

Under the Second Five Year Plan, for the period 1957-62, import priorities are given to the following commodities:

(a)   Industrial and agricultural materials such as chemicals,
      finished steel products, wool tops, fertilizers, insecti-
      cides, etc.

(b)   Special engineering products not made in China and not
      conveniently obtainable from the Soviet bloc.

    (c)   Equipment of which China's production has, so far,
been lagging, such as railway equipment, telecommunications equipment, etc.

    (d)   Light tractors and other agricultural equipment, such
as irrigation pumps, etc.

    (e)   Manufactured consumer goods which China does not
produce.

China has alloted limited resources to pay for these goods. [23]

Beginning in 1954, new export commodities began to
appear on the list of exportable goods from China in her trade
agreement with small nations, e.g., steel plates and structural
steel for export to Burma and Egypt, and machine tools, textile machinery, and other industrial equipment destined for
Indonesia. Exports of Communist China in 1958 reportedly included equipment for paper and cement factories, rolled steel
machine tools, diesel engines, rubber tires, sewing machines,
and woolen textiles. [24]

The appearance of these new exports should not be interpreted to mean that China has already achieved exportable surplus in these commodities, nor to mean that China can now
produce them more cheaply than most nations. They may be
exported while there is still a shortage of them in China. Their
costs of production may be higher than that of the international
market, but they are exported at a loss. The purpose of exporting such items may be political in nature for the propaganda
value.

BALANCE OF PAYMENTS

Because of the lack of information on the economy of Communist China, it has been extremely difficult to estimate her
merchandise trade and her balance of payments. Information
is lacking on the transportation expenses and insurance charges
in connection with her imports and exports. It is likely that,
for these, she has a net out-payment. There is no information on
the accounts of travel. Because very few foreigners are allowed to visit China, the amount that China can earn from
tourists is certainly very small. There is no information on
private investments abroad and returns from these investments,

but both are expected to be small. Russia does not have any
direct investment in China. Russia's original copartnership
interests in railroads, mining, and harbor fields in Manchuria
and Singapore have all been transferred to China. All Russian
economic transactions in Communist China are covered by loan
agreements. All the capital goods, raw materials, and technical services sent to China are bought by China on credit, and
China now has to repay the loans plus interest. Russian loans
received by China and Russian loan services paid by China in the
period 1953-57 are given in Table 51. These include the estimated yearly repayments of 10 per cent of the principal Russian
loans plus 1 per cent interest. For 1953, there was only the
interest payment, as repayment of the principal did not start
until 1954. [25]

A large source of in-payments for China has been the remittances from overseas Chinese to invest in land or business
activities in China, to support their relatives and families, or
to support other activities. These remittances, prior to World
War II, were usually estimated at U. S. $100 million annually:
a major source of in-payment to meet the trade deficit. This
amount has been dwindling since the Communists took over in
China, mainly because of the sovietization program, which has
made it impossible for overseas Chinese to invest their money
in China, and the restrictions imposed by Western countries on
the remittances: for instance, those imposed by the United States
government in December, 1950. The Communist Chinese government has taken a few measures to encourage the overseas
Chinese to send funds in. It allows the overseas Chinese remittances to be deposited in banks in foreign currency, without
having to convert them into Chinese yuan immediately, in order
to escape the effect of inflation. It has established an Overseas
Chinese Investment Corporation to channel funds into industries
in Fukien province, the home province of many overseas
Chinese, with a government guaranteed interest of 8 per cent.
Banks in Hong Kong estimate the overseas Chinese remittance
at 128 million yuan for 1952, 77 million yuan for 1953, and 167
million yuan for 1954. 170 million yuan, or about U. S. $73
million, is a safe estimate for the annual remittances since
1955. [26]

Table 51 indicates Communist China had a deficit in payments yearly from 1953-57, although it had for the same period

Table 51

Balance of Payments for Communist China, 1953-57
(in million yuan)

	1953	1954	1955	1956	1957
1. Inpayments					
A. Exports	3,525	4,050	4,935	5,568	5,200
B. Overseas Chinese remittances	80	160	170	170	170
C. Russian loans	438	884	1,657	117	23
Total	4,045	5,095	6,760	5,855	5,395
2. Outpayments					
A. Imports	4,595	4,440	7,635	5,297	4,755
B. Payments for Russian loans	26	127	508	604	621
C. Loans granted to other nations	1,592	628	456	404	508
Total	6,213	5,195	8,599	6,305	5,885
3. Balance	-2,168	-100	-1,839	-450	-490

Sources: Choh-ming Li, Economic Development of Communist China, University of California Press, Berkerley, 1959, p. 184. Trade figures given here vary somewhat from those given in Table 45. The United Nations Economic Commission for Asia and the Far East gives much larger figures for the loans granted to other nations. See Economic Survey of Asia and the Far East, 1957, Bangkok, p. 103. The United Nations figures are used instead of Li's figures on the loans granted to other nations for the years 1953-55.

a surplus balance with the free world.

Since 1958, there have been some changes in the international trade balances of Communist China. It had a surplus balance of U.S. $127 million with the Soviet area in 1958, and a surplus

Table 52

Communist China's Export Surplus with the Free World
(in millions of U. S. dollars)

Year	Exports	Imports	Surplus
1950	534.70	452.10	82.60
1951	524.70	446.20	78.50
1952	369.90	272.50	97.40
1953	432.70	287.40	145.30
1954	375.40	294.00	81.40
1955	494.40	316.60	177.80
1956	643.30	433.40	209.90
1957	658.90	526.80	132.10
Total	4,034.00	3,029.00	1,005.00

Sources: Choh-ming Li, Economic Development of Communist
China, University of California Press, Berkerley,
1959, p. 150 and p. 156. However, Huges and Luard,
The Economic Development of Communist China,
Oxford University Press, London, 1959, p. 130, give,
estimates that are much smaller: 40 million pounds
for 1955, 67 million pounds for p956, and 100 million
pounds for the first half of 1957.

balance of U.S. $166.5 million for 1959. Its trade with the
Soviet area was balanced in 1960, with no surplus and no deficit.
For the period of 1958-60, it had a trade deficit with Western
Europe of about U.S. $100-$250 million annually. It had a trade
deficit with Australia of about U. S. $20 million annually and
a trade deficit with New Zealand of about U. S. $20 million an-
nually. But it had a trade surplus with Asian countries of
about U. S. $230-320 million annually. Therefore, as a whole,
Communist China, for the period 1958-60, had a small trade surplus with the free world, at about U. S. $40-70 million annually.
Since the over-all trade surplus of Communist China was not
large enough to take care of its repayments for Russian loans,
it had deficits in international payments. Consequently, it
suffered a loss of international reserves. For the period from

1950-60, its specific outflow, including gold sold to Russia and silver sold to England, was estimated at U.S. $30 million. That is why Communist China has been anxious to expand its exports to Asian countries, where it has had continuous surplus balances to relieve the international payments pressure.

SYSTEM OF TRADE CONTROL

International trade is, to all intents and purposes, a state monopoly in Communist China. Trade is regulated through the control of foreign exchange, the tariff system, the bilateral barter trade agreements, and the licensing of exports and imports. The operation of trade activities is almost entirely by state corporations. The result is that the volume of trade with the free world suffered, but a favorable balance of trade with the free world has been achieved.

Foreign exchange is controlled in China. Exporters are required to surrender their foreign-exchange proceeds in return for exchange deposit certificates issued by designated banks. Importers have to purchase these certificates through designated banks for foreign-exchange settlements with foreign merchants. It is designed to prohibit foreign exchange from going into the black market. The policy aims to conserve foreign exchange, and to channel all foreign transactions through the designated banks. Designated banks will buy and sell foreign exchange according to the official rate, so that the rates are under control and made effective.

Prior to July, 1950, official exchange rates were not uniform. The United States dollar was quoted at different rates in Shanghai and Canton. This shows the lack of effective central control of foreign exchange. Up to February, 1951, official exchange rates exhibited a great deal of flexibility. The policy of the Chinese Communist government was to fix the official rates of exchange at a level reasonably close to the free market rates.

In December, 1952, the rate was 24,620 jen-min pi (Communist China's currency) per United States dollar.

After the monetary reform in 1955, the exchange rate quoted by the People's Bank was 2.345 yuan per American dollar and

0. 427 yuan per Hong Kong dollar. [27]

To facilitate the imports of essential supplies and to encourage the export of native products, the People's Bank sometimes grants loans to the state import and export corporations
for their trade transactions. The transactions must first be approved by the proper trade authorities, and the applicant corporations must make a deposit with the bank in yuan in the
amount of 30 per cent of the value of the transactions.

Tariff regulation is another way to control trade. Communist China's import and export tariffs, together with the Provisional Tariff Regulations, were promulgated on May 10, 1951,
and came into effect on May 16. With a few exceptions, the
tariff rates have remained unchanged to the present. There
are tariffs on both imports and exports. The guiding principle
is to protect China's domestic production and to regulate her
trade, with a view of promoting the economic reconstruction of
the country. Goods necessary for reconstruction and for the
livelihood of the people are charged low rates or admitted free.
But manufactures or semi-manufactures, which China can produce in large quantities now or has the potentiality of developing in the near future, are charged with rates high enough to
cover the difference in costs of production between the domestic
and foreign-made articles. All luxuries and nonessentials are
charged extremely high duties. According to the tariff, commodities are classified into 17 categories, 89 sections, 939
numbers, and 1, 864 items. 100 per cent ad valorem duties
are collected from silk products, synthetic fiber products, and
other luxury items. There is also 100 per cent ad valorem
duty on tea because tea is an important cash crop of China. There
is a 100 per cent ad valorem duty on sugar, probably for
revenue purpose. A very large group of commodities are in
the 15 per cent and 30 per cent categories, evidencing the protective nature of the tariff. [28]

There are two columns of duty rates in China's tariff: the
general tariff rates and the minimum tariff rates. For goods
imported from a country having a commercial agreement with
China with reciprocal reduced tariff rates provided, the minimum rates will apply; for goods from other countries, the
general tariff rates, which are higher, will apply.

Duties on imports are assessed on the basis of c. i. f value at the port of entry in China.

The value of imports or exports, if calculated from a foreign currency, is converted to yuan by the Customs at the average rate of exchange between buying and selling quotations of the People's Bank of China, unless the conversion rate has been agreed on by the proper authorities. [29]

As stated before, the foreign trade of Communist China is almost entirely handled by state corporations. This transition took place in the period from 1950-53. In 1950, private exporters handled about 82 per cent of the foreign trade of South China, and state corporations handled the balance. By 1953, the situation was reversed, with the latter handling about 90 per cent of the trade. Before the Communists took over, there were over 1,000 private exporter-importers in Canton. By 1952, the number had been reduced to less than a hundred, and most of them have become agents of the state corporations, though retaining their old company names. [30] For instance, if a British firm wants to ship goods into China, inquiries may begin with the Chinese representatives attached to the office of the Chinese Commercial Counsellor at the Chinese Legation in London. All negotiations regarding the permit, the transaction, the price and volume, and the terms have to be conducted with the state import or export corporation in Peking. Sometimes it is necessary to inquire at the Chinese Mission at Berne, Switzerland. The reason for this is that the Chinese Legation at Berne is often used as the starting point for Chinese trade officials visiting Western Europe. [31]

Before 1958, the usual form of payment used by Chinese authorities for their imports was an irrevocable letter of credit confirmed in London with prompt payment on presentation of documents. From 1958 on, China began ask for documentary credit of 30 days. As time went on, the period was extended, whenever possible, to 60, 90, and in some cases, to 120 days. Another change, in 1958, was the omission of the Bank of China in London from the credit confirmation. The effect of this change was that in the event of nonpayment, the British exporters' only redress was against the Bank of China in Communist China. [32]

As to the actual control of exports and imports, there are
three types of operational procedure. The first of these is
trade with Russia. The objective is to import sufficient industrial and strategic equipment and supplies to carry out the five
year economic plans. The volume of imports from Russia is
not limited by the volume of exports to Russia. The trade does
not have to be balanced. Import surplus is financed by long-
term loans. Trade agreements are negotiated with Russia,
from time to time, according to the need for equipment and
supplies. Since 1949, a Council of Mutual Economic Aid has
existed in Moscow, charged with the task of coordinating the
economic plans of the Soviet Bloc. Communist China is not a
member of this Council, but sends observers to its meetings.
Trade relations among the Communist countries are studied by
this Council, which takes into consideration needs and capabilities of the different countries. [33]

Secondly, there is trade with other Communist countries.
There is no long-term planning of China's trade with Communist
countries other than Russia. Trade agreements are made annually according to the needs of that year. The agreements
specify the kinds of commodities to be exchanged, the volume,
and the total value for each side, the terms, and the general
conditions. Normally, the trade is conducted on a barter basis.
If there is any surplus import, the type of payments will be
specified. But before the end of the year, there may be a change
in the needs. Then a protocol will be negotiated to change the
volume or contents of the trade. To carry out the agreement,
specific contracts will have to be signed with the state corporations under the scope of the agreement to specify the delivery,
the definite amount, and the price of the particular commodities.
The objective is still to acquire sufficient supplies to carry out
the construction program of the five year plans. But here the
barter system is used. China would not normally import more
than she can export to these countries. The trade in this area
is not as indispensable as that with Russia, and the term of
agreements may not always be carried to the full. [34]

The third type of control procedure is applied to trade
with the free world. Four levels of control authorities carefully
scrutinize and regulate the trade in commodities, classified into
four groups according to their importance and strategic value.
The relative importance of the export or import commodities

determines the level of authorization required. The four
categories of commodities and the proper authorization
agencies are:

(a) Permitted commodities including textiles, metals,
    general machine tools, and medicines for which
    there is no state corporation in control. Only the
    written permission from the local FTCO (Foreign
    Trade Control Office) is needed to export or im-
    port these commodities.

(b) Special commodities including bristle, vegetable
    oil, peanut oil, coal, mineral oil, gasoline, hard-
    ware, rubber products, tungsten, antimony, tin,
    and other industrial materials for which there are
    no state export or import corporations to exercise
    monopolistic control. Authorization for import-
    ing or exporting these commodities must be ob-
    tained from one of the proper state corporations which are
    the only suppliers of these commodities. These
    state corporations determine the prices and quanti-
    ties and other trading terms. Decisions are made
    at Peking, where most of the headquarters of the
    state corporations are located.

(c) Limited commodities including aircraft, motor ve-
    hicles, telecommunications equipment, photographic
    equipment, military equipment, and other military or
    strategic materials. Authorization for importing or
    exporting these items must be obtained directly from
    the Ministry of Foreign Trade in Peking.

(d) Prohibited commodities including coins, gold, silver,
    nickel, copper, government documents, antiques, and
    contraband. Authorization of importing or exporting
    these items must be obtained from the Committee of
    Fiscal and Economic Affairs, of the Government Ad-
    ministration Council, which is the highest trade author-
    ity of Communist China.[35]

The purpose of the control system is to set up a monopolistic control of trade by the state corporations, to protect the
country's monetary system, to prevent contraband and military
equipment from going into private hands, in addition to the gen-

Table 53

Communist China's Trade with Southeast Asia for
1938, 1948, 1952–62

(a = in millions of U. S. dollars;   b = percentage of total trade of
Southeast Asian countries)

Amount of China's Imports

		1938	1948	1952	1953	1954	1955	1956	1957	1958	1960	1962
Burma	a	3.8	13.4	0.1	1.3	0.1	17.5	14.4	9.1	3.0	6.6	17.1
	b	2.2	5.9	0.03	0.5	0.04	7.7	5.9	4.3	1.5	2.9	6.7
Ceylon	a	---	---	25.9	50.8	46.5	25.5	28.3	35.6	16.3	25.3	28.0
	b	---	---	8.2	15.4	12.2	6.3	11.0	10.1	4.5	6.8	7.5
Hong Kong	a	7.3	70.6	91.0	94.5	68.4	31.8	23.8	21.6	27.3	21.0	14.9
	b	4.7	17.4	17.8	19.5	16.1	7.1	4.2	4.1	5.2	2.8	1.8
India	a	4.8*	17.4	6.5	2.5	3.7	14.3	8.0	8.5	7.2	11.8	0.4
	b	0.8*	1.3	0.5	0.2	0.3	1.1	0.6	0.6	0.6	0.8	---
Indonesia	a	13.7	1.6	---	---	2.3	6.2	11.7	26.3	43.4	35.4	...
	b	3.6	0.4	---	---	0.3	0.7	1.3	2.7	5.7	4.2	...
Malaya &	a	2.1	7.1	---	1.8	6.4	4.2	7.8	24.2	38.8	31.0	...
Singapore	b	0.2	0.9	---	0.2	0.6	0.3	0.6	1.8	3.0	1.8	...
Pakistan	a	---	9.9	83.8	7.2	26.1	31.7	15.9	9.5	7.6	14.8	1.6
	b	---	1.6	15.7	1.6	7.3	7.9	4.7	2.8	2.5	3.7	0.4
Total	a	31.7	120.0	207.3	113.1	153.5	131.2	120.0	134.8	146.8	147.3	72.3
	b	1.8	2.9	4.0	2.6	3.4	2.6	2.4	4.4	4.4	1.3	0.7

Amount of China's Exports

		1938	1948	1952	1953	1954	1955	1956	1957	1958	1960	1962
Burma	a	1.4	5.0	2.3	1.5	0.5	2.3	22.2	12.5	16.6	24.9	28.6
	b	1.8	2.8	1.2	0.8	0.2	1.3	11.2	4.2	8.1	9.6	13.2
Ceylon	a	0.1	0.9	6.8	43.9	33.3	16.8	28.1	17.6	31.9	27.8	8.5
	b	0.1	0.3	1.9	12.9	11.3	5.5	8.2	5.9	8.8	6.7	2.4
Hong Kong	a	73.9	108.4	145.3	150.0	121.1	151.1	181.7	197.9	244.5	207.5	212.3
	b	39.5	20.7	21.9	21.9	20.1	23.2	22.7	22.0	30.3	19.2	17.6
India	a	5.9*	3.6	32.4	1.9	3.2	5.4	17.5	10.9	11.1	6.8	2.5
	b	1.0*	0.2	1.9	0.2	0.2	0.4	1.0	0.5	0.6	0.3	0.1
Indonesia	a	2.0	11.7	1.9	2.1	3.5	9.9	30.2	27.0	41.8	57.0	...
	b	0.7	2.9	0.2	0.3	0.6	1.6	3.5	3.5	8.1	9.9	...
Malaya &	a	5.3	53.6	39.4	34.3	28.5	37.8	43.1	52.2	79.2	73.0	79.3
Singapore	b	1.6	6.3	3.1	3.3	2.8	3.0	3.1	3.7	5.2	4.3	4.4
Pakistan	a	---	20.8	2.2	3.3	1.6	0.2	0.5	7.8	10.3	4.0	4.2
	b	---	5.1	0.4	0.9	0.5	0.05	0.1	1.8	2.5	0.7	0.6
Total	a	88.6	204.0	230.3	237.0	191.7	233.5	324.3	325.9	444.1	409.7	352.5
	b	5.9	4.3	4.0	5.2	4.4	2.5	5.8	5.0	4.9	3.9	3.6

* Including Pakistan

Source: Shao Chuan Leng, "Communist China's Economic Relations with Southeast Asia," American Institute of Pacific Relations, Far Eastern Survey, Vol. 28, No. 1, p. 45.

eral supervision of trade.

In order to achieve a favorable balance of trade, Communist China not only wants the imports and exports of the country to balance each other in total value at the end of the year, but she also wants to have each transaction of an export to be paired off with an import in equal value in the manner of barter. In other words, no export will be authorized until there is a corresponding import to go with it, so that the payments of these two can be cleared. If there is a difference between the value of the export and the corresponding import, it should not be more than 3 per cent of the value of the export or 3, 000 Hong Kong dollars. Trade with the West is conducted on this barter basis. If a trade agent has been authorized to carry out a barter trade and, completed the export, cannot bring about the import, he is subject to penalties.

To carry out a transaction of barter trade, a private trade agency may follow one of four procedures and have the chosen procedure approved by government authorities for the particular transaction.

(a) Direct barter--This is when a trade agent attempts to import certain industrial materials and to export certain native products of the same value. His first step is to go to the Foreign Trade Control Office to apply for the authorization of the two way transaction. The FTCO may approve, reject, change the volume, or suggest a price. The foreign-exchange proceeds from the export will be used to pay for the import. If there is a difference in the values between the export and the import, payment will be made through a designated bank.

(b) Clearing process--This occurs when a trade agent, at a given time, wants to import a certain commodity to China but has not arranged for any export. Authorization of this import is applied for and may be given him on the condition that, within a stipulated period of time, he must undertake an export of similar value to complete this barter. If he cannot go through with this export, he must find another trade agent to export a supply of goods at similar value to complete this barter in order to relieve him of this obligation. However, by this clearing process, eventually all the imports will be paired off with corresponding exports.

(c) Link process--This is similar to the clearing process, only the order of import and then export is reversed.
First a trade agent is authorized to export, but within a stipulated time period, he must import a certain supply of goods of
similar value.

(d) Back to back barter--This procedure is used when a
foreign exporter wants to export foreign commodities to China
and another foreign importer wants to import Chinese products from China, of similar value. The two may come together,
and their transactions will be paired off as a barter. The Foreign Trade Control Office gives them authorization for this
transaction. After their goods have been delivered, the foreign
importer will pay the foreign exporter. [36]

Using the four procedures, Communist China is assured
that for each import there will be an export to follow (or vice
versa), or that the outgoing and incoming transactions will proceed
simultaneously. Thus an unfavorable balance of trade can be
prevented. These procedures, plus the trade drive by the
state corporations to promote exports, have made it possible
for Communist China to create a favorable balance of trade
with the free world. Of course, all this causes red tape, time
delay, and inefficiency, and as a consequence, the total volume
of trade with the free world may suffer.

There is also a commodity control for trade. The Communist government classifies commodities for export into
three groups, according to their relative importance. Commodities for import are also classified similarly. A certain
export commodity of one group must be paired off with another
import commodity from the group of corresponding importance.
In other words, the government would not allow a premium export commodity to be exported in exchange for a low priority
import commodity.

Classifications for Export and Import Commodities. [37]

Exports   Imports

Group A--Premium Exports   Group A-- Strategic and Essential Imports of Great Importance to China

For instance: bristle, soya beans, antimony, wolfram, tin, tungsten, tung oil, coal, coke, etc.

For instance: cotton, electric generators, machine tools, arms, ammunition, wood pulp, explosives, petroleum products, chemicals, precision instruments, etc.

Group B--High Ranking Exports

For instance: vegetable oils, beans, grains, etc.

Group B--High Priority Imports

For instance: hardware, bicycles, motorboats, newsprint, cement, photographic supplies, etc.

Group C--Dispensable Exports

For instance: tobacco, china, sundry goods, handicraft products, etc.

Group C--Low Priority Imports

For instance: soaps, paper products, processed foodstuffs, leather goods, etc.

While countries in Western Europe, under the Common Market system, are moving toward free trade, Communist China has joined the iron curtain countries along the road to the opposite direction. China has become a land of proliferating bureaucrats, who delight in creating controlling agencies on top of controlling agencies and regualtions within regulations. The effect of the prevailing situation, both economic and political, on trade is one of restraint rather than encouragement.

To summarize, the trade of Communist China is undergoing a change due to the determined industrialization program of Peking. The composition of her imports has changed, with capital goods and industrial materials taking an increasing share. The composition of her exports has not changed much as yet, but is expected to be modified with increasing importance for her light industrial goods as she moves further along the course of industrialization. As to the future volume of her trade, there will be some growth, but there are limiting factors. Her trade with Russia and the Soviet Bloc may expand if Communist China can obtain more loans from Russia. This may prove difficult in view of the differences that have

developed between the two countries. Her trade with the free
world will expand, but the limiting factors are the cold war and
the complicated system of trade controls, and the low level of
production in Communist China.

Notes to Chapter 7

1. C. F. Remer, Three Essays on the International Economics
    of Communist China (Ann Arbor: the University of Michigan
    Press, 1959), p. 215; Chohming Li, Economic Development
    of Communist China (Berkeley: University of California
    Press, 1959), pp. 177-78. The total trade for the world in
    1954 is put at approximately U.S. $155,000 million.

2. Alec Nove and Desmond Donnelly, Trade with Communist
    Countries (London: Hutchinson & Co., Ltd., 1960), pp. 149-50.

3. Hsin Ying, Foreign Trade of Communist China (Hong Kong:
    Union Research Institute, 1954), pp. 106-11.

4. Li, op. cit., pp. 192-93.

5. Remer, op. cit., pp. 143-48.

6. Li, op. cit., pp. 172-77. The official rate of exchange was
    1 yuan to 2 rubles in 1951 and 1 yuan to 1 ruble in 1956.
    See United Nations Economic Commission for Asia and the
    Far East, Economic Survey of Asia and the Far East, 1958,
    Bangkok, p. 35.

7. Los Angeles Times, July 5, 1961.

8. Los Angeles Times, December 27, 1964, Section 1, p. 2.

9. T.J. Hughes and D.E.T. Luard, The Economic Development
    of Communist China (London: Oxford University Press,
    1959), p. 130; Ying, op. cit., pp. 88-100. Trade figures
    given here for 1950-53 are somewhat larger than those
    in Table 45.

10. Remer, op. cit., pp. 195-99; Ying, op. cit., p. 112.

11. E. F. Szczepanik, Economic and Social Problems of the Far East (Hong Kong: University of Hong Kong Press, 1962), pp. 143-45.

12. Remer, op. cit., p. 206, and Ying, op. cit., p. 112.

13. Shao Chuan Leng, "Communist China's Economic Relations with Southeast Asia," American Institute of Pacific Relations, Far Eastern Survey, XXVIII, No. 1 (New York: American Institute of Pacific Relations, January, 1959), pp. 1-11.

14. Leng, op. cit., p. 7; Los Angeles Times, October 18, 1964, Section F, p. 8.

15. Leng, op. cit., p. 7; also Remer, op. cit., pp. 186-87.

16. Leng, op. cit., p. 7; and Remer, op. cit., pp. 189-91.

17. Leng, op. cit., p. 7; and E. F. Szczepanik, The Economic Growth of Hong Kong (London: Oxford University Press, 1958), p. 158.

18. Los Angeles Times, October 18, 1964, Section F, pp. 1,8.

19. Leng, op. cit., p. 7; Ying, op. cit., p. 127.

20. Los Angeles Times, October 18, 1964, Section F, pp. 1, 8.

21. Leng, op. cit., p. 8.

22. Los Angeles Times, October 18, 1964, Section F, pp. 1, 8.

23. Nove and Donnelly, op. cit., p. 152.

24. Hughes and Luard, op. cit., p. 129.

25. Li, op. cit., p. 183.

26. Hughes and Luard, op. cit., p. 125; Li, op. cit., p. 182;
    Yuan-li Wu, An Economic Survey of Communist China
    (New York: Bookman Associates, 1956), p. 468. Wu
    does not fix the specific volume but considers it is below
    the prewar level of U.S. $100 million.

27. Li, op. cit., p. 5, pp. 254-55; Wu, op. cit., pp. 486-93.

28. Ying, op. cit., section on trade control; Ta Kung Pao
    (a Chinese newspaper), Trade with China, Hong Kong,
    1957, pp. 38-39.

29. Ta Kung Pao, op. cit., pp. 38-39.

30. Ta Kung Pao, ibid., section on trade organization; Remer,
    op. cit., p. 125; Nove and Donnelly, op. cit., pp. 150-1;
    Ta Kung Pao (a Chinese newspaper), Trade with China,
    Hong Kong, 1957, pp. 41-54, where a detailed list of trade
    corporations and agencies with their addresses are given.
    Remer classifies the state corporations into general,
    exporting, and importing according to their titles. Actually,
    they each handle a group of commodities whether for export
    or import.

31. Nove and Donnelly, op. cit., pp. 150-51.

32. ibid., pp. 150-51.

33. Hughes and Luard, op. cit., pp. 123-25.

34. Wu, op. cit., pp. 483-84; Remer, op. cit. The latter
    contains a detailed description of the known trade agree-
    ments, protocols, and contracts signed by Communist
    China from 1949 to mid-1957.

35. Ying, op. cit., p. 46.

36. Ying, loc. cit.

37. Wu, op. cit., p. 497.

CHAPTER **8** TRADE OF AUSTRALIA

Australia is an important source of raw materials and foodstuffs such as beef, mutton, dairy products, wheat, wool, hides and skins, and is also a good market for capital goods. Australia was rapidly industrialized during and after World War II, and is a producer of sizeable volumes of manufactured products. Australia, with a per capita income of U. S. $1,240 a year, is among the richest nations in the Pacific.

POSTWAR DEVELOPMENT

Australia has come a long way since the time the first European colonists settled in Sydney in 1788. It is now an independent parliamentary democracy in the British Commonwealth. It is a large country of 2,974,579 square miles, with a small population of 11 million people of predominantly British stock. It is the world's leading wool producer; leading producer of lead; the third largest producer of zinc. Industrialization in Australia has reduced the importance of primary production in its economy. The wool industry used to be so important that it was said that the cities of Australia rode on the back of the sheep. Although now wool is still the leading product, it amounted to only a third of the output of the economy in 1963, despite the fact that wool output has increased 70 per cent since World War II.

The number of factories in Australia has more than doubled since 1940; electric power output has increased from five billion kilowatt hours to about 26 billion; ingot steel production has more than trebled, to 4 million tons annually. Australia now has a thriving automobile industry. There are fourteen companies assembling cars in Australia, with a capacity of 400,000 vehicles a year. Two out of three families in the country own a car. The center of automobile industry is in

Victoria, where Ford spent 30 million dollars in 1963 on plant
expansion, and General Motors 40 million. The 99 per cent
Australia-owned company, Holden, started production in 1963.
Manufacturing employs some one million people, more than one
fourth of the work force. Now only one eighth of the work force
is engaged in primary industry.

The government of Australia is embarking on bold projects
to speed up the economic development of the country. For instance, the Snowy Mountain Hydroelectric Authority was established in 1949 to turn the Snowy River and its tributaries
through mountains to feed into the Murray and Murrumbridgee
Rivers, with the aim of using the water to irrigate some 3,000
square miles of land and to generate electric power with a capacity
comparable to that of the Tennessee Valley Authority. The project is scheduled to be completed in 1975.

Australia has ample space and natural resources, but
there are two major obstacles in the way of fast development:
the lack of population and capital. Australia is getting more
of both. Immigrants, mainly from Europe, come in at the rate
of 100,000 a year. The "White Australia" policy designed a
century ago to check Asian immigration has been only slightly
modified. Now a trickle of Japanese, Chinese, and other
Asians are permitted to take up residence each year. The
population is still small for such a vast land. It has a density of
3.6 persons per square mile as compared to India's 349 per
square mile.

Because Australia is making fast progress, it has become a
land of opportunities. Foreign capital is coming in large
amounts for the high rate of return and security, as the government has demonstrated its ability to keep peace and order and
to protect property rights. The United States investment alone,
in 1963, exceeded $100 million.

All these changes going on in the economy of Australia
certainly have had profound effect on its foreign trade. Her
exports of manufactured goods have increased in value, and
she began to export some capital equipment to Asian countries. [1]
In 1953, both her exports and her imports were four times as
large as those in 1938. There were no serious difficulities
with her balance of trade, with favorable balances for some

years and unfavorable balances for others. From 1953 on
there has been an unfavorable movement of the terms of trade
due to the lowering of export prices. Australia's producers
of exports suffered a loss of purchasing power due to the decline of the terms of trade. Because of this, unfavorable
balances of trade occurred more often than in earlier periods.

Table 54

Trade of Australia
(in millions of U. S. dollars)

	Exports	Imports	Balance
1938	530.0	527.0	3.0
1948	1649.2	1411.2	238.0
1949	1749.6	1422.1	327.5
1950	1481.9	1353.8	128.1
1951	2038.0	2422.3	-384.3
1952	1688.8	1979.0	-290.2
1953	1976.8	1470.8	506.0
1954	1659.3	1869.2	-209.9
1955	1747.4	2160.4	-413.0
1956	1887.4	1963.8	-76.4
1957	2202.5	1944.7	257.8
1958	1652.6	2057.4	-404.8
1959	2001.4	2122.8	-121.4
1960	2060.9	2362.2	-301.3
1961	2376.2	2096.2	280.0
1962	2362.7	2265.1	97.6

Source: United Nations, International Monetary Fund and In-
         ternational Bank for Reconstruction and Development,
         Direction of International Trade, New York, Series T,
         V. IV, No. 1/2, pp. 298-301; Series T, V. VI, No.
         10, pp. 271-73; Series T, V. XI, No. 9, pp. 363-66;
         Annual 1958-62, pp. 269-70.

Australia has a large international trade for the size of

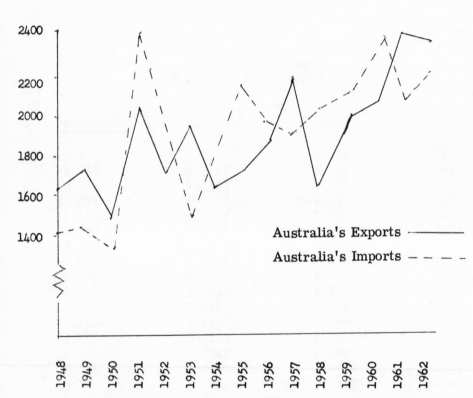

FIGURE 14
TRADE OF AUSTRALIA
(in millions of U.S. dollars)

Australia's Exports ————
Australia's Imports — — — —

Source: International Monetary Fund and International Bank
for Reconstruction and Development, Direction of
International Trade (New York: United Nations),
Series T, V. IV, N. 1/2, pp. 298-301; Series T,
V. VI, N. 10, pp. 271-73; Series T, V. XI, N. 9,
pp. 363-66; Annual 1958-1962, pp. 269-70.

the population. Its imports in recent years range from 16 per
cent to 24 per cent of the gross national product, and its exports from 16 to 23 per cent. Corresponding figures for the
United States average approximately 6 per cent and 5 per cent
respectively. [2] Imports fluctuate right along with exports.
Peaks of exports in 1949, 1951, 1953, 1957, and 1961, were
followed by peaks of imports in 1949, 1951, 1955, 1960, and
1962. Dips of exports in 1950, 1952, and 1958, were followed
by dips in imports in 1950, 1952, and 1961.

DIRECTION OF TRADE

A very significant change in the trade of Australia in the
postwar period is the change of the direction of her exports.
From the percentage figures of the shares of various areas
and countries for the selected years 1938, 1948, and 1959, it
is very clear that the sterling area, the traditional market
for Australian exports, has declined in importance. The sterling area is still the biggest buyer of Australian exports and
the United Kingdom the leading customer, but the share of
Australian exports to the United Kingdom has dropped greatly.
The United Kingdom bought more in absolute figures, but is
less important as a market compared to prewar days.

In the postwar period, North America and Asia have not
only increased their purchases from Australia in dollar value,
but also increased their shares of Australian exports as compared to prewar days. The United States has been making
steady gains in her share of Australian exports throughout
the postwar period. Japan bought very little from Australia
in the years immediately following the war, but as Japan has
recovered industrially, she has been making tremendous gains
as an important buyer of Australian goods. [3]

Australia is reorienting its trade away from its traditional
trade markets in the United Kingdom and the sterling area as a
whole. Its commercial outlook is in the direction of America
and Asia. Australia made about $880 million from sales
in Asia over the period from 1957 to 1961. When the United
Kingdom announced in July, 1961, its intention to seek entry into the European Common Market, Australia increased
its efforts to tap the vast trade potential in America

FIGURE 15
LEADING NATIONS RECEIVING AUSTRALIAN
EXPORTS AND SUPPLYING ITS IMPORTS, 1962
(in millions of U.S. dollars)

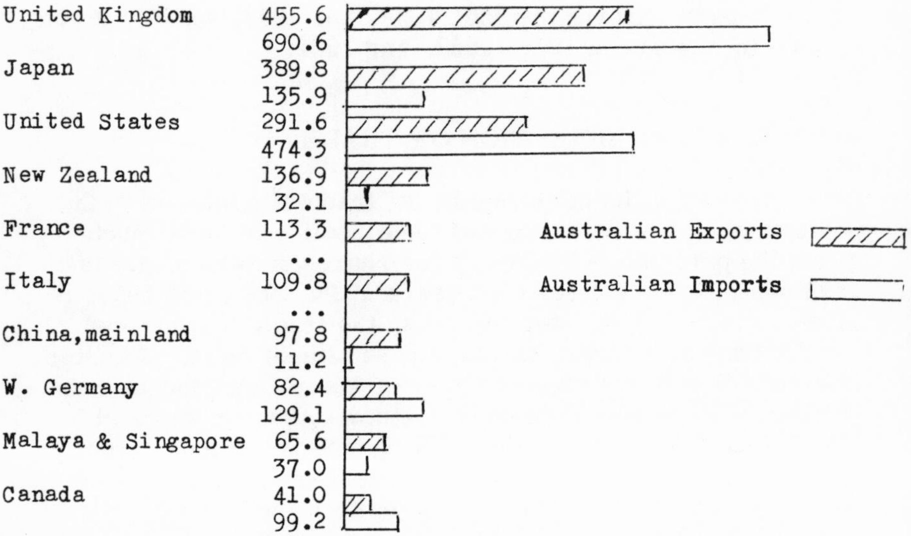

United Kingdom	455.6	
	690.6	
Japan	389.8	
	135.9	
United States	291.6	
	474.3	
New Zealand	136.9	
	32.1	
France	113.3	Australian Exports
	...	
Italy	109.8	Australian Imports
	...	
China,mainland	97.8	
	11.2	
W. Germany	82.4	
	129.1	
Malaya & Singapore	65.6	
	37.0	
Canada	41.0	
	99.2	

Source: International Monetary Fund and International Bank
for Reconstruction and Development, Direction of
International Trade (New York: United Nations),
Series T, V. IV, N. 1/2, pp. 298-301; Series T, V.
VI, N. 10, pp. 271-73; Series T, V. XI, N. 9, pp.
363-66; Annual 1958-1962, pp. 269-70.

and Asia in the hope of replacing the markets it expects to lose
in the United Kingdom. Exports to Japan for the twelve months
to June 30, 1960, showed that Japan had made purchases totalling 161,700,000 Australian pounds, or the equivalent of U.S.
$355,740,000--an increase of 27 million Australian pounds
over the previous year. This forecasts future closer ties between Australia and Japan in trade. [4]

In 1959, the leading nations as markets of Australian exports, in the order of their importance, were: the United
Kingdom, Japan, the United States, New Zealand, France,
Italy, Mainland China, West Germany, Belgium, and Luxemburg, Malaya and Singapore, and Canada. Of the major exports of Australia, wool, in 1956, went mainly to the United
Kingdom, but by 1964, Japan became the best market. Meat
and butter still go to the United Kingdom primarily. Wheat
recently has gone to Communist China in large quantities.

Regarding the imports of Australia: The sterling area is
still the most important area of supplies and the United Kingdom the leading supplier. But the same trends revealed in
the export trade are discernible in imports. The relative
importance of the different areas and countries has changed.
The United Kingdom cannot supply the equipment and goods
to keep pace with the industrial progress in Australia. As
indicated in Table 56, the share of the United Kingdom in
Australian imports has declined in the postwar period, and
so has the share of the sterling area as a whole. While nonsterling Europe's share in 1962 surpassed the prewar level,
Asia's share has improved but is still below the prewar level.
The countries which have made gains in their shares of
Australia's imports in the postwar period are the United States,
West Germany, the Netherlands, Japan, Malaya and Singapore.

Factors in favor of the sterling area's keeping its lead in
Australian trade are, among others: traditional associations which
provide established business connections with British firms
and individuals; easy payment procedure as the Australian
pound is still closely related to the pound sterling; the available shipping facilities provided by the British; the commercial methods and techniques in common; and the political
affinity. But all these have not prevented the other industrial
powers from gaining ground in Australia. Australia's pur-

Table 55

Destination of Australia's Major Exports, 1955

	Value (in million Australian pounds)	Destination	Percentage
Butter	25	United Kingdom	85
Meat	58	United Kingdom	75
Wheat & Flour	66	United Kingdom	22
		Japan	12
		New Zealand	9
		Indonesia	8
Wool	338	United Kingdom	25
		Japan	19
		France	16
		Italy	9
Cres & concentrates of silver, lead, zinc	9	United States	
		United Kingdom	
		Belgium-Luxemburg	
Refined silver, lead, and zinc	26	United Kingdom	
		United States	
		Ceylon	
Iron & steel, processed	4	New Zealand	
		Japan	

Source: Australia's Continuing Development, pp. 61-62.

chases from the United States have been handicapped by the dollar shortage. Japan and West Germany will be very promising sources of supplies for Australia. [5]

In 1959, the leading nations sending merchandise to Australia, in the order of their importance, were: the United Kingdom, the United States, Japan, West Germany, Canada, Indonesia, Iran, India, Malaya and Singapore, and the Netherlands.

Of the major sources of Australia's important imports, ma-

Table 56

Direction of Australian Trade

	1938	1948	1959	1962
Australian Exports (in percentage of her total exports)				
North America	9.9	10.1	12.1	14.0
Sterling Area	75.4	66.8	44.4	...
Non-sterling Europe	20.4	24.4	20.4	...
Asia	10.4	13.0	23.5	30.7
United States	7.9	8.3	9.5	12.3
United Kingdom	63.4	43.5	27.0	19.3
Japan	4.3	0.8	13.6	16.5
Australian Imports (in percentage of her total imports)				
North America	24.1	12.2	11.0	25.3
Sterling Area	53.4	56.7	46.6	...
Non-sterling OEEC	10.3	6.0	13.7	...
Asia	17.4	11.4	14.4	16.1
United States	16.4	9.4	12.8	20.9
United Kingdom	42.8	41.7	31.9	30.5
West Germany	4.0	---	4.9	5.7
Netherlands	0.5	0.9	1.8	1.3
Japan	4.9	---	3.6	5.2
Malaya and Singapore	0.9	1.0	1.5	1.6

chinery, tools, and equipment are still mainly from the United Kingdom. Transportation equipment is from the United Kingdom, the United States, and Germany. Iron and steel products are

Table 57

Sources of Australia's Imports, 1955
(in millions of Australian pounds)

	Value	Sources
Raw Materials		
Tobacco	16.2	United States, Rhodesia
Cotton, raw	6.4	United States, Pakistan, Mexico
Petroleum, crude	44.3	Borneo, Middle East, Indonesia
Rubber, crude	15.2	Malaya, Papua
Copper	3.6	Rhodesia, Belgium Congo, Union of South Africa
Iron and Steel	38.9	United Kingdom, United States
Textile		
Bags	10.2	India
Cotton yarn	2.5	United Kingdom
Rayon, silk yarn	2.5	United Kingdom
Carpets, linoleum	10.0	United Kingdom
Silk, rayon piece-goods	4.8	United Kingdom
Cotton, linen piece-goods	37.2	United Kingdom, Japan
Machinery, equipment		
Transport equipment	98.6	United Kingdom, United States, Western Germany
Electric equipment	35.5	United Kingdom
Other machinery	109.5	United Kingdom

Source: Australia's Continuing Development.

from the United Kingdom and the United States. Textile material and products are from the United Kingdom and Japan.

COMPOSITION OF TRADE

The most important change in the composition of the exports of Australia is the decline of wool and butter, which once were her chief exports. Wool is her biggest export item, but, with the exception of 1957, wool prices have not been good. Wool's share in Australia's total exports has declined from 48.8 per cent in 1952, to 40.0 per cent in 1959. Butter amounted to 7.5 per cent of Australia's total exports in 1938, but only 2.6 per cent in 1959.

In the postwar period, some food items have gained importance to make up for the decline in butter. These are fish, barley, and fruits. Other crude materials gained importance to make up for the decline in wool: for instance, hides and skins and mineral fuels.

Because of the progress made in industries in the early postwar period, Australia has improved her exports of manufactured products: for instance leather goods, metal products, chemicals, and paper. Australia has also become an exporter of some machinery, electric equipment, motor vehicles, and tractors.[6] However, in the 1950's, exports of manufactures had fallen from 12 per cent to 6 per cent of production, and constituted only 13 per cent of her total exports. Exports of manufactures did not grow with the industries. This was largely due to the keen competition in the Far East and the high tariff and severe import controls practiced by the Far Eastern countries. Manufacturing in Australia is operated on a small scale due to the lack of manpower. Consequently, it may not have the efficiency to compete in the world market in such fields as textiles, paper, paint, rubber tires, chemicals, and electric appliances where in the 1950's there was excess capacity.

About Australia's imports: Because of her progressive industrialization program, there was, from 1952 to 1959, an increase in her imports of crude materials and machinery and transport equipment, both in their value and in their share of the total imports.

There was, during the years from 1952 to 1959, some decline in the imports of manufactured consumer products: for instance, petroleum products, paper and paperboard, miscellaneous fabrics, and textile products. This can be attributed to the growth of the local industries to provide a higher degree of sufficiency. 7

BALANCE OF PAYMENTS

In the postwar period, Australia has a tendency of unfavorable balance of payments for goods and services. The situation is not so much due to deficits in the merchandise trade as due to the large outpayments for transportation, insurance, returns for foreign investments, and government purchases. The deficit is balanced by the private capital that continues to come in. There is no need for much international bank or official loans. Australia has a large outshipment of gold, but this is because Australia is a gold producer. Gold is a merchandise for export. Outshipment of gold for monetary reasons has been rare. Her official holdings of gold and foreign exchange have fluctuated but show no signs of long-run deterioration.

An interesting development in the international payments of Australia, in the postwar period, is apparent upon analyzing her payments with the various areas. From the information on exports and imports in Table 56 on the direction of trade, it is evident that, in the years from 1956 to 1959, Australia had an unfavorable balance with the sterling area and also an unfavorable balance with the United States. Consequently, Australia has a shortage of pounds and American dollars for making payments.

During the same period, from 1956 to 1959, Australia had a favorable balance with nonsterling Europe and also a favorable balance with Asian countries. In other words, Australia has been earning foreign exchange from nonsterling Europe and Asia to meet the payments to the sterling area and the dollar countries. Therefore, it is reasonable to believe that Australia will double her efforts to promote her trade with nonsterling Europe and Asia, be-

Table 58

Australia's Holdings of Gold and Foreign Exchange
(in millions of U. S. dollars)

	Total	Gold	Foreign Exchange
1952	1,032	112	920
1953	1,362	117	1,244
1954	1,133	138	995
1955	835	144	691
1956	953	107	845
1957	1,321	126	1,195
1958	1,120	162	958
1959	1,226	154	1,072
1960	843	147	696

Source: International Monetary Fund, International Financial
Statistics, Washington, D. C. , 1961, December
issue, p. 46.

cause with the proceeds from these areas   she can buy more
of the needed capital equipment and essential materials from
the sterling areas and the dollar countries.

The exchange rate for buying and selling pounds sterling
has been fixed since 1931 at 1. 25/1. 255 Australian pounds
sterling. From 1939 to 1951, Australian rates for nonsterling
currencies have fluctuated in a manner paralleling the sterling
rates for these currencies. Since 1951, the sterling and dollar
rates have been fixed, and, therefore, the Australian rate for
the dollar is also stabilized. [8]

Australia has a fine investment climate for foreign capital.
There is no restriction on the remittance of capital funds to
Australia, except that exchange-control approval must be
obtained. Exchange-control approval is also required for remittance abroad of net income resulting from foreign investment. There is an agreement between the United States and

Australia to eliminate double taxation on investment income.
Foreign investment has come to Australia mainly from the
United States, the United Kingdom, and New Zealand. Most
of the capital inflow is for investment in oil and mineral ex-
ploration and in manufacturing. The proportion of portfolio
investment in foreign investment has increased. A substantial portion of profits is reinvested, but the amount of remittance overseas creeps up steadily. The investment from
the United States has tripled from the accumulated $201
million in 1950, to $601 million in 1957. One half of the
United States investment is in manufacturing. [9]

TRADE CONTROLS

The first commonwealth tariff, introduced in 1901, was a
mild revenue tariff. The 1908 tariff rates were raised for
protection purposes and preference was given to British
goods. This was the beginning of the dual column tariff.
From 1914 to 1918, World War I stimulated industrial development in a wide range of industries. The tariff of 1920
was intended to protect these new industries growing out of
the war, and the margin of preference for British goods was
widened. The Industrial Preservation Act of 1921 imposed
special duties on goods coming from countries with depreciated
currencies. In 1921, a Tariff Board was set up to advise the
government on trade and tariff. In 1927, a special committee
was appointed to investigate the tariff policy, and in 1929 the
committee made a report. It warned the government not to
raise tariff rates, mainly for the reason that high prices and
higher cost would make Australian products uncompetitive in
the world market. But the depression caused the markets for
Australian goods to decline, and higher tariff rates resulted in
the period 1929 to 1930. There were 50 per cent surcharges on
a number of items and total import prohibition on others.
When the world market collapsed after 1930, Australia sought
shelter within the sterling area. The Ottawa Conference of
1932 launched a strong Imperial Preferential System. This
was achieved not by lowering tariff rates for British Commonwealth products, but by raising rates against non-Common-
wealth products. The United Kingdom, in return, granted
lower rates on Australian goods. The Imperial Preferential

System benefited some industries, but harmed others. Industries finding good markets in the United Kingdom benefited: for instance, dairy products, meat, sugar, and fruits. But industries depending largely on markets outside the United Kingdom suffered, as other countries raised their tariff rates in retaliation against the dual column tariff system. Therefore, there were in Australia as in the United Kingdom, mixed feelings toward the Imperial Preferential System.

In 1936, tariff rates were raised on a number of commodities: for instance, cotton and silk piece goods from Japan and cars from the United States. In 1938, as Australia gained efficiency in agricultural and iron and steel products, she was able to compete in the world markets. Subsequently, there was a trend toward lower tariff rates and freer trade. During World War II, Australia adopted an import licensing system to protect certain desired war industries. Industries were classified into three categories:

(1)   Rigid licensing of imports was instituted to protect those industries desired for permanent establishment in Australia.

(2)   Temporary licensing of imports was instituted to protect those industries not desired for permanent establishment but which were necessary to meet the exigencies of war, and assistance of liquidation was to be given after the war.

(3)   No licensing for other industries.

Australia now has a three column tariff: the preferential rates for the British Commonwealth of Nations; the most favored nation rates for the most favored nations group including the United States; and the general tariff rates to the remaining nations. Since 1947, Australia has been a member to the General Agreement on Tariffs and Trade (GATT); and the margin of preferential and most favored nation rates have been bound against any increase. [10]

Balance of payments crises occurred in 1951, 1954, and 1955, and in those years import licensing of varying degrees was put into operation. Improvement of wool prices in 1957 resulted in a substantial, but not complete, lifting of import licensing. The lowering of wool prices in 1958 and 1959, and the shortage of U.S. dollars, led Australia back to import licensing again. But by October, 1960, with improvement in balance of payments, import licensing was lifted except for a few luxury items.[11]

Notes to Chapter 8

1. Australia's Continuing Development (Melbourne: Australia and New Zealand Bank, Economic and Statistics Department, 1953), pp. ix-xi.

2. Australia's Continuing Development, op. cit., p. 31.

3. Australia's Continuing Development, loc. cit.

4. Australia's Continuing Development, op. cit., p. 64; The Los Angeles Times, January 1, 1962, Section 1, p. 13.

5. Australia's Continuing Development, op. cit., p. 64; The Los Angeles Times, January 1, 1962, Section 1, p. 13.

6. Bertram Stevens, New Horizon (Sydney: Peter Huston, 1946), p. 31, and Australia's Continuing Development, op. cit., pp. 57-65.

7. J.B. Condliffe, The Development of Australia (London: Free Press of Glencoe, 1964), pp. 114-18.

8. International Financial Statistics (Washington, D.C.: International Monetary Fund, 1961).

9. The Australian Market, (New York: J. Walter Thompson Co., 1959), pp. 38-39; Condliffe, The Development of Australia, op. cit., p. 124.

10. U.S. Department of Commerce, Bureau of Foreign Commerce, World Trade Information Service, Economic Reports, Part 1, No. 55-21, p. 5.

11. ibid., No. 60-7, p. 21.

CHAPTER 9 TRADE OF INDIA

India, a typical nation of Asia in that it is highly aware
of its nationalistic political accomplishment, is very earnest in its efforts to achieve rapid military and economic
build-up. India has maintained a neutral foreign policy in
the cold war, and has gained for itself a prominent position
in world affairs. Neither side in the cold war can afford to
lose India to the other camp, and large amounts of economic assistance have come from the United States, Russia,
the United Kingdom, Canada, Australia, New Zealand, and
various international financial organizations. The government of India has taken the leadership in pursuing an economic development program through a number of Five-Year
Plans. The first Five-Year Plan covered the period 1951-56,
the second 1956-61, the third 1961-66, and the fourth 1966-71.
A continuous theme in these plans has been the emphasis on
heavy industries and social overhead. As a result, India has
a wide industrial basis in heavy industries and is rapidly gaining self-sufficiency in capital goods in a number of fields. In
1962, it was reported that India was self-sufficient in sugar
manufacturing machinery, produced 34 per cent of the domestic requirements of machine tools, 64 per cent of textile machinery, 75 per cent of electric motors and 85 per cent of
diesel engines. In 1962, it was also self-sufficient in light
capital goods such as typewriters, sewing machines, household refrigerators, and radios.[1] Although capital-goods industries have improved, the over-all progress for industry
and mining has been rather poor. Industry and mining remained
constant, about 17 per cent of national income for the period
1951-60. For that matter, the growth of national income at
constant prices was about 3.4 per cent annually for the period
1951-60. With the fast increase of population for the period,
the growth of per capita product was about 1.4 per cent annually.[2]

International trade, as far as its size is concerned, has
never played a large role in the Indian economy. In the
1951-60 decade, exports did not grow with production. The
total value of its exports actually fell from 5. 8 per cent of
national product in 1950, to 5. 1 per cent in 1953, and 4. 3
per cent in 1960. While the value of world trade increased by
about 55 per cent in the period 1951-60, the value of
India's exports in 1960 was 13 per cent lower than in
1951.[3]

Imports of goods and services had traditionally been
of much the same size as exports, but in the period of the
second plan, from 1956 onward, imports rose substantially.
They were financed either by a withdrawal from India's
sterling balance or by loans and grants from abroad. Despite their small size, India's imports are vital to its economy because of the capital goods and raw material content
which are badly needed in the country's economic development.

There are a number of reasons for the stagnation of
India's exports, some of which are summarized as follows:

First, the partition of India and Pakistan has cut off
the raw jute and raw cotton supplies for India's jute manufacturing industry and cotton textile industry, which were
major export industries of India. Before partition, India
had the complete monopoly of the world's raw jute and was
the world's largest jute manufacturer. After the partition,
East Bengal, the jute growing region, went to Pakistan, but
the jute factories are highly localized near Calcutta in
India. The strained economic relations of the two countries
caused a great decline in the production and exports of jute
manufactures for India. Second, the world market for jute
manufactures has greatly declined. The development of
shipping techniques has reduced the demand for jute manufactures, which are used largely in packaging agricultural
products. The bulk handling techniques in international
shipment has eliminated the use of gunny sacks, and the
small package method for local distribution of agricultural
products has substituted paper bags for gunny sacks.
Third, India's tea trade has faced keen competition from

Ceylon, though India is still the world's largest producer and exporter of tea. Tea is cheaper than coffee and cocoa, but its world demand has declined due to its low income elasticity. Fourth, India's share of world trade in cotton textiles has declined due to the keen competition from Japan, Hong Kong and Pakistan. Furthermore, the world trade in cotton textiles itself has shown no strong tendency to expand because of the industrialization of Asian and African countries which has helped these countries to become more and more self-sufficient in cotton textiles. India has not made much technical progress in the cotton textile industry. Consequently, its exports are predominantly grey cotton goods of coarse and medium grade, the very types in which the developing countries will first become self-sufficient. Fifth, India's export of coal and coke has not expanded much, due to the growing domestic demands. Sixth, the government, until recently, has not shown much interest in export promotion. On the contrary, there were often export duties and controls to keep raw materials at home to meet the growing requirements of domestic industries at the expense of the export trade. [4] Seventh, the decline of exports in value for the period 1951-60 was largely due to the 37 per cent drop of export prices rather than to a decrease in the quantity of exports. The quantity of export actually increased 10 per cent in the period.

Since 1960, exports have not expanded very rapidly. The peak of $1610.5 million was barely over the 1951 level. Imports, meanwhile, have increased sharply, almost doubling in volume over the decade 1951-60. They rose from 5.5 per cent of national product in 1950 to 11.0 per cent in 1957. After stringent restriction, the percentage was reduced to 8.4 per cent in 1958 and 7.3 per cent in 1959. [5]

In the postwar period, there was usually a deficit in the balance of trade because of the increase in the imports of food, raw materials and capital goods and the sluggishness of exports.

There is an interesting relationship between the exports and imports of India. They fluctuate closely together. Peaks of exports in 1951, 1957, and 1960 brought about peaks of imports in 1951, 1957, and 1960. Dips of exports in 1950, 1953, and 1958 brought about dips of imports in the same

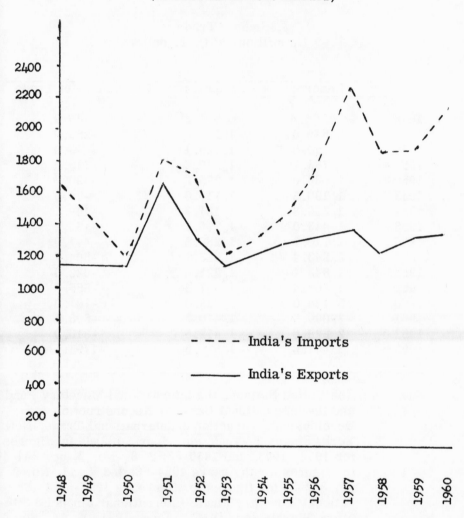

FIGURE 16
TRADE OF INDIA
(in millions of U.S. dollars)

- - - - India's Imports

———— India's Exports

Source: International Monetary Fund and International Bank for
Reconstruction and Development, Direction of International Trade (New York: United Nations), Series T,
V. 5, N. 8, pp. 182-84; Series T, V. 8, N. 7, pp.
244-46; Series T, V. 11, N. 9, pp. 332-34;
also, International Monetary Fund, International Financial Statistics (Washington, D.C.: International
Monetary Fund, June, 1961), V. 14, N. 6, pp. 36-39.

287

Table 59

India's Trade
(in millions of U. S. dollars)

	Imports	Exports	Balance of Trade
1938	575. 4	621. 3	45. 9
1948	1, 616. 0	1, 363. 0	-253. 0
1950	1, 150. 0	1, 146. 1	-3. 9
1951	1, 785. 2	1, 610. 2	-175. 0
1952	1, 686. 0	1, 295. 3	-390. 7
1953	1, 190. 2	1, 116. 0	-74. 0
1954	1, 290. 8	1, 181. 7	-109. 1
1955	1, 413. 0	1, 276. 1	-136. 9
1956	1, 710. 7	1, 268. 8	-441. 9
1957	2, 243. 4	1, 378. 7	-864. 7
1958	1, 843. 4	1, 221. 4	-622. 0
1959	1, 863. 4	1. 307. 8	-555. 6
1960	2, 124. 0	1, 333. 0	-791. 0
1961	2, 006. 0	1, 410. 9	-595. 1
1962	2, 228. 6	1, 412. 6	-816. 0
1963	2, 401. 6	1, 610. 5	-1791. 1

Sources: The United Nations, the International Monetary Fund
and the International Bank for Reconstruction and
Development: Direction of International Trade, New
York, Series T, V. 5, No. 8, pp. 182-84 for figures
for 1938, 1948, and 1950-53; V. 8, No. 7, pp. 244-46
for figures for the years 1954-56; and V. 11, No. 9,
pp. 332-34 for figures for the years 1957-59; International Monetary Fund: International Financial Situation, Washington, D. C., June, 1961, V. 14, No. 6,
pp. 36-39 for figures for 1960.

years: 1950, 1953, and 1958.

There was a shortage of foreign exchange. Consequently,
controls over trade were instituted. In 1949, the Indian cur-

rency was devalued by 30.5 per cent, in line with other sterling countries. The devaluation and trade controls succeeded in turning the balance of trade to favorable in 1949 and keeping the deficit at a very low level in 1950. [6]

India's imports increased greatly in the postwar period: from 3,601 million rupees in 1946 to 10,114 million rupees in 1960. This increase was not caused by prices. In fact, import prices on the whole declined slightly, with only a few years showing some increases. The average unit value for imports for the period 1953-60 was 99, with 1953 as the base. The increase of imports was due to the increase in quantity of goods. The quantum index for 1957 was 168, and that for 1960, 166, with 1953 as the base. This is explained by the large amounts of machinery, equipment, and materials needed for the economic development program.

DIRECTION OF TRADE

In the postwar period, there has been a significant change in the direction of the trade of India. Her trade with countries in the sterling area and countries of Asia has declined in importance though not in the absolute. Her trade with other areas has gained importance: for instance, her trade with the United States and Canada, with the countries of the Organization for European Economic Cooperation, with Middle East countries and with the Soviet area. This breaking away from the Commonwealth in trade and gaining more trade with other areas may be a result of the economic independence brought about by political independence and the industrialization program being carried out in the country. This is clearly shown in Table 60.

There has been a decline in the share of India's exports to the sterling countries since 1943. India's exports to the sterling area countries amounted to 41 per cent of her total exports in 1909, and they rose to 65 per cent in 1943. Since then, the exports gradually decreased to 47.5 per cent in 1959. India's imports from the sterling area countries amounted to 70 per cent in 1909, but gradually decreased to 56.6 per cent in 1938. After the war, they were further re-

duced to 30.9 per cent in 1959. The sterling area has become less important to India in the matter of trade; however,
it still is considered a major area of trade.[7]

There has been a decline in the share of India's imports from
the United Kingdom since the turn of the 20th century. India's
imports from the United Kingdom were 62.8 per cent of India's
total imports in 1909. They gradually decreased to 30.8 per cent
in 1938, and were reduced to 16.9 per cent in 1962. Other countries are gradually replacing the United Kingdom as suppliers of
materials and capital goods to India. For instance, India has been
buying more imports from the United States than from the United
Kingdom since 1959. The United Kingdom is still the country
taking the biggest share of India's exports. Her share increased to 34.2 per cent in 1938. After the war, the share was
reduced to 21.8 per cent in 1948, but increased to 27.6 per cent
in 1959. Then there was a reduction to 23.6 per cent in 1962.[8]
The United Kingdom is able to maintain her large share of Indian
exports because of her investments in tea plantations, jute and
cotton industries, and mineral properties. She also has
large holdings in shipping facilities.

There has been, generally speaking, a decline in the
share of India's trade with Asia as a whole. India imported,
from Asia, 31.2 per cent of her imports in 1938, but this
share was reduced to 11.5 per cent in 1959. Japan
was an important supplier of materials, providing 9.7 per
cent of Indian imports in 1938. The war cut off Japanese
imports, and India was able to find supplies from other
Asian nations, whose share of Indian imports rose from 21.5
per cent in 1938 to 28.9 per cent in 1948. After the war, as
Japan started on the road to economic recovery, she managed
to increase her share in Indian imports, but the share of
India's imports from other Asian nations has continuously declined. The same story goes for India's exports to the rest
of Asia, whose share has declined from 24.6 per cent of
Indian imports in 1938 to 18.3 per cent in 1959. Japan was
a big buyer of Indian exports, taking 8.7 per cent in 1938. During
the war, India lost the Japanese market, but she was able
to develop markets in other Asian nations, which took 27.3 per
cent of Indian exports in 1948 as compared to 15.9 per cent in
1938. However, in the postwar period, Japan has made a
comeback. Japan's share in Indian exports increased from 1.0
per cent in 1948 to 5.5 per cent in 1959. Meanwhile, the share

of Indian exports bought by other Asian nations declined, probably
due to the competition from Japan. India was able to increase
the Asian nations' share of her trade only in the absence of competition from Japan during the war. After the war, as soon as
Japan's economy had recovered sufficiently to regain markets
in Asia, Asia's share of Indian trade declined. [9]

The trade between India and the United States has shown
tremendous expansion since World War II. Before the war, the
United States played an insignificant role in India's trade. In
1913, the United States provided 2.6 per cent of Indian imports.
This share was increased to 9.5 per cent in 1918 because of
World War I. After the war it settled back to 6.2 per cent in
1938. Since then the share has steadily increased, reaching 23.4
per cent in 1962. Since 1959, the United States has overtaken the
United Kingdom as the number one supplier of India's imports.
The only limiting factor on imports from the United States is
India's ability to pay. There has been a dollar shortage since the
balance of trade between India and the United States turned unfavorable for India in the postwar period. In 1913, India sent
8.7 per cent of her exports to the United States. Because of
World War I, this share was increased to 13.8 per cent in 1918,
but settled back to 8.5 per cent in 1938 because of the depres-

Table 60

Direction of Trade of India

	1938	1948	1951	1959	1962
Exports (percentages of India's exports)					
North America	9.8	17.8	21.3	18.5	20.3
United States	8.5	15.9	18.6	15.3	16.8
Canada	1.3	1.9	2.2	2.4	3.4
Latin America	2.7	7.0	6.1	2.4	2.4
Sterling Area	52.0	56.2	54.1	47.5	....
Non-sterling, OEEC	18.1	9.9	10.9	10.1	....
Soviet Area	1.4	1.8	1.9	7.0	11.6
Other	16.0	7.3	5.7	14.5	....
	100.0	100.0	100.0	100.0	100.0
Western Europe	49.3	29.2	33.9	39.0	....
United Kingdom	34.2	21.8	25.8	27.6	23.6
West Germany	5.1	0.5	1.3	3.2	2.3
Middle East	3.8	4.8	5.4	9.2	6.2
Africa	2.8	3.2	4.2	3.0	....
Asia	24.6	28.3	20.1	18.3	14.2
Japan	8.7	1.0	2.4	5.5	4.7
Australia	1.7	5.2	6.0	3.8	2.8
Imports (percentages of India's imports)					
North America	6.8	22.1	26.5	24.8	29.3
United States	6.2	20.3	23.7	22.0	23.4
Canada	0.6	1.7	2.6	2.5	1.3
Latin America	....	3.1	....	....	....
Sterling Area	56.6	39.8	42.6	30.9	....
Non-sterling OEEC	16.8	11.1	12.6	25.2	....
Soviet Area	1.2	1.0	....	3.5	9.6
Other	18.6	22.9	18.4	15.6	....
	100.0	100.0	100.0	100.0	100.0
Western Europe	45.6	35.9	26.4	44.4	....
United Kingdom	30.8	28.6	16.8	19.4	16.9
West Germany	8.5	0.4	3.0	13.3	9.4
Middle East	5.6	12.6	13.4	9.9	5.5
Africa	4.0	2.9	3.4	4.3	....
Asia	31.2	30.1	25.4	11.5	11.4
Japan	9.7	1.2	2.6	4.6	5.3
Australia	1.5	4.9	2.1	1.3	1.7

sion. Since then the American share of India's exports has
increased to 16.8 per cent in 1962.[10] In the twenty-one
years from 1938-59, trade between the United States and
India increased more than sixfold, from U. S. $92.8 million
to U. S. $611.0 millions. This was the result of the lend-
lease program during the war, the foreign aid and technical
assistance programs after the war, and the growing United
States investments in India and abundant supplies obtainable
in the United States.

Trade between Canada and India, though still quite
small, has great possibilities for future development. Ever
since 1938, Canada's share of exports and imports to India
has grown constantly. This is due to the fast economic progress made in Canada during and after World War II. Canada
has become a supplier of manufactures, capital goods, and
metals to India. The balance of trade between the two countries in the postwar period has often been unfavorable to
India; therefore, there has been a shortage of Canadian dollars for
India to make payments.[11]

India had a well-developed trade with European countries in 1938. The trade was interrupted during the war. In
the postwar period, as the countries in the Organization for
European Economic Cooperation progressed gradually on
the road to recovery, their trade with India steadily improved. Although they took only 10.1 per cent of Indian exports in 1959, which was below the 1938 level, they supplied
25.2 per cent of India's imports in 1959, a larger share than
that of 1938. West Germany has done exceedingly well, supplying 13.3 per cent of India's imports. West Germany has
become a competitor of England and the United States in the
field of capital goods for India.

The Middle East and Africa have been playing an increasingly important role in trading with India; their share
of India's trade in 1959 surpassed that of 1938. In recent
years, there has been an increase in the trade between
India and the Soviet Area, mainly Russia. Australia has
also increased her trade with India, and she has become a
growing market for Indian exports.

The bulk of India's trade is with a small number of countries where she can obtain capital goods, materials, and food. The United Kingdom and the United States, together, took 42.2 per cent of India's trade in 1959.

FIGURE 17
LEADING NATIONS RECEIVING INDIA'S
EXPORTS AND SUPPLYING ITS IMPORTS, 1962
(in millions of U.S. dollars)

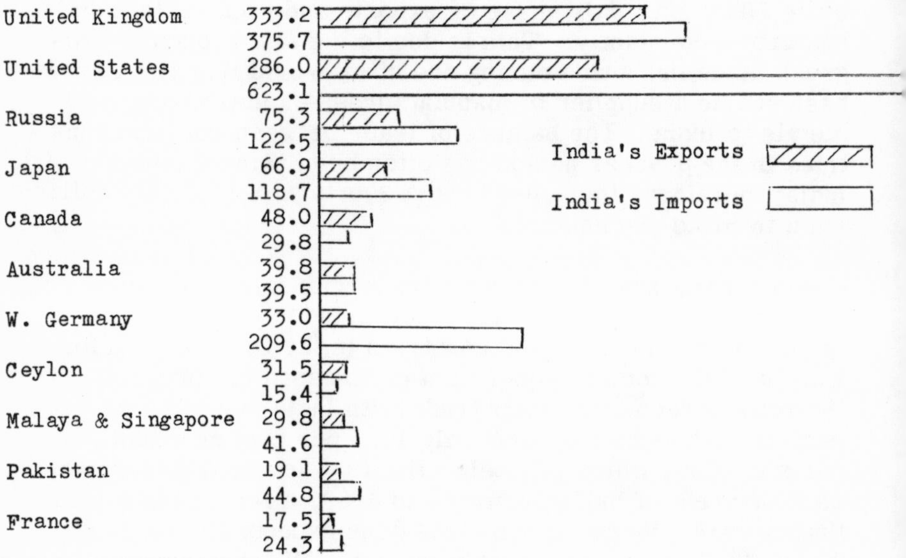

United Kingdom	333.2	
	375.7	
United States	286.0	
	623.1	India's Exports
Russia	75.3	India's Imports
	122.5	
Japan	66.9	
	118.7	
Canada	48.0	
	29.8	
Australia	39.8	
	39.5	
W. Germany	33.0	
	209.6	
Ceylon	31.5	
	15.4	
Malaya & Singapore	29.8	
	41.6	
Pakistan	19.1	
	44.8	
France	17.5	
	24.3	

Source: International Monetary Fund and International Bank for Reconstruction and Development, Direction of International Trade (New York: United Nations), Series T, V. 5, N. 8, pp. 182-84; Series T, V. 8, N. 7, pp. 244-46; Series T, V. 11, N. 9, pp. 332-34; also, International Monetary Fund, International Financial Statistics (Washington, D. C. : International Monetary Fund, June, 1961), V. 14, N. 6, pp. 36-39.

COMPOSITION OF TRADE

The major exports of India are tea, cotton fabrics, jute bags and sacks, and leather goods. Tea and jute manufactures are the two traditional major exports of India. In 1959 they still amounted to 38.1 per cent of the total value of exports of that country. Cotton fabrics and leather goods are newly developed exports, growing rapidly in importance during World War II, and in the post-war period. This new development, if it continues to be pursued, will help to broaden the base of India's exports to relieve the country from too much dependence on the markets of tea and jute manufactures.

Before World War II, India exported a large quantity of raw cotton (238 million rupees for 1938), but her export of cotton fabrics was small (48 million rupees for 1938). During the war, India captured part of Japan's cotton textile markets in Asia, the Middle East, and Africa, and consequently there was a boom in India's exports of cotton fabrics. India's export of cotton fabrics increased to 362 million rupees in 1948, and to 631 million rupees in 1954, while her export of raw cotton decreased to 140 million rupees in 1948 and to 101 million rupees in 1954. Of course, now with Japan having recaptured most of her lost markets in cotton textile, India's export of cotton textile declined somewhat. However it remains an important sector of India's exports.[12]

Tea gained importance in India's exports during World War II and continues to be important. It has always been a major commodity of India. The export of leather goods also grew steadily. In 1938, India exported only 42 million rupees of leather goods, but in 1959 she exported 285 million rupees worth, showing an increase of over sixfold.

Manufactured goods and equipment have become increasingly important in India's exports. India was originally a colonial country, exporting mainly food, crude raw materials, and agricultural products. But as the country has been undergoing industrialization, her exports of manufactured goods and equipment have increased. In 1938,

her exports of manufactured goods, articles, and equipment
amounted to 23. 0 per cent of the total value of her exports;
but, in 1961, they amounted to 43. 9 per cent (which, however,
was slightly smaller than in 1951). India's exports of manufactured goods are chiefly products of light industries such
as cotton and jute textiles and leather goods. This reflects
the initial stage of India's industrialization. [13]

In the postwar period, India's major imports of food included dried milk, wheat, rice, copra, and spices. The import of rice fluctuated, depending on the harvest in India.
The import of wheat steadily increased. The partition of
1947 has caused India to depend more on the imports of food,
because a large section of the food producing area is now in
Pakistan. India has tried to increase her production of
food to reduce this dependence on foreign supplies, but she
has not yet solved her problem. Food for some time to
come will remain as a major category of imports. [14]

India's imports of crude materials and minerals have included, in the postwar period: wool, cotton, jute, crude
petroleum, aviation gasoline, kerosene, diesel fuel, lubricants, and rubber. Her industrial progress requires these
materials. India's imports of raw cotton and, to some extent, her imports of raw jute have increased. This gain can
be traced to the partition, as cotton and jute producing areas
are in Pakistan. [15]

India's imports of manufactured goods include chemicals,
coal tar dyes, vitamins, antibiotics, medicine and phar-
maceuticals, manufactured fertilizers, plastics, newsprints,
rayon yarn, pig iron, steel ingots, structural steel, coated
or galvanized steel, plates and sheets, railway rails, copper
and brass manufactures, aluminum and manufactures, zinc,
and alloys. All these are largely industrial materials.
This is another indication of India's industrial progress.
Before World War II, India's imports were of an entirely different nature. The imported manufactures then were
consumer goods such as textiles, leather goods, glassware,
watches, clocks, toys, bicycles, sewing machines, etc.
Now, with her industrialization underway, most of the
former goods imports can be replaced with domestic pro-

ducts. [16]

India has become a good market for capital goods. She
is importing ever-increasing amounts of equipment and machinery, including: steam generating boilers, aircraft engines,
diesel and other internal combustion engines; agricultural
tractors, machine tools, rolling mill and foundry machinery;
conveying, hoisting, mining, and excavating machinery;
paper and pulp mill machinery; textile mill machinery; air
conditioning and refrigeration machinery; electric generators, transformers, switch gear converters, insulated wire
and cables; passenger autombiles, commercial vehicles,
railway coaches; and photographic equipment. [17] As mentioned early in the chapter, India has recently improved its
self-sufficiency in capital goods in a few fields. India exports to the United Kingdom: tea, jute manufactures, leather
goods, oil seeds, tobacco, raw and waste cotton, coir and
matting, wool, wool yarn and wool manufactures, hides and
skins, manganese, oils and fats. India is still a supplier of
raw materials to the United Kingdom. India imports from
the United Kingdom: machinery, vehicles, cotton manufactures, chemicals, drugs, electric appliances, iron and steel
manufactures, nonferrous metals and manufactures, woolen
textiles, cutlery and hardware, silk and rayon yarns, pottery
and glassware, paper and cardboards. India's trade with
the United Kingdom still follows the early colonial tradition. [18]

India exports to the United States: raw jute, jute cloth,
goat and lamb skins, lac, cashew nuts, sandalwood, coir
matting, coir yarn, tea, castor seed, and spices. India imports from the United States: machine tools, mining machinery,
typewriters, gas engines, tractors, oil crushing and refining
machinery, automobiles, trucks, buses, chassis and parts,
raw cotton, pharmaceutical products, toilet articles,
tobacco, and liquor. India's trade with the United States is quite
similar to her trade with the United Kingdom, with the
United States serving as a supplier of heavy industrial equipment. India, before World War II, enjoyed a favorable trade
with the United States, but after the war there was an unfavorable trade for India. [19]

India's exports to Japan follow the general pattern, in-

cluding raw cotton, raw jute, oilseed, metal ores. India's
imports from Japan include light industrial manufactures
such as clocks, matches, drugs, medicine, earthenware,
porcelain, glassware, hardware, paper and paper boards,
cotton manufactures, and silk and rayon manufactures.
India also imports capital goods from Japan, but not as
much as she does from the United Kingdom and the United
States.[20]

Canada has also become a significant trader with India.
India imports from Canada wheat and chemical fertilizers.[21]
India exports to Canada tea, jute manufactures, wool carpets,
spices, and vegetable.

India exports to Australia items similar to those to
Canada and she imports from Australia food, raw wool, liq-
uors, oils, metal ores, machinery, and mill work.[22]

India is an exporter of light industrial manufactures and
agricultural products. She is successful in developing markets in the Middle East and Africa. Her exports to Asia
have met tough competition from local producers.

In order to pursue her industrialization program, India
requires a large volume of capital equipment and industrial
raw materials. Her imports could be much larger than they
have been, if only she had the ability to pay. In recent years,
she has been drawing from her foreign-exchange reserve which
she accumulated during World War II to pay for her trade deficit in part, and she has depended heavily on grants, aid, and
loans from other nations and international organizations.
The difficulty in payments will continue to be a factor in restricting her trade and economic development for some time
to come.

In the postwar period, due to England's concentrated
efforts on the reconstruction program at home, she has not
been able to supply India with the necessary capital equipment and industrial materials. This has resulted in the
tremendous expansion of India's trade with the United States
and Canada. Gradually, India's imports from these two

countries surpassed her exports to these two countries with a
consequent unfavorable balance of trade for India. India has
had a dollar shortage, and this shortage will be a serious factor limiting her trade with these two countries. Investments
from the United States will be encouraged and are expected
to expand. These investments will provide a large source
of dollars for India to meet the shortage.

BALANCE OF PAYMENTS

Before World War II, because of the decline of prices of
raw materials and large home-charge payments to England,
India had an adverse balance of payments. India had to export gold to the amount of $1.2 billion U.S. for the eight
years from 1933-41 to meet the deficit.[23] During World
War II, the Allies bought large quantities of supplies from
India, and India's imports were curtailed due to the shortage
of shipping and exchange controls. Large trade surpluses
were recorded each year. There was also considerable
Allied military spending in India. Becuase of all these, India
was able to repay its external debts to over $120 million U.S.
and also to accumulate a large foreign-exchange reserve of
about $5.2 billion U.S.[24] India came out of the war a credi-
tor nation. India turned over all her foreign-exchange reserve to England, which serves as a custodian of the pool of
foreign exchange for the entire Commonwealth of nations. The
account is kept in pounds sterling and by agreement England
will release specific amounts to India on a yearly basis.
Out of the account, a sum amounting to $600 million U.S.
was transferred to Pakistan after the partition in 1947. After
independence, the government expenditures of India increased
due to the large defense spending and the payments made to
England for the purchase of British railways and other assets,
as England began to withdraw capital investments from India.
India has been withdrawing funds from the foreign-exchange
reserve. In 1955, the reserve declined to about $1.8 billion
U.S. [25] India has been using her foreign reserves to pay for
the needed supplies in her economic reconstruction, during
her first Five-Year Plan, 1951-56, and her Second Five-Year
Plan, 1956-61. By 1960, India's reserves declined to $670

million U. S.

Table 61

India's Gold and Foreign-Exchange Reserve
(in million of U.S. dollars)

	Reserve Bank and Government	Reserve Bank	Gold	Foreign Exchange
1952	1,976	1,729	247	1,482
1953	1,862	1,765	247	1,518
1954	1,867	1,782	247	1,535
1955	1,866	1,791	247	1,544
1956	1,435	1,360	247	1,113
1957	942	872	247	625
1958	722	644	247	397
1959	814	695	247	448
1960	670	566	247	319

Source: International Monetary Fund, International Financial
Statistics, August, 1961, Washington, D. C. p. 148.

In 1960, India's foreign-exchange reserve with the Reserve
Bank had declined to $319 million U.S. Before long, India
will not have any reserve to pay for her merchandise unfavorable balance. Her imports will have to be reduced unless
she can improve her exports or find other ways for making
payments.

Transportation and insurance have brought in a net receipt
for India. Private donations, including personal and institutional
remittances and Ford Foundation grants, have also helped India
to meet the adverse payments. Private capital has been flow-
ing out of India. This is mainly due to the fact that British
nationals are liquidating their assests in India and sending
their capital back to England. Official donations including grants
from Australia, New Zealand, Canada, the United Kingdom, the

United States, and other countries are another source of in-
payments. The long-term official capital increased heavily
from 1957 to 1960. This shows a tremendous increase in
borrowing from the United States, Russia, and the International Bank of Reconstruction and Development.

There has also been a change in the pattern of payments
with different regions of the world. Before World War II,
India had a deficit with the sterling area, but a surplus with
Canada and the United States. During the war, India's imports from the sterling area declined due to the shortage of
supplies in those countries, but India's imports from Canada
and the United States began to increase. In recent years,
India generally has a surplus with the sterling area, but a large
deficit with Canada and the United States. India has also developed a deficit with the OEEC countries because she has been
importing, heavily, capital equipment and supplies from that
area. India has a surplus balance with Latin American countries. India's balance with Far Eastern countries has been
fluctuating. [26]

In 1947, Britain allowed India to convert her assets
freely in the Empire foreign-exchange pool into dollars or any
other hard currencies. In 1949, India was admitted to full
membership in the sterling area. There was no quantitative
limitation on the drawings from the central pool to meet her
dollar needs, but India's drawings must be approved by the
Commonwealth. The sterling area is a voluntary arrangement. It is designed to serve the interest of the solvency of
the sterling area as a whole. India's drawing must be agreed
upon by Britain on a yearly basis. From 1951 to 1952, India
had no difficulty in meeting the dollar needs; in fact, she had made a
net contribution to the central pool yearly. This was mainly
due to her jute manufactures sales in the United States--a
source of dollar earnings. But from 1955 to 1960, there was
a serious deficit in payments to dollar countries, and
large drawings from the central pool have been made to
meet the needs. [27]

Foreign investments have been an important source of in-
payments for India. Immediately after independence, the

Indian leftists advocated the expropriation of foreign capital in India, but the government turned a deaf ear to the demand. British capital was treated on an equal basis with native capital. Domestic investment outlays in India are 7 to 9 per cent of the national income, which is inadequate to meet the capital need.

Foreign investments were estimated at $1,399 million in 1957, of which four fifths were held by British nationals. The British investments were mainly in the fields of tea plantation, utilities, transportation and financial institutions.

The United States was able to obtain an agreement from the Indian Government in 1957 to guarantee no confiscation and free conversion from rupee to dollar for the remittance of profits, dividends, and interests.[28] The United States investments in India have grown rapidly, with the 1956 investments at $98 million--almost three times that of 1948 at $34 million.[29] The United States investment in 1959 amounted to $136 million. About 70 per cent of this was in the petroleum industry and the rest in pharmaceuticals, office equipment, batteries, aircraft parts, jute products, tires and tubes, and beverages. There have been some investments from Switzerland and West Germany. The investment from West Germany rose from a quarter of a million dollars in 1948 to 5.7 million dollars in 1956.[30]

The fourth Five-Year Plan, for the period from 1966 to 1971, calls for a total expenditure of $45 billion with about $1.5 billion from private foreign investment. The current third Five-Year Plan, from 1961 to 1966, scheduled $23 billion expenditure with about $300 million from private foreign investment. This means the Indian Government hopes to increase foreign private investment in the next five years to five times what it was in the past five-year period. Most of the private foreign investment is expected to come from the United States. The return on Indian investment is from 10 per cent to 20 per cent depending upon the industry, according to M. Gopala Menon, resident director of the Indian Investment Center in New York. India is looking for investments in heavy engineering, petro-chemical, electrical, oil refining, electronics, farm equipment, and sea food processing industries. It is believed that India will need one more Five-Year Plan before its economy is self-generating and independent of external assistance. India's first Five-Year Plan was launched in 1951 with expenditures totaling $6 billion, 90 per cent of which was internal capital; its second Five-Year Plan with $10 billion expenditures, 80 per cent of which was internal capital. [31]

The investment policy of India is still based on the law of 1949 with a few recent modifications. It can be briefly summarized as follows:

1. No restriction or limitation on foreign private investments.

2. No restraint in remitting profits.

3. In the event an enterprise financed by foreign capital is nationalized, fair compensation will be made.

4. Major interest in ownership and effective control are to be in Indian hands.

5. Foreign investments should be in manufacturing, but not in trading, commerce, or financial enterprises.

6. The manufacturing projects should fit into the government five-year plans.

7. The projects should conserve Indian foreign exchange by reducing or stopping imports, or earn foreign exchange through exports.

8. The projects should contribute to the training of Indians in advanced techniques.

9. The projects should be located in areas acceptable to the Indian government.

10. New companies pay no tax on up to 6 per cent of the capital employed for a period of five years.

There are also tax rebates and exemptions. [32]

Recently there has been some restriction in the repatriation of foreign capital. In 1958, foreign capital investments were classified into two categories: those invested
before 1950, as old capital, consisting of capital from the
sterling area, Norway, Denmark, and Sweden, and those
invested after 1950 as new capital. Old capital is allowed
free repatriation. New capital invested in high priority projects is allowed free repatriation, but new capital invested
in low priority projects is not allowed repatriation in the
first ten years.

In recent years, India has depended heavily on foreign
loans and grants as a source of foreign exchange. The
Colombo Plan under the supervision of Britain calls for a
pool of 1, 868 million pounds to be used for the rehabilitation and reconstruction of the Commonwealth nations in
Asia in the period from 1951-57. Two thirds of the fund
was to be spent in India, with the rest spent in Pakistan,
Ceylon, Malaya, and British Borneo. The emphasis was
on transportation, communication, and agriculture taking
66 per cent of the expenditures. Industry and mining would
take 10 per cent of the expenditures and the rest of the fund
would go to housing, education, health, fuel, and power.
While capital goods would come from the Commonwealth as
a whole, the training of personnel would be conducted in
Canada, Australia, and New Zealand. The fund for the
Colombo Plan includes government loans, private investment, loans from the International Bank, and drawings from the central pool of reserves by the members.[33]

The United States, Canada, and the International
Bank have been generous in providing loans and grants to
India. In the ten years from 1949 to 1959, the Indian
government received approximately $2. 5 billion U. S. in
loans and grants. About $2.2 billion U. S. came from the
United States including the Wheat Loan of 1951, the Commodity Loan of 1956, Export Import Bank Loan, and loans
from the Development Loan Fund. In addition, there are
about $78 million U. S. of private donations. The In-

ternational Bank of Reconstruction and Development in the period from 1949 to 1957 made a total of $232 million U.S. of loans including the railway loans of 1949 and 1957, the Industrial Credit and Investment Corporation loan of 1955, and the Tata Sons loans of 1955 and 1957. Canadian government loans, in the period from 1949 to 1957, amounted to about $75 million U.S. [34]

SYSTEM OF TRADE CONTROLS

Before World War I, India had no protective tariff. India was, under the British Empire, a colonial source of supply of raw materials and handicraft merchandise. There were custom duties for revenue purposes. During World War I, it was realized that India, for the sake of defense and self-reliance, should be allowed some degree of industrialization, and for that protective tariffs might be needed. In 1921, as a result of the recommendation of a Fiscal Commission which studied the situation, the policy of protective tariffs was gradually introduced. Under the protective tariffs, the steel and sugar industries developed. There were sentiments in India for more protective tariffs and industrialization, but the Indian Government, as an institution of the British Empire, intervened to safeguard the international obligations of the British Empire. There were often occasions of conflict between the Indian Legislature, representing the protection sentiments, and the Indian Executive branch, safeguarding the interest of the British Empire. The Fiscal Commission recommended protective tariffs on a limited basis. A triple formula was adopted as a basis for granting protective tariffs to industries.

First, the industry must have the natural advantages of plentiful supplies of raw materials, cheap power, sufficient labor, and a large home market so that, given the protection, it would have a chance to develop.

Second, the protective tariff must be necessary, and the industry would not have a chance to survive without it.

Third, the protective tariff would be of a temporary nature, and eventually the industry could develop to meet world competition.

The Fiscal Commission recommended the establishment of an Indian Tariff Board and it was appointed in 1924. Before World War II the Tariff Board, following the principles of the triple formula, granted protective tariffs to a few industries including iron and steel, cotton textiles, sugar, paper and pulp, matches, salt, magnesium, chloride, plywood, and tea. The Provisional Collection of Taxes Act of 1931 authorized the basic revenue tariff. Over 700 items are specified on the Imperial Tariff Schedule. Of these, about 40 are on the free list, over 100 are subject to protective duties ranging from 10 per cent to 120 per cent ad valorem, and the remainder are subject to revenue duties ranging from 3 per cent to 100 per cent ad valorem. [35] The protective tariff for the iron and steel industry was removed in 1947. A number of industries requested protection but were denied by the government. They included chemical, oil, coal, and cement.

After World War II and her independence, India started the process of industrialization. As a result, additional protective tariffs were granted by the Tariff Board to a large number of industries, including plastic goods, glassware, slate and pencil, sericulture, rayon, phosphates, cotton cloth, yarn, gold and silver thread, wire, bicycles, caustic soda, bleaching powder, and calcium chloride.

As a member of the General Agreement on Tariffs and Trade (GATT), India was successful in obtaining concession of tariffs for 25 per cent of its total exports in exchange for concession granted to 20 per cent of its imports. India received concession on its exports of jute goods, cotton piece goods, carpets, rugs, mats, etc., and gave concessions on imports of capital goods, essential raw materials, food, and consumer goods, which were greatly needed for her reconstruction.

Protection for industries is given for short durations. After expiration, the cases will be reviewed and many may be denied further protection. In 1952, there were 42 industries under protection. Of these, 30 industries were covered by duties not too much higher than the revenue

duties. The twelve industries protected by high tariffs were:
soda ash, calcium chloride, photographic chemicals, coated
abrasives, sericulture, plastics, bicycles, cotton textile
machinery, starch, alloy, tools and special steel grinding
wheels, and iron and steel machine screws. [36]

In order to promote exports, an Export Advisory Council
and an Import Advisory Council were established under the
Ministry of Commerce, in 1954. India is ready to reduce its
protective tariffs in exchange for advantages for its exports. [37]
During the period 1952 to 1959, protection was withdrawn from
thirty-one industries, claim for protection was rejected for
eight industries, and initial protection was granted to seventeen
industries. In 1959, the average ad valorem rate for duties
of India was 16.5 per cent. As of January, 1961, there were
twenty-eight industries on the protected list. The Tariff Board
has usually granted protection for three years, subject to
review at the end of the period. There are cases where ten-
year periods of protection were granted. [38]

The tariff of India provides for both standard and preferential rates. The standard rates apply to the United
States and most countries, while the lower preferential
rates apply to the sterling area and Burma.

Trade with the Commonwealth nations is governed by
the preferential tariffs. The system can be traced as far
back as 1897 when Canada reduced her duties in favor of
the United Kingdom against other nations. In 1902, the
Colonial Conference passed a resolution requesting all
other colonies to follow Canada's lead. This preferential
tariffs system was extensively practiced by the colonies;
in 1922, there were preferential tariffs in twenty-six
colonies giving reduced tariffs to the United Kingdom and
to each another. The United Kingdom departed from the
principle of free trade in 1915 and raised protective tariffs on
industries. The United Kingdom gave reciprocal preferential tariffs to her colonies.

In 1932, at the Imperial Economic Conference at
Ottawa, a series of trade agreements was concluded among
the Commonwealth nations on the basis of reciprocal pref-

erential tariffs. India, as a member, participated in these
agreements. Preferential tariffs have been a much debated
issue ever since. Those in favor argued that India was able
to maintain a flourishing trade because of the all-round
tariff reduction among the Commonwealth nations. India
could find good markets for her exports in the Commonwealth
while there were trade difficulties in other parts of the world.
Those against the tariffs argued that India was thus bound to
the British Empire and had to maintain high duties to the rest
of the world, consequently suffering the retaliation of high
tariffs of those nations. India would not have a good chance to
develop her trade with the rest of the world.

Agreements were signed between Commonwealth nations
from time to time, to revise the preferential tariffs. For instance, tariffs governing the British--Indian trade were defined by the 1939 agreement. India allowed a preference of
10 per cent ad valorem to British goods such as chemicals,
paints, piece goods, woolen carpets, sewing machines, etc.,
and that of 7.5 per cent ad valorem on motorcycles, scooters,
and buses. Britain in return granted: free admission for
certain Indian goods such as raw jute, mica slabs, etc.; a
preference of 10 per cent ad valorem to linseeds, castor
seeds, ground nuts, leather, soya beans, and spices; and a
preference of 15 per cent ad valorem to jute manufactures,
cordage, cables, ropes, and twine, castor oil, rapeseed oil,
ground nut oil, paraffin wax; and a preference of 20 per cent
to coir mats and matting, cotton manufactures, and jute
sacks. [39]

To some Indian commercial interests the preferential
tariffs are advantageous in promoting trade within the Commonwealth, but disadvantageous in so far as the trade with
the rest of the world is concerned. It is a sacrifice of the
world trade for the Commonwealth trade. India will have
to balance the gain against the loss. As the direction of the
trade of India has undergone a significant change in the postwar period, with the trade with the United Kingdom and the
sterling area on the decline and the trade with Canada, the
United States and European countries on the rise, preferential tariffs have become more of a burden than a help.

However, on the other hand, trade within the Commonwealth has been more stable than that of the world as a
whole. Keeping the preferential tariffs may provide a
more stable trade within the Commonwealth nations.

Before World War II, there was little control over
foreign exchange. On the outbreak of the war, the Indian
Government delegated to the Reserve Bank the authority to
regulate and control foreign exchange. All dealings of foreign exchange had to be transacted through authorized
dealers and banks. No restrictions were placed on the exchange of the Empire currencies, but exchange of non-
Empire currencies was controlled, especially the U.S.
dollar and other hard currencies, as there had been shortages
of these currencies since 1942. To conserve foreign exchange and shipping space, the government established a
system of licensing imports during the war. Gold transactions were also controlled by the Reserve Bank. Imports
of gold were generally allowed. Exports of gold were only
allowed to go to the United Kingdom or the United States
and the proceeds in sterling pounds and dollars were to be
sold to the Reserve Bank. After the war, the licensing of
imports and foreign-exchange control have been revised,
sometimes tightened and sometimes liberalized, as required by India's position of international payments. In
order to deal with the critical adverse balance of payments,
Indian authorities began tightening import restrictions in
1957. Import quotas were cut from some 509 relatively
nonessential items. At the same time it was announced
that import licenses for capital goods would be issued only
to businessmen if there was foreign investment of foreign
credit to pay for these imports.

Foreign trade is handled by private enterprise, with
thousands of exporter-importers participating in trade
transactions. In 1956 a few state trading corporations
were established to handle the trade of iron ore, manganese ore, chemical fertilizers, cement, and salt. These
agencies are mainly for handling trade with Communist
countries, where trade is conducted through state monopolies. [40]

Notes to Chapter 9

1. United Nations, Economic Survey of Asia and the Far East, 1963, pp. 43-44.

2. United Nations, Economic Survey of Asia and the Far East, 1961, p. 89.

3. Manmohan Sing, India's Export Trends and the Prospects for Self-Sustained Growth (Oxford: Clarendon Press, 1964), p. 11.

4. Sing, op. cit., pp. 43, 72, 96-97.

5. United Nations, Economic Survey of Asia and the Far East, 1961, p. 89.

6. Kewal Krishna Dewett and Gurucharan Sing, Indian Economics (Delhi: Premier Publishing Co., 1951), pp. 404-12.

7. G. D. Binani and T. V. Rama Rao, India at a Glance (Calcutta: Orient Longmans Ltd., 1953), p. 1594.

8. Dewett and Sing, op. cit., pp. 408-15.

9. B. B. Ghosh, Indian Economics and Pakistan Economics (Calcutta: A. Mukherjee and Co., 1949), pp. 517-18; B. N. Ganguli, India's Economic Relations with the Far East and Pacific Countries (Bombay: Orient Longmans Ltd., 1956), pp. 19-21, 160-61.

10. T. N. Ramaswamy, Full Employment for India (Benares, India: Nande Kishore & Brothers, 1946), p. 249; H. Venkatasubbiah, Indian Economy since Independence (Bombay: Asia Publishing House, 1958), pp. 200-201; Ganguli, op. cit., p. 32, pp. 285-86; K. C. Ghosh, Economic Resources of India and Pakistan (Calcutta: K. P. Basu Publishing Co., 1956), pp. 320-21; Dewett and Sing, op. cit., pp. 418-19.

11. Ganguli, op. cit., pp. 262-66.

12. Dewett and Sing, op. cit., p. 411.

13. B.B. Gosh, op. cit., pp. 485-86; Ganguli, op. cit., pp. 16-17.

14. The Indian Market (New York: J. Walter Thompson Co.,
    1959), pp. 30-32; Ganguli, op. cit., pp. 16-17.

15. The Indian Market, op. cit., pp. 30-32; Binani and Rao,
    op. cit., p. 1594.

16. The Indian Market, op. cit., pp. 30-32; Dewett and Sing,
    op. cit., pp. 408-9.

17. Dewett and Sing, op. cit., pp. 408-9.

18. Dewett and Sing, op. cit., p. 417.

19. Dewett and Sing, op. cit., p. 417.

20. Ganguli, op. cit., pp. 154-161.

21. Ganguli, op. cit., p. 262.

22. Ganguli, op. cit., pp. 223-26.

23. International Monetary Fund, Balance of Payments
    Yearbook, Washington, D.C., 1955, Vol. VI,
    p. India-7.

24. Balance of Payments Yearbook, loc. cit.

25. Balance of Payments Yearbook, loc. cit.; H. Venkatasubbiah,
    Indian Economy Since Independence (Bombay: Asia Publishing
    House, 1958), pp. 230-31.

26. International Monetary Fund, Balance of Payments Year-
    book, Washington, D.C., 1955, Vol. VI, p. India-10.

27. Venkatasubbiah, op. cit., pp. 233-34; G.B. Jathar and
    S.G. Beri, Indian Economy (London: Oxford University
    Press, 1949), pp. 306-7.

28. Celia I. Herman, Investment in India (Washington, D.C.:
    Government Printing Office, 1961), pp. 122-23.

29. Binani and Rao, op. cit., pp. 377-79; The Indian Market, op. cit., p. 38.

Foreign Investment in India, 1956
(in millions of U.S. dollars)

Great Britain	853
United States	98
Switzerland	17
Pakistan	9
Germany	6
Other	80
Total	1,063

30. The Indian Market, loc. cit.

31. Los Angeles Times, December 19, 1964, Section II, p. 8.

32. Herman, op. cit., pp. 1-2; Los Angeles Times, December 19, 1964, Section II, p. 8.

33. New Horizon in the East (London: His Majesty's Stationery Office, 1950), pp. 32-35.

34. Venkatasubbiah, op. cit., p. 237; P.T. Bauer, United States Aid and Indian Economic Development (Washington, D.C.: American Enterprise Association, 1959), p. 108.

35. Herman, op. cit., pp. 124-25.

36. Dewett and Sing, op. cit., p. 409, pp. 446-70, 480-81. Venkatasubbiah, op. cit., pp. 246-48; Binani and Rao, op. cit., pp. 506-7.

37. Venkatasubbiah, op. cit., pp. 242-43; B.B. Ghosh, op. cit., pp. 506-7.

38. Herman, op. cit., pp. 124-26.

39. Ghosh, op. cit., pp. 513-15; Dewett and Sing,
    op. cit., pp. 473-77.

40. Venkatasubbiah, op. cit., p. 244; Binani and Rao,
    op. cit., pp. 1601-1718. There is a list of 117
    pages of exporters and importers.

CHAPTER 10 TRADE OF SOUTHEAST ASIA

A common characteristic of the trade of Southeast Asia, comprising Hong Kong, Burma, Thailand, Malaya, Singapore, South Vietnam, Laos, and Cambodia is that it reflects the underdeveloped economy of these countries in the sense that they are exporters of foodstuffs and raw materials. Malaya and Singapore had a trade boom during the Korean War, because of their entrepôt trade in rubber and tin. The other countries of this area, with the exception of Hong Kong, have not made much economic progress, except to regain, with varying degrees of success, their trade position of the prewar colonial days. Economic progress in this area is slow, due to the lack of technical capability, shortage of capital, lack of established business institutions, and the general political instability. Wars and Communist activities have further complicated the situation and have made fast economic progress impossible. All the nations in this area have a narrow range in the composition of their exports, consisting of two or three major items, with varying combinations of rice, rubber, tin, and tea. The trade of Malaya, Singapore, and Burma is basically balanced. Their early recovery in the production of rice, rubber, and tin, and the high prices they received for these commodities in the postwar period have enabled them to balance their trade with payments. Trade controls in these countries are mainly intended to protect their export prices, to extract a larger amount of government revenues from trade, and to encourage native citizens to participate in trade activities. The trade of South Vietnam, Cambodia, and Laos has shown serious adverse balances. Consequently, there is instability in foreign-exchange rates.

TRADE OF MALAYSIA

British Malaya, situated at the far eastern end of the British Commonwealth of nations, was an important dependent of the United Kingdom until 1957, when the Federation of Malaya became a fully sovereign and independent nation. In 1963, Singapore, Penang, Sarawak, and British North Borneo joined the Federation of Malaya to form the new Malaysia state. This new nation in Asia with its ambitious government and energetic people has the potential of becoming a land of promise.

The economy of Malaysia is slightly better than the economies of Southeast Asian countries, with comparatively good systems of roads, railways, ports, coastal transportation and communication services, power facilities and financial installations. The per capita national income was estimated in 1963 at about U.S. $266. The role of foreign capital and enterprise, particularly European and Chinese, and the role of foreign labor, particularly Chinese and Indian, have been of special significance in the economic development of Malaysia.

Malaysia is the world's largest producer of tin, and is second only to Indonesia in the output of natural rubber.

The economy of Malaysia can be described in three levels: at the bottom, the peasant economy producing rice and fish; at the second level, the plantation and mining economy producing rubber and tin; and at the top, the international trade economy which is centered at Singapore, Penang and Kuala Lumpur.

The peasant economy involves a large majority of the natives. Rice and fish are produced by traditional methods, using intensive manual labor. The record of about 1,000 pounds of rice per acre a year is better than that of India, but not as good as those of Japan and China. Rice is the main food supply for the people. Malaysia does not have too large a population, but it is far from self-sufficient in its rice output. About one half of the domestic demand must be met by imports. Fish, coconuts, and other farm products are produced for food and for cash. Except for the

short periods of prosperity, such as in 1951, the peasants live
in poverty most of the time, getting in and out of debt depending on the harvests of the year.

The plantation and mining economy involves some natives,
but mostly it is in the hands of Europeans and Chinese. While
the prices of tin and rubber fluctuate violently, the supply of
these commodities tends to be inelastic. Rubber takes about
seven years to grow. When production starts, it is almost
impossible to make output adjustments. If a plantation is
abandoned once, it will deteriorate, and its rehabilitation is
costly. The same conditions apply in tin mining.   A tin dredge
is expensive. If there should be any cutting back in output,
the overhead costs of equipment will become too great.
European holdings in rubber and tin are usually large-scale
operations, while the Chinese holdings are generally small,
using old fashioned methods. For the Chinese operators, the
productivity is low and the profit margin is slim. Fluctuations of the market for rubber and tin will hit both the European and the Chinese, but the damage may be more severe
for the latter group as their operations are often too small
to stand the loss. Manufacturing accounted for about 10 per
cent of gainful employment in 1955. Most industrial activities are concentrated in fields associated with primary producing and trading activities or in fields where there are
particular advantages of location in serving the domestic
market.

The most prosperous sector of the Malaysian economy is at
the international trade level. The trade of Malaysia is
mainly of two kinds: first, the importation of goods for internal consumption and the exportation of raw materials produced in Malaysia; and secondly, the large entrepot trade
which dates even before the development of the rubber and
tin industries. The main trading centers are Singapore in
the south, Penang in the north, and Kuala Lumpur in the
middle. All these centers serve primarily the well developed western part of Malaya, while the eastern part is for
the most part underdeveloped jungles with some trading
activities carried on through small coastal ports.

Brunei is not part of the newly established Malaysia.

The Deleware-sized British protectorate sultanate has a population of 94,000 and is, in contrast to the poverty in Asia,
very rich in oil and affluent in financial aspects. Since Shell
first started tapping its Seria field on the western edge of
the country, more than 500 million barrels have been exported. Production from more than 300 wells has tapered
off since the peak year of 1956, and it was thought that Brunei
might run out of oil by the end of the century. An estimated
240 million barrels remain in the Seria field. However, new
offshore finds made in 1963 appear to rule out this unpleasant
possibility. Brunei has a budget surplus every year and no
external debt. There is no income tax, and yet the government can provide for its citizens adequate services. All
education is free. There are noncontributory old age
pensions, school meal programs, disability compensation,
and free medical care for every one. The sultanate has a
stock portfolio worth $267 million from which it earned
$12.3 million in dividends in 1963. Total revenue from all
sources in 1963 amounted to $36 million, double Brunei's
expenditures. Brunei's economy is based on its oil industry which accounts for 80 per cent of its gross national
product. [1]

Historical Development

Malaya and Singapore have been, since their establishment, important trade centers for Asia. Before the founding
of Hong Kong, the British trade with South China came at
least partly through Malaya and Singapore. With their free
trade policy, they also captured part of the European trade
with Indochina, Indonesia, and the Philippines. Singapore
became the logical center for the collection and grading of
miscellaneous spices, forest products, and other raw materials known collectively as "Straits produce." This produce was controlled by the Chinese and European merchants
of Singapore. Marketing services, insurance facilities, and
shipping accommodations were provided at Singapore.

The establishment of Hong Kong provided an alternative
and more superior entrepôt for the trade of South China.
Thus, the collecting and distributing trade with China was
lost. Similarly, in the 19th century encouragement of

direct shipments to Europe from Indochina by the French and
from Indonesia by the Dutch took away much of the entrepôt
trade.

In the 20th century, imperial preference was introduced.
This undermined Malaya and Singapore's free trade position
and reduced their tradewith nonempire nations. Trade controls and foreign-exchange restrictions, practiced by the
French and the Dutch, also reduced the importance of Malaya's
and Singapore's position as trade centers.

The development of tin mining and the rubber industry
saved the day. They added far more to Malaya's and Singapore's profit than the contraction of their field of entrepôt
trade could take away. Singapore and Penang became important centers of rubber milling and tin smelting, serving
not only Malaya, but the neighboring countries as well.
There was also an expansion of the rice and opium trade
through Malaya and Singapore for the Far East. Malaya and
Singapore became a center for the oil trade in the Far East
when the oil industry was developed in Burma and Indonesia.[2]

After World War II, there was a boom in the rubber
trade and many rubber dealers in Malaya and Singapore
made fabulous fortunes in a short time. Rubber could be
shipped from Indonesia and other sources, at very low
cost, to Malaya and Singapore where it was graded and processed. Rubber then was shipped to the Far East and the
United States for a good price.

In 1946 the United States started her stockpile program
and became the largest buyer of rubber. The price of rubber under the agreement with the United States was stable.
The devaluation of the British pound in 1949 caused the
price of rubber to climb momentarily. In 1950, when China
and Russia bought rubber from Malaya and Singapore, the
price of rubber increased again: for instance, from Malaya,
45 cents per pound to $2.40 cents per pound. After the
Korean War started, due to the embargo against Communist
countries, the United States became the major buyer; the
price of rubber fluctuated around $2.00 Malayan per
pound.[3]

In recent years the entrepot trade of Malaya and Singapore has amounted to about half of their total trade. About 90 per cent of the entrepot trade is conducted in Singapore and the remainder in Penang. There has been a continuing decline in the trade in "Straits produce," but there has been some improvement in the trade of rubber. There has been a spectacular increase in the volume of trade in Western products such as machinery, manufactures, materials and foodstuffs, which are brought to Singapore from Western countries and are distributed throughout the neighboring countries. In spite of the decline from the extraordinary peak of 1951, the volume of cotton piece goods and other textile manufactures trade, in 1953, was still three or four times as great as in prewar years. The trade in condensed milk, canned fish, cigarettes, and beverages is above the prewar levels. The entrepot trade of petroleum products has increased three or four fold above the prewar volume and has been rising steadily in recent years. [4]

Because of the large scale trade activities at Singapore, the city has become a financial and manufacturing center for Malaya and Southeast Asia, with a large number of banks, brokerage offices, processing factories, stock exchanges, warehouses, and transshipment facilities all crowded into this small area. In the early postwar years, Singapore, with about one sixth of the population of Malaya, had more than one third of its income. The separation of Singapore from Malaya may have reduced somewhat the high concentration of income in Singapore, as some aspects of the business activities have been diverted to Kuala Lumpur. Meanwhile, both Sarawak and Brunei were attempting to develop ocean ports of their own.

In the postwar period there has been a tendency for imports of Malaya and Singapore to exceed exports in value by a small margin, with the exception of the Korean War period when there was a big expansion in exports and a large margin of favorable balance of trade resulted. From 1956 to 1958, imports grew faster than exports in quantities, but import prices were weaker than export prices, thus leaving Malaya and Singapore slightly favorable terms of trade.

Table 62

Trade of Malaya and Singapore
(in million Malayan dollars)

	Imports	Exports
1946	793	720
1947	1,368	1,323
1948	1,791	1,764
1949	1,853	1,721
1950	2,915	4,014
1951	4,756	6,074
1952	3,873	3,917
1953	3,238	3,020
1954	3,140	3,105
1955	3,822	4,156
1956	4,153	4,166
1957	4,410	4,171
1958	4,096	3,726
1959	5,647	5,913
1960	6,229	6,394
1961	6,193	5,935
1962	6,483	6,043
1963	6,813	6,178

Source: Statistical Office, United Nations, Yearbook of International Trade Statistics, New York, 1958, p. 194.
Prior to 1955 base period weights are used for quantum indexes and current period weights for the unit
value indexes. Beginning 1955, the unit value indexes are computed with the weights of 1949.

Imports of Malaya fluctuate with exports quite clearly.
Peaks of exports in 1951, 1957, and 1960 were matched by
peaks of imports in the same years. Dips of exports in 1953,
1958, and 1961 were followed by dips in imports in 1954, 1959,
and 1961 (usually a year behind).

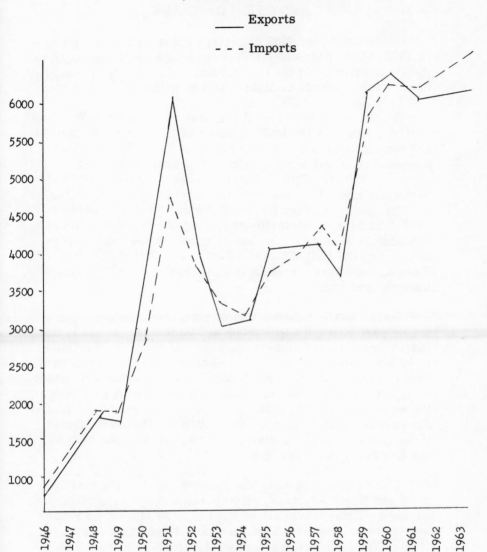

FIGURE 18
TRADE OF MALAYA AND SINGAPORE
(in millions of U.S. dollars)

_____ Exports

- - - Imports

Source: Statistical Office, United Nations, Yearbook of International Trade Statistics (New York: United Nations,
1958), p. 194.

321

DIRECTION OF TRADE

Since the Federation of Malaya gained her independence in 1957, there has been some decline in Malaya's exports to the United Kingdom; but the sterling area is still the leading buyer of the exports of Malaya and Singapore.

In 1938 and 1948 and at the peak of the Korean War, the United States was the leading buyer of the exports of Malaya and Singapore; but in the latter part of the 1950's the United Kingdom regained her position as the leading-buyer nation. By 1960 the United States was again the leading buyer. Japan has made fantastic gains as a buyer country, taking, in 1957, more than ten times the value of her purchases in 1948. The major countries receiving the exports of Malaya and Singapore in 1962, arranged according to their importance, are the United States, Japan, the United Kingdom, Russia, Indonesia, West Germany, France, Italy, Australia, Canada, and India.

So far as the export trade of rubber is concerned, a major part of it goes to Europe and America. In 1956, one fourth went to the Common Market, one fourth to the United Kingdom, two fifths to the United States and Canada, 5 per cent to the European Free Trade nations, and the remainder to Japan and other nations. The export trade of tin follows the same pattern. In 1956, sixty per cent went to the United States and Canada, fifteen per cent to the Common Market, three per cent to the United Kingdom, and one per cent to the European Free Trade nations.

The Common Market has become, next to the sterling area and North America, an important market for Malaysian exports. External tariffs of the Common Market on rubber and tin have been low: 3 per cent and 10 per cent respectively. These rates are comparatively insignificant. So far Malaysia is much concerned about whether it wants to be affiliated with the Common Market. However, if Malaysia should develop later a large export trade in vegetable oils, the high rates of the Common Market tariffs on vegetable oils may present a problem.

    While Singapore and Kuala Lumpur handle the trade of all
Malaysia, Penang is a port of Northern Malaya. It handles largely
the trade with Northern Sumatra, southern Burma, and southern
Thailand. All of these are somewhat isolated areas. Penang has
a small industry which is mainly confined to processing a few of
the region's exportable commodities: for example, tin smelting,
coconut oil production, rubber milling, and saw milling.

FIGURE 19
LEADING NATIONS RECEIVING EXPORTS OF
MALAYA AND SINGAPORE AND SUPPLYING THEIR
IMPORTS, 1962
(in millions of U.S. dollars)

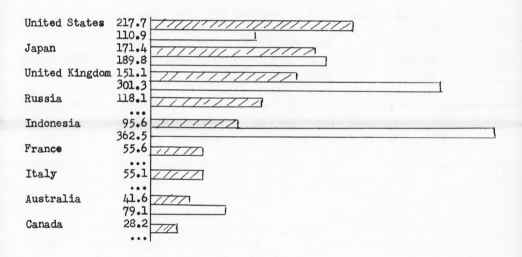

Nation	Exports	Imports
United States	217.7	110.9
Japan	171.4	189.8
United Kingdom	151.1	301.3
Russia	118.1	...
Indonesia	95.6	362.5
France	55.6	...
Italy	55.1	...
Australia	41.6	79.1
Canada	28.2	...

Source: International Monetary Fund and International Bank for
        Reconstruction and Development, Direction of Inter-
        national Trade (New York: United Nations), Series T, V. 11,
        N. 9, pp. 353-55.

As far as supplying the imports of Malaya and Singapore in the postwar period (while the sterling area has been able to maintain its leading position), Asia has made tremendous gains in importance, supplying, in 1957, more than double the value it supplied in 1948. The major countries supplying the imports of Malaya and Singapore, in 1962, arranged in the order of their importance, were: Indonesia, the United Kingdom, Japan, the United States, Mainland China, Australia, Hong Kong, Western Germany, and the Netherlands.

COMPOSITION OF TRADE

The major exports of Malaya and Singapore consist of three groups: rubber, mineral ores, and vegetable oils. The three groups amount to 90 per cent of the total exports in value in the postwar years. Among the mineral ores are tin, iron, gold, and aluminum. Vegetable oils include palm oil, coconut oil, oilseeds, and copra. These commodities, together with pepper and forest products, make up the contents of the exports of Malaya and Singapore often referred to as the "Straits produce."

The most important export commodity of Malaya and Singapore is rubber. Rubber is not a native plant but was brought to Malaya from Brazil. In the 1880's, commercial plantation of rubber in its experimental stage was successful throughout the entire area. By 1919 about one half of the world's output of rubber was produced in Malaya. The profit then was so high that 40 per cent yield on the capital was not uncommon. Between World War I and World War II, the Malayan government, due to rice shortages, discouraged too-rapid expansion in rubber plantation, but without much success. Commercially speaking, even in the worst depressions, rubber producers were better off than rice producers. After World War I, the price of rubber was stabilized by the Stevenson Scheme which provided a rigid formula based on the previous quarter's average price, for the restriction of outputs of participating countries. This brought about a short period of prosperity to Malaya and Singapore. The scheme collapsed in 1928 due to mainly two reasons: (1) the development of synthetic rubber by the United States--reducing the world demand for natural rubber, and (2) the steadfast refusal on the part of the Dutch government to cooperate in limiting the output of the Dutch Indies. While Malaya and Singapore limited their output of rubber, the Dutch Indies expanded its output. Malaya and Singapore, in the long run, were hurt by the Stevenson Scheme. At the beginning of the scheme, Malaya and Singapore had fifty per cent of world's planted area of rubber, but by its end, they had lost their leading position. After 1928 the price of rubber dropped, and, by 1932, it was about one fortieth of what it had been in 1925. In 1932 the Dutch government joined in a second restriction scheme which lasted until the Japanese occupation. The basis for the second scheme was to restrict outputs of rubber for the various producing countries in order to ensure a 7.5 per cent return after allowing all costs including depreciation and replanting provisions. In the postwar period, the price of rubber has fluctuated violently, depending very much on American consumption and stockpiling of rubber. During the Korean War the price of rubber climbed considerably. In 1955, there was a rise in the price of rubber and, consequently, there was a favorable balance of trade for that year. From 1956 on, there has been a decline in the price of rubber. [5]

Prior to World War II, Malaya and Singapore participated in an international restriction program for the export of tin. The cut in tin export for Malaya and Singapore was severe because quotas for the various producing countries were based on the 1929 output--a low level output for Malaya and Singapore. The cost of production of tin in Malaya and Singapore was lower than that in Bolivia and Nigeria, but Malaya and Singapore could not enjoy a competitive position because of the international restriction program. In the postwar period, the recovery of the tin industry was slow, and until 1949 the small output had been bought entirely by the United Kingdom. It was during the Korean War period that heavy American stockpiling raised the price and stimulated rapid recovery of the industry. [6]

Iron ore is abundant, but the iron industry had not developed because of the scarce and poor quality supply of coal in Malaya and Singapore. Iron ore is exported to Japan and

Europe. Aluminum ore is also exported. There is no aluminum smelting industry in Malaya and Singapore because of the absence of cheap electric power. [7]

The imports of Malaysia include a large variety of commodities. Approximately one third of the imports (in value) are foodstuffs for domestic consumption, of which rice from Burma, Thailand, and Indochina is the most important item. Another one third consists of manufactured goods supplied by the United Kingdom, India, Continental Europe, America, and Japan. Part of these goods are for domestic consumption, and part are to be re-exported to the neighboring countries. The remaining one third are raw materials or semi-processed materials, principally rubber, tin, oil, copra, rattans, and forest produce obtained from the neighboring countries for further processing or re-exporting to the world.

BALANCE OF PAYMENTS

The international payments position of Malaya and Singapore has been, on the whole, very sound. For the forty-three years from 1895 to 1938, the balance of trade of Malaya and Singapore had always been favorable. This was mainly due to the development of the rubber and tin industries under the British control.

In the period between World War I and World War II, Malaya and Singapore were regarded by the United Kingdom as important sources of United States dollars. During the postwar period the trade balance for Malaya and Singapore has been satisfactory. There were years with trade deficits, but the large trade surpluses during the Korean War more than offset the deficits. The export surplus for 1951 was nearly $2 billion Malayan. There were trade deficits for 1957 and 1958, but again a trade surplus appeared in 1959.

Investment income payments are usually in the negative for Malaya and Singapore. This is due to the heavy foreign investment in Malaya and Singapore, for which

dividends and profits have to be made yearly. Private donations are also usually in the negative, on account of the large
numbers of Chinese and Indians constantly making remittances to their families and relatives in their home countries.
These negative items in the balance of payments are offset
by the positive items such as transportation income, official
donations, and official and bank capitals.

Although Malaysia has a persistently favorable balance
of trade with dollar and European currency areas, she has
an uncertain balance with other countries, particularly Indonesia and Japan.

Balance of payments for Malaysia is a very important
matter to its economy because of the relatively large size
of its trade. Exports of domestic products constitute over
a third of the gross national product. Imports for domestic
consumption also amount to a third of the gross domestic
expenditures. [8] Therefore, any problem in its balance of
payments will have significant repercussions on its economy.

Malaysia's earnings of foreign exchange through exports fluctuated a great deal due to the unstable markets
of rubber and tin. This makes it necessary for Malaysia
to maintain much higher reserves of sterling balances
than would be required where the international structure
is more stable.

Under the present currency system, which requires
the currency issue to be backed at least 100 per cent in
sterling, fluctuations in export earnings tend to be reflected at once in corresponding movements in internal
liquidity and, consequently, in patterns of spending on imported goods and services. Balance of payments deficits
are, in this way, corrected without a persistent or serious
drain on sterling balances, and it is not likely for an exchange problem to develop.

However, in case there is a deficit fiscal policy or a
policy to increase credits of commercial banks, an increase
of domestic expenditures will lead quickly to an increase

Table 63

Federation of Malaya and Singapore Balance of Payments
(in millions of U. S. dollars)

	1956	1957	1958	1959
A. Goods & Services	206	-19	-147	464
Exports, f.o.b.	4,010	3,978	3,562	4,240
Imports, c.i.f.	-4,152	-4,408	-4,094	-4,124
Transportation	229	271	239	234
Investment income	-181	-146	-93	-114
Others	300	286	239	228
B. Private Donations	-267	-283	-288	-270
C. Private Capital	42	56	51	56
D. Official Donations	12	29	35	40
E. Official & Bank Capital	112	103	-63	-232
Long term-capital	8	-1	-10	49
Short-term capital				
Net IMF position	---	---	-3	-2
Other short-term capital	104	104	-70	-279
Monetary gold	---	---	---	---
F. Errors & omissions	-105	114	432	-58

Source: International Monetary Fund, International Financial
Statistics, Washington, D. C., February, 1962,
p. 305.

in the demand for imports. If there is no corresponding increase in earnings through exports, the balance of payments
will be in difficulty. The margin for financing development
through budget deficits or liberal credit policies, without
creating balance of payments difficulties, is consequently very
narrow.

Before 1957, Malaya and Singapore received large sterling receipts arising from expenditures of British forces
stationed in this area. This source of foreign exchange has
ceased to exist. The availability of financial resources presents one of the most difficult problems for the economic

development of Malaysia. Recent government outlays have
been raised substantially, and taxes are becoming heavier.
Domestic savings for long-term investments are inadequate.
Foreign private and government capital will have to be
attracted to meet the needs of the economic development program of Malaysia, unless domestic savings can be effectively
encouraged.

Malaya and Singapore are members of the sterling area,
and their dollar earnings are deposited in the dollar pool at
London, from which they are allocated yearly withdrawals. [9]

Exchange Rate

The exchange rate has been maintained by Malaya at the
fixed relationship of 8.57 Malayan dollars to one pound sterling since 1906. The Malayan dollar is tied to the pound
sterling. For instance, following the devaluation of the pound
sterling in 1949, the Malayan dollar was also devalued in the
same proportion. The Malayan dollar has been very stable.
The par rate--that is the midpoint annual average rate--has
fluctuated only between $3.05 to $3.07 Malayan to one United
States dollar in the period from 1952 to 1958. [10]

Trade Control

Singapore and Penang are, generally speaking, areas of
free trade. There are no restrictions on imports from the
sterling area and soft currency countries. As members of
the sterling area, they have some restrictions on imports from
the Soviet area and from hard currency countries such as the
United States. From mid-1948 there have been restrictions
on the importation of textiles, trucks, and automobiles from
hard currency countries. Since 1949 no importation of foodstuffs from the hard currency countries has been allowed.
Singapore and Penang prepare annual import programs which
are submitted to the United Kingdom authorities. This enables
production in the British Commonwealth of Nations to be planned so as to meet the import requirements of Singapore and
Penang with a view of minimizing their dollar expenditures.
Since 1950, there have been export duties on rubber, tin, tin
ore, coconuts, and palm products for revenue purpose. [11]
The Federation of Malaya levies import duties, the average

rate of which in 1956 was 16 per cent ad valorem.   The tariff
is for revenue purpose. [12]

Imports are also regulated by licenses. For most import
commodities, open general licenses are issued. For imports
from hard currency countries they are issued for six-month
terms and for those from soft currency countries twelve-month
terms. Each license covers only the importation of one particular
supply and has to be surrendered after that transaction is completed. The purpose is for the government to regulate the
imports from hard currency countries, so that the earnings
of hard currencies can be used for buying only the items considered essential for the economic life of Malaysia.

The future of the trade of Malaysia and, for that matter,
the future of the economic development of Malaysia depends
a great deal on the future of the rubber and tin trade. Of
these two industries, rubber is by far the more important.
At least ten people are employed in the rubber industry
for every one in the tin industry. A substantial expansion
in the tin industry is considered unlikely. Therefore, Malaysia
will have to gamble its future on the rubber industry, which
is the largest earner of foreign exchange for the country.
The future of the rubber industry depends on its ability to
compete with other natural rubber producers such as Indonesia and Libya, on the one hand, and with the synthetic
rubber industry in industrial countires, on the other hand.
The Federation of Malaya completed its first five-year
plan of 1956-60, and began carrying out its second five-
year plan for 1961-65. In that second five-year plan, the
government scheduled a total of $376 million for capital ex-
penditure of which $333 million was allocated to economic
and social development. Priorities were assigned to those
primary industries which are responsible for the major part
of the country's output. The rubber replantation scheme
received the largest single allocation. Other priority industries include cocoa, coconuts, coffee, oil palms, hemp,
pepper, pineapples, ramie, and tea. [13]

In the planning for economic development, Malaysia em-
phasizes private enterprise, with the government's part
limited to the sector where there is the need for large business organizations, capital, and advanced techniques

such as power, irrigation, transportation, and communication. Cement and fertilizers are under government operation, and fishery may be a field for the government to enter. The international Bank for Reconstruction and Development advocates more government efforts for the expansion of vocational training facilities, assistance in technical and market research, and improvement in the industrial credit system. The consensus is that manufacturing and trade in general should be left to private business.

There are difficulities in the industrialization of Malaysia. A major factor unfavorable to its industrialization is that, except for its deposits of iron ore, Malaysia is relatively poorly endowed with the complex of basic materials usually associated with advanced industrial development. Convenient sources of cheap electric power are lacking; domestic supplies of fuels are very limited and of poor quality.

Another difficulty in the development program is still the shortage of capital. With the population growing at the rate of 3 per cent per year, national income must be promoted to match this growth; otherwise, not only will there be no improvement, but the present standards of living cannot even be maintained. In 1957, the capital formation, estimated at 8 per cent of the national income, was far from being adequate.[14]

The Federation of Malaya is one country where the Western investor is not plagued with fears of nationalization, frozen profits, bureaucratic red tape, and endless procrastination and squeeze. Most of the capital came from the United Kingdom, and the remainder from Hong Kong, Japan, and the United States. To encourage investment, guarantees were given that there would be no nationalization of private firms or discriminatory legislation. In 1958, a law was passed which gave pioneer status to new industries which were officially approved. Both Malayan and Western firms were offered complete relief from income tax for two to five years, depending on the amount invested. They were assured of protective tariffs, the waiver of import duties on essential imports and the free transfer of profits abroad. Many foreign firms are increasing their investments in Malaysia, including Shell, Esso, Unilever, and Dunlop. Foreign assets are reported to have increased 16 per cent from 1955 to 1962.[15]

A factor in favor of industrialization is that Malaysia possesses a much higher degree of enterprise, business experience and skills than most Asian countries. Established habits and disciplines conducive to manufacturing operations and efficient marketing and commercial systems create an environment favorable to industrial growth. What is likely to happen is the development of a rather large range of light industries on a small-scale basis.   It seems that some further expansion of rubber processing, vegetable oil processing and tin smelting can be considered.

TRADE OF HONG KONG

Hong Kong, with 400 square miles of territory and a population of three million, is a thriving community. Its national income for 1960 was estimated at Hong Kong $5,000 million (equivalent to U.S. $875 million) and an average annual wage for an unskilled worker of Hong Kong, $1,800 (equivalent to U.S. $315). It compares favorably with most of the Asian countries in the standard of living of the people. Since the Communist conquest of mainland China, Hong Kong has been making fast progress in industrialization. It enjoys ample supplies of capital, labor, and, above all, enterprise. Many Shanghai capitalists succeeded in transferring funds to Hong Kong for industrial and commercial development before Shanghai fell into Communist hands. The large refugee population has provided an almost inexhaustible supply of both skilled and unskilled labor and kept the wages in relation to productivity. Among the refugees from mainland China are many enterprising businessmen, bankers, and technicians, providing the necessary know-how and drive for the industrialization of Hong Kong. A firm government pursuing a liberal policy in relation to trade, a stable currency linked to sterling but using a system of exchange control much more liberal than any other in the sterling area, and a well-developed system of education have all helped the recent economic growth.

Postwar Development

Hong Kong ranks fifth among the Asian countries in the total value of trade. Those with larger trade are Japan,

China, India, and Malaya. With deep-water harbors, excellent
storage facilities, low port dues, and duty-free entry for most
goods, it has served as an important distribution center of
trade between China, Southeast Asia, and the rest of the world.
Before the outbreak of the Sino-Japanese War in 1937, it was
estimated that about two thirds of the colony's exports were
local products and one third re-exports. [16] In 1962, 73 per
cent of exports were local products and 27 per cent re-exports.

Table 64

Trade of Hong Kong
(in millions of Hong Kong dollars)

	Imports	Exports	Balance
1946	934	797	-137
1947	1,550	1,258	-292
1948	2,078	1,604	-474
1949	2,903	2,474	-429
1950	3,802	3,755	-47
1951	4,892	4,460	-432
1952	3,788	2,913	-875
1953	3,875	2,740	-1,135
1954	3,436	2,420	-1,016
1955	3,720	2,540	-1,180
1956	4,567	3,127	-1,250
1957	5,150	3,022	-1,928
1958	4,594	2,993	-1,601
1959	4,949	3,278	-1,671
1960	5,864	3,938	-1,926
1961	5,970	3,930	-2,040
1962	6,657	4,387	-2,270
1963	7,412	4,991	-2,421

Source: The United Nations, Yearbook of International Trade
Statistics, New York, 1959, Hong Kong.

In the postwar period, Hong Kong generally had an unfavor-

FIGURE 20
THE TRADE OF HONG KONG
(in millions of Hong Kong dollars)

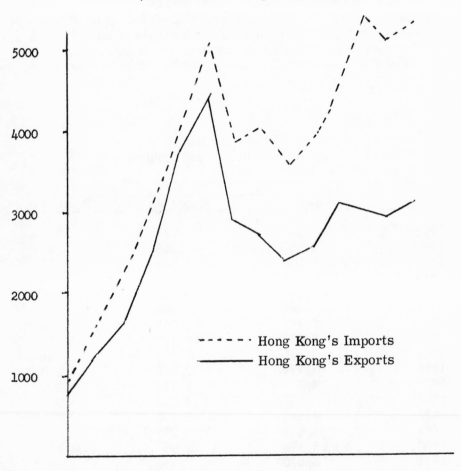

Source: International Monetary Fund and International Bank for
Reconstruction and Development, Direction of Interna-
tional Trade (New York: United Nations), Series T, V. 11,
N. 9, pp. 269-70; Annual 1958-1962, pp. 339-40.

able balance of trade. This was largely due to the increasing
volume of imports needed to supply the growing population whose
ranks were swelled by the huge influx of refugees. These
repeated unfavorable trade balances were met by the inflow of
funds either in the form of foreign investments or remittances sent in by overseas Chinese.

In 1950 and 1951, there were sizeable increases in the
value of both the imports and the exports; this was due to the
boom brought about by the Korean War. From 1951 to 1954,
both imports and exports dropped, as the Korean War boom
collapsed and the United States, the United Kingdom, Canada,
and Japan imposed an embargo on the shipment of all strategic materials to China, Hong Kong, and Macao. From 1954
on, as the embargo and restrictions were gradually relaxed,
the trade of Hong Kong began to recover.

The imports and exports of Hong Kong fluctuate together
closely. Peaks of exports in 1951 and 1956 were matched by
peaks of imports in 1951 and 1957. Dips of exports in 1954
and 1958 were matched by dips of imports in the same years,
as shown in Figure 20.

Direction of Trade

The major countries of destination of Hong Kong's exports in 1958, arranged in the order of their importance,
were: the United Kingdom, Malaya and Singapore, the United
States, Thailand, Indonesia, mainland China, Japan, Australia, Formosa, and Portuguese Asia.

The sterling area is a very important market for Hong
Kong; its share of Hong Kong's exports in the postwar period
not only has increased in value but also in percentage. The
United Kingdom, Malaya and Singapore, and Australia are
buying increasing amounts of Hong Kongs exports, and also
have improved their shares of Hong Kong's total exports.

Hong Kong's exports to the United States declined considerably in 1952 and 1953, owing to severe restrictions imposed by the United States on imports presumed to be of
mainland-Chinese origin. The total value of trade between
Hong Kong and the United States during 1952 dropped to about

FIGURE 21
COUNTRIES OF DESTINATION FOR HONG KONG'S
EXPORTS AND SOURCES OF ITS IMPORTS, 1958
(in millions of U.S. dollars)

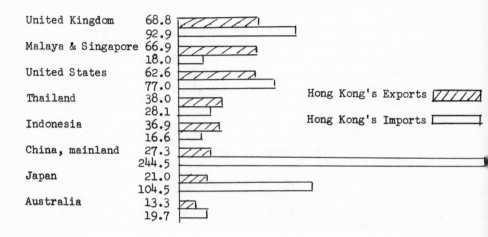

Source: International Monetary Fund and International Bank for
Reconstruction and Development, Direction of International
Trade (New York: United Nations), Series T, V. 11, N. 9
pp. 269-70; Annual 1958-1962, pp. 339-40.

one third of its 1950 level. After lengthy negotiations, the list of
local manufactures which could be shipped and brought back by
tourists to the United States under certification of origin was extended in 1953. However, the value of Hong Kong's exports to the
United States during the first nine months of 1953 declined further
and was only one half of that of the corresponding period in 1952.
After 1955, Hong Kong's exports to the United States began to
recover rapidly. [17]

Mainland China was a big market for Hong Kong's exports in 1946, taking 39.3 per cent of the total. Following the Communists conquest of China, by the end of 1949 the market for Hong Kong's exports also disappeared. For one thing, the Communist Chinese Government encouraged direct trading with foreign countries. For another, it aimed at confining exports and imports to essential commodities. By 1958, mainland China's share of Hong Kong's exports was reduced to 5.2 per cent. [18] There had also been a decline of Hong Kong's exports to Japan, South Korea, and the Philippines in 1957 and 1958, due to the application of the production origin restrictions. The result was a decline of Hong Kong's exports to Asia. Asia took 72.5 per cent of Hong Kong's exports in 1948, but only 51.2 per cent in 1958.

However, Hong Kong's exports to some Asian countries, such as Indonesia, Thailand, and Formosa, increased considerably during the postwar period. [19] As of 1958, the major countries supplying Hong Kong's imports were the following, arranged in order of their importance: mainland China, Japan, the United Kingdom, the United States, Thailand, West Germany, Switzerland, Australia, Malaya and Singapore, and Indonesia.

Although the sterling area has been supplying Hong Kong with goods of increasing value, its share in Hong Kong's imports has declined in percentage from 27.7 per cent in 1948 to 22.4 per cent in 1958. The same goes for the United Kingdom: from 14.4 per cent in 1948 to 11.5 per cent in 1958. The North American share of Hong Kong's imports declined in dollar value and in percentage. This is also true in the case of the United States, mainly due to the embargo and the dollar shortage. However, there has been a fast increase in Hong Kong's imports from the nonsterling OEEC countries, both in value and in importance. This is especially noteworthy with the imports from West Germany, the Netherlands, and Switzerland. The manufactured goods and capital equipment from these countries have made great inroads into the markets of Hong Kong and from there to Southeast Asian countries. Asian countries have improved their share in Hong Kong's imports. Mainland China has improved her share from 20.7 per cent in 1948 to 30.4 per cent in 1959. Japan has also improved her share from 3.8 per cent in

1948 to 13.0 per cent in 1958. The large influx of Chinese refugees into Hong Kong in the postwar period has made Hong Kong more dependent on the food supplies of mainland China and cheap consumer goods from Japan.

Composition of Trade

Because of the fast increase of population in Hong Kong in the postwar period, there has been a corresponding increase in the import of food, beverages, tobacco, and manufactured consumer goods to meet the needs of the population. For the same reason, there has been a decline in the exports of these items, as domestic consumption has reduced the exportable surpluses.

Hong Kong has developed some minor industries producing light consumer goods for export to Asian countries. These exports, in addition to the re-export of manufactured goods and capital equipment from Europe and North America, are reflected in the increase of exports of such commodities as cotton fabrics, textile products, enamelled household utensils, footwear, lacquers, paints, preserved fruits, plastic articles, iron, steel, and aluminum ware, cement, and furniture. [20]

Tariffs

Hong Kong is an open port. There is no duty for exports or imports. There are, however, excise taxes for five groups of commodities, either imported or manufactured in the colony for local consumption. These are liquor, tobacco, mineral oils, toilet preparations and proprietary medicines, and table waters. A preferential rate of tax for liquor of Empire origin is levied at approximately 80 per cent of the rate for non-Empire product. Locally produced beer is allowed a further preferential margin on Empire beer.

A drawback on exports is permitted on duty-paid commodities manufactured locally. This means that if a businessman paid taxes on some imports and he had manufactured exports out of these imports, he, then--upon shipping these exports out of Hong Kong--will be refunded the taxes paid on these imports.

Trade Controls
_____

There are four groups of imports for which special licenses are required.

(1) Dutiable commodities such as petroleum, liquor, tobacco, and methyl alcohol.

(2) Goods dangerous to public health and safety, such as arms, ammunition, explosives, narcotics, and chemicals.

(3) Strategic commodities such as electrical equipment, transportation equipment, and atomic energy equipment.

(4) Restricted commodities such as gambling equipment, sugar, rice, meat, radio sets, gold, diamonds, silver, and coal.

Since 1951 (when the United States imposed an embargo against Communist China, North Korea, and North Vietnam), new groups have been added to the restricted list, such as: metals, minerals, rubber products, precision and scientific instruments, and machinery parts and tools. [21]

For exporting to the United States, certificates of origin are required to show the commodities are not made in Communist China. These certificates can be obtained at Hong Kong General Chamber of Commerce, the Chinese General Chamber of Commerce, the Indian Chamber of Commerce, or the Department of Commerce and Industry for a small fee. There is a small amount of exemption for tourist purchases. [22]

Foreign-exchange control in Hong Kong is a rather complicated matter. There are different procedures for transactions with different areas. Generally speaking, there are three areas:

(1) Scheduled area, commonly known as the sterling area, including the British Commonwealth of Nations except Canada, British protectorates, British trust

territories, Burma, Iceland, Ireland, Jordan, Libya, and Middle Eastern countries. There is no restriction on the conversion between Hong Kong dollars and the currencies of this area.

(2) American account area, including: Canada, Bolivia, Columbia, Costa Rica, Dominican Republic, Ecuador, Guatemala, Haiti, Honduras, Liberia, Mexico, Nicaragua, Panama, the Philippines, El Salvador, Venezuela, and South Korea, in addition to the United States. This is often known as the dollar area. The conversion from Hong Kong dollars to American is done at the open market, and the rate is much higher than the official rate. Conversion at the official rate is only allowed for external accounts for the import of a few essential commodities.

(3) Transferable account area, including countries other than the two above mentioned groups. Special permits are required for the conversion between Hong Kong dollars and the currencies of these countries. [23]

Notes to Chapter 10

1. Los Angeles Times, Los Angeles, December 5, 1963, Section VIII, p. 8.

2. T. H. Silcock, The Economy of Malaya (Singapore: Donald Moore, 1957), pp. 8-12.

3. Joan Wilson, The Singapore Rubber Market (Singapore: Eastern Universities Press, 1958), pp. 34-36.

4. Louis Chick and others, The Economic Development of Malaya (Baltimore: Johns Hopkins University Press, 1955), p. 133.

5. Silcock, op. cit., pp. 17-26.

6. Silcock, op. cit., pp. 14-15.

7. Silcock, op. cit., pp. 26-27.

8. International Bank of Reconstruction and Development,
    Economic Development of Malaya (Baltimore: Johns
    Hopkins Press, 1955), p. 22.

9. Dun J. Li, British Malaya, the American Press, New
    York, 1955, pp. 37-40; United Nations, Economic Com-
    mission for Asia and the Far East, Economic Survey
    of Asia and the Far East, Bangkok, 1953, p. 98.

10. International Monetary Fund, International Financial
    Statistics, Washington, D.C., March, 1962, p. 186.

11. Economic Survey of Asia and the Far East, op. cit.,
    New York, 1948, p. 438; 1949, p. 267.

12. Robert J. Barr, American Trade with Asia and the
    Far East (Milwaukee: Marquette University Press,
    1959), p. 35.

13. Barr, op. cit., p. 34.

14. Silcock, op. cit., pp. 40-1.

15. Economic Survey of Asia and the Far East, op. cit., 1962,
    pp. 16-22.

16. Economic Survey of Asia and the Far East, op. cit., New
    York, 1948, pp. 234-36.

17. ibid., 1953, pp. 55-56.

18. B.N. Ganguli, India's Economic Relations (Bombay:
    Orient Longmans, 1956), p. 86.

19. Economic Survey of Asia and the Far East, op. cit., 1953, p. 56.

20. Economic Survey of Asia and the Far East, op. cit., 1953, p. 55.

21. Hong Kong, Department of Commerce and Industry, Directory
    of Commerce, Industry and Finance (Hong Kong: Marklin
    Advertising Ltd., 1961), pp. 80-85.

22. loc. cit.

23. Directory of Commerce, Industry and Finance, op. cit., p. 89.

The economic structures of the Far Eastern nations are
quite different from one another since the countries have ex-
perienced varying stages of economic development and industrialization. It would be difficult to generalize about the trade
of this region. What is said to be true in one instant may not
apply in another. Furthermore, there have not been enough
years of postwar development for certain definite trends to be
established. It is necessary to keep this complexity of the subject matter in mind when the common characteristics of trade
or the general patterns of economic development are being
discussed.

The Far East no longer forms an economic entity; the Cold
War has cut it into two halves. On one side is Communist Asia
including Communist China, North Korea, and North Vietnam,
with their trade oriented toward the Soviet Bloc. On the other
side is the free Far East comprised of the rest of this region,
with its trade oriented toward the West. The Soviet Bloc has
tried to push through an economic offensive to capture some
of the trade of free Far Eastern countries, but so far it has
not made much progress. It has seldom gained more than 8
per cent of the trade of the entire free Far East region. However, within this region there is a group of neutral countries
(for instance, India, Indonesia, Burma, and Ceylon) where
the Soviet Bloc has made some inroads into their trade.

Japan is vitally interested in regaining her trade with continental Asia, especially with Communist China, but her attempts to reopen this trade have been obstructed by the embargo.
Japan has succeeded in gradually obtaining liberalization of the
embargo provisions allowing more items to be sent to Communist China. However, there is little hope that Japan will
regain its prewar position in the trade with mainland China unless the Cold War issues are satisfactorily resolved. Under
these circumstances, the trade of the Far East will continue

to develop in two camps, with a pro-West trade growing in the free Far East and a pro-Soviet Bloc trade developing in Communist Asia.

The Far East has undergone a political transistion from colonial status to independent nations in the course of World War II or shortly thereafter. The war and the postwar economic difficulties of the Western nations and their loss of political control in the Far East have inevitably weakened their economic position in their former colonies. The United Kingdom's share in the trade of the Commonwealth nations in the Far East in 1960 was smaller than in 1938. France's share in the trade of Vietnam, Cambodia, and Laos, in 1959, was much smaller than that in 1953. The United States share in the trade of the Philippines in 1958 was much smaller than that in 1938. The Netherlands suffered the most severe loss in the trade of Indonesia, with its share in the trade of Indonesia reduced to insignificance in 1959. As the Western powers were losing their grip on the trade of their former colonies, an opening was presented to other advanced industrial powers to go in and exploit the situation. Consequently, West Germany and Japan, whose positions were strengthened by their remarkable economic recovery in the postwar period, availed themselves of this opportunity to obtain increasingly larger shares of the trade of free Far East. The United States, although suffering a reduction in its share of the trade of the Philippines, has gained larger shares of the trade of other free Far Eastern nations.

A major difficuluty undermining the trade of the Far East is the imbalance of international payments for the current accounts of goods and services of the various nations. Some are more fortunate than others in this respect. Japan, Burma, Australia, New Zealand, Malaya, Singapore, Ceylon, and Pakistan do not have basic problems with their international payments, but due to the price fluctuations of their exports, they may from time to time suffer some deficits in international payments. There is no need for these nations to resort to severe restrictive tariffs which are long-term measures to limit imports, but temporary import restrictions through licensing and quotas will be employed when the need arises. Some nations, Taiwan and Thailand included, are less fortunate in that their imports tend to exceed exports chronically.

In these countries, military build-up or industrialization program will have to be financed through long-term borrowing
or foreign aid. For countries such as South Korea, South
Vietnam, Cambodia, and Laos, imports exceed exports out
of all proportion and a serious basic imbalance of their international payments exists. Their exchange rates will be
unstable, and they will have exchange controls for years to
come.

          What will happen to the trade of the Far East in the
future? An analysis of the postwar development reveals
a few outstanding factors which will have a long-run im-
pact on the patterns of commercial activities of the nations in the region.

ECONOMIC DEVELOPMENT
THROUGH INDUSTRIALIZATION

          The postwar development of international trade of the
Far East has a great deal to do with the economic development of the area as a whole and should be studied in that
context. The central theme of the economic development
of the area has been industrialization. Through industrialization, the different countries hope to improve their national
income in the aggregate and in the per capita sense. Industrialization is pushed through under government leadership and planning with varying scope and effectiveness. In
the case of Japan and Malaya, there is complete freedom
of enterprise. The governments do not dictate to their
businessmen decisions concerning production and marketing.
The Japanese Government only proclaims certain guiding
principles, forecasts the future development requirements,
and applies certain restrictive or encouragement measures.
Its final goal is not to improve the public sector of the economy at the expense of the private sector, but, on the contrary,
to benefit private business. These are the countries where
the capitalistic philosophy prevails. To the other extreme,
there are Communist China and Indonesia, where planning
is very extensive in scope and major decisions of production, the allocations of resources, and distribution of commodities are made by the governments; in these countries the

public sector has gained at the expense of the private sector.
These are the countries where Communism or state social-
ism flourishes.   Between these extremes are the majority
of the Far Eastern countries.

Although the promotion of industrial output has been the
emphasis in all these countries, there is a big difference in
the types of manufacturing to be promoted first: a problem
of assigning priorities in planning.   In Hong Kong and Malaya,
where production decisions are entirely left to private enterprise, the emphasis has been on consumer goods.   In this case
initial capital requirement is small, the turnover of capital
is fast, and business can expect better chance of good quick
returns.   However, there may be the danger of the heavy
industries falling behind and creating long-range development
difficulties.   In mainland China and India, where there is a
large public sector, the government takes the initiative in
making many production decisions.   Their emphasis has
been on heavy industry, such as the iron and steel, machinery,
and transport equipment manufacturing fields.   The government is also engaged in power, water, transportation and communication facilities.   In these fields, large amounts of capital are required, and there are no quick returns.   The immediate economic growth will be slow, but because of the
building up of the industrial base, economic growth in the
future may be better assured.

How successful has been industrialization in the Far
Eastern countries under government planning?   The results have not been uniform.   Some plans were too ambitious
while others were too conservative.

As indicated in Table 65, Taiwan, Japan and South Korea
had high planned rates of growth of over 5 per cent.   The
planned rate is about right for Taiwan as it agrees with her
actual rate of growth for 1960 and 1961.   The planned rate
for South Korea is too ambitious, and her actual growth in
1960-61 was behind.   However, the planned rate is too conservative for Japan, as compared to the actual rate of growth
of 1961-62.   Most of the Far Eastern countries (including
Burma, Ceylon, India, the Philippines, and Thailand)
set their planned rates of growth at about 5 per cent

Table 65

Planned and Actual Growth Rates of Gross National Product
(selected Far Eastern countries, in constant prices)

	Planned Period	Planned Rate of Growth	Actual Rate of Growth	
			1960	1961
Burma	1961-64	5.9	8	-2
Ceylon	1959-68	5.9	7	4
Taiwan	1961-64	8.0	8	8
Malaya	1961-65	4.1	9	5
India	1961-.5	5.6-6.0	7	..
Indonesia	1961-69	3.7	1	..
Japan	1961-70	7.8	13	14
South Korea	1962-66	7.1	2	3
Pakistan	1960-64	4.4	6	4
Philippines	1959-66	5.9-6.0	4	6
Thailand	1961-66	6.0	12	4

Source: United Nations, Economic Survey of Asia and the Far
East, 1962, p. 179.

annually. Of these countries, some have attained their goal in
1961 and others have not. Lower rates, of around 4 per cent a
year, were planned for Malaya, Pakistan, and Indonesia. While
Malaya and Pakistan will have no difficulties in attaining their
goal, Indonesia's showing in 1961 was disappointing. Since
there are countries with some of their actual rates of growth
surpassing their planned goal and others failing to attain the
goal, the over-all experience for the Far Eastern countries in
carrying out their economic plans for 1961 was not all unsatis-
factory.

Judging by the figures in Table 66, the annual rate of
growth of the Gross National Product of the Far Eastern countries in the second half of the 1950's, ranging from 2.6 per
cent to 9.7 per cent, compares not unfavorably with the
Western countries--the United States at 3.3 per cent and the

Table 66

Annual Rate of Growth of Gross National Product
1953-54 to 1960-61
(at 1960 prices)

	Gross National Product	Primary Sector	Industrial Sector	Manufac- turing
Burma	4.5	3.2	8.4	9.3
Ceylon	4.0	1.7	5.6	5.3
Taiwan	6.3	5.0	7.2	5.5
Malaya	3.2	2.9	5.9	...
India	3.4	2.0	3.5	...
Indonesia	2.6	3.8	0.02	...
South Korea	4.5	3.6	11.1	13.8
Pakistan	2.7	1.2	8.0	7.1
Philippines	5.1	1.0	8.8	9.5
Thailand	5.6	4.6	6.9	4.9
Weighted average	3.6	2.3	5.2	4.9
Japan	9.7	3.5	6.5	6.7
Australia	3.8	-0.3	4.7	4.4

Sources: United Nations, Economic Survey of Asia and the Far
East 1962, p. 192 and p. 196; op. cit., 1963, pp. 34-5.

United Kingdom at 2.5 per cent. Because of the fast population
growth in the Far Eastern countries, the annual rates of growth
of per capita product are behind the Western countries.[1] Because of the emphasis on industrialization in their economic development, all the countries listed in Table 66 for the period
1953 to 1960 had faster growth in the industrial sector than in
the primary sector.

For the period 1953 to 1960 Burma, Taiwan, South Korea,
Pakistan, the Philippines, and Japan achieved more than 6 per
cent growth in manufacturing. Of course, these very high

percentage rates of manufacturing growth should be considered
in the light that most of these countries, except Japan, start
with a very small industrial sector, accounting for about 10 per
cent of their national income.   Therefore, a small increase
in the manufacturing output in dollars would register a very
high percentage growth.

The industrialization of the Far Eastern countries does
not necessarily mean a decline in agricultural output   if we
do not assume fixed supplies of resources.   There was steady
growth in agricultural output in these countries, except Austr-
lia, during the period from 1953 to 1960.   There was adequate
manpower to meet the requirements of both industrial and
agricultural developments.   Industrialization could have diverted capital away from agriculture.   However, in the case of
Japan, high rate of capital formation has made it possible for
the high rates of growth for both industrial and agricultural
sectors.   In the case of Taiwan, the high rate   of growth   of
both sectors was due to the fact that industry and agriculture
are complementary to each other as part of the industries dealt
with the processing of agricultural products.   In the case of
South Korea, the fast growth in both sectors was probably
largely due to foreign aid.   In the case of Thailand, some of its
industries obtain their capital partially from foreign private
investments   rather than compete entirely with agriculture for
the domestic capital.   In the case of India, Pakistan, and the
Philippines, although economic planning placed emphasis on industry, there was also the policy of self-sufficiency in food production so that agriculture was not entirely neglected.

We may still argue theoretically whether this change to
industrial development is really doing the Far East any good.
We may still point out that, by the change, there may be inefficiency and waste in industrial production resulting in high
prices and poor quality of commodities, and that by going back
to agricultural specialization there may be better growth in real
national income.   However, since the Far East has made a start
in industrialization, found that is is not impossible, and has begun
to attain some degree of success, it probably has passed the
point of no return in this adventure.   For the next decade or so,
so far as government policies are concerned, this pursuit of
economic development through industrialization will most likely

remain as their central theme.

Trade and the related international economic activities have greatly facilitated the development programs of the Far Eastern countries. The contribution of trade to underdeveloped countries with an open economy has been very ably summarized by Fei and Ramis in four aspects: First, through trade these countries are able to obtain the imports of capital goods and raw materials which are necessary to improve their production and efficiency. Second, a whole range of technological alternatives developed in the West become available for these countries to pick and choose from to suit their resources, environment and development strategy. Whether they choose wisely or not, the opportunity is there. Third, through better international economic contacts, additional sources of capital can be promoted to finance the development projects of these countries. These sources of foreign capital include private foreign capital, private donations, foreign aid, and foreign loans. Fourth, the role of the export sector is to provide in itself an additional source of savings available for the expansion of the export industries. [2]

The contribution of export trade to economic development is clear in that the export trade promotes the markets of the agricultural, mining, and manufacturing sectors. However, the contribution of the import trade to economic development is not apparent. Ordinarily, imports competing with domestic production may reduce the domestic markets for domestic products. Imports of luxuries may reduce domestic savings and retard growth. However, the import of capital goods and materials which are noncompetitive will facilitate economic growth of domestic production. There are both beneficial and not so beneficial effects of imports. In the Far East, by import control and foreign-exchange control, imports competing with domestic production and imports of luxuries are greatly reduced, and imports of noncompetitive capital goods and materials greatly encouraged. Consequently, imports have a large investment content which is beneficial to economic development. Furthermore, foreign aid, foreign private capital, foreign private donations, and foreign loans have been promoted to improve the investment of these coun-

tries through imports. Therefore, imports to the Far Eastern
countries have assumed an important role in the economic development process.

Since there is a capital shortage in the Far Eastern countries, foreign sources of capital are necessary to augment investments to promote and sustain the expansion of production.
Imports financed by both current accounts and foreign capital
accounts make the necessary noncompetitive capital goods
and materials available to these countries to speed up economic development. [3]

For Hong Kong and Singapore, where their trade sector is
large and their production sector is largely engaged in the
processing of trade items, the economic development of these
two areas depends greatly on their trade.

Japan has a predominant industrial sector and trade is
promoted to support its industrial sector. The economic development of Japan has been accelerated by its trade. It can
be said that trade is the engine of growth for Hong Kong, Singapore, and Japan.

However, for the other countries of the Far East, the
trade sector is small in the economy, and the agriculture and
mining sectors are predominant. Because of the stagnant export trade of the traditional primary products, trade cannot
promote a spectacular rate of growth of the agricultural and
mining sectors, although it has successfully promoted the industrial sector of these countries. The over-all effects of trade
in economic development vary from magnificent to insignificant for the different countries, depending largely on how
large the industrial sector is. For these countries of the Far
East, trade is not the engine of growth, but, as Fei has pointed
out, trade plays a possibly important but essentially facili-
tating or supporting role. [4]

Because of economic development through industrialization, there have been some significant changes in the import
trade of the Far Eastern countries. If imports are classified
into food, other consumption goods, materials chiefly for con-

sumption goods, materials chiefly for capital goods, and capital goods, the relative positions of these component groups of imports have changed.

As indicated in Table 67, in the 1950's the consumption goods composition of imports has declined for all the countries listed with the exception of Hong Kong, where there has been a large influx of population coming from Communist China faster than the domestic consumption industries could provide for. Although the food composition of imports has increased for Malaya and Singapore, South Korea, and Pakistan, there is a decline in the composition for consumption goods other than food, so that the combined consumption-goods composition of imports has declined for these countries. In the case of Japan, there has been an increase in the import composition for consumption goods other than food in the 1950's. The reason is that Japan has become advanced in industrialization and there has been a change of emphasis from light industries to heavy industries, resulting in the increase in consumption goods imports. The percentages of imports for capital goods have increased for all listed countries in the 1950's and the percentages of imports for materials chiefly for capital goods have also increased for all listed countries except Hong Kong, Indonesia, and the Philippines.

This change in the composition of the imports for the Far Eastern countries indicates that these countries have been successful in carrying out their trade controls and in promoting the manufacturing of consumption goods. Trade controls include protective tariffs, import controls, and foreign-exchange controls. Domestic production is thus encouraged to replace imports of consumption goods achieving a higher degree of sufficiency.

Because of this, the prospects for the West to sell consumption goods to the Far East would not be very bright, but the prospect for selling capital goods and materials would be excellent.

There has been over-emphasis on the tariff reduction to promote trade with the Far East. It is often the hope that,

Table 67

Composition of Imports
(percentage distribution)

	Food	Other Consumption Goods	Materials Chiefly for Consumption Goods	Materials Chiefly for Capital Goods	Capital Goods
ECAFE Region					
1951	23.0	19.0	35.2	8.4	14.4
1961	14.5	11.6	32.2	17.7	24.0
Burma					
1951	10.0	41.6	19.7	11.9	16.7
1961	9.9	28.8	13.9	14.8	32.6
Cambodia					
1955	10.9	51.9	10.6	9:6	17.0
1961	10.2	37.6	6.1	16.9	29.2
Ceylon					
1951	43.6	20.5	13.2	5.1	17.6
1961	39.2	19.7	11.5	9.7	19.9
Taiwan					
1951	16.3	13.4	39.3	4.9	26.1
1961	10.7	6.1	41.1	7.3	34.8
Malaya & Singapore					
1951	20.7	29.1	32.6	6.4	11.5
1961	22.0	24.6	22.6	13.4	17.4
Hong Kong					
1951	17.8	20.5	38.0	10.3	13.4
1961	23.8	26.0	27.8	7.1	15.3
India					
1951	31.5	6.2	33.1	7.5	21.7
1961	11.7	5.9	25.5	8.9	48.0
Indonesia					
1951	18.0	39.8	15.2	5.3	21.7
1961	12.8	26.6	25.4	4.3	30.9
Japan					
1951	24.2	1.8	58.1	12.7	3.2
1961	11.0	2.1	44.7	30.4	11.8

Table 67--Continued

	Food	Other Consumption Goods	Materials Chiefly for Consumption Goods	Materials Chiefly for Capital Goods	Capital Goods
South Korea					
1951	3.4	21.9	59.2	10.6	4.9
1961	13.3	10.4	47.2	11.4	17.2
Pakistan					
1951	6.7	39.3	26.8	7.0	20.2
1961	17.9	8.7	15.5	11.8	46.1
Philippines					
1951	20.8	37.9	12.5	9.4	19.4
1961	16.6	10.1	22.6	5.8	44.9
Thailand					
1951	13.6	45.4	9.4	6.5	25.1
1961	7.6	31.7	13.9	10.1	36.7
South Vietnam					
1955	11.7	52.6	13.9	7.2	14.6
1961	11.3	23.4	21.6	11.8	31.9

Source: Economic Survey of Asia and the Far East 1962, pp. 208-10.

by reciprocal commercial agreements or by GATT conferences, tariffs in the Far East can be drastically revised downward to allow large flow of goods and services to the Far East. This hope is not well-founded. For the Far Eastern countries imports are classified into consumption goods and capital goods and materials. Tariff policies for the two groups are not uniform. For consumption goods, especially of the luxury goods type, and the types competing with domestic production, rates are high. Unless there is a change in policy, the economic development through industrialization will call for these high rates; negotiation, whether bilateral or multilateral, would not accomplish much to bring about drastic reduction, although there have been some minor reductions in recent years. However, for the imports of capital goods and

materials, the rates are low (or these goods enter entirely
free of duty) because these imports are required by the development programs of these countries. Any tariff on capital goods
could be easily transferred to the importer through higher
prices because of the inelastic demand. Also, there is no
reason for high tariff rates to be imposed in the first place
because imported capital goods are not competing with any
domestic production, which is nonexistent. For capital goods
on which Far Eastern countries would not mind tariff reductions, the rates are already low. For consumption goods,
where the Far Eastern countries would insist on the protective
rates, there is not much likelihood that the rates would be
lowered. There could be some "trade offs," i.e., reduction of
tariffs on consumption goods by the Far Eastern countries in
exchange for the reduction of tariffs for their exports by the
West. Tariff negotiations probably would not exert much substantial effects on the trade of the Far East.

        Even if the tariff barriers are overcome somewhat, there
will be foreign-exchange controls to make large improvement
of imports of consumption goods unlikely. The different
governments of the Far East, conserving the short supply of
foreign exchange for capital goods and imports, cannot afford
to allow much foreign exchange to be used for consumption
goods. Importers of consumption goods will face serious
exchange diffuculities. Furthermore, as the light industries
start to develop, there will be keener competition in the Far
East.

        The future of the trade between the West and the Far
East lies in the trade of capital goods and materials. There
is a mutual interest in the promotion of this trade by both
sides. Because of the comparative capital surplus in the
West and the advanced stage of technological development,
capital goods and materials have become increasingly important in the export trade of the West. In the Far
East, due to the industrialization program, capital goods
have also become an increasingly important component of
their import trade. For the capital goods and materials to
go to the Far East, tariffs will be low, foreign exchange
for making payments will be readily available (as the foreign
exchange controls are aimed at conserving the supplies

of foreign exchange for this purpose) and there will be no domestic competition to contend with. The trade of capital goods
and materials from the West to the Far East is a promising
field with golden opportunities. The promotion of this trade is
beneficial to both sides.

There has been a generally pursued policy of promoting
exports for the Far Eastern countries in order to serve two
purposes: to expand the markets of their exports and to use
export expansion to stimulate domestic production. This is
particularly essential when the domestic market is too small.
Second, exports are promoted so that their foreign-exchange
earnings can be increased to expand their capacity to import
and to better balance the payments. For instance, the fast
economic growth in Japan has from time to time induced imports to grow much faster than the foreign receipts of the
country would allow. The ensuing balance-of-payments difficulities have repeatedly led to internal adjustments, resulting in temporary slowing down of economic growth. The
history of the past ten years thus testifies to the existence of
a foreign-trade or balance-of-payment ceiling to Japan's economic growth. Export promotion would serve the purpose of
improving the country's foreign-exchange earnings and raising
the ceiling of its economic growth.

The Far Eastern countries have followed a policy of
promoting the exports of manufactures. The purpose of this
policy is to promote industrialization in these countries.
By promoting the exports of manufactures it is hoped that
the manufacturing sector will earn the necessary exchange
to buy the imports of capital goods and materials to sustain
fast growth. In this respect the Far Eastern countries have
made some progress. The promotion of exports of manufactures has improved their share of the total exports of
these countries. If we use chemicals, manufactured goods
and miscellaneous manufactured articles (SITC section 5, 6,
and 8) to represent manufactures in general, their percentages in the total exports have improved in the period 1955 to
1961 for all listed countries except Burma, India and
Japan as indicated by Table 68. In 1961 India had 43.9 per
cent of its total exports in manufactures. This percentage
was a great deal larger than those of most Far Eastern

Table 68

Percentage Distribution of Exports
(by Major SITC Sections)

	0, 1	2	3	4	5,6,8	7
Burma						
1955	83.2	13.5	0.2	---	3.0	---
1961	80.3	16.9	0.6	---	2.2	---
Ceylon						
1955	69.0	23.8	---	6.1	0.8	---
1961	70.9	21.3	---	6.4	0.8	---
Taiwan						
1955	87.6	3.9	0.6	0.1	7.8	---
1961	56.4	4.7	2.5	0.1	35.1	1.3
Hong Kong						
1955	12.7	10.7	0.1	1.0	72.3	3.1
1961	9.0	6.8	0.2	0.5	78.4	4.3
India						
1955	30.1	19.5	1.9	2.0	45.0	0.3
1961	34.9	18.0	0.9	1.0	43.9	0.6
Indonesia						
1955	13.6	60.4	22.9	2.5	0.4	0.1
1961	12.8	50.2	33.1	2	0.8	0.1
South Korea						
1955	6.2	81.6	2.7	0.2	7.8	1.3
1961	22.7	52.2	5.5	0.3	11.6	2.2
Malaya & Singapore						
1955	7.0	59.7	9.3	2.5	16.3	1.5
1961	7.5	55.6	7.7	2.5	19.7	2.4
Pakistan						
1955	10.2	83.1	---	---	6.0	0.3
1961	9.9	62.9	---	---	26.2	0.9
Philippines						
1955	34.4	59.2	---	4.2	2.2	---
1961	34.7	55.7	---	2.9	6.3	---
Thailand						
1955	52.4	45.8	---	0.1	1.5	---
1961	53.8	43.7	---	0.1	1.8	---
Japan						
1955	6.8	4.9	0.4	0.9	74.7	12.3
1961	6.3	3.1	0.5	0.8	63.7	26.6

0.   Food   1. Beverages & Tobacco   2. Crude materials

3.	Mineral fuels & Lubricants	4.	Animal, vegetable oils and fats
5.	Chemicals	6.	Manufactured goods
7.	Machinery & Transport Equipment	8.	Miscellaneous manu-factured articles

Source: Economic Survey of Asia and the Far East 1963,
          p. 37.

countries, although it declined slightly in the period 1955-61.
The percentages of exports for machinery and transport
equipment (SITC section 7) have also increased for most of
the listed countries with the fastest increase for Japan as
indicated in Table 68. Of course the capital-goods content
of the exports of the Far Eastern countries except Japan is
still insignificant. About 90 per cent of Japan's exports
consisted of manufactures and capital goods in 1961, and in
the period of 1955 to 1961 there was a change of emphasis
in the exports from light manufactures to heavy capital goods.
Again, as indicated by Table 68, the percentages of exports
for crude materials (SITC section 2) have declined for the
listed countries except Burma and Taiwan. This indicates
a great need for crude materials by the growing manufacturing industries of the majority of Far Eastern countries.

In their colonial days, the Far Eastern countries exported crude materials and imported manufactures. During
the period 1955 to 1961, in the exports of these countries,
the shares of crude materials had decreased and the shares
of manufactures had improved. Although the period is
short and the changes are small, it is still an indication
of the breaking away from the colonial pattern. It signifies
some degree of success in their policy of economic development through industrialization.

FOREIGN AID

From July 1, 1945, to September 30, 1960, the United
States had bestowed on the world a total of $85 billion of

grants and credits. Sir Roy Harrod of Oxford University re-
gards the foreign aid of the United States as almost incredible,
as he states, "It constitutes a measure of generosity which is
new in human history; only two decades ago no one would have
believed it possible."[5]

In the days of dollar shortage, foreign aid made available
the needed liquidity and undoubtedly helped American trade a
great deal. Now there is a dollar shortage in many nations.
But the problem of the over-all world dollar shortage is not
as serious as in the immediate postwar years, and, therefore,
the basis of foreign aid should be re-examined. When the
United States had a surplus balance of payments and a large
gold reserve, foreign aid was not too costly to the United
States. Now the situation is different. The gold reserve
of the United States is low, and the country has been suffering unfavorable balance of payments. To continue large-
scale foreign aid is costly. In providing foreign aid, the
United States has accomplished a feat of heroic proportions
in helping the West and the underdeveloped world to recover
and grow, but it would be unrealistic to expect the United
States to bear this tremendous burden indefinitely.

Of the $85 billion dollars of American foreign aid, about
$23.5 billion, or one fourth, has gone to the Far East, where
most countries suffer dollar shortage. Foreign aid has promoted American trade with these countries, because, without
it, they could not have bought as much as from the United
States as they did. Foreign aid in these countries has certainly promoted economic stability and political order and
has contributed to the mutual defense efforts to keep them
out of the Communist sphere of influence. In a broad sense,
foreign aid has been partially successful in achieving its objectives.

The American foreign aid was an emergency measure
to help out the war-devastated parts of the world, and it has
been extended to meet the urgent needs of the underdeveloped world. It should not be considered a cheap source
of capital to be supplied indefinitely. The time has come
to acknowledge that rendering assistance to the underdeveloped world is not the sole responsibility of the United

States. With the dwindling gold reserve in this country and
the unfavorable balance of payments in recent years, sharing
the burden with the flourishing nations of the West is a neces-
sity.

A few Western countries have given foreign aid to the
Far Eastern countries. The United Kingdom, Canada, Australia, and New Zealand have all made their contributions.
Of course, these sources of foreign aid are largely given to
the Asian countries of the sterling area.

When foreign aid eventually comes to an end, the Far
Eastern countries, in order to sustain their economic development, will have to double their efforts in promoting
foreign investments and sources of credits from international
and other agencies, unless the domestic capital formation
has become adequate.

FOREIGN INVESTMENT AND LOANS

A major cause of deficits in international payments for
the Far Eastern countries is the very large requirements of
imports of capital goods and materials. Since these countries
will not want to reduce the imports of capital goods and
materials lest their economic development slow down, they
will have to promote better sources of domestic or foreign
capital.

The Far East is poor in capital, and the accumulation of
capital through savings is slow because of the low standard of
living and high propensity to consume--except in Communist
China where by economic planning, consumption is kept low
and savings are forced. Even there the program has been only
partially successful due to the unchecked population increase.
Consequently, foreign capital has become an important factor
contributing to economic growth and trade promotion in Far
Eastern countries. There are a number of ways through which
long-term foreign capital can be raised: bonds, bank loans,
private investment, and corporation investment.

Bonds are the traditional form of long-term capital. New York and London are still important sources of capital where Australia, New Zealand, India, and Japan sell bonds to individual investors.

Commercial bank loans are usually limited to short-term credits, but recently they have begun to include some medium-term credits. The reason for banks going into the medium-term field (for periods of more than 180 days) is to meet the needs for such credits caused by the increase of capital goods and materials in international trade. The Export-Import Bank of the United States is an important source of credits for foreign merchants to buy supplies from the United States. The International Bank for Reconstruction and Development has been making long-term loans to a number of countries in the Far East including Australia, India, Japan, and Thailand. Loans made by this bank are on the basis of specific projects, which include electric power, transportation, communications, agriculture, forestry, and manufacturing fields. So far the Bank has not suffered a single default of payments; this can be attributed to the strict standards required in awarding loans and the careful scrunity in approving projects by a competent staff of many nationalities. Actually, the standards of the Bank have been so strict that the need of capital for many worthy projects is, for a large part, left unfulfilled. To fill this gap, the International Financial Corporation and the International Development Association, affiliates of the Bank, have been established. The International Financial Corporation, since 1958, and the International Development Association, since 1961, have been making "soft loans" in the Far East. "Soft loans" are also carefully made on sound economic principles. They have easier terms for borrower nations, such as lower interest, longer terms, and easier deferment for principal repayments. These loans may be payable in local currencies to avoid the difficulties in the conversion of currency. By June, 1963, the three agencies together had made a total of $2,674 million of loans in the Far East. [6] These international financial agencies should be considered big steps forward in providing the needed capital for economic development of the Far East and other underdeveloped areas.

Portfolio investment in equities is made by individuals:
for instance, an American investor's buying of shares of stock
of a Philippine corporation. Corporation direct investment
is made when an American corporation establishes a branch
factory in the Philippines. The difference between the two
is this: As a stockholder, there is little participation in the
business management, while as an owner of a branch factory, there is control in management. Of course, an in-
between situation is the joint venture: that is, the creation
of a company in the Philippines with joint ownership of an
American corporation and a Philippine corporation. This
will give the American corporation partial control. Portfolio investment in the Far East is often considered too
risky for investors. Corporation direct investment may
face various types of restrictions and limitations by the
borrower nations, because of the fear of domination by
foreign corporations. Joint venture seems to be a compro-
mise and has gained popularity as a channel for foreign investment. Private long-term investments, whether through
bonds, bank loans, portfolio or corporation direct investment, all tend to have a healthy effect on economic
growth and international equilibrium. It is the new blood
injected to the underdeveloped countries in the Far East to
speed up their economic growth. It supplements domestic
capital in providing capital for business activities where
domestic capital is inadequate or unavailable. Foreign investment moves from low interest countries to high interest
countries; therefore, it will reduce the interest differential
in the world and promote the equilibrium of supply and demand of capital in the long run. Foreign investment in promoting new business activities will improve employment in
the Far Eastern countries. It does not necessarily reduce
the employment of domestically financed activities because,
in the Far Eastern countries, there is a large reservoir of
labor supply to more than meet the needs for both types of
activities. As the foreign investment comes into the Far
Eastern countries to utilize the cheap labor supply, it will
improve the demand for labor and, in turn, bring up the
wage rates. Therefore, it is a factor in eventually reducing the wage differentials in the world. This, of course,
does not mean that an American company in the Philippines
pays the same wage to American and Filipino employees for

doing the same job. Filipino employees are usually paid
lower rates than American employees, but much higher than
local rates, thus narrowing the wage gap between nations.
New economic activities, financed by foreign capital and participated in by local people, will provide experience for the
local people. The local people, working side by side with
foreign technical personnel, will be able gradually to gain
the necessary technical knowledge. This is beneficial to
the people individually and to the nation as a whole in promoting its economic progress. Of course, a great deal
depends on the education system of these countries, and the
personnel management policy of foreign corporations. To
generalize, there are reasons to believe that foreign investment has become an important vehicle for equalizing the
returns on labor and capital among nations and for the
spreading of technology throughout the world. It is a factor working toward equilibrium in the long run.

Foreign investment in the Far East has been low. Of
the $30 billion corporation direct investment of the United
States in the world in 1959, the share for the Far East was
only $3.1 billion. The blame for this lack of interest in
the Far East can be laid at the door of the Far Eastern
countries themselves. In the immediate postwar years
some Far Eastern countries confiscated foreign capital; some limited foreign investment to 50 per cent, or less,
of the capital for companies in certain industries; some did
not allow the invested foreign capital to leave the country;
some only allowed repatriation of capital after a prescribed
number of years; some did not allow the returns to foreign
investment to leave the country; some forced the returns
to foreign investment to be converted to foreign currency
for remittance at discriminatory rates; and some applied
high tax rates on the profits for foreign investment. There
were all kinds of regulations and restrictions which made
the Far East a risky area for foreign investments, deny-
ing these countries a source of capital which was badly
needed. Some of the regulations and restrictions grew
from short-run balance-of-payments considerations, as
they were designed to reduce the out-payments for dividends,
profits, and interests. Here nationalistic emotions replaced rational thinking, and immediate gains were pre-

ferred to long-run development. The result was a short-
sighted policy. A long-run view is to create a favorable atmosphere for foreign investments. Economic growth should
be given primary concern, and improvement in investment
is necessary for the growth. The people of the Far East
must realize that if foreign capital is needed, then they
should be prepared to pay the high interest, profits, or
dividends for it. For the promotion of foreign investment,
there is need for mutual trust and sincere cooperation
between the creditor and borrower nations. There are
mutual reponsibilities. Any tendency to monopolize the
market on the part of creditor nations, or any exclusion-
ary or discriminatory policy on the part of the borrower
nations, will destroy this atmosphere and make foreign
investment difficult.

In recent years many leaders in the Far East have
gradually realized the importance of foreign investment
and have adopted positive policies for attracting private
foreign investments. Taiwan, the Philippines, and South
Korea welcome foreign capital in the productive fields
which will expand their exports and reduce their imports.
Taiwan does not allow foreign capital in sugar and petroleum industries which are state monopolies. India does
not allow foreign capital in iron and steel, heavy casting
and forging of iron and steel, heavy machinery, and
heavy electric machinery industries, but allows joint
ventures for foreign and domestic capital in iron and steel
structures, iron and steel pipes, special steel, nonferrous metal and alloys and a number of heavy industries.
Pakistan lists a group of 82 light manufacturing industries
for foreign capital to go in, for instance: petrochemical,
cotton textile, soda ash, caustic soda, drugs, etc. Australia and New Zealand leave the choice of fields of foreign
investments open, only the central banking authorities
need be consulted on royalty payments. [7] All these may be
indications that probably there is the beginning of a new
approach to foreign investments or a more rational
policy for the economic development of the Far Eastern
countries.

IMPROVEMENT IN TRANSPORTATION

The Far East is now experiencing a rapid growth in the field of transportation, providing more adequate services at lower costs than ever before. In the developing nations of the area, railroads are being built, airports constructed, air lines organized, and coastal shipping, inland waterway shipping and the trans-Pacific shipping expanded. Japan has a thriving shipbuilding industry. Oil tankers, among the largest in the world, are being built by Japan to carry oil from the Middle East to the Far East and to the Western Hemisphere. While, formerly, weeks or months were required to travel in the Far East, now trips can be made by air in a few days. The Far East is located so far away from Eruope and the American continent that it was often thought of as a land of mystery and seclusion: a situation growing out of the lack of facilities and high costs of transportation. Transportation improvements in the Far East should be regarded as a major breakthrough, because transportation costs constitute an important part of the costs of production and distribution. Any substantial reduction of these costs certainly would promote the trade of the Far East. Not only is the total volume of the trade expected to increase, but the content of the trade may change in nature. Before transportation improvements, bulky or perishable commodities were kept out of the international market in the Far East, but they may now enter the international market with growing volume and importance. Machinery, equipment, mineral ores, basic metals, chemicals, fuels and many other essential indüstrial materials required for the economic development of the Far Eastern countries can now be shipped cheaply in large quantities. Improvements in transportation facilities certainly will accelerate the economic development of these countries and enlarge their trade.

BUSINESS FLUCTUATIONS

Trade is affected by the economic conditions of the trading countries. A recession or depression will reduce their imports and exports, while prosperity will improve them. Business fluctuations of big and advanced countries tend to have strong effects on the economy of small and poor countries while the effect of fluctuations in the latter on the former is negligible. Let us distinguish the effects of business fluctuations in two categories: foreign repercussions and backwash effects. Foreign repercussions refer to the effects of one country's business fluctuations on the national income of other countries through trade. Backwash effects refer to effect of fluctuations of foreign countries on the national income at home. For the Far Eastern countries, the foreign repercussion effects are small, but the backwash effects are important. A recession in Malaya will reduce Malaya's imports from the United States, but this will not hurt the economy of the United States much, as Malaya buys only a small share of the exports of the United States. However, during a recession in the United States, the United States, a major buyer of Malayan rubber, will buy less; the price of rubber will drop, and it is likely a recession will develop in Malaya also. Of course, this is due to the fact that Malaya depends more on its trade with the United States than the United States depends on its trade with Malaya. The great depression in the United States in the early 1930's was a predominant factor of the world depression, to say nothing of the depression in the Far East, and for the same reason, the Korean War prosperity in the United States in 1951 to 1953 brought about the increase of trade and prosperity for most of the Far Eastern countries. The future of the trade of the Far East depends not only on the stability or prosperity of the Far Eastern countries, but also, or in a sense even more so, on the stability and prosperity of the West.

ECONOMIC FRAGMENTATION

The Far East in the postwar period has a tendency toward economic fragmentation: a process of breaking up the region into many small economic units, each trying to promote self-sufficiency within narrow territorial limits. Burma, India, and Pakistan were at one time members of a single economic unit with free flow of goods among them. Now they are independent and separate from one another, with increasing economic barriers being erected among them to obstruct economic development. Pakistan produces raw jute and raw cotton, but has little manufacturing facilities, while India has the facilities but does not have adequate supplies of raw jute and raw cotton. French Indochina was, at one time, one economic unit, but it has now been divided into four government units with little economic integration among them. The Philippines enjoyed free trade with the United States before World War II, but now there are increasing tariff barriers. Political independence is desirable for the peoples of the Far East. For anyone who is familiar with the peoples of the Far East and their aspirations, it is very obvious that political independence has been probably their most cherished goal. However, economic fragmentation--that is, trying to base the economy on a very narrow territorial base--is not going to promote fast growth. The peoples of Asia must learn to preserve and promote economic cooperation on an international scale and still preserve political independence. The experience of the Common Market in Europe provides a valuable lesson for the people of the Far East. The organization of customs unions of small groups of nations may be looked into to provide a wider territorial base necessary for a fast-growing economy.

The free Far East can be regarded by the West as an economic frontier where the West has a great deal to offer in the development of this frontier and, thereby, a great deal to gain in return. A frontier offers an opportunity for progress, but it does not promise that the path will be easy. There will be difficulties, setbacks, and problems, but, then, all frontier experiences are compounded of hard work and enterprise. When the West comes to the free Far East with the intention of rendering a helping hand to promote its national income and standard of living in exchange for some opportunities of trade and investment, the free Far East can accommodate the West and, in doing so, help itself. This will provide a sound basis for a joint adventure with mutual benefits. The promotion of the national income of the free Far East will naturally bring about improvement of the trade of this region with the West. A prosperous Far East will provide a better basis for peace, order and stability for that part of the world and a better environment for democratic ideals and human dignity to flourish.

Notes to Chapter 11

1. United Nations, Economic Commission for Asia and the Far East, Economic Survey of Asia and the Far East, New York, 1961, pp. 11-15.

2. John C.H. Fei and Gustav Ramis, Development of the Labor Surplus Economics (Homewood, Ill.: Richard D. Irwin,Inc., 1964).

3. John C.H. Fei and Gustav Ramis, A Study of Planning Methodology with Special Reference to Pakistan's Second Five Year Plan (Karachi: The Institute of Development Economics, 1960), pp. 2-6.

4. Fei and Ramis, Development of the Labor Surplus Economics, op. cit., p. 306.

5. Roy Harrod, The Dollar (New York: W.W. Norton & Company, Inc., 1963), p. xii.

6. International Bank of Reconstruction and Development, World Bank Group in Asia, a Summary of Activities, Washington, 1960.

7. Economic Survey of Asia and the Far East, op. cit., 1963, pp. 71-73.

BIBLIOGRAPHY

BOOKS

Agarwala, Amar Narain. The Economics of Underdevelopment. New York: Oxford University Press, 1963.

Alexander, Robert Jackson. A Primer of Economic Development. New York: The Macmillan Company, 1962.

Allen, George C. A Short Economic History of Modern Japan 1867-1937. London: Allen and Unwin, Ltd., 1962.

_____. Japan's Economic Recovery. London: Oxford University Press, 1958.

Allen, Robert L. Communist Economic Warfare. (Committee on Un-American Activities, House of Representatives; 86th Cong., 2d sess.) Washington, D.C.: Government Printing Office, 1960.

Allen, Roy George Douglas, and Ely, J. E. International Trade Statistics. New York: John Wiley & Sons, 1953.

Allen, William R., and Allen, Clark Lee. Foreign Trade and Finance. New York: The Macmillan Company, 1959.

Alpert, Paul. Economic Development: Objectives and Methods. New York: Free Press of Glencoe, 1963.

American Academy of Political and Social Science. Communist China and the Soviet Bloc. Philadelphia: American Academy of Political and Social Science, 1963.

American Tariff League, Inc. The United States in World Trade; a Contemporary Analysis and a Program for the Future. New York: American Tariff League, Inc., 1958.

Anderson, Erwin O. Japan's Foreign Investment and Joint Ventures Abroad. New York: Columbia University Press, 1959.

Anstey, Vera. The Economic Development of India. 4th ed. London: Longmans, Green and Company, 1952.

Aubrey, Henry G. United States Imports and World Trade. Oxford: The Clarendon Press, 1957.

Australia and New Zealand Bank, Ltd., Economics and Statistics Department. Australia's Continuing Development. Melbourne: Australia and New Zealand Bank, Ltd., 1953.

_____. Investment in Australia. Melbourne: Australia and New Zealand Bank, Ltd., 1960.

Australia Institute of Political Science. Economic Growth in Australia. Sydney: Angus and Robertson, 1962.

Babcock and Wilcox of Australia, Ltd. The Australian Manufacturer's Directory. Sydney: Babcock and Wilcox of Australia, Ltd., 1959.

Babu, V. Vithal. Economic Conditions in India. Delhi: Atma Ram & Sons, 1951.

Balassa, Bela. The Theory of Economic Integration. Homewood, Ill.: Richard D. Irwin, Inc., 1961.

_____. Trade Prospects in Developing Countries. Homewood, Ill.: Richard D. Irwin, Inc., 1964.

Banerjea, Pramathanath. A Study of Indian Economy. 6th ed. Calcutta: University of Calcutta Press, 1951.

Barr, Robert J. American Trade with Asia and the Far East. Milwaukee, Wisc.: Marquette University Press, 1959.

Basch, Antonin. Financing Economic Development. New York: The Macmillan Company, 1964.

Bastable, C. F. The Theory of International Trade. New York: The Macmillan Company, 1903.

Bauer, Peter T. Economic Analysis and Policy in Underdeveloped Countries. Durham, N. C.: Duke University Press, 1957.

_____. The Economics of Underdeveloped Countries. London: Nisbet, 1957.

_____. Indian Economic Policy and Development. New York: Frederick A. Praeger, 1961.

_____. United States Aid and Indian Economic Development. Washington: American Enterprise Association, 1959.

Berrill, Kenneth. Economic Development with Special Reference to East Asia. New York: St. Martin's Press, Inc., 1964.

Bharadwaj, Ranganash. Structural Basis of India's Foreign Trade; a Study Suggested by the Input-Output Analysis. Bombay: Bombay University Press, 1962.

Binani, G. D., and Rama Rao, T. V. India at a Glance. Calcutta: Orient Longmans, Ltd., 1953.

Boeke, J. H. Economics and Economic Policy of Dual Societies. New York: Institute of Pacific Relations, 1953.

Braifanti, Ralph J. Administration and Economic Development in India. Durham, N. C.: Duke University Press, 1963.

Buchanan, Norman Sharpe. Approaches to Economic Development. New York: Twentieth Century Fund, 1955.

Bureau of National Affairs, Inc. International Trade Reporters Survey and Analysis of Current Development. Washington, D. C.: Bureau of National Affairs, Inc., 1954.

Business Dictionaries, Ltd. British Commonwealth and Empire Trade Index, 1960-1961. Manchester: Business

Dictionaries, Ltd., 1962.

Camps, Miriam. The European Common Market and American Policy. (Center of International Studies.) Princeton: Princeton University Press, 1956.

_____. Trade Policy and American Leadership. (Center of International Studies.) Princeton: Princeton University Press, 1957.

Caves, Richard E. Trade and Economic Structure. Cambridge: Havard University Press, 1933.

Chand, Gyan. The New Economy of China. Bombay: Vora and Co. Ltd., 1948.

Chao, Kuo-Chun. Economic Planning and Organization in Mainland China, 1949-1959. Cambridge: Harvard University Press, 1960.

Challiab, Raja Jesudess. Fiscal Policy in Underdeveloped Countries with Special Reference to India. New York: The Macmillan Company, 1960.

Cheng, Chu-yuan. Communist China's Economy, 1949-1962. South Orange, N. J.: Seton Hall University Press, 1963.

_____. Economic Relations between Peking and Moscow, 1949-1963. New York: Frederick A. Praeger, 1964.

Cheng, Yu-Kwei. Foreign Trade and Industrial Development of China. Washington: The University Press of Washington, D.C., 1956.

Chick, Louis and others. The Economic Development of Malaya. Baltimore: John Hopkins Press, 1955.

Cohen, Jerome B. Japan's Postwar Economy. Bloomington: Indiana University Press, 1958.

Committee for Economic Development. The European Common Market: Its Meaning to the United States. New York: Committee for Economic Development, 1959.

Condliffe, J. B. The Development of Australia. London:
Free Press of Glencoe, 1964.

Cook's Business Directory of Australia and New Zealand,
1952-1953. Sydney: Cook's Australian Directory, Ltd.

Copland, Sir Douglas Berry. The Adventure of Growth; Essays
on the Australian Economy and its International Setting.
Melbourne: F. W. Cheshire, 1960.

_____, and Barback, R. H. The Conflict of Expansion
and Stability; Documents Relating to Australian Economic
Policy, 1945-1952. Melbourne: F. W. Cheshire, 1957.

Cowan, Charles Donald. The Economic Development of
China and Japan. New York: Frederick A. Praeger, 1964.

Crane, Robert I. Aspects of Economic Development in South
Asia. New York: Institute of Pacific Relations, International Secretariat, 1954.

Datta, Bhabatosh. Economic Development and Exports of
India. Calcutta: World Press, 1962.

Dewett, Kewal Krishna, and Singh, Gurucharan. Indian Economics. 5th ed. Delhi: Premier Publishing Company,
1961.

Dewhurst, J. Frederick, Coppock, John O., Yates, P.
Lamartine, and associates. Europe's Needs and Re-
sources. New York: Twentieth Century Fund; London:
Macmillan and Company, Ltd., 1961.

Directory of the State of Singapore, 1960-1961. London:
The Diplomatic Press and Publishing Company, 1961.

Eckstein, Alexander. The National Income of Communist
China. New York: Free Press of Glencoe, 1961.

The Economist Intelligence Unit, Ltd. The Commonwealth
and Europe. London: Whitefriars Press, 1960.

Enke, Stephen. Economics for Development. Englewood Cliffs, N. J.: Prentice-Hall, 1963.

Erhard, Ludwig. Germany's Comeback in the World Market. New York: The Macmillan Company, 1953.

_____. Prosperity through Competition. New York: Frederick A. Praeger, 1958.

Federation of British Industries. A Trade in Transition. London: Federation of British Industries, 1961.

Federation of Indian Chambers of Commerce and Industry. Silver Jubilee Souvenir. New Delhi: Chamber of Commerce, 1952.

Fei, John C., and Ranis, Gustav. Development of the Labor Surplus Economy. Homewood, Ill.: Richard D. Irwin, Inc., 1964.

Felber, John E. Guide for American Soviet Trading. Newark, N. J.: Internal Import Index of New Merchandise Printing Consultants Publishers, 1960.

Firth, Raymond William. Capital Saving and Credit in Peasant Societies. London: Allen and Unwin, Ltd., 1964.

Friedman, W. G., and Pugh, R. C. Legal Aspects of Foreign Investment. Boston: Little, Brown and Company, 1959.

Fujii, Shigeru. Japan's Trade and Her Level of Living. Tokyo: Science Council of Japan, 1955.

Furtado, Celso. Development and Underdevelopment. Berkeley: University of California Press, 1964.

Ganguli, B. N. India's Economic Relations. Bombay: Orient Longmans, 1956.

Ghati, B. G. Asia's Trade. Bombay: Oxford University Press, 1948.

Ghosh, Alak. Indian Economy: Its Nature and Problems.
    Calcutta: The World Press Private, Ltd., 1962.

Ghosh, B. B. Indian Economics and Pakistan Economics.
    Calcutta: A Mukherjee and Company, Ltd., 1949.

Ghosh, K. C. Economic Resources of India and Pakistan.
    Calcutta: K. P. Basu Publishing Company, 1956.

Gill, Richard T. Economic Development, Past and Present.
    Englewood Cliffs, N. J.: Prentice-Hall, 1963.

Guth, Wilfred. Capital Exports to Less Developed Countries.
    Dordrecht: Reidel, 1963.

Haberler, Gottfried. International Trade and Economic De-
    velopment. Cairo: National Bank of Egypt, 1959.

_____. A Survey of International Trade Theory. Princeton:
    Princeton University Press, 1961.

Hancock, W. K. Wealth of Colonies. Cambridge: Cambridge
    University Press, 1950.

Harrod, Sir Roy Forbes. International Trade Theory in a
    Developing World. London: Macmillan and Company,
    Ltd., 1963.

_____. Toward a Dynamic Economy. New York:
    The Macmillan Company, 1948.

Herman, Celia I. Investment in India. Burea of Foreign
    Commerce, United States Department of Commerce.
    Washington, D. C.: Government Printing Office, 1961.

Higgins, Benjamin H. Economic Development: Principles, Problems
    and Policies. New York: W. W. Norton & Company, Inc., 1959.

Hirschman, Albert O. The Strategy of Economic Develop-
    ment. New Haven: Yale University Press, 1963.

Hoffmeyer, Eric. Dollar Shortage. Amsterdam: North-
    Holland Publishing Company, 1958.

Hollister, William W. China's Gross National Product and
  Social Accounts, 1950-1957. Glencoe, Ill. : Free
  Press, 1958.

Hoselitz, Berthold F. Sociological Aspects of Economic
  Growth. Glencoe, Ill. : Free Press, 1960.

Hughes, Trevor Jones. The Economic Development of Communist China, 1949-1960. London: Oxford University
  Press, 1961.

Hunsberger, Warren Seabury. Japan and the United States
  in World Trade. New York: Harper and Row, 1964.

Hunter, Alex. The Economics of Australian Industry.
  Parkville: Melbourne University Press, 1963.

Imlah, Albert H. Economic Elements in the Pax Britannica.
  Cambridge: Harvard University Press, 1958.

Irving National Bank. Trading with the Far East. New York:
  Irving National Bank, 1919.

Iyengar, S. Kesava. A Decade of Planned Economy. Mysore,
  India: The Indian Academy of Economics, 1961.

Jacoby, Erich H. Agrarian Unrest in Southeast Asia. London:
  Asia Publishing House, 1961.

Jathar, G. B. , and Beri, S. G. Indian Economics. 8th ed.
  Madras: Oxford University Press, 1949.

Johnson, Harry G. International Trade and Economic Growth.
  London: Allen and Unwin, Ltd. , 1958.

Kamioka, Kazayoshi. Japanese Main Export Commodities.
  Tokyo: Tokyo News Service, 1961.

Kenen, Peter B. Giant Among Nations. New York: Harcourt
  Brace and Company, 1960.

Khan, Nasir Ahmad. Problems of Growth of an Underdeveloped
  Economy - India. Bombay: Asia Publishing House, 1961.

Kindleberger, Charles P. Foreign Trade and the National Economy. New Haven: Yale University Press, 1962.

_____. The Terms of Trade, a European Case Study. New York: John Wiley and Sons, 1956.

The Kobe Chamber of Commerce and Industry. Kobe Directory. Kobe: Chamber of Commerce and Industry, 1957.

Kovner, Milton. The Challenge of Coexistence, a Study of Soviet Economic Diplomacy. Washington, D.C.: Public Affairs Press, 1961.

Kuznets, Simon Smith. Economic Growth, Brazil, India and Japan. Durham, N. C.: Duke University Press, 1958.

Lewin, Pauline. The Foreign Trade of Communist China. New York: Frederick A. Praeger, 1964.

Lewis, W. A. The Theory of Economic Growth. London: Allen and Unwin, Ltd., 1955.

Levin, Jonathan V. The Export Economies; Their Pattern of Development in Historical Perspective.. Cambridge: Havard University Press, 1960.

Li, Choh-Ming. Economic Development of Communist China. Berkeley: University of California Press, 1959.

_____. Industrial Development in Communist China. New York: Frederick A. Praeger, 1964.

Li, Dun J. British Malaya. New York: The American Press, 1955.

Linder, Staffan Burenstan. An Essay on Trade and Transformation. New York: John Wiley and Sons, 1961.

Liu, Ta Chung, and Yeh, Kung Chia. The Economy of the Chinese Mainland: National Income and Economic Development 1953-1959. Princeton: Princeton University Press, 1965.

Loeber, Thomas S. Foreign Aid, Our Tragic Experiment.
New York: W. W. Norton & Company, Inc., 1961.

Loganathan, C. (Chief Executive of the Bank of Ceylon).
Democracy and Economic Development in Asia. Colombo:
Nadaraja, Ltd., 1957.

Malenbaum, Wilfred. Prospects for Indian Development. New
York: Free Press of Glencoe, 1962.

Manoilesco, Mihail. Theory of Protection and International Trade.
London: P. S. King and Son, Ltd., 1931.

Marshall, Alfred. Money, Credit and Commerce. New York:
The Macmillan Company, 1923.

Mason, Edward S. Promoting Economic Development; The
United States and Southern Asia. Claremont, Cal.:
Claremont College, 1935.

Matsui, Kiyoshi. Essays on International Trade. (Economics
Series No. 29). Tokyo: Science Council of Japan, 1958.

Matsumura, Yutaka. Japan's Economic Growth 1945-1960.
Tokyo: Tokyo News Service, 1961.

Meade, J. E. Balance of Payments. London: Oxford University Press, 1951.

_____. A Geometry of International Trade. London:
Allen and Unwin, Ltd., 1952.

_____. The Theory of Customs Unions. Amsterdam:
North Holland Publishing Company, 1955.

_____. Trade and Welfare. London: Oxford University
Press, 1955.

Meier, Gerald M. International Trade and Development. New
York: Harper and Row, 1963.

Melville, L. G. and others. Australia's Postwar Economy.
Sydney: Australian Publishing Company, 1945.

Meyer, F. V. The European Free Trade Association. New
    York: Frederick A. Praeger, 1960.

Mezerik, Avrahm G. Financial Assistance for Economic
    Development. New York: United Nations, 1959.

Mikesell, Raymond F. United States Economic Policy and
    International Relations. New York: McGraw-Hill Com-
    pany, 1952.

Myrdal, Gunnar. Beyond the Welfare State: Economic Plan-
    ning and Its International Implications. New Haven:
    Yale University Press, 1963.

_____. An International Economy. New York: Harper
    and Brothers, 1956.

_____. Rich Lands and Poor. New York: Harper and
    Brothers, 1957.

National Bureau of Economic Research. Capital Formation
    and Economic Growth. Princeton: Princeton University
    Press, 1955.

National Industrial Conference Board, Inc. Economic Unity
    in Europe, Progress and Problems. New York: Na-
    tional Industrial Conference Board, Inc., 1960.

Nove, Alec. The Soviet Economy, an Introduction. New
    York: Frederick A. Praeger, 1961.

_____, and Donnelly, Desmond. Trade with Com-
    munist Countries. Institute of Economic Affairs. Lon-
    don: Hutchinson & Co., Ltd., 1960.

Nurkse, Ragnar. Patterns of Trade and Development. New
    York: Oxford University Press, 1961.

_____. Problems of Capital Formation in Underde-
    veloped Countries. Oxford: Basil Blackwell, 1953.

Nurul, Islam. Foreign Capital and Economic Development:
    Japan, India and Canada. Ruthland, Vermont: Charles
    E. Tuttle Company, 1960.

Ohlin, Bertil. Interregional and International Trade. Cambridge: Harvard University Press, 1933.

The Oriental Economist. Japan Economic Yearbook. Tokyo: The Oriental Economist, 1959.

Perkins, James Oliver Newton. Britain and Australia. Parkville: Melbourne University Press, 1962.

Puthucheary, J. J. Ownership and Control in the Malayan Economy. Singapore: Eastern University Press, Ltd., 1960.

Pryor, Frederick L. The Communist Foreign Trade System. Cambridge: The M.I.T. Press, 1963.

Ramaswamy, T. N. Full Employment for India. Benares: Nand Kishore and Brothers, 1946.

Ramsay, G. D. English Overseas Trade during the Centuries of Emergence. London: Macmillan and Company, Ltd., 1957.

Ranis, Gustav. The United States and the Developing Economies. New York: W. W. Norton and Company, 1964.

Reddaway, W. B. The Development of the Indian Economy. Homewood, Ill.: Richard D. Irwin, Inc., 1962.

Remer, C. F. Three Essays on the International Economics of Communist China. Ann Arbor: University of Michigan Press, 1959.

The Research Institute of Japan. Japan Trade Guide. Tokyo: The Research Institute of Japan, 1960.

Rimalov, Viktor Vladimirovich. Economic Cooperation between the USSR and Underdeveloped Countries. Moscow: Foreign Language Publishing House, 1962.

Rosenstein-Rodan, P. N. Capital Formation and Economic Development. Cambridge: The M.I.T. Press, 1964.

Rostow, Walt Whitman. The Stages of Economic Growth. New York: Cambridge University Press, 1960.

Sapir, Michail. Japan, China and the West. Washington: National Planning Association, 1959.

Sayers, Richard Sidney. Central Banking in Underdeveloped Countries. Cairo: National Bank of Egypt, 1956.

Scope Book, Ltd. The Scope Yearbook of Industry, Trade and Finance. London: Scope Books, Ltd., 1950.

Sen, Surendra Nath. Central Banking in Underdeveloped Money Markets. Calcutta: Bookland Private, 1956.

Shenoy, B. R. Indian Planning and Economic Development. New York: Asia Publishing House, 1963.

Silcock, T. H. The Economy of Malaya. Singapore: Donald Moore, 1957.

Singer, Hans Wolfgang. International Development: Growth and Change. New York: McGraw-Hill, 1964.

Singh, Manmohan. India's Export Trade and the Prospects for Self-Sustained Growth. Oxford: The Clarendon Press, 1964.

Sinha, Manas Ranjan. A Decade of Economic Development and Planning in India. Bombay: Asian Studies Press, 1962.

Sovani, N. V. Economic Relations of India. Bombay: Oxford University Press, 1949.

Stern, Robert Mitchell. Policies for Trade and Development. New York: Carnegie Endowment for International Peace, 1964.

Stevens, Bertram. New Horizon. (Australian Institute of International Affairs, New South Wales Branch.) Sydney: Peter Huston, 1946.

Szczepanik, E. F. Economic and Social Problems of the Far East. Hong Kong: University of Hong Kong Press, 1962.

Ta Kung Pao. Trade With China. Hong Kong: Ta Kung Pao, 1957.

Taussig, F. W. International Trade. New York: The Macmillan Company, 1927.

Thompson, Warren S. Population and Progress in the Far East. Chicago: University of Chicago Press, 1959.

Torrens, R. Letters on Commercial Policy. London: London School of Economics and Political Science, 1958.

Tsang, Chih. China's Postwar Markets. (Institute of Pacific Relations, International Secretariat.) New York: The Macmillan Company, 1945.

Tsuru, Shigeto. Essays on Japanese Economy. Tokyo: Kimokuniya Bookstore Company, 1958.

Tung Chi Chu Pan She. Major Aspects of the Chinese Economy through 1956. Peking: Tung Chi Chu Pan She, 1958.

Vakil, Chandalal C. Economic Consequences of Divided India. Bombay: Vera and Company, 1950.

Venkatasubbiah, H. Indian Economy since Independence. Bombay: Asia Publishing House, 1958.

Viner, Jacob. The Custom Union Issue. New York: Carnegie Endowment for International Peace, 1950.

_____. International Trade and Economic Development. Oxford: The Clarendon Press, 1953.

_____. Studies in the Theory of International Trade. New York: Harper and Brothers, 1937.

Wilson, Joan. The Singapore Rubber Market. Singapore: Eastern University Press, 1958.

Wolf, Charles, Jr. Foreign Aid: Theory and Practice in
    Southern Asia. Princeton: Princeton University Press,
    1960.

_____, and Sufrin, S. C. Capital Formation and
    Foreign Investment in Underdeveloped Areas. Syracuse:
    Syracuse University Press, 1955.

Wood, G. L. Australia: Its Resources and Development.
    New York: The Macmillan Company, 1947.

World Market Publication, Inc. The Waste Trade Directory
    of Dealers and Consumers in the United States and
    Canada and Leading Importers and Exporters in all Im-
    portant Centers of the World. New York: World Market
    Publication, Inc., 1961.

Wright, Philip G. Trade and Trade Barriers in the Pacific.
    Stanford: Stanford University Press, 1935.

Wu, Yuan Li. An Economic Survey of Communist China. New
    York: Bookman Associates, 1956.

Yamada, Isamu. Theory and Application of Interindustry Anal-
    ysis. Tokyo: Kinokuniya Bookstore Company, 1961.

Yin, Helen, and Yin, Yichang. Economic Statistics of Main-
    land China. Cambridge: Harvard University Press, 1960.

Ying, Hsin. The Foreign Trade of Communist China. Hong
    Kong: Union Research Institute, 1954.

Zupnick, Elliot. Britain's Postwar Dollar Problem. New
    York: Columbia University Press, 1957.

                    PERIODICAL ARTICLES

Bardhan, Pranab. "External Economics, Economic Develop-
    ment and the Theory of Protection," Oxford Economic
    Papers, XVI (March, 1964).

Bhagwati, J. "Pure Theory of Internal Trade," Economic
    Journal, LXXIV (March, 1964).

Cairncross, A. K. "International Trade and Economic Development," Economica, XXVIII (August, 1961).

Chenery, Hollis B. "Comparative Advantage and Development Policy," American Economic Review, LI (March, 1961).

Haberler, Gottfried. "Some Problems in the Pure Theory of International Trade," Economic Journal, LX (January, 1950).

Hagen, Everett E. "An Economic Justification of Protectionism," Quarterly Journal of Economics, LXXII (November, 1958).

Haring, Joseph E. "Export Industrialism and Economic Growth," Western Economic Journal, I, No. 2 (Spring, 1963).

Kravis, Irving B. "Availability and Other Influences on the Commodity Composition of Trade," Journal of Political Economy, XVIII (April, 1956).

_____. "Wage and Foreign Trade," Review of Economics and Statistics, XXXVIII (February, 1956).

Lancaster, Kelvin. "Heckscher-Ohlin Model, a Geometric Treatment," Economica, XXIV (February, 1957).

Lewis, W. A. "Economic Development with Unlimited Supplies of Labor," Manchester School of Economic and Social Studies, XX (1954).

Mehta, F. "The Effects of Adverse Income Terms of Trade on the Secular Growth of Underdeveloped Countries," Indian Economic Journal, VI (July, 1958).

Metzler, L. A. "Graham's Theory of International Values," American Economic Review, XL (June, 1950).

Michaily, Michail. "Factor Proportion in International Trade," Kyklos, XVII (1964).

Morgan, Theodore. "The Long-Run Terms of Trade between
    Agriculture and Manufacturing," Economic Development
    and Cultural Change, VIII (October, 1959).

Myint, H. "The Classical Theory of International Trade
    and the Underdeveloped Countries," Economic Journal,
    LX (June, 1958).

Nanavati, Sir Manial, and Vakil, C. N. "India Speaking,"
    The Annals of the American Academy of Political and
    Social Science, CCXXXI (1944).

Prebisch, Raul. "Commercial Policy in Underdeveloped
    Countries," American Economic Review Papers and
    Proceedings, LXIII (May, 1950).

Singer, H. W. "The Distribution of Gains between Investing
    and Borrowing Countries," American Economic Review
    Papers and Proceedings, LXIII (May, 1950).

                REPORTS AND OFFICIAL DOCUMENTS

Bureau of the Census, United States Department of Com-
    merce. U.S. Exports of Domestic and Foreign Mer-
    chandise. FT420. Washington, D.C.: Government
    Printing Office, December, 1961.

_____. U.S. Foreign Trade Summary Report,
    1956. Washington, D.C.: Government Printing Office, 1956.

_____. U.S. Import Duties Annotated for Statis-
    tical Reporting. Washington, D.C.: Government Printing
    Office, 1960.

_____. U.S. Imports of Merchandise for Con-
    sumption. FT110. Washington, D.C.: Government Printing
    Office, December, 1961.

Bureau of Statistics, Office of the Prime Minister. Japan's
    Statistical Yearbook. Tokyo: Government Printing
    Office, 1963.

Commonwealth Bureau of Census and Statistics. Commonwealth of Australia Overseas Trade. Canberra: Bureau
of Census and Statistics, 1959, 1960.

Consultative Committee of the Colombo Plan. The Tenth
Annual Report of the Consultative Committee of the
Colombo Plan. Kuala Lumpur, Malaya: Government
Press, 1961.

Department of Commercial Intelligence and Statistics,
Ministry of Commerce and Industry. Directory of Ex-
porters of Indian Products and Manufactures. Delhi:
Government of India, 1955.

Department of Economic Affairs, United Nations. Measures
for International Economic Stability. New York: United
Nations, 1951.

_____. Relative Prices of Exports and Imports of
Underdeveloped Countries. New York: United Nations,
1949.

Department of Economic and Social Affairs, United Nations.
Establishment of Industrial Estates in Underdeveloped
Countries. New York: United Nations, 1961.

_____. The International Flow of Private Capital. New
York: United Nations, 1959.

_____. The Quest for Freer Trade. New York:
United Nations, 1955.

_____. World Economic Report. Lake Success, New
York: United Nations, 1948-54.

_____. World Economic Survey. Lake Success, New
York: United Nations, 1955-62.

Department of Economics and Statistics. Statistical Outline
of India. Bombay: Tata Industries, Ltd., 1959.

Economic Commission for Asia and the Far East, United Nations.
Economic Survey of Asia and the Far East. Lake Success,
New York: United Nations, 1947-62.

_____. Foreign Investment Laws and Regulations
in the ECAFE Region. Bangkok: Committee on Industry and
Trade, March, 1950.

_____. Intra-regional Trade Statistics. Bangkok:
United Nations Department of Economic and Social
Affairs, 1960.

_____. Regional Market Arrangements with Refer-
ence to the ECAFE Region. Bangkok: United Nations,
1961.

_____. A Study of Trade between Asia and Europe.
Geneva: United Nations Department of Economic and
Social Affairs, November, 1953.

Economic Planning Agency. New Long-Range Economic
Plan of Japan 1961-1970. Tokyo: The Japan Times,
Ltd., 1961.

Foreign Trade Section, Tokyo Metropolitan Government.
Buyers' Guide of Tokyo. Tokyo: Foreign Trade
Section, 1959-60.

General Statistical Board of the Council of Ministers,
USSR. Forty Years of Soviet in Facts and Figures.
Moscow: Foreign Language Publishing House, 1958.

Hill, Dumond Peck. Staff Memorandum on the Communist
Economic Offensive. 85th Cong., 2d Sess. Washington,
D.C.: Government Printing Office, March 4, 1958.

Intelligence Branch of the Commonwealth Economic Committee. Commonwealth Trade with the United States,
1948-1957. London: His Majesty's Stationary Office,
1959.

International Bank for Reconstruction and Development.
The Economic Development of Malaya. Baltimore:
Johns Hopkins Press, 1955.

_____. The World Bank and International Develop-
ment Association in Asia. Washington, D.C., 1962.

International Monetary Fund. Balance of Payments Yearbook, V, VI, VIII, IX. Washington, D.C.: International
Monetary Fund, 1954-60.

_____. International Financial Statistics, XIV, No. 6. Washington, D.C.: International Monetary Fund, 1963.

Ministry of Foreign Affairs. Japan's Foreign Trade. Tokyo: Ministry of Foreign Affairs, 1958.

_____. Statistical Survey of the Economy of Japan. Tokyo: Ministry of Foreign Affairs, 1959.

Organization for European Economic Cooperation. Foreign Trade by Origin and Destination and by Commodities, 1951-1952. Paris: Organization for European Economic Cooperation, 1953.

Statistical Office, United Nations Department of Economic and Social Affairs. Yearbook of International Trade Statistics, 1959. Vol. I. New York: United Nations, 1960. Yearbook of International Trade Statistics, 1953, Vol. I, New York: United Nations, 1954.

United States Tariff Commission. Postwar Development in Japanese Foreign Trade. Washington, D.C.: Government Printing Office, March, 1958.

ABOUT THE AUTHOR

Alfred K. Ho draws upon his intimate knowledge and background of Far Eastern affairs to make this comprehensive study of Far Eastern trade patterns. Educated at Yenching University, Peking, he has traveled extensively in China, Japan, Hong Kong, and the Philippines and served with the Chinese Supply Commission (a Lend Lease agency in Washington, D. C.) during World War II. He returned to China to become an Assistant Professor at Yenching University from 1946-48.

Back in the United States in 1951, Dr. Ho was a Research Associate at Stanford Research Institute in Palo Alto, California, until 1953. His research there included study of the economy of Communist China. From 1958-66 Dr. Ho was Associate Professor of Economics at Los Angeles City College. At present he is an Associate Professor of Economics at Western Michigan University in Kalamazoo, Michigan. He has spent several summers as a visiting Assistant Professor at the University of California in Los Angeles.

Mr. Ho received his master's degree from the University of California in Los Angeles and was awarded a doctorate from Princeton University.